THE BEGINNINGS OF DIALECTIC THEOLOGY

VOLUME ONE

THE BEGINNINGS OF DIALECTIC THEOLOGY

Edited by James M. Robinson

Part I translated by Keith R. Crim

Part II translated by Louis De Grazia and Keith R. Crim

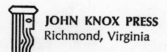 JOHN KNOX PRESS
Richmond, Virginia

The Beginnings of Dialectic Theology is a translation of Teil 1. pp. 37-49; 77-218, 322-347 (© 1962 Chr. Kaiser Verlag), and Teil 2. pp. 11-218 (© 1963 Chr. Kaiser Verlag), of *Anfänge der dialektischen Theologie*, published by Chr. Kaiser Verlag, Munich.

English translation © M. E. Bratcher 1968
Library of Congress Catalog Card Number: 67-12941
Printed in the United States of America
24-0475

Contents

PART II: CHRISTIANITY AND CULTURE

1. RUDOLF BULTMANN

2. FRIEDRICH GOGARTEN

The Plight of Absoluteness

Introduction

KARL BARTH is almost universally regarded as the greatest theologian of our times. The literature about his theological achievement gives every indication of becoming as voluminous as that related to the theologies of other church fathers. Far beyond his own denomination, far beyond the confines of Protestantism, the quality of what he has done has led to his *de facto* canonization as a *doctor ecclesiae*.

A concomitant of this sheer achievement has been an awe-inspired tendency on the part of Barth's closest followers to attend and interpret the construction of the *Church Dogmatics* as a stance more appropriate in the presence of such grandeur than would be their own more feeble attempts at theological construction. Thus we face the prospect of a generation of *epigoni,* a Greek term originally referring to the posterity of heroes whose role is that of custodians of the glorious heritage, but used more recently in German theology to describe the generation that followed upon the brilliant epoch of German idealism, and specifically upon the theology of Friedrich Schleiermacher. Or, to find an analogy perhaps more fitting for Barth, we are in a situation in which the theologian may feel inclined to play Beza to Barth's Calvin, Melanchthon to Barth's Luther—the outcome of which was in the seventeenth century a Protestant scholasticism centuries after the age of scholasticism was supposed to have ended. Since another scholasticism is hardly a live option today, the danger is that such a trend within Barthian circles would lead to a generation that would simply ignore the greatest theologian of our times.

Perhaps a fresh look at *The Beginnings of Dialectic Theology* is the antidote needed to prevent such an inappropriate course of events. For those beginnings have in large part been lost from sight by a generation that did not share in them. Much of the decisive material is inaccessible, scattered in obscure journals and lost in the periodical stacks of older university libraries. In 1962-1963 Jürgen Moltmann sifted through this material and collected the most important speeches, reviews, and articles into two German volumes entitled *Anfänge der dialektischen Theologie, The Beginnings of Dialectic Theology;* in 1966 Walther Fürst edited a third volume, containing primarily material from the early period of the confrontation with Nazism.

The period covered varies somewhat from theologian to theologian, but is defined by Moltmann as extending "from the criticism of the

given situation to the first positive grasp of one's own position."[1] The
collection under each theologian's name includes not only material by
him, but at least in some cases also critiques of him. The English
translation is a selection from and rearrangement of the German series.
The first volume includes as Part One, "From Religious Socialism to
Barthianism," the section on Barth derived from the years 1919-1924,
and the "Beginnings of Barthianism" in 1933. However, three essays
by Barth are omitted, since they were already available in English in
the Harper Torchbook *The Word of God and the Word of Man*. They
are the essays of 1920 on "The Christian's Place in Society" and
"Biblical Questions, Insights and Vistas," and the essay of 1922 on
"The Word of God and the Task of the Ministry." They have been
replaced by material that Moltmann says would have been included
in his collection, had it not already been made readily available in
German in the third volume of Barth's collected essays of 1957,[2]
namely, the famous public correspondence of 1923 between Barth and
Adolf von Harnack. Of course to fill out the picture with regard to
Barth in this period one must also consult the two commentaries too
large for inclusion in this collection of essays, the *Romans*—of which
only the completely rewritten second edition of 1922 is available in
English—and *The Resurrection of the Dead* of 1924, a commentary on
1 Corinthians, especially chapter 15. The present volume should also
be read in conjunction with the Barth-Thurneysen Correspondence,
1914-1925, published by John Knox Press in 1964 under the title
Revolutionary Theology in the Making.

An expression coined by Schleiermacher to refer to Frederick the
Great and used by Barth to refer to Schleiermacher himself[3] can
equally well be applied to Barth: "It was not a school he founded,
but an era." The truth of this is apparent when one considers the
theologians brought together into this series on *The Beginnings of
Dialectic Theology*. They are the great theologians of the first half of
the century, representing the major alternatives to Barthianism as well
as Barthianism itself. Thus Part Two of the present volume, "Christianity and Culture," consists of the early writings of Rudolf Bultmann
and Friedrich Gogarten, who form the focus of the other major pole
in German theology. With regard to Bultmann, also, much stemming
from the period of the "beginnings" could not be included with the
present collection, but is available elsewhere in English. His standard
work on form criticism, *The History of the Synoptic Tradition* of 1921
appeared in English in 1963, and his *Jesus and the Word* of 1926 has
been in English since 1934. *Existence and Faith: Shorter Writings of
Rudolf Bultmann* includes a sermon of 1917 and three articles from

the '20s. The main articles from the '20s are in the first of Bultmann's
four volumes of collected essays under the general title *Glauben und
Verstehen*. Hence the amount of material by Bultmann in the present
collection is relatively limited, but does serve to fill in gaps in this
decisively formative period.

The early writings of Gogarten have not become available in
English, and indeed he has until recently been little recognized in the
English-language world.[4] Hence it is necessary for us to be reminded
that originally his was a more prestigious voice than any other within
the group. Barth rightly referred to him as a "dreadnought on our
side and against our opponents."[5] It was Gogarten's article of 1920
entitled "Between the Times" that provided the title for the subsequent journal of dialectic theology. His essay of the same year on "The
Crisis of Our Culture" created a sensation when presented before the
prestigious society of German liberal theology, so much so that the
poet Wilhelm Schäfer believed he was listening to Luther himself: "He
was aflame with divine demonic, as was the case with Jesus when he
overturned the tables of the moneychangers in the temple."[6] Hence
it was Gogarten who led in the debate with dominant cultural trends
of the day, from Anthroposophy, in vogue at that time, to religious
socialism, represented by Emil Fuchs (no kin to Ernst Fuchs, but father
of the famous atomic spy). His debate with his teacher Ernst Troeltsch,
then Germany's dominant philosopher of religion, is indicative of the
offensive he led. Indeed Gogarten functioned as dialectic theology's
philosophical theologian, having begun with a critique of Fichte and
then moved into dialogue with such figures in German culture of the
time as Ferdinand Ebner and Eberhard Grisebach. It is in this role
that Barth was not able to function, and where his first doubts about
Gogarten came to expression.[7] On the other hand it is none other
than Gogarten who came to grips most intensively with the revival of
the study of Luther in the '20s. In these regards the later affinities
between his recent work and that of Bultmann, on the one hand, and
Gerhard Ebeling, on the other, were anticipated.

Volume Two of the English edition is also to be divided into two
parts. Part One, "The Point of Contact," will include the material
relevant to the position that was long the dominant form dialectic
theology took in America—that of Emil Brunner and Heinrich Barth,
who is the brother of Karl Barth, but, as a philosopher, more of a
Brunnerite than a Barthian. Part Two, "The Confrontation with
Nazism," will document the way in which especially Karl Barth and
Rudolf Bultmann in their theological writing took an unambiguous
stand against Nazism at a time when most theologians—not excluding

those in social ethics—were tacitly or explicitly going along with the regime.

If these great theologians who were the first Barthians in turn became major alternatives to Barth, the next generation that grew up in the *Kirchenkampf* of the Confessing Church tended to produce a flood of less distinguished and more faithful Barthians. The outstanding exceptions tended to be hybrids, such as Dietrich Bonhoeffer, with an ingredient of Anglo-Saxon influence, and Gerhard Ebeling, more a product of Marburg and Zürich than of Basel. The third generation of Barthians has however tended to involve more such independent spirits. Some began under Barth's influence and either repudiated him or were repudiated by him; these today tend to be located at the most varied positions on the theological spectrum, from Wolfhart Pannenberg's replacement of the theology of the word with universal history as revelation, to Heinrich Ott's philosophical theology, Eberhard Jüngel's advocacy of the new hermeneutic, and Paul van Buren's *Secular Meaning of the Gospel.*

Perhaps the first such unorthodox Barthian, if this term is defined from the position of the *Church Dogmatics,* is the early Barth himself. One may compare the situation, structurally at least, with that of the later Heidegger, who has variously distanced himself from *Being and Time,* partly by limiting himself to more of a historical defense of its necessity at its given time than to a present support of its specific formulation, and partly by saying that what it was really seeking to do was not what it was taken to be achieving by those who first attributed to it epochal significance. In a somewhat analogous way Barth has distanced himself from his *Romans.* Indeed, the later Barth's suspension of the normative validity of his early writings extended as far as his *Christliche Dogmatik im Entwurf,* the first volume of which appeared in 1927 and was promptly heralded by Gogarten with an interpretation theologically inacceptable to Barth.[8] Conceding the relative justification of such an interpretation of his work thus far, Barth discontinued the *Christliche Dogmatik im Entwurf* and rewrote the first volume under the new title *Kirchliche Dogmatik* (1932 ff.) — the *Church Dogmatics* with which we are familiar in English.

This unorthodox Barthianism forms the content of *The Beginnings of Dialectic Theology.* To invite the reader to a fresh study of this material is not only to propose a fresh examination of its relation to subsequent theology, but also to invite in the process a fresh study of the subject matter of theology itself. Individual readers may reach varying conclusions from such a confrontation of this source material with its intended subject matter. One may conclude that Barth's basic theological insight was better implemented in the theological systems which others of the dialectic theologians produced than in his own; another that there was no basically new insight but only a temporary one-sidedness within the given theological spectrum; still another that a basically new insight was lost sight of and still calls for adequate development.

To be sure, the standard view is that this dialectic theology is the beginning of a development that reached its most consistent and purified consummation in the Barthianism of today, just as one option for interpreting the radical theologies of Jesus, Paul, and John is to find their logical consummation in the deutero-Pauline, early Catholic Church that composed the canon. Yet before one affirms such a parallel one should recall the frequent criticism of the early Barth to the effect that if he was going anywhere it was more nearly toward Marcion than toward the early Catholic Church. Indeed, in the foreword to the second edition of *The Epistle to the Romans* Barth said, with evident empathy: "Paulinism has always found itself on the edge of heresy, and we must really marvel what harmless and inoffensive books most commentaries on Romans and other books about Paul are." The present collection of material by, for, and against the early Barth is, in distinction from most current literature about Barth, not absolutely harmless and inoffensive. To open it is to open a Pandora's box of unfinished business. Paul Schempp's "Marginal Notes on Barthianism" shows that already in 1928 the radical movement with its devastating critique of given alternatives had, with something of a thud, come down to earth as itself an "ism." "Barth has a following because his theology corresponds better to the present intellectual climate than do other theologies . . ." "One could almost say that the discussion of Barth is gradually beginning to be as boring and comfortable as is a theological retreat." ". . . the literature *for* Barth is almost entirely . . . no better than that *against* Barth." Thus Schempp marks the transition from the beginnings of dialectic theology to Barthian*ism*.

In his "Departure from *Zwischen den Zeiten*" in 1933 Barth repudiated Gogarten, declaring that their joining forces had been one big "misunderstanding," as their polarization into an "anthropological" and a "theological" orientation had tended to suggest and Gogarten's joining of the "German Christians" in contrast to Barth's choice of the "Confessing Church" tended to confirm. Although Gogarten a decade earlier had threatened to withdraw because of what he felt to be the inadequately radical stance of his partners,[9] he does not now think the situation calls for disbanding. In his attempt to present his case in the introduction to his *Judgment or Skepticism* he defines the common point of departure as a two-front war against liberalism's harmonizing of Christianity with culture, on the one hand, and conservatism's separating of religion from concrete reality into a sacral preserve, on the other. Yet if he succeeds in suggesting, as Bonhoeffer was later to argue, that the Confessing Church was leading to an introverted pietism whose outcome would be a return to conservatism, he hardly proved his claim that his own choice of the German Christian side was basically different from the *Kulturprotestantismus* he initially opposed. Moltmann rightly comments: "It is indeed striking, the extent to which they saw each other in terms of what in the beginning they had been united in protesting against."[10] Thus the mutual declaration that the other side had not transcended the traditional cleft between conservative and liberal would tend to suggest the skeptical thesis that there was indeed no basic transcending of antecedent alternatives with a new grasp of—or, as they put it, a being grasped by—the subject matter of theology. The continuation, precisely in Switzerland, of the antecedent party lines of "positives" vs. "freethinkers" and the analogous polarization of Barth's theology of the word vs. Bultmann's kerygmatic theology, which is in turn being overlaid today to some extent by the polarity between Wolfhart Pannenberg's universal history as revelation vs. Gerhard Ebeling's hermeneutical theology (both more explicitly dependent on pre-Barthian alternatives than had been any German theology since World War I), might suggest to some a reading of twentieth-century German theology along lines not fundamentally different from the perennial conservative-liberal dichotomy of American theology. And Moltmann (perhaps unwittingly) tends to support such a thesis in tracing the "misunderstanding" back to the very beginning when Barth's theology of the word was heard in terms of an "I-Thou" philosophy of language, and then forward to today's cleft between the Barthians and the new hermeneutic. However, before thus declaring the matter decided, one should reflect on Moltmann's further observation: "Under certain circumstances more could lurk in [the beginnings of dialectic theology] than [the dialectic theologians] themselves were subsequently able to develop."[11]

This possibility can be illustrated for our times, when the "death of God" issue seems to separate contemporary theological debate from that of the past, by recalling Gogarten's blunt statement in his initial essay of 1920 entitled "Between the Times": "And we raise the question, in all seriousness, whether today there are any men who can really conceive of God." This was echoed by Barth: "The theologian finds himself in the extraordinary situation of having to talk of what one cannot talk. His standpoint is the point on which one cannot stand." *"As theologians we should talk of God. But we are humans and as such cannot talk of God. We should know both—our duty and our inability—and thus give God the glory.* That is our plight. Everything else is by comparison child's play." The dialectic theologians regarded this Kafka-esque plight as paradoxically healthy. "There was finally an opportunity to raise questions about God. The times fell asunder and now time stands still. For one moment? For an eternity? Must we not be able to hear God's Word now? Must we not be able to see his hand in his work now? Therefore we cannot yet run from one period to another, however much we would like to. The decision must first be made here. Until now we could do nothing wholeheartedly. We have been standing between the times for so long. This is a terrible human plight. For there everything human crumbles in disgrace, including everything which was and is to be. But now if we fully comprehend this plight, we can ask about God."

Yet they did proceed to move from the one time to another— Gogarten to the German Christians, Barth to the system of the *Church Dogmatics*. And seen from outside, their movement can give the appearance of simply replacing one concept of God with its opposite. "The subject matter of theology is God, and the reproach against liberal theology is that it treated not God, but man. God means the radical negation and dissolution of man. Hence the theology that has God as its subject matter can only have the 'word of the cross' as its content, which is however an 'offense' for man."[12] Yet in the case of Barth's *Romans* Bultmann went to great pains to show that God is not just an inference from man's limitation. "This negation of the world is no standpoint, but *the experiencing of divine judgment.* That 'No' is not the presupposition in a logical inference; rather, if it is a real 'No,' it contains the 'Yes' in itself."

We for our part should avoid the temptation to place that time "between the times" simply in the graph—visible in retrospect—of the success story of dialectic theology, for that would in effect avoid the issue, stultify the question. One may also recall Bultmann's recent warning, expressed in a different context, against conceptualizing the relation between continuity and discontinuity in history simply as a dialectic. "To call it dialectic does not indeed seem to me fitting, for it does not do justice to the element of decision."[13] Hence the proper purpose of the study of the beginnings of dialectic theology is not simply to explain the shifts in the history of contemporary theology as "background material" for the present theological situation, but rather to inquire if its openness to the issue at stake in theology will clarify for us our confrontation with that issue in our situation.

In order to catch sight of the full sweep of Barth's trajectory from the social gospel to Barthianism one should recall his point of departure as an activist in the "religious-social movement" led by Hermann Kutter and Leonhard Ragaz, which was the Swiss counterpart to the American "social gospel." An essay of 1911 can serve to document this Barth of religious socialism before the transformation in his thought had begun.[14] Barth was then vicar in the German-speaking parish of Geneva; a referendum was being held in the Canton of Geneva to legalize gambling so as to be able to compete with the neighboring French resorts. Barth launched into the debate with the full involvement of social action, and unequivocally identified the will of God with one side of a concrete political choice: "It is here, if anywhere, that we are dealing with a question which is *no* question, but where it is certain a priori that we must take sides, and how we are to take sides. For here it is not a question of what one might call Christian ideology, where Yes and No, pro and con, can vary widely even among Christians and theologians, as we all know. Rather it is simply and clearly a matter of the real content of life that we all are to cherish, extend, and protect. It is a matter of the Kingdom of God in the hearts, of Christian character, the moral conscience oriented to the norms of Jesus. He who realizes what games of chance are knows a priori that they ruin a person's attitude—and hence knows what he should do. If we did not know, we would be well advised to pack our bags." The cliché of the opposition to the effect that "we respect religion, but leave us in peace," is rejected flatly, and instead the basic distinction between believers and unbelievers is shifted from the traditional distinction between church members and non-members to that between the two sides of a referendum. Specifically religious topics as well as theology are ultimately superfluous *epiphenomena* upon the body politic, whose good is by definition the will of God.

The essays collected in the present volume begin at the time of the first edition of *The Epistle to the Romans,* before Barth became a dialectic theologian, but when he was moving away from religious socialism into a sort of *Heilsgeschichte.* The German "Christian-social" leader Friedrich Naumann had so identified the will of God with certain concrete political objectives such as full employment, minimum wage laws, and the like, that these absolutized ends tended to justify the means—such political compromises necessary to get legislation passed as the armaments race and the entry into World War I. Barth recognized this dilemma for what it was, indeed as indicative of the human plight, and characteristic of man's relation to God. Hence he recognized that when Naumann ignored the contradiction in his position and simply championed a political program as man's unambiguous relation to God, he was betraying his ignorance of God and worshiping an idol. Barth saw more sensitivity to the dilemma in the Marxist radicalism that withdrew Russia from the war. "Is it possible that the godless Social Democrats (they were fighting against the church!) understood God better than the church did? Was it possible that the church needed to repent and turn to the God of the godless?" This anti-clerical radicalism was transmitted to Barth, to be sure, in a much less worldly context, namely, by Christoph Blumhardt, who, however, also "meant something other than what the church meant when *he* spoke of 'God.' " (The church of our day might do well to canonize Barth a bit less and take to heart what he said a bit more!) Barth's paradoxical hearing of God among the godless included a quite positive, "optimistic," liberal side: ". . . *all* men, *all* relationships and movements, particularly of the 'worldly' life," are brought under God's promise by the gospel. One thinks of Bonhoeffer, who ended up finding God's promise in—a band of assassins.

The ongoing debate was, however, not carried on in such categories "out in the world," but rather in the seemingly more protected, bourgeois mode of the village pastor's dilemma in giving his explanation of a historical document from the pulpit and thus maintaining that his explanation is God speaking. No doubt this exegetical cast given to the revolutionary theology made it more palatable to many church people—just as it risked losing a hearing for it among the more secular. Full justice can be done the hermeneutical debate only by hearing it in terms of the other dimensions which it originally had in view—or, conversely, by recognizing the hermeneutical debate carried on at the exegetical level to be just an acute instance of man's pervasive quest for abiding meaning in a relativistic age, in which sense the encompassing issue is seen as itself hermeneutical. "The dilemma of our task is only the sign of the dilemma of all human tasks. . . . Our task can be classified within the whole of known human life, within nature and culture, only at the point where the question arises how this whole is in turn to be classified in God's world and creation."[15]

The materials in the present volume that deal with the first edition of *The Epistle to the Romans* are so bad, so floundering, that one can really wonder how any good thing could come out of such a beginning. How much more orderly and manageable the tacit policy of liberalism had seemed, in that, while recognizing God's freedom not to conform to our established procedures for knowing him and hence acknowledging such knowledge to be in the final sense his gift, it felt that the only sensible thing to do was to keep calm, not wring one's hands, but rather carry through those established procedures as intelligently as possible and hope for the best. Barth's policy is initially simply to throw a monkey wrench into this machinery by constantly repeating that this best-laid plan in no way actually assures knowledge of God; for the sake of this higher truth he is even willing to risk otherwise quite disreputable formulations. Indeed, all parties in this debate about the first edition, and not just the *advocatus diaboli*, Adolf Jülicher, use the language provided by the previous theological generation. Thus one can, from the point of view of dialectic theology, polemically dismantle this prelude to the movement as simply the last feeble gasp of the old. However, we might do it more justice by recognizing both the fateful givenness of any language world, which will inevitably continue to have its say, and at the same time recognizing that the real hermeneutical task is to listen in such a given language world for any new event in which a new grasp of the subject matter may be coming to expression. The first edition and the discussion about it are after all the birth pangs of the second.

The preface to the first edition of *The Epistle to the Romans*, shocking as it was to Jülicher in terms of a beginner's presumption, is even more shocking when studied in terms not of personalities but of subject matter. It does bring the disquieting "monkey wrench" to expression, but in such stumbling fashion as to reveal how hermeneutically naïve the exegesis was. "All my attention has been directed to seeing *through* the historical to the spirit of the Bible, which is the eternal Spirit." Man cannot, however, get through the historical in the sense of going beyond his finitude. He can, in studying a text or a historical encounter, move beyond causal explanation and objective classification to a grappling with the subject matter involved—what existentialistic interpretation later treated in terms of the text's understanding of existence. Or, as Barth put it: "What once was serious is still serious today, and what today is serious, and not just arbitrariness and whim, stands also in direct relation to what was formerly serious." Yet though one shares the assumption—rightly designated by Hans Jonas as the "metaphysical a priori of the student of the history of ideas"[16]—that issues that are basic crop up repeatedly, they do so in historically conditioned, varying forms. Hence one must recognize that there is no one instance of the least common denominator; it can be approximated—as an abstract construct, not a reconstruction of a reality ever actually given—only by the mediation of what Hans-Georg Gadamer calls a hermeneutical "fusion of horizons."[17] Thus the concepts of moving beyond the human to the divine, of a historically unmediated contemporaneity, were at best ambiguous, inviting the tag "pneumatic exegesis,"[18] a designation of increasing embarrassment to the dialectic theologians, which was finally explicitly rejected by Bultmann in his effort to work out a defensible hermeneutic for Barth's exegesis.

Emil Brunner's enthusiastic review of the first edition of *The Epistle to the Romans,* useful as it may have been at the time in gaining a hearing for Barth, does not in retrospect do more than pose the problem more acutely. Brunner rightly acknowledges the value of Barth's criticism of psychologism, but he is incapable of advancing to a tenable alternative. Knowledge of God is compared to the compelling force of rational reflection, in that for both the question of validity is independent of the type of psychological experience accompanying them. Here Bultmann saw more acutely than did Brunner, and pointed out that though Barth is in this way able to distinguish faith from psychic, historical occurrence, he does not thereby distinguish it from intellectual life; rather the Barthian contrast between world and God is conceptualized analogically to that between nature and culture, with the result that "a bit of the radicalism of the concept of faith is broken off," in that "God is made a part of the world." To be sure, Bultmann himself proceeded to analyze faith, if not in terms of intellectual life, still in those of human existence, e.g., as "eschatological existence."

Brunner escaped from this dilemma only at the expense of postulating a supernaturalistic *deus ex machina.* The writings of Paul are not the views of a historically conditioned man, but rather "the truth which God speaks" coming from "an area which is inaccessible to our natural and empirical experience of knowledge as well as to natural logic both as a whole and in each separate point." We catch sight of the origin and connection of the thoughts only from "the specific inner necessity for the knowledge of God with its organic connections." For this one needs no "arts of modernization." "The Letter to the Romans applies itself as soon as it is understood . . ." Of course the whole problem is how to reach that understanding. Brunner appeals to 1 Corinthians 2:15 as the alternative to scholarly method, and thus falls through the door open to "pneumatic exegesis." Barth's exegesis is thus held to appeal not to our reason, "but to our original understanding of God. . . . that part of our souls which is not imprisoned in the temporal and finite, but has remained an undisturbed reservoir for the voice of God, undistorted by the 'culture' and adaptation to the world of merely human knowledge." (Brunner neglects to reveal the identity of this secret faculty.)

It is consistent with this ambivalence in Brunner's Barthian position that the world's fallen state, our "godlessness," once described, is said not to be a description of "our real, present condition," which is instead tempered by divine or supra-history breaking into our history. This leads to the advocacy of biblical "realism," i.e., the view that faith is not a new understanding of the world, but a confrontation with "new facts." This overcoming of the "platitudes of liberalism" thus points toward the crudities of *Heilsgeschichte*. In any case we do not here have to do with a truly dialectic position. It is not without importance that this Brunnerite reading of the first edition, possible though it was in terms of what Barth had written, focused rather well upon precisely those things that Barth sought to overcome in the second. The "steady, unexpressed appeal to that divine reservoir in us" may have been what made the first edition of Barth's *Epistle to the Romans* intelligible and acceptable to the very first Barthians who joined the movement before the second edition was published. But it was precisely that which was eliminated in the second. In the preface to the second edition Barth says the positive reviews of the first edition so "dismayed" him that he awoke to "self-criticism." For this we are indebted, among others, to Brunner. Thus he reveals quite clearly the transitional nature of the movement at the beginning, as it presupposes the very position it intends to repudiate. It brings to mind the jibe directed at Kant's system to the effect that one cannot enter it without assuming a *Ding an sich,* but cannot go through it to its logical outcome without giving up that assumption.

Jülicher's is the thankless task of presenting the case for the older generation of theologians oriented to the critical historical method. To some extent his role is to present pedantic details that disprove Brunner's overly hasty reassurances as to Barth's competence in exegetical detail. But Jülicher also succeeds in showing that these errors are part of a pattern that furthers Barth's material position. If Barth's position necessitates distortion of the text, this would for Jülicher serve to discredit Barth's theology as materially diverging from Paul; but it could, as in the case of Bultmann's review of Barth's *Resurrection of the Dead*,[19] lead to the recognition of the necessity of material internal criticism, i.e., the recognition that Paul's formulations are not always consistent with his own basic position, with the implication that the exegete, rather than simply declaring that Paul always said what he should have said to be consistent, must examine critically each Pauline formulation as to whether it is consistent with the central Pauline point.

Of course sometimes it is perhaps Jülicher who is superficial, as when he opposes Barth's reading of Paul's comments about Judaism, the Establishment of his day, in terms of the established Christian church today. This is not a slip, an inaccuracy, on Barth's part, but rather the result of the hermeneutical assumption that what was brought to expression in terms of a concrete specific situation by Paul has its equivalent in concrete specific situations today that are not necessarily the same as those to which Paul was referring. This in turn is related to the hermeneutical assumption that the ultimate meaning of the text is not confined to the specific stage the writer reaches in moving in a certain direction, but is also to be examined in terms of that direction as such and its ultimate outcome. That is to say, here there is a hermeneutical dissensus between Jülicher and Barth comparable to Krister Stendahl's reaction to Luther's defining the topic of Romans as the doctrine of justification by presenting the counterclaim that its topic is Paul's plans for his trip to Spain. What is at stake is the validity of Jülicher's claim: "Much, perhaps even very much, may someday be learned from [Barth's] book for the understanding of our age, but scarcely anything new for the understanding of the 'historical' Paul." At least for the second edition of Barth's *Epistle to the Romans,* the subsequent history of Pauline research, e.g., that of Bultmann, might tend to disprove that claim.

Barth's effort to try Romans on for size in the concretion of his own existence proved to be a heuristic tool for exposing aspects of the historical Paul's understanding of existence that had hitherto been overlooked. The fact that Barth brought this understanding of existence to expression in the language of his own situation does not mean that it was not Paul's understanding of existence he had grasped and communicated. Of course Barth did not in one attempt fully grasp Paul, and hence the hermeneutical circle of using one interpretation as no more than the working hypothesis for the next should be presupposed in any evaluation of the role of Barth's exegesis. This factor, together with that of changing situations, means that exegesis must go and has gone beyond Barth's *Epistle to the Romans*—as Barth himself has repeatedly said. In Germany, where the role of the Jew is a theological issue and post-Bultmannian trends are evident in theology, one can observe Käsemann's return to Schlatter's criticism of Barth, similar to that of Jülicher, that the theme of chapters 9-11 is "the dying and rising again of Israel," and that this theme is central to Romans. This notwithstanding, Jülicher's attempt to eliminate Barth's book as only "practical" and Barth as after all a "Gnostic" is ultimately the attempt of *Kulturprotestantismus* to retain its control over the accepted meaning of the New Testament. Jülicher is right in relativizing Barth as symptomatic of "a period in the history of culture that is not historically oriented," but he does not succeed in ruling out of bounds Barth's basic challenge to the accepted "Paulinism" of the day. Barth does show that Paul's positive theological affirmations about the church are not unambiguously a vindication of the established churches of today.

Gogarten, whose essay "Between the Times" was included by Jülicher in his attack upon the modern "Gnostics," seeks to answer Jülicher. His argument that every student of history comes to the text with his own questions—Kierkegaard's "subjectivity"—valid though it is, was subsequently to be improved by the emphasis that this working hypothesis with which one gains access to the depth dimension of a religious text—what Bultmann would call a "pre-understanding"—is constantly open to revision in the light of the text. Thus the new hermeneutic proposes to attain openness to the text's own existential questions, and to this extent seeks an objectivity that had been lacking in the critical historical method's focus of exegesis upon the more superficial level of fact. Gogarten further denies that Christianity's definition as a historical religion is to be taken either as defining the critical historical method current in that day as the most suitable theological method or as regarding the working out of the effects of Jesus' activity through the course of history as the revelation in history. The "original eternal deed of God" is distorted into a human product by historiography and by the use made of it for man's own purposes in the course of the history of the church. Hence the meaningful thing to do is to stop interfering with this action of God. Yet here too the lines of criticism are clearer than those of the suggested alternative.

Jülicher's *Kulturprotestantismus* was simply shocked at Barth's rejection of politics and of the history of Christendom as proof of Christianity's validity, and of the established church's claims for itself. Although Barth may have been something of a bull in a china shop on such concrete matters, we must realize he was not in any ivory tower, and that his china breaking was child's play compared to the damage done subsequently by the other alternative. The way things were moving was sensed by Barth in his criticism of Paul Althaus' book in 1922: "Now the 'earnestly tested historical calling of a nation' (p. 66) becomes at once a truly mystic quantity, somehow raised to the heavens above the profane alternatives, which are termed 'accidental parliamentary majority' or 'international court of justice.' The vocation of a nation should be a 'question of transcendent depth' (p. 65) because here the 'irrational' and the 'creative deed' are at home (p. 66), and politics is now suddenly 'in its depths a religious matter.'" This can be compared with a letter of February 26, 1922, to Thurney-

sen, in which Barth sketches in the context of his theological debate
with Hirsch (whose academic career concluded in his being dismissed
in the denazification procedures of 1945): "More dangerous is the
fact that the political question plays a part in the *foreground* of our
discussions which are apparently so remote from the world. He deals
with it with sinister passion, filling the air continually with such
words as 'war-guilt lie,' 'humiliating peace,' 'enemy league,' etc."[20]
After all, Naumann's involvement in concrete politics had led him
to shift his terminology from "Christian social" to "national social."[21]

Barth's preface of 1921 to the second edition of his *Epistle to the
Romans* emphasizes the "vigorous change of position" between the
two editions: ". . . no stone from the first work has remained on another"; the second "offers now an entirely different view"; Barth fears
he has exposed himself to the charge of "too great flexibility"; he
recognizes better than do his critics "the real weakness of the first
edition . . . what could and should have been said in almost devastating
manner." The motto from Galatians 1:17 at the opening of the preface
points the direction: "I did not go up to Jerusalem . . . but went away
into Arabia." That is to say, rather than steering a course in a more
conventional direction, as the reviews of such early Barthians as Emil
Brunner would suggest, Barth moved, under the influence of such
radicals as Oberbeck, Kierkegaard, and Dostoevsky (all absent from
the first edition), out into a more isolated, desert position than that
of the first edition. The *Heilsgeschichte* of the first edition gave way
to "dialectic" theology.

On March 26, 1922, Barth wrote to Thurneysen passing along a
comment he had received from a Swiss student in Marburg: "Bultmann
not only has given his lecture on my *Romans* but has spent the last six
hours of his course working over it alone. He takes 'fearful pains' to
understand me. He sees that this takes time and has given the lecture
and the course 'more the form of a study group.' 'Instead of a critic
we are met with an advocate.' . . . No criticism of details, only the
question whether the ideas are Pauline. And in fact it is also Bultmann's view that the submission to the crisis is the Pauline obedience
of faith."[22] It is this lecture by Bultmann, written as he first worked
through the second edition of *The Epistle to the Romans* into the
Barthian dialectic theology, which is included in the present volume.
His approach to Barth is revealed in the way he describes him as carrying on in a new way the argument for "the autonomy and absoluteness
of religion" that Schleiermacher's *Discourses on Religion* and Otto's
Idea of the Holy—and Paul in Romans—had in their way sought to
carry through. Thus Bultmann understands Barth to be presenting a

new grasp of the nature of true religion, although he agrees to use Barth's preferred designation, the nature of *faith*. One can also anticipate Bultmann's own description of the task as that of establishing the document's understanding of existence. Bultmann's attempt to locate Barth's role in the mainstream of Protestant theology, as well as his transposition from "the original form of a commentary" into a more analyzable topical discussion, the penetration of his own analysis that moves beyond misleading formulations and facile though frequent misunderstandings to seek what is really being said, the serious and successful attempt to make sense of a very uncanny document, the critical rigor that never gives way to adulation—these traits made Bultmann's review the door of entry for critical scholarship into dialectic theology, and today it is still the best introduction to what Barth was groping for. Bultmann was in fact the most important convert Barth made by the second edition. "I must confess, however, that the new edition made a much deeper impression on me than the first did." To be sure, in retrospect one can detect on the fringes anticipations of the subsequent parting of the ways. Barth's letter to Thurneysen continued: *"Unfortunately, unfortunately,* he [Bultmann] goes on: 'The relation of "I" and "not I" I [Barth] understand according to the word of Hermann Hesse: "Each one seeks to become himself!" ' "[23] Here one can detect an anticipation of Bultmann's correlation of faith with authentic existence, as it was subsequently to be expressed in Heideggerian terms, and of Barth's subsequent rejection of such "existentialistic interpretation."

The designation "dialectic theology" was not simply a tag hung onto the movement in 1922 by some spectator, as Barth suggested in the bitterness of closing down *Zwischen den Zeiten* in 1933. This view was all too one-sidedly appropriated by Moltmann,[24] who prefers the designation "theology of the word of God," as being more in line with such an interpretation of the early Barth as that of Torrance. For at the time of the second edition of *The Epistle to the Romans* Barth clearly invited such a designation. In the preface to the second edition he expresses his suspicion that those who complain of his complexity are really advocating "a direct, non-paradoxical, not merely believable truth," in contrast to which Barth prefers to speak "dialectically," to exegete in "a dialectic movement as inexorable as it is elastic," to attain "the *inner dialectic of the subject matter.*" The commentary affirms: "The grace of creation, like the grace of redemption, is nowhere present as a given condition among other given conditions. It is the imperceptible relation in which all given conditions stand, and knowledge of it is always and everywhere dialectic."[25] Or, as Barth put it in his debate with Harnack in 1923: "I do not sever [faith from what is human], but I do contest any continuity from the one to the other. I maintain a dialectic *relationship* which points to an *identity* which cannot be carried out and therefore also is not to be asserted." Bultmann explains: "Naturally all this does not lead to a metaphysical dualism; it is not a matter of a 'balance between two situations' [cf. Brunner!], but of a 'dialectic' contrast between God and the world, of a 'duality which is established only in being transcended, and the transcendence of which is its establishment!' "

Bultmann further observed that Barth's talk of a point (the life of Jesus) where the vertical and horizontal lines visibly intersect unwittingly contradicts "a purely dialectic . . . contrast between God and the world"; furthermore what Barth defined as visible about Jesus is not visible to the historian's eye, but is rather the retrospective interpretation based on the Easter faith (e.g., Phil. 2:6-11). Thus Bultmann clarified Barth's position in terms of his own dialectic kerygmatic theology, in which the earthly Jesus was not a direct revelation of God, nor the Easter experience a direct presence of the man Jesus. Easter is understood as the dialectic revelation of God's eschatological action in Jesus' action and passion recurring in the witness to him. Barth for his part gradually gave up the dialectic intention and redefined the undialectic revelation as the Lucan 40 days of bodily resurrection appearances[26]—quite a departure from *The Epistle to the Romans,* where he had said Jesus' resurrection is "no event of historical extent *beside* the other events of his life and death, but the 'unhistoric' relationship of his *whole* historic life to its origin in God."[27] Here, as in other respects, the history of the beginnings of dialectic theology cannot be read in terms of a Barth following a consistent and unambiguous course to the *Church Dogmatics* with lesser figures on all sides falling into misunderstandings or distortions of his original intention.

Tillich echoes Bultmann's criticism of Barth's dialectic. "The imperceptible, non-objective character of faith is broken down. There is a point at which the direction of faith is bound by an objective historical factor. The recognition of an empirical fact has been accepted into the act of faith. Into this opening, however, heteronomy, law, and absolutistic religion break in unhindered." "It is my fear that the way in which he [Barth] and Gogarten use dialectic will unintentionally lead on beyond the dialectic position to a very positive and very undialectic supernaturalism . . ." Tillich sees this taking place "in the doctrine of revelation, in the doctrine of absolute contingency, and the like." That is to say, Tillich anticipated the situation which Bonhoeffer was to brand as "revelation positivism." Tillich for his part has arrived at the "certainty that there can be a justification of the 'irreligious' and of the 'atheist' and of the one who 'blasphemes the Son of Man,' if only the spirit of truth is not blasphemed." Tillich's position is based on his analysis of the *kairos* or situation in which the culture finds itself. "For example, it is impossible for one who is aware of this situation to speak of God as if this word could directly convey to him its essential richness. Therefore we must speak of the *unconditioned.*"

It is at this point that Gogarten, similarly analyzing the situation, draws a more radical inference by appeal to Nietzsche. ". . . I could understand it if someone resolutely turned his back on all theology, but in addition also on all theology camouflaged as philosophy or philosophy of culture." Rather than replacing the term "God" with talk of the unconditioned, one should "determine resolutely to speak of another 'thing,' " for example, "the reality of our life, the reality of man." However he does not, on such terms, see any reality to our life, but would think more in terms of what T. S. Eliot called "hollow men." It is for this reason that Gogarten remains a theologian: ". . . for us there is no reality outside that of the God who was revealed in the man Jesus Christ."

Seen from outside the theological dialectic this seems quite negative, an absolutizing of the dialectic movement *ad infinitum,* a position from which one can hardly move to a philosophy of culture. Hence Tillich advocates "a real transcending (and not an inner-dialectic one) of the dialectic position . . . from the starting point of the unconditioned"; he wishes to "make conscious the non-transcending position which is contained even in the proclamation of the crisis," to comprehend "the Yes which is the presupposition of the No." He calls for "faith in the unity of judgment and revelation, even in the human spirit. . . . Intellectual life is also supported by the unity of grace and judgment." In this way nature, man, history, culture in its widest sense, as well as theology, are dialectic movements, paradoxes, that share a common positive basis in the unconditioned.

Barth's reply is that he is of course aware that it is God that is at work in the dialectic. But he questions that the dialectic itself can ever be transcended by man "on the basis of the unconditioned"; ". . . who transcends here? Is it an intellectual act of the philosophical theologians? If so, in what does it then consist? How do I accomplish this transcending of something 'really' and in addition 'on the basis of the unconditioned'? Are we not confronted here with a philosophical story in the style of Baron von Münchhausen? If not (i.e., if 'transcendence' by means of some kind of divine act), how do I recognize such a transcendence coming from such a different quarter? To what extent is my knowledge of it not dialectic all over again?"

Bultmann calls attention to the distinction between dialectic in the philosophical sense of an unending approximation to the truth in the question-and-answer procedure of Socratic dialogue, and dialectic theology which has to do with "one particular question—the decisive question of man in his existence. And there is likewise one particular answer—the justification of the sinner by God." No movement of thought advances beyond this question and this answer, for they are not stages in the movement of abstract thought but the reality of man's situation and the event of God's grace. Just as Bultmann questions whether the term "dialectic" should not be avoided in order to keep this distinction clear, he also opposes the use of the term "paradox" to justify all kinds of obscurity and the appeal to mystery that plagues theology to such an extent. "In fact, Christianity is not concerned with one or more paradoxical statements, and we might ask whether paradoxical language is not better dispensed with, since the terminology of paradox as well as that of dialectic is loaded with philosophical connotations. But there can be no serious doubt that our talk of paradox refers to paradoxical *event,* namely, the event in which God is gracious to the sinner. As a statement it is not paradoxical in the least—it is understood quite well by the world; but as an event it is completely incomprehensible. The paradox, therefore, is that the statement (for one can speak of an event only in a statement) about God's grace for the sinner can be uttered as a true statement."

Here the dialectic theologians are in agreement with philosophical theology's criticism of the common appeal to "dialectic" and "paradox." Tillich's *Systematic Theology* argues that dialectic thinking does not involve "genuine logical contradictions," but rather "transforms the static ontology behind the logical system of Aristotle and his followers into a dynamic ontology, largely under the influence of voluntaristic and historical motives rooted in the Christian interpretation of existence."[28] In a somewhat similar way Charles Hartshorne argues that "the metaphysico-theological paradoxes" are "avoidable with more refined techniques."[29] Traditional metaphysics stands in contradiction to the understanding of God as historic, and no appeal to the mystery of God should be permitted to obscure or justify the resultant confusion in Western thought. Rather this confused situation should be exposed for what it is, and the inference drawn that a new metaphysic would be free of such "paradoxes." This rejection of what is simply illogical and the denial of "any insolubility in principle of the conceptual problem"[30] might well have been acceptable to the original dialectic theologians, if the escape clause "in principle" could be correlated to their definition of dogma as eschatological: God ultimately makes sense, and hence any complacency over the present state of theology is illegitimate, even though any claim to have achieved that theological ultimacy is, in the light, e.g., of 1 Corinthians 13, *theologia gloriae* or perfectionism. Just as it is the prophetic task of the ministry to transcend any given *status quo* in the light of that promised future, it would be the responsibility of theology not to take with ultimate seriousness traditional metaphysics and the resultant dilemmas for thought, but to seek to transcend them, trusting in the ultimate rationality of God.

Bultmann himself does not embark upon such a clarification of the doctrine of God; rather, in order to retain the recognition of the reality and the concreteness of the encounter with God, he directs his efforts toward a comparable reinterpretation of man. "If God is the object of our human talk, then we must realize that in order not to carry on philosophical dialectics and not to speculate, we must speak of *ourselves*. It has been clearly enough stated that this does not mean "of our experiences." It should be equally clear however that we are then speaking "of our *reality*, in which alone we have our being before God." ". . . the object of theology is nothing other than the conceptual presentation of man's existence as determined by God —that is, as man must see it in the light of Scripture." Hence Bultmann moved from the traditional metaphysical understanding of man to man's "historical nature," and found in the work of the early Heidegger the philosophical equipment needed for his recasting of theological anthropology.

If at this point Bultmann anticipated Germany's radical theologians for whom God-talk is no longer possible, and left it for subsequent philosophical theologians to concern themselves with an analogous reinterpretation of the nature of God, we should not ignore the fact that it is Barth who is the common source of America's death-of-God theologians. Of course, "Barthianism" consists in America, as in Europe, of a meeting of the later Barth's move to the right with conservatism's opening itself to influence from the center. But behind this standard Barthianism lie potentialities in the beginnings of dialectic theology that are only now, in quite diverging and surprising ways, entering into combinations with current trends to form the theological alternatives of our day.

NOTES

1. *Anfänge*, I, xi.
2. *Gesammelte Vorträge*, III: *Theologische Fragen und Antworten*, 1957, pp. 7-31.
3. *Die protestantische Theologie im 19. Jahrhundert* (Zollikon: Evangelischer Verlag, 1946), p. 379. Eng. tr. *Protestant Thought: From Rousseau to Ritschl*, tr. by Brian Cozens, 1959, p. 306.
4. Cf. now Larry Shiner, *The Secularization of History (Introduction to the Theology of Friedrich Gogarten)*, 1966, which indicates the recent interest in Gogarten's theology.
5. *Revolutionary Theology in the Making*, p. 53.
6. Cited by Moltmann, *Anfänge*, II, 94. The lecture was presented at the meeting of the "Friends of *Die Christliche Welt.*"
7. *Revolutionary Theology in the Making*, p. 110: ". . . Gogarten went on in such a way that I preferred to hide myself in silence because otherwise we could easily have gotten in trouble with each other 'in front of the enemy.' The final picture then was this: Gogarten, the possessor of a knowledge concerning whose source and content he was unable to give any kind of account, the others pressing him all the more eagerly but always fruitlessly, and finally departing shaking their heads. The Christological problem is dealt with and solved by him with the help of a speculative I-Thou philosophy."
8. Cf. Gogarten, "Karl Barths Dogmatik," *Theologische Rundschau*, n.F. I (1929), 60-80; "Das Problem einer theologischen Anthropologie," *Zwischen den Zeiten*, VII (1929), 493-511.
9. Cf. Barth's letter to Thurneysen of July 21, 1924, in *Revolutionary Theology in the Making*, p. 188.
10. *Anfänge*, I, xi.
11. *Ibid.*, x.
12. Bultmann, *Glauben und Verstehen*, I, 2, cited by Moltmann, *Anfänge*, I, xv.
13. *Glauben und Verstehen*, IV (1965), 194.
14. "Wir wollen nicht, dass dieser über uns herrsche!" *Kirchenblatt für die reformierte Schweiz*, 1911, issue 21.
15. *Anfänge*, I, 216; *The Word of God and the Word of Man* (Harper), pp. 213 f. (*Das Wort Gottes und die Theologie*, p.176).
16. *Augustin und das paulinische Freiheitsproblem. Ein philosophischer Beitrag zur Genesis der christlich-abendländischen Freiheitsidee*, *FRLANT* 44, n.F. 27, 1930, 2. Aufl. 1965, p. 24 of the second edition.
17. *Wahrheit und Methode: Grundzüge einer philosophischen Hermeneutik*, 1960, p. 289.
18. Ph. Bachmann, "Der Römerbrief verdeutscht und vergegenwärtigt," *Neue Kirchliche Zeitschrift*, 33 (1921), 518, referred to Barth's "pneumatic-prophetic exegesis" and thus inaugurated the term vigorously debated in the last half of the 20's.
19. *Glauben und Verstehen*, I, 38-64.
20. *Revolutionary Theology in the Making*, pp. 87-88.
21. Cf. *Die Religion in Geschichte und Gegenwart*, third edition, IV (1960), 1383.
22. *Revolutionary Theology in the Making*, p. 94.
23. *Ibid.*
24. *Anfänge*, I, xii.
25. P. 113 of the second German edition of *The Epistle to the Romans* (Eng. tr., p. 135) cited by Bultmann, below, p. 109 (*Anfänge*, I, 129).
26. *KD*, I, 2 (1938), 126 (*CD*, I, 2, 1956, 114).
27. P. 177 of the second German edition of *The Epistle to the Romans* (p. 175 of the eighth reprint of the second edition, 1947, Eng. tr., p. 195) cited by Bultmann, below, p. 117 (*Anfänge*, I, 138).

28. *Systematic Theology*, I (1951), 56. Cf. also p. 57: "Paradox points to the fact that in God's acting finite reason is superseded but not annihilated; it expresses this fact in terms which are not logically contradictory but which are supposed to point beyond the realm in which finite reason is applicable. . . . There is, in the last analysis, only *one* genuine paradox in the Christian message—the appearance of that which conquers existence under the conditions of existence. Incarnation, redemption, justification, etc., are implied in this paradoxical event. It is not a logical contradiction which makes it a paradox but the fact that it transcends all human expectations and possibilities. It breaks into the context of experience or reality, but it cannot be derived from it. The acceptance of this paradox is not the acceptance of the absurd, but it is the state of being grasped by the power of that which breaks into our experience from above it. Paradox in religion and theology does not conflict with the principle of logical rationality. Paradox has its logical place."

29. *The Divine Relativity: A Social Conception of God*, 1948, p. 3.

30. *Ibid.*, p. 5.

PART I

From
Religious Socialism
to Barthianism

1

The Debate with
Religious Socialism

PAST AND FUTURE:
Friedrich Naumann and Christoph Blumhardt
   Karl Barth

BASIC PROBLEMS OF CHRISTIAN SOCIAL ETHICS:
A Discussion with Paul Althaus
   Karl Barth

PAST AND FUTURE:

Friedrich Naumann and Christoph Blumhardt*

Karl Barth

It is not intended to be a judgment of men and of human affairs when I use the designation "Past and Future" for two men who have recently died and who both occupied a position of decisive, determinative importance in the life of the past decades—Friedrich Naumann and Christoph Blumhardt. Their paths met, ran parallel for a while, and then separated widely. For them, the great question of our day, socialism, became both promise and fate (take it as you will). In their interpretation of life both took positions—positions between which one must make a choice. Even today there will be no lack of clever persons who would like to "do justice" equally to Naumann and Blumhardt. We would have to regard this impartiality as the worst form of underestimating them *both*. The uncommitted observer who takes no one and nothing seriously is impartial. To take a person seriously means to understand him in the context of those things which move him to action. And that means a conscious renunciation of impartiality. I should like to honor both these dead men by taking them seriously through participating in that which motivated them, that is, through saying No to one and Yes to the other, not, to be sure, as a judge, but as a partisan. It is not a question of personalities, but of the ways, of the positions, of the totality of their direction and lifework. Personal questions are dealt with elsewhere and do not concern us here. It is not a question of praise or blame, but of recognition of the issue and its movement. History does not praise or blame, but it does continually carry out through its decisions a choice and a rejection. Without choice and rejection, without taking sides, it is not possible to have a fruitful relationship to significant persons and events. "Because you are lukewarm," it says in the Bible, "and neither cold nor hot, I will spew you out of my mouth." Therefore, beginning with the title, I confess at once my coldness here and my warmth there, and believe that in this way I can do justice to both the dead of whom I will speak better than those who are all too just.

FRIEDRICH NAUMANN

The church was the home of this German member of the Reichstag, leader of the Democratic (leftist liberal) Party, and writer,

---

* From *Neuer Freier Aargauer*, XIV (1919), issues 204 and 205.

Friedrich Naumann. It was the orthodox Lutheran Church of Saxony, but that was accidental; it could just as well have been the Catholic or the Mohammedan—in any case, *the* church, for which the relationship of the world to the divine is an a priori, fixed, ordered, unchanging connection which merely needs religious explanation and transfiguration. God is as he is, and the world is as it is, and besides man's nearest duties and sorrows there is nothing for him to do but to have "religion," that is, to quietly honor the inscrutable, and to be as optimistic as possible in his relations, through submissiveness and morality, to the conditions of this dark vale of earth. In his religious views Naumann underwent great changes: from a positive Christianity to modern theology, and from there again to Darwinism. But in his basic concept of the inescapable constancy of the relationship between God and the world he always remained the typical pastor. This was not easy for him. There is an uncomfortable moment when an upright man begins to reflect with open eyes both about religion and about life. Religion? Yes, what does religion mean and what help is it; what is the *truth* of religion when life with its ordinances and relationships, the whole raging course of the world as it is, so notoriously bypasses the love and righteousness of "God," of which religion speaks? Does religion consist in the subterfuge of calling fate "God"? And life? *Must* everything really be as it is, with all the sorrow and injustice, all the irrationality and disorder of the course of the world? Is there nothing *new* under the sun? Are not perhaps those right who struggle against *this* life, who would like to *reform this* life? May it not finally be that the divine begins where religion ceases?

The young Naumann also reached this dangerous and narrow pass. As a helper in the *Raues Haus,* a well-known charitable organization in Hamburg, as pastor in an industrial community in Saxony, and then as industrial chaplain in Frankfurt am Main he became acquainted with the situation of modern workers, as well as the efforts of Social Democracy, and at the same time began to read the New Testament with new eyes. He found in it a message so radical, so revolutionary, directed so precisely to a *transformation* of the world, that as a result the church's pretty balance between God and world seemed to him to threaten to fly apart. He was then very near to the sacred fire, very near to understanding the God whom the church does not understand. He had an inkling of the transience of the present world, and that behind all its appearances a new world was striving to be born. He had an inkling that something might not be in order between Jesus and present-day Christianity, that perhaps Jesus might not be the one whom all the churches bearing his name worship and honor—that is, the mild Savior who in the name of God blesses and transfigures all that exists—but that "God" might not only *mean* help, deliverance, transformation, but could *be* all this in life. Is it possible that the godless Social Democrats (they were fighting against the church!) understood God better than the church did? Was it possible that the church needed to repent and turn to the God of the godless?

It was a beautiful spring, full of hope for many Christians far beyond the boundaries of Germany, when Naumann began (in the mid-nineties of the last century) to raise these questions together with his friends and in connection with the court pastor Stöcker, who had been similarly aroused. I still remember the subtitle of his newspaper *Die Hilfe* in those days (as a schoolboy I sometimes saw it on my father's desk), "Help for God, help for one's brother, help for the State, help for oneself," and the impression these strong words made on me, although I scarcely understood them. It was widely felt that something very powerful, great, and new was coming. *But it did not come*. Oh, there was an Evangelical Social Congress at which year after year many learned and pious men gave wonderful lectures on the relation of Christianity to the social question; there were "Evangelical Labor Societies" and "Christian Trade Unions"; there was a "Christian Social Program," which tried to contrast the false socialism with the true socialism, which was related to the church, as Catholicism still tries to do today.

But remarkably, simultaneously with the complete loss of power and success of this type of activity, it became evident that all those who had undertaken it, and in particular Naumann, had lost that fundamental insight to which he had once come so near. To be sure, in his meditations, later collected under the name *Gotteshilfe* (which many a lazy pastor has since then raided for sermon material!), he continued to depict in glowing colors the "social Jesus," the Jesus of the poor and oppressed, sketched according to the picture of St. Francis of Assisi. It is, however, worthy of consideration that Naumann passed from this theme more and more to a religious veneration of nature and of modern culture. By the sea, in the mountains, in the desert (he became a great traveler), in the roar of machinery, in the bustle of great cities, in the iron structure of the Eiffel Tower in Paris and of the Frankfurt railway station, he now sought and found all sorts of revelations of God. *Why not?* God speaks everywhere. But without his noticing it, everything that existed began to be surrounded with a peculiar halo of religion—the State and the Hohenzollerns and the Prussian military, the German citizen with his incomparable "efficiency," capitalism, trade, enterprise, in short, the whole Germany of Kaiser Wilhelm, which reached the zenith of its brilliance about the turn of the century. Overnight the flag of "Christian socialism" changed into that of a "national socialism," and in 1903 disappeared completely into the museum of "liberalism." Then came Naumann's journey to Palestine, on which he made the discovery that Jesus could not possibly have been the practical social reformer whom we need, for if he had been, the streets and roads in that land would be in better condition! Then came the insight that the much praised friend of the poor, Francis of Assisi, must have been a good, noble fool, who has nothing to teach us in the age of the telegraph and express trains. This led finally to setting up that new trinity of democracy, industry, and world power (ballot, reinforced concrete, and armored ships), to whose proclamation Naumann, who had now completely gone over to politics, from then on dedicated his life.

How could this have happened? A truly tragic second conversion (if a first had ever occurred) had taken place. In the search for a new understanding of God and the world he had come to the point where it became inescapably clear to him, that *either* God is that which the New Testament calls God—but then "God" means the conversion of not only a few, but of all things, the renewal of the whole world, a transformation of life, in which not one stone can remain on another; then faith means commitment to this reformation, the preparation for it, counting on it as the most certain fact; then the Social Democrats are right, and not the social reformers; then the most radical Social Democrats are not yet radical enough; then acceptance of Social Democracy is only a little, obvious, very insufficient, poor and temporary *part payment* of what a "Christian" today owes to his faith. *Or,* Naumann now had to say, God is that which binds man with necessity to his nature and to the general laws of nature, which throws him into the struggle for existence, which, although not without religious and moral by-products, supplies the drive for self-preservation and racial instinct and teaches him to use them. Man cannot, O profound insight, get out of his skin. Faith then means the courageous taking up of the struggle for existence under the given conditions *and* incidentally the sad attempt to find meaning in the nonsense of life that arises from this. The church then is right in its teaching of maintaining the equilibrium. There is nothing new under the sun. Socialism, however radical it is, rests on a fatal misinterpretation of "reality." Social reform with careful protection of capitalism; democratization with deep respect for the Kaiser and the military; development of personality, but preferably only in the realm of "German inwardness"—are the highest and the ultimate that are to be expected, demanded, and achieved.

Naumann decided for the *or*. Confronted by the choice between the visible and the invisible, between the possible and the impossible, with a heavy heart, but finally deliberately and resolutely, he grasped the visible and possible. The stormy conflict between religion and life, God and world, was solved in a sensible arbitration, a *both-and* that gave both sides their due. Naumann was back where he had started— with the God who acts inscrutably, with the religion of the soul which may seek comfort and power in the world, but does not seek victory *over* the world.

When I met him in person a few years ago, I had the impression, in contrast to his books and essays which were written with immovable certainty, of a man who is not so certain of his affairs, because he secretly knows of something better than what he speaks. This uncertainty was in any case the best, the living, the eternal in him. But he no longer spoke this better which he knew. In his lifework the neo-German ideal conquered the insights of his early years. "All religion is now right for us, whether it is the Salvation Army or Islam, if it only helps us to hold out through the war," he told us then in so many words. On the ground which he chose, Naumann was an excellent, useful man. After the New Testament finally became a closed book for him, he was one of the most influential men of the new Germany (according to some, the most significant political mind after Bismarck!), a famous and ever-ready speaker in parliament or in public, the spiritual head of left-wing German liberalism. His name was mentioned last autumn in connection with the choice of a new president of the Reich. "All these things will I give thee, if thou wilt fall down and worship me." As far as the Social Democratic movement is concerned, he had always the warmest interest in the movements for trade unions and cooperatives, but he no longer understood the heart, the spirit, of socialism, indeed, no longer wanted to understand it. Untiringly he preached reason, moderation, and opportunism to the Social Democrats, and August 4, 1914, the dark day on which the German Social Democrats betrayed socialism, was the fateful symbol of the character of his own lifework.

He followed the affairs of the church from a distance with a certain mild superiority, as one who has looked behind the scenes and no longer lets himself be taken in. He looked back on his own path with that sad smile with which one recalls the ideals and errors of his youth. In the often-mentioned book *Mitteleuropa,* he finally showed what he expected of the future—an industrialized Germany, strengthened by Austria-Hungary, Holland, Switzerland, and other small countries, which would be the preliminary citadel of German world rule. This future was past before it became present. Raw reality strangely deserted in the most insolent manner this man who had given himself so fully and trustingly to "reality." If anything has been condemned as false, abolished, and annihilated through the present world catastrophe, then it is the religious and political thought-world of Friedrich Naumann. One cannot pass so close to truth and escape unpunished. His figure is the embodiment of the tragic greatness, guilt, and shame, not only of his people, but of our whole age.

CHRISTOPH BLUMHARDT

Blumhardt, who died on August 2, also started out as a pastor. But his path had nothing in common with the church, although his work, in contrast to the very active course of Naumann, outwardly was very nearly that of a pastor. His lifework, surprisingly modest and unpretentious, consisted of the direction of the spa Boll near Göppingen in Württemberg, which he had taken over from his father, and of the pastoral care of the guests who came there from near and far because of him. Even when the leaders of the church later recognized the new, strange element in him and tried to persuade him to give up the title of pastor, this did not bring about the slightest change in the character of his activity. It was only the confirmation that Blumhardt meant something other than what the church meant when *he* spoke of "God." His inner disposition was so free and so radical that it allowed him, even demanded of him, to be "pastor" with or without the title.

It is not possible to speak of Blumhardt without thinking of his father, Rev. Johann Christoph Blumhardt (1805-1880), one of the most remarkable men of the nineteenth century, who in the difficult experiences of his congregation in Möttlingen near Calw found his way through to a completely new, or rather, the oldest, insight in Christendom. The first stanza of a song he wrote during those struggles became symbolic of this new insight, first in Möttlingen and later in Boll. The awkwardness of the form stands in remarkable relation to the power and earnestness of the meaning.

Jesus ist der Siegesheld
Der all seine Feind besieget.
Jesus ists, dem alle Welt
Bald zu seinen Füßen lieget.
Jesus ists, der kommt mit Pracht
Und zum Licht führt aus der Nacht.

Jesus, the victorious hero,
Conquers every foe.
At the feet of Jesus soon,
The whole world shall bow.
Jesus, glorious, out of night
Leads us onward to the light.

That was the atmosphere in which the younger Blumhardt (born 1842) grew up. That unhappy word "religion," which contains also the inflexibility of the "real" world, this word, with which man, tired of life, turns to the distant unknown, was no longer used in Möttlingen and Boll. The "God" about whom these men inquired and to whom they witnessed was the *living* God. This was true in the double sense that they wanted to understand him as the Bible does, as the one who lives, from whom new deeds, power, and proofs are to be expected, and that they wanted to seek for and await his Kingdom not only in the souls of individual men or in a distant heaven, but above all and first of all in life, precisely in the "real" life of men on earth. Once more the relation of God to the world appeared to them as a mighty, historical process, a movement, a victorious struggle, which must end with the renewal of all things. The cheap assertion by all the churches, so often in contradiction to the facts, of the omnipotence and dominion of God *is* not true, but it *becomes* true through the victory of Jesus on earth. (And for this reason "Jesus, the victorious hero"—not merely the friend of souls or the preacher of morality, but the herald and bearer of divine might on earth.)

In connection with this struggle and in the light of this coming victory, the two Blumhardts sought to understand the situation of the world. The church's interpretation that the world as a whole was and would remain wicked, while somehow in the details much could be modified, eased, and improved by religion, they turned upside down, and said, even without religion there is much that is good and hopeful in the particulars, many reminders of the divine in the world; still as a whole it needs and awaits a thoroughgoing redemption and renewal, not through religion, but through the real power of God. What appeared again in Boll that was new and in accord with the New Testament can be comprehended in one word: *hope*—hope for a visible and tangible appearing of the lordship of God over the world (in contrast to the simple, and so often blasphemous, talking about God's omnipotence); hope for radical help and deliverance from the former state of the world (in opposition to that soothing and appeasing attitude which must everywhere come to a halt before unalterable "relationships") ; hope for all, for mankind (in contrast to the selfish

concern for one's own salvation and to all the attempts to raise up
religious supermen and aristocrats) ; hope for the physical side of life
as well as for the spiritual, in the sense that not only sin and sorrow,
but also poverty, sickness, and death shall one day be abolished (in
contrast to a purely spiritual ideal of the so-called "religious-moral"
life). To believe in "God" meant, for the two Blumhardts, to take this
comprehensive hope seriously, more seriously than all other considerations; to regard and deal with everything on the basis of this hope;
to place one's self and one's life in all particulars in the great light of
this hope. This new insight is all along the line and in all points down
to the present day a total contrast to the general religion of churches
and pastors of all denominations.

What was original in the younger Blumhardt was precisely that
he did not feel that he had to be original, as is usually the way of sons
in relation to their fathers. He merely continued to be true to the
insights of his father concerning God and the world, which were indeed
those of the Bible. He represented and expressed them in *his* day;
that means, however, in *our* day, the period of the end of the nineteenth century and the beginning of the twentieth. Thus it is natural
that in time much that his father had placed great hope in assumed
less importance for him; for example, the visible church with its
forms, experiments, and successes; theology with its points of doctrine
and its historical erudition; foreign missions and the activities of
Christian societies with their rather doubtful self-assurance and busywork. The question mark which the new insights placed over the
whole of former Christianity became even clearer for him than for his
father. But he also saw more clearly the light of the promise and the
faith into which *all* men, *all* relationships and movements, particularly
of the "worldly" life are brought by the gospel; as a result, he focused
his attention on a variety of spheres and areas of life to which his
father's eyes had not been fully opened.

One thing stood out ever more clearly: that there was contained in
the new insight, because of the forgiving, redeeming love which
included here everything human, a comprehensive attack on the bases
of present-day society, culture, and church. Blumhardt had a fine,
keen ear for the sighing for redemption which runs through all of
creation and mankind. And therefore he could not come to terms at
any point with what now is abiding and of valid. It was the burden
of his life, and also his joy, that always and everywhere he not only
could but had to believe in the new that will be born out of the old.
So in Boll, as perhaps nowhere else, that patience was preached which
arises out of the strongest opposition, and the opposition which is

likewise embedded in the greatest patience. But above it all there always stood the great divine "Forward!" Because God lives, not only a few of man's affairs but all of them must become different. Despite all religion, man has endured, engaged in, and borne too much non-sense, injustice, and misfortune, not only to his own hurt and shame, but above all to the dishonor of the name of God and to the damage of the love of Christ. Because God lives, man must awake from sleep, the sleep of honor and piety, in order to give again to the whole of his life, not only to isolated, rather superficial relationships, the meaning which today he has lost.

Blumhardt was as little deceived as Naumann was over "reality," over the nature of man. He did not expect to make it different through preaching, agitating, and instructing, but neither did he renounce taking into account the necessary conversion of man. He trusted in the *real* reality, in the *natural* nature of man, in the manifestation of that which is now still hidden in man, in a new outpouring of the *Holy Spirit*. Because he believed in God, he also believed in man, and be-cause he believed in man, he also believed in the renewal of the world. If the gift "from above" were to be understood again and find a ready soil, all things would be possible. In the meantime, however, he af-firmed joyfully and hopefully, as signs and harbingers of the coming victory of Jesus Christ, everything that seemed to him to point toward the renewal of the world which was in preparation.

He, like Naumann, was a great friend of nature and of natural science. The concept of evolution occupied him as much as it did the former. But he learned from nature not the desolate and destructive doctrine that we all must complete the circle of our existence according to eternal, great, ironclad laws, but the joyous message of the inex-haustibility of the possibilities of life, which became for him, as it had once for Paul (1 Corinthians 15), a parable of the resurrection. He, like Naumann, had an open eye for the wonders of modern technology, for the progress of the human spirit in knowledge and ability. But he did not lose himself in admiration of man and his works, did not lose sight of the chief issue, the question of the true liberation and reviving of human existence for which even the highest cultural achievements could at best be parable and preparation. Like Naumann, Blumhardt had a liking for travel in distant lands. But what he brought home was not the knowledge of all sorts of strange facts and with it the depressing truth that man is the same everywhere, but always new stimuli and the new possibility of believing in the men of all lands and peoples and having hope for them. "All that is perishable is but a parable," but still a parable of the *imperishable*.

His path too, as did Naumann's, finally crossed that of Social Democracy. But he did not succumb to the temptation which then came to those civic-minded men who were concerned with this phenomenon, the temptation to affirm the practical, liberal, and attainable in socialism—that is, the trade union and cooperative movements— and to shrug their shoulders compassionately over the incomprehensible utopianism of the final goal of socialism. That is what Naumann did, and it corresponded to his position in regard to the New Testament. Blumhardt, however, readily recognized precisely in the radicalism and the teleological thought of the socialists the parable of the Kingdom of God for our time. This protected him from the further temptation to which Naumann and Stöcker succumbed, that of wishing to place a "Christian" socialism alongside Social Democracy, a project which was doomed to die. If the godless have understood God better than the Christians have, then it cannot be the task of the latter to try to outdo them through a "Christian" imitation. We should rather give God the honor, and in this case give the godless their due. This is what Blumhardt then did; not content with multiplying the unnumbered host of the "socially minded" in the bourgeois camp, to the shock and loss of almost all his friends, he openly entered the Social Democratic party of Württemberg and for a number of years even let himself be elected to the local legislature. This step was a completely unpolitical, simple, and obvious confession before God and man of his living belief in the future. In this was the proof of the fact that he was serious about this belief. It cost Blumhardt his title of pastor, the larger number of his former adherents, and the remainder of the confidence which "Christian" circles still had in him. The great astonishment that the hope for the Kingdom of God could mean this is still reflected in the forced explanations with which even his closest friends try to explain this step and where possible to deny its basic importance.

Blumhardt was in other ways much imitated by those around him, although he stressed most strongly that each must travel his own path in freedom. In a remarkable way his friends have made the *greatest* use of the freedom *not* to be Social Democrats! But that is another matter! Blumhardt's secret was his endless movement between hurrying and waiting, between lively participation in the fullness of what is and astonished inner waiting for that which seeks to be through the power from on high. In his relation to God, he achieved also a vital relation to his own time. No world war and no revolution could make him a liar. At one time Naumann and Blumhardt knew each other. I was later once in the strange position of carrying greetings from Naumann to Blumhardt, most probably the last such greetings. The former understood the latter in matters of hurrying and setting to work, but less well in matters of waiting and listening. On the other hand, there are some friends of Blumhardt who understand very effectively how to wait without hurrying, how to deal with and to rejoice again and again in the great thoughts of the Kingdom of God, and at the same time to follow the course of the world with a smile. In the one case as in the other they change the new insights into that which the church has always said. The unique element, and I say it quite deliberately, the prophetic, in Blumhardt's message and mission consists in the way in which the hurrying and the waiting, the worldly and the divine, the present and the coming, again and again met, were united, supplemented one another, sought and found one another. It is no wonder that this man made a strange, forbidding, baffling impression on so many. He was of necessity a stranger among all those who were willing and able to feel at home in present-day society, church, and world. It is also no wonder that many others, who in all types of personal difficulties and sorrows sought comfort and counsel, found in Boll the answer that no one else was able to give, but without committing themselves to that which was *his* concern for man, *his* great cause. Many others became neither his enemies nor his friends, but they heard the message and were infected by the restlessness, moved by the strong emotion, and gripped by the faith which were in this man. His uncomprehending opponents and his grateful followers will be silenced in time. He himself will remain alive among all who can grasp what was the issue in his life—the victory of the future over the past.

BASIC PROBLEMS OF CHRISTIAN SOCIAL ETHICS:

A Discussion with Paul Althaus*

Karl Barth

It is rewarding for us who are chastised with the name of "religious socialists" to concern ourselves with Paul Althaus, because—more than he wants to admit—he is a fellow seeker, a man of basic questions and not of assured basic answers. In his book he does not offer us a disposition of the problems which claim our attention, but a contribution toward basically sharpening them. This is done partially in opposition to our thoughts, and partially also merely in underlining insights which, as he well knows (pp. 12, 32, 59), have long been discussed in our small circle as well. We really have no occasion to be on guard lest "one bring dispassionate objections to bear on us" (p. 31); rather we are thankful that this occurs on the basis of the exigencies of the situation and not from the safe harbor of one who already knows, is already decided, who merely dispenses oracles from some special source. Althaus is not such a mastermind. He also knows Luther well enough not to use him to strike us dead, but rather to remind us of what is alive, of what is at stake, in the present crisis. I gather that he would like to have finished us off more thoroughly than he succeeded in doing. But he has sufficient insight and integrity to submit himself entirely to the pressure of the problem, and as a result he gets no further than really opening up the question. "We simply cannot let the new Christian radicalism confuse our consciences in relation to law, fatherland, State, and military service, in the name of Jesus and the Sermon on the Mount," he says on page 32, and in this he openly states the motive which brings him to write against us, as it already has so many others. But he also said a few pages earlier: "By the command to love, Jesus leads those who are his into the greatest peril and uncertainty. . . . He does not speak against law, State, the military, social stratification, but he also does not speak for them. . . . Jesus confronts us with the difficult question. We cannot find the answer in what he says" (pp. 28 f.). It is to be hoped that Althaus sees *who* it is who "confuses" the consciences here, if he wants to express it that way! He also concludes at the decisive point with the

---

* From *Das Neue Werk*, IV (1922), pp. 461-472. Barth is replying to Althaus' *Religiöser Sozialismus: Grundfragen der christlichen Sozialethik* (Gütersloh: Bertelsmann), 99 pp.

statement that we cannot pass "through all that without distress of conscience," and even says explicitly: "The inner distress is a proof of the deepest obedience to Jesus" (pp. 89 f.) . Moreover he will certainly not let himself miss seeing that the "solution" of Luther, with which the book closes, is precisely good and Christian insofar as it offers no solution, and that wherever it was understood as a solution the immediate consequence was gross misconduct. Perhaps Althaus should discuss with those who are basically closer to his position, such as Emmanuel Hirsch (p. 90) , why it is that his book did not turn out to be less ambiguous, more devastating. We can only rejoice in the fact that he has taken a stand at a point where we are able to enter into discussion with him.

First, Althaus agrees with us in the general thought that there is a will of God not only for the behavior but also for the conditions of souls and in an ultimate metaphysical sense there is no "independent law" of conditions over against this will. He knows that the realization of this objective will of God is the duty and task of the Christian community, which is not static, not motivated merely by pastoral concerns (pp. 43-46). He even undertakes (pp. 78-79) to base this concept on Luther and regrets the silence of Lutheranism concerning the development of economic and social life. He blames the church for having left Stöcker alone, and in this way once again missed the hour of destiny (p. 52) by having "failed to recognize, kept silent, and smothered" the critical power of the fundamentals of the gospel in relation to economic life (p. 50; cf. pp. 59 f.) . If we miss something here it is a clear and forceful presentation of how far the gospel possesses this power to criticize society. In any case this is not made clear in the chapters about Jesus and Paul. Althaus surely does not mean that little bit of humanitarian teaching on love that can be inferred from the Synoptics if one is sufficiently color blind. But how is it that in just this context he knows so little how to begin to deal with the *eschatology* of the New Testament, and on the other hand that it has made apparently no impression on him at all that the Social Democrats are today so fundamentally in advance of the church (long before there was a Stöcker!) that for the latter there is very little left to do this time but to feel ashamed of itself? But it is enough for us to see that Althaus knows of that "critical power," in any case does not dispute it, and perhaps even notices something of the fact that the church should today apply it above all to itself.

Althaus, in the second place—in the context of those general thoughts—agrees with us in recognizing the relative right of a way of life, let us express it carefully, which is more oriented in the direction of socialism (pp. 50-52). He cites approvingly Tillich's statement that Christianity has a greater affinity for certain (this means for the socially oriented) forms of the organization of society than for others (p. 50). To be sure, he rightly reminds us "religious socialists" that the natural law, Calvinist, Western ideal of democracy and of socialism is only one ideal among others (pp. 47-50), that Christianity turns its criticism just as much against unrestricted private capitalism as against rigid socialism, that there is therefore "no formula for the right economy," that in the struggle of the two ideals which stand over against each other today only a knowledge of the subject matter and a live conscience can decide from case to case (pp. 55-58). He criticizes here our dilettantism, absolutism, and nomism (pp. 58 f.). But he nevertheless spares—and as a Lutheran that is much to his credit—at least in this context, the most evil of all theological doctrines, the doctrine of the ordinances of creation, or the God-willed social class structures. His sympathy belongs clearly to the "organic, aristocratic" ideal of the State, but he does say of it (unfortunately in agreement with the well-known accusation of the Entente ideologists) nothing more than that it is "deeply rooted in German history and in the thinking of the German classes" (p. 49). He declines, however, and this is the point, to give it a religious basis. He is, rather, inclined to admit that all politics consists at best in service to the whole based on mutuality, and is not Christian love (p. 40), although this insight (p. 65) suddenly appears clouded again, and although the religious socialists are once more roughly attacked just before the end, because they do not want to admit that "national politics" could be something else besides "naked egoism" (p. 93). These are inconsistencies which the author himself must iron out and which I would rather not hold him to. For in another place he shows understanding even for the fact that, in the famous opposition of the two "ideals," strictly speaking it is a matter not only of the struggle of one ideal against the other, but of the struggle of the ideals themselves against the hard necessities of existence (p. 55), of the contest of spirit and matter, life and work (p. 59). He certainly perceives that this is admitting the relative advantage of the "Calvinistic" ideal, and that he has rightly made Tillich's statement about the "greater affinity" his own. He demands therefore that "Christendom" not let this struggle cease again (p. 59). Yes, he goes so far in the discussion of the Lutheran concept of authority as to expand it so that even the economic-political liberation of an oppressed class, and thus the activity of a labor leader, becomes an office of "authority" which can be a part of the Christian task (pp. 91-92). Althaus would need only to apply the same thought to pacifism as well (pp. 61-71) in order to come still closer to us. That here too he might perceive the relative possibility of rejecting the existing order as clearly as that of recognizing it, that here too he might become aware of the relatively greater right of rejection, that here too he might renounce the evil, romantic justification of existing conditions, is certainly only a question of time and of further reflection.

In the third place, Althaus is in agreement with us in the interpretation that the position of the Christian in society can basically be only inconsistent. What irritates him about us is the primitive and naïve manner in which we occasionally, in answering the difficult question of the practical application of Christianity, simply, directly, and untiringly appealed to democracy, socialism, communism, anarchism (p. 47), or even still do. If I concede to him that this naturally is not possible, he will perhaps on his side concede to me the privilege of referring for a few years, inconsistently and indirectly, for instructional purposes, to these possibilities, just as the modern Lutherans, for example, for more than a generation have referred to the old Prussian state. Surely he sees not only the mote in his brother's eye! No, he knows well, that even his own—that is, the Lutheran—solution, the paradoxical doctrine of the two realms, is at least under suspicion of being "a compromise, a relaxation of the absoluteness of Jesus, or even a sophistical solution" (p. 88). Between Scylla and Charybdis, between the old and new secularization of Christianity, he is obviously seeking his own middle way. We are glad that he perceives the impossibility of both, and that he is still unable to preserve intact the illusion of a third possibility satisfactory to all. We are glad that particularly the chapter on Luther, in which he obviously in an extraordinary manner intended to correct the "confusion of spirits" which we instigated (p. 74), accomplishes nothing, absolutely nothing, other than to make clear that the realization of the will of God in the world is all along the line (even the "hearts," even the "consciences," of Christians are in the world!) the task and the hope, but also the question and the confusion of the Christian; that here there is no road, but only steps, no accomplishment, but only intention, no "Christianity" which is in any sense triumphant, but—here I would like to confront the prophet with a "sober objection"—at best a heathendom, striving, struggling, believing, in the entire distress and under the entire promise which have come upon it from God in Christ.

These are my formulations, which Althaus will presumably reject. In this I am perhaps indicating all the more clearly what conclusion I draw from my statements. Behind the Lutheran teaching of the two realms there still stands dominant the teaching of justification by faith

alone. That which Luther hated and combated in the Baptists and
others was moral, religious dogmatism. Hence it is adapted least of all
to the erection of a new "Christian" dogmatism of a conservative
stamp. Man is in the wrong; no assertion of "ethics" may lure us
away from this conclusion of "dogmatics." I am not now overlooking
the fact that Althaus asserts in strong terms that Luther's "solution"
signifies the practical overcoming of the dualism of world and Kingdom of God (pp. 77-87), and that there is a unified moral stance
(thus in itself justified) of the Christian. But all of us, like Luther
himself, as well as Althaus, only assert this and do not demonstrate it,
much less make it a method by which one could somehow attain to
this rightness. "This unity is real only in that it includes the powerful
tension between intention and work" (p. 87). But this means that it
is, precisely insofar as it is reality, no unity; it is not given in some
"stance" or other, not even that of the so-called "Christian"; it rests
on Christ, on the forgiveness of sins; it is the unity of the new man.
If our "professional dealings" as such were simply "dealings in love,"
if it were not a "dangerous and seductive matter," if it did not signify
any longer the "mighty tension" which brings peril to our conscience
(pp. 89 f.), then we would be rid of God, rid of the threat as well as
the promise which comes from him. That our office, our professional
activity, is service, a work of love (p. 85), is true (whether it is now
war service or the pastorate!) never directly, never otherwise than on
the detour by way of an "in-spite-of" of unprecedented paradoxical
nature. We will never be able to assert it otherwise than with grim
humor, whereby we are comforted a little that this paradoxical nature
is also proper to God's activity itself, which, burning with love, still
uses force (p. 85). In as far as Althaus has really not led us out beyond
this paradox, not a step backward to the fleshpots of the land of Egypt
and not a step forward to that activity of the Christian in society
which is assured and justified in itself and of which the religious
public on the right and on the left longs to hear, *we* are in any case
one with *him*. He is really not the man (because he himself really
already knows too much) to step, in pastoral concern and armed
with Luther, between us and the confused spirits. If he admits this,
he will surely turn around from the top step of the pulpit, from where
he is still speaking to us, climb down, and in "comforted despair" take
his seat beside us on the little bench of poor sinners, where there no
longer exists any appreciable difference between the Lutheran and the
religious-socialist concept of "building the world" and "keeping away
from the world."

What really separates Althaus from us, what presumably hinders him from recognizing as legitimate the interpretation of his position given here, from leaving the pulpit steps and joining us, is not the specifically "religious-social" problem. I surmise that concerning them, assuming elasticity on his side, I could quickly come to agreement with him. We are not, however, unequivocally united in what we call "God." Therefore in the same insight into the same materials we place the emphasis so differently. Therefore we read Luther as well as the Bible through such different eyes. Therefore, presumably, we take in practice such entirely different positions to the questions of the present day. Even this contrast is naturally relative and therefore hopeful. The chasm which divides men from God is absolute; the chasms which divide men from one another are relative, even when it must be so for the sake of God. Even so, there are great, basic disagreements which are hard to remove, and they must be recognized openly. What does Althaus really mean when he speaks of God and his will? I am surely not doing him an injustice when I prepare the way for answering this question by another question. In what connections does he become interested, eager, eloquent, so that the reader must notice that this is what the man really wants to say to us? In the book under discussion I find two such occasions of zeal: first, where the author speaks of the elementary conditioned nature of our life, and second, where he speaks of what he calls the "attitude and obligation of the heart" (p. 76), "congregation" or "Christendom." At these two points he evidently sees himself somehow confronted by ultimate realities in the sense that the possibilities and necessities which confront him at these two points somehow coincide directly and immediately with the possibility and necessity of the will of God. Because at these two points he now (even though with slight doubts!) believes he knows (that which he can know as little as we can!), he has written his book against us. What could he have against us if he did not feel that he had this knowledge of God? And it is because at these points he now sets up only human answers (instead of being satisfied that here the human question about God is unavoidable) that his book has turned out so uneven and full of contradictions. For those points at which one no longer dares to question further are the source of all arbitrariness and contradictions in thought. Althaus sees much more of the dialectic which arises at just these two points than many others do; it is a pity that he did not see a little more of it!

Let us begin with the first. On page 34 Althaus asks the serious question, whether love can be thought of as the only structure of the world. I would answer Yes to this question. The love which is "thought of" in the Sermon on the Mount is either an illusion or the only "structure of the world." God's love is surely the crisis of all that we call love for God and for man. To take part in this love is the way from life through death to life. As a reminder of this we stand under the hard but meaningful law of a world order that all along the line is anything but love. To believe, however, means to affirm the love of God as the only conceivable structure of the world, despite the fact that the only world order which we know confronts us in the most pronounced manner as non-love. Althaus thinks otherwise. He seems not to notice at all that the questions raised by the Sermon on the Mount deal with God and the either-or of faith, and that good taste (not to speak of anything more) must prevent him from answering here with a "both-and." But he says quite confidently, "The answer can only be a negative one," therefore, it is not conceivable that love is the only structure of the world; there is still another. Where, in contrast to religious-social optimism, he should have, with his own sensitivity for what is decisive, spoken of the enigmatic nature of the world order which we know, of the hiddenness of God's creation, of the darkness in which faith must commit itself to the love of God, he spoke instead about the "very elementary necessity of law and the State." He remembers of course that Luther customarily spoke above all of the reign of sin here, therefore of the *problematical* nature of this which is elementary. But he quickly bypasses this. He knows better. "Everyone knows . . ."—Yes, that is it, everyone. From this it necessarily follows that God will not be spoken of here. Thus everyone knows that ". . . governance by natural law and law in personal relationships are the two basic presuppositions of all personal as well as of all social life" (p. 35). Of what life?, we ask curiously. Of the "higher," "historical," "moral" life, we are informed incidentally and rather uncertainly (pp. 35-37). But what if the Sermon on the Mount is dealing with *eternal* life, as Luther's opinion certainly held? What then is the meaning of the "reasonable" but really all too simple proof (pp. 35 f.) that communism and anarchism are not practical, that a little order here below is wiser than the free sway of love? What is the meaning of the all too illuminating reference to the value of power and the State "for the development of personal morality, for all educative effectiveness in the Kingdom of God" (p. 37)? What is the meaning of the all-too compromising reminder of church law (p. 39)? How does Althaus know that "in the Kingdom of God" there is education? Where is it written that the love which is spoken of in the Sermon on the Mount needs a basis which must first be secured, regulated, even created, by law (p. 37)? Not one single genuine "enthusiast" has proven to be teachable by means of such an appeal to the eternal iron necessities of the world and their meaning for salvation, and the reason is that when someone comes to him with *that*, he has the gospel on his side against his Lutheran mentor, the gospel that speaks of God and of faith and not of what "everyone knows," of ultimate things and not of penultimate. One cannot do without the "misunderstanding of human nature and the simple necessities of historical life" (p. 37), so strongly censured by Althaus, where it is a matter of hearing the message of Christ. Insofar as we hear it, we certainly do not hear something else, and insofar as we are still hearing something else, we are not hearing the gospel.

The same line of thought meets us a second time and in more detail in pages 62-73, for me the *worst* part of the book. It deals with pacifism. Althaus asks, what is the concrete content of the norms of righteousness in world politics? I would answer again, that their highly concrete content is the righteousness of God, so concrete that no one kind of political righteousness could be identical with it even in the slightest. It is the scales on which the peoples are weighed in their conscientious as well as in their conscienceless decisions, in their peaceful as in their warlike destinies, the pressing, burdensome, highly disquieting, highly actual question in all politics, the deadly poison for all—the pacifistic as well as the nationalistic—ideologies with which man seeks to escape the truth. Althaus answers differently. The "living movement" of history which we know really seems to him to coincide with the realization of the will of God and therefore the process of thinking oneself into the "organic laws" of history (how can the naturalism of these formulae not be offensive to him?) seems as significant as an at least partial recognition of the will of God (p. 62). When in the life of the nations its power rises (e.g., England?) "as the capacity for historical life and historical dominion" (p. 63), then he sees that there in earnest right arises. Now the "earnestly tested historical calling of a nation" (p. 66) becomes at once a truly mystical quantity, somehow raised to the heavens over the profane alternatives which are termed "accidental parliamentary majority" or "international court of justice." The vocation of a nation should be a "question of transcendental depth" (p. 65), because here the "irrational" and the "creative deed" are at home (p. 66), and politics is now suddenly "in its depths a religious matter" (p. 65; since on p. 40 the religious socialists were to be refuted, it reads differently there).

Now everything is possible. Now war can no longer be called murder, but rather a "mighty self-measuring of the nations for leadership and for the future" (p. 67). Now, sight unseen, we are to "live through the competition and die the death," no longer call war as fate an ethical problem, but leave its abolition to "the eschatology of faith" (p. 69). Now the Christian conscience has only a twofold task, deciding whether wars are necessary or unnecessary, and avoiding personal hatred in war (pp. 94-96), as if this unspeakably inadequate and questionable solution corresponded somewhat better to the level of the Sermon on the Mount than does the indecisiveness of the pacifists! Where does Althaus get the right to praise the irrational as a consecrated sanctuary? How does he know about the "transcendental depth"? How is it that the concept "Prussia" or "Bavaria" should possess higher dignity than the concept "League of Nations"? With what reason and on what ground does he dare to reject Luther's teaching of the sinful conditionality of the elementary bases of society without the simplest attempt at refutation (p. 71)? How is it that in his enthusiasm for people, State, war, etc., he totally forgets to consider original sin and to develop the problem of ethics on that basis? But, one moment! "A deep premonition tells us that this state of history is connected with the separation of man from God by sin, even as physical death is" (pp. 69, 95). Certainly a very deep premonition! But why merely a premonition? Why is it not taken seriously? How does Althaus come to identify its content with "the irrational element of life itself," with "the course of fate or (!) predestination" (p. 71), to treat as something given what is no more and no less than a problem, but in the New Testament is, significantly enough, the problem that has been basically overcome? Why is it not vital to faith in God and in the living Christ to forget the ineradicable limit of all moral ordering of the world: life as nature, fate, and struggle; indeed to forget it as such an ineradicable limit, that is to say, to contrast it as the perishable to the imperishable, as what is totally dissimilar to it, incomparably less than it in significance and dignity? How should it be more pious "to bow before the God who has placed us in this world under such laws of life" (p. 72)? Who is this God then? Is he really God? He is "life itself" (p. 71), the life that itself still stands under the law of death. If faith in God and Christ is resurrection faith, I should think it would be essential for it to be resolute, unromantic, disrespectful disbelief toward *this* God. And again, the most inadequate, rationalistic pacifist, in his protest against war as the manifestation of that which has absolutely no right to exist, has the New Testament on his side.

The second point at which Althaus becomes animated is "Christendom," the "congregation," the Kingdom of God as the "lordship of the gospel in the heart" (p. 38). He rightly contrasts "Christianity" with all kingdoms and organizations as something specifically different. He rightly expects great things of it, ascribes significance to it in relation to social politics, although somewhat less clearly in relation to world politics. But it is just this—great things, significance, the caution, the mere both-and—which causes us offense here also! Can it really be "that the Christian lives and acts always in the Kingdom of God, but cannot understand his total actions as such in terms of the Kingdom of God" (p. 90)? Not "his total actions"? Well then, as I turn myself against Althaus' *position*, I would like to ask: A part of them? Who is it that teaches us to understand even a part of our actions as action for the Kingdom of God? Is there then perhaps a "Christendom"? Does Althaus think he knows this entity? "Even a reign of peace in the world remains worldly in nature," he says in one place against the pacifists (p. 39). Yes, but is this not also true of a world reign of peace in the hearts of men to be established through perhaps mission or evangelization? Or is the skepticism which he brings to bear on a political reign of world peace to be turned into credulity when it is a question of the church? Even of this reign and its establishment (thus of missions, as an example) the objection raised against Friedrich Wilhelm Foerster must be repeated: "How can something like that be mentioned in the same breath with Jesus' words about commitment of life?" (p. 41). That "entirely personal something" (p. 28) in which, according to Althaus, the socialism of Jesus consists, is surely not identical with any definite Christianity realized in these or those persons. Or is it? In Althaus I read sentences like the following: "In the midst of performing his duties to the order of the world, yes, precisely through them, the Christian fulfills Jesus' command of love" (p. 76). "The Christian can, even in undertakings of raw, hard work in the life of law, the State, and war, live completely according to the spirit of the Sermon on the Mount" (p. 77). "Every judge and official and statesman who is also a moral person or a Christian lives inwardly by authority of these thoughts of Luther" (p. 88). "The Christian fulfills," "the Christian can completely," "the Christian lives"—where does Althaus, who is so sober in relation to the *political* realization of the will of God, get the certainty with which he asserts its *psychological* realization? Surely it is not the case that the spirit of the Sermon on the Mount and Jesus' commandment to love are things that are possible, attainable, and feasible spiritually but not politically and socially? There is surely no difference: The inner life, even the religious, even the Christian religious life, stands under the same judgment under which Althaus (and we agree with him) sees the outward life. If Althaus were to dispute this, I would say to him that he has not yet perceived the judgment under which outward life stands; yes, that by a retreat, through the help of Luther, into inwardness he is in fact seeking to escape it; that his turning from outer to inner politics means first of all the creation for man of a religious "mighty fortress" where he can be assured he is justified before God—protected—the rest of his worldly activity confirmed as well, surrounded by a soft, transfiguring glow of God's will; that at the basis of the removal of eschatology from ethics there lies the intention of making the former harmless and of removing the latter from the threatening shadow of the former *ad majorem gloriam hominis.* Althaus desires that as little as I do, but I confess that his book has greatly strengthened my deep mistrust of the sinister connection between Lutheran inwardness and Lutheran worldliness. Whoever can bring the will of God into such dangerous proximity to the little bit of experience of heart and conscience of so-called Christians and the little bit of "common life of the congregation" will also of necessity bring it into the quite fatal proximity to history, nature, and fate. The psychological immanence of God of necessity brings the cosmic in its train. Or am I doing Althaus an injustice when I surmise that he does not ascribe "transcendental depth" to the "congregation" as he does to the national State only because this is obvious for him? Does he not really see in the complex heart–conscience–Christendom –church a kind of ultimate reality, from which he thinks he can discern the ultimate will of God, and in which he can identify an occurrence of the will of God? If so, then I would term the lack of feeling for distance, the obscuring of the *critical* character of the concepts "congregation" and "creation," which is revealed in this, the point in his book which I find most objectionable. That Althaus really does this, however, is unequivocally clear in the desperate attempt on the last pages to add to the "attitude of the soul" (described as "inner abstinence from the world"), an "outward renunciation" as a postulated function within the congregation, taking up into the program of Christian ethics voluntary poverty, celibacy, political detachment (even refusal of military service?), for the sake of the "organic-biological" communal life of the congregation, thus making what is individual not the limit but the real subject matter of ethics. Why is it that Luther himself did not come to this idea? Because for him "congregation" and "creation" marked the distance as well as the communion between God and the world, a dialectic which Althaus did not see through. Thus it is in vain that he defends himself against the suspicion that his completing of the concept of the congregation is the renewal of the dual morality of Catholicism. The motive that moves him to this is really not a new one, for Catholicism also is concerned with the "total life of the congregation," with the bad

conscience of a merely inward Christendom that demands a supplement. And what is betrayed in Althaus' new attempt at this old possibility is only the deep uncertainty of the entire religious-social and
non-religious-social Protestantism in relation to the concepts of justification and forgiveness of sins, which, if recognized in their critical
power, would smoke out the hiding place of a mere Christianity of the
heart or of the conscience as well as the never-never land of an
"organic-biological" congregation, and would present man at every
point as the one who can never be justified, and who is entirely and
for all time cast on the mercy of God. It is precisely in this thought
that the deep rightness of Lutheranism against religious socialism consists. It knows, or it says it knows, what we have at times forgotten—
that even in the best life all our doings are in vain. It is thus all the
more regrettable when in this book its representative ends with mild
ambiguity in just this respect. With this pietistic-churchly line of
thought he will hardly be able to instruct any of us, because he shows
us only too well that he is a patient in the same hospital where we are.
A "solution" by the "direct action" of individuals has really played a
role in our movement, and a fateful one. That is something that
Althaus did not need to tell us.

If I have spoken sharply, I have done it only for the sake of clarity.
The book remains a congenial phenomenon, because even in its inner
flaws it is a proof that the ice is melting. I was given the occasion for
speaking out by the fact that Althaus gave me—I do not know whether
to say the honor or the shame—of counting me one of the most "moderate" of the religious socialists. I hope that what is involved in "moderation" has become clear to him in the process.

2

A Discussion of
Barth's *Epistle to the Romans*

FOREWORD TO THE FIRST EDITION
  Karl Barth

THE EPISTLE TO THE ROMANS BY KARL BARTH:
An Up-to-Date, Unmodern Paraphrase
  Emil Brunner

A MODERN INTERPRETER OF PAUL
  Adolf Jülicher

THE HOLY EGOISM OF THE CHRISTIAN:
An Answer to Jülicher's Essay: "A Modern Interpreter of Paul"
  Friedrich Gogarten

FOREWORD TO THE SECOND EDITION
  Karl Barth

KARL BARTH'S *EPISTLE TO THE ROMANS*
IN ITS SECOND EDITION
  Rudolf Bultmann

KARL BARTH'S *EPISTLE TO THE ROMANS*
  Adolf Schlatter

FOREWORD TO THE THIRD EDITION
  Karl Barth

FOREWORD TO THE FIRST EDITION
Karl Barth

Paul spoke to his contemporaries as a child of his age. But much more important than this truth is the other, that he speaks as a prophet and apostle of the Kingdom of God to all men in all ages. The differences between then and now, there and here, must be considered. But the purpose of this consideration can only be the recognition that these differences have *no* significance for what really matters. The critical historical method of biblical research has its place; it points to a preparation for understanding that is never superfluous. But if I had to choose between it and the old doctrine of inspiration, I would resolutely choose the latter. It has a greater, deeper, more important place because it points directly to the task of understanding, without which all preparation is worthless. I am happy that I do not have to choose between the two. But all my attention has been directed toward seeing *through* the historical into the spirit of the Bible, which is the eternal Spirit. What was once a serious matter is still serious today, and what today is serious, and not just arbitrariness and whim, stands also in direct relation to what was formerly serious. Our questions, if we understand ourselves aright, are the questions of Paul, and Paul's answers, if their light illumines us, must be our answers.

> Das Wahre war schon längst gefunden,
> Hat edle Geisterschaft verbunden,
> Das alte Wahre—fass es an!

> The true was found long ago,
> It bound together noble spirits.
> The old and true—hold it fast!

Historical understanding is a continuous, more and more honest and penetrating conversation between the wisdom of yesterday and the wisdom of tomorrow, and these are one and the same. With respect and gratitude I remember here my father, Professor Fritz Barth, whose whole lifework has been an application of this insight.

It is certain that it was more natural for all ages which hungered and thirsted after righteousness to take a positive, active position alongside Paul instead of one of the passive detachment of an observer. Perhaps we are now entering such an age. Unless I deceive myself, this book can now already perform a certain limited service. The reader will get the feeling that it was written in the joy of discovery. The powerful voice of Paul was new to me, and I imagine that it must also be new to many others. But at the end of this work it is clear to me that there is much here that is still unheard and undiscovered. It is thus intended as nothing more than a preliminary work which invites others to join in. If only many who are better qualified would come in order to dig more wells there! But if I should be deceived in the joyful hope of a joint new search and quest for the message of the Bible, then this book has time to—wait. The Letter to the Romans itself is also waiting.

THE EPISTLE TO THE ROMANS BY KARL BARTH:
An Up-to-Date, Unmodern Paraphrase*

Emil Brunner

The Epistle to the Romans by Karl Barth is an astonishingly objective and—in the Schillerian sense—naïve book. Objective insofar as it concerns itself solely to present to us the recognized truth as clearly and unambiguously as possible, and to take no account of the doubts, misgivings, and particular needs and wishes of the reader. Naïve in that it simply presents itself without reflecting on its relationship to other, similar undertakings—with the single exception of the Foreword. It goes straight on its own course without looking to left or right or to the rear, without indicating its "position" in reference to other standpoints and paths. It completely lacks a Greek "chorus" which would provide glosses for what occurs on the stage—certainly not a common occurrence in our subjective and reflective age. Precisely in this book, however, the reader will feel very strongly the need for a "chorus," for reflection that justifies and deliberates, because in method and content it deviates from the usual more than other books. Thus I ask the author and the readers for permission to play the role of leader of the chorus.

The first impression is probably astonishment and surprise. Among present-day exegetical literature the book appears as an erratic block, like a faithful yeoman with a halberd and a suit of armor in a machine gun company. It may seem at first to some a "naïve" book in the common sense that the author is not quite "up with the times," that he remains stuck in long outdated views, and dares to present us with the "whole" Paul with such obvious authority only because he is not acquainted with and cannot properly evaluate the great, purifying work of modern critical theology and historical science. Naturally, with so well-equipped a theologian as Barth that can be only appearance. He makes us aware, not only in the Foreword, but also—without pointing it out with his finger—in the work itself, that he is well acquainted with the methods and results of modern biblical studies, and beyond this—in contrast to many recent works—knows how to extract what is valuable from the older interpreters. The few text-critical observations that are scattered through the work indicate

* From *Kirchenblatt für die Reformierte Schweiz*, XXXIV (1919), issue 8, pp. 29-32.

thoroughgoing scientific preparation, and it would surely have been very easy for the author to shine in the usual way by means of scientific apparatus. He rejected this for the same reason that his work as a whole is so "unmodern."

The implicit presupposition of the whole book and of all his individual thoughts is the recognition that our developmental-historical, "scientific" thought—the pride of modern times and the new theology —is of merely relative significance and its results of merely relative truth. The point of view of the church fathers and the Reformers, now apparently outgrown, who made an absolute division between the "Word of God" as absolute truth and the "word of man," contained more truth than the now dominant historical-relative view of the Bible. What Paul wrote was not the "theological views" of a particularly brilliant or religious man of a specific cultural circle arising out of the various elements of tradition, experience, logic, imagination, etc., but rather, the truth which God speaks. Just as little as research into the occurrences in the brain or into the mental conditions of thought is able to explain thought as such, or the cogency of lines of thought —however valuable they may be otherwise—so little can all historical-psychological research methods explain the thoughts and lines of thought in the Letter to the Romans—whatever helpful auxiliary functions they may perform. The real, the creative birth and development of these "thoughts" occur in an area which is inaccessible to our natural and empirical experience of knowledge as well as to natural logic both as a whole and in each separate point. In basic and decisive matters neither research in the biography of Paul nor the study of Hellenism or late Judaism, valuable as these researches are, so to speak, for the physiology of Pauline thought, give us insight into the origin and train of thought of the Letter to the Romans. This is given only by the specific inner necessity for the knowledge of God with its organic connections. On the formal side, Barth's main purpose is to show that the Letter to the Romans is a tree of knowledge which is an organic outgrowth of the knowledge of God in Christ. Paul himself was certainly conscious of this specific, "supernatural" character of his knowledge. "The unspiritual man does not receive the gifts of the Spirit of God . . . The spiritual man judges all things, but is himself to be judged by no one." How far this claim is justified by Barth's work must be determined by the analysis of the content. If, however, this is really the case, if the assumed "theology" of Paul in its foundation and structure springs from the specific "logic" of the knowledge of God, then this means nothing less than that the biblical studies of our day have overlooked the essential thing. Inasmuch as they, despite

Paul's warning, judge "spiritual things unspiritually," that is, by other standards, and thus, in order to be "scientific," remain strange to the object of their study and outside it, they are in that situation which Kutter so delightfully characterized in his description of those people who instead of looking at the picture in the picture book, analyze its paper and color because the proper task of considering and understanding the picture seems to them to be "unscientific." Thus critical historical theology speaks entirely beside the point; it "holds the parts in its hand" more firmly and neatly than former generations, and "unfortunately lacks only the spiritual bond."

But now, instead of solidifying this "if" to "that" in difficult and debatable investigations in the theory of knowledge,* Barth has chosen the more fruitful task of presenting the evidence for his interpretation by giving the thoughts of the Letter to the Romans in their direct testimony and their organic connections without trying to prove anything. It is intended that they should explain themselves, not to our intelligence—for that is "of this world"—but to our original understanding of God. He expects them to find admission to that part of our souls which is not imprisoned in the temporal and finite, but has remained an undisturbed reservoir for the voice of God, undistorted by the "culture" and adaptation to the world of merely human knowledge. Already here in the "presuppositions" there is a dualism at work which governs the whole book and with which Barth, on Paul's side, stands over against our present-day developmental monism—the dualism of the Fall, the break in principle with the optimistic concept of evolution which rules almost undisputed over our religious, moral, and scientific thought.

"The times are out of joint," not merely in the sense of a moral platitude, but in the cosmic sense. The whole world of space and time with its brutality, its subterranean chaos, and its chaotic beginnings; human life with its bestial origins and elements; all this sad exile of the spirit in the bondage of nature; this humiliating fact that first the spirit is bound and made dull, speechless, and impotent by the "elements of this world"; all this miserable necessity of a development— this is not normal, not the situation created by God, not what was "in the beginning," but the product of a disturbance, arising out of man's primal turning away from God, out of the "Fall." What happens in this fallen world no more follows the original will of God than the process of decomposition of a corpse follows the normal life functions of the body. Our world is not a "cosmos" in the true sense, but a dis-

---

* I made an attempt in this direction in my work *Das Symbolische in der religiösen Erkenntnis* (1914).

turbed cosmos. Hence all that is senseless and purposeless: suffering, sickness, the powers of destruction, death; hence the processes of decay in the spiritual life: error and sin, the deadly analytics of our reasoning faculties and of our individualistic, egoistic wills. Even the organic nature of humanity is destroyed through the disappearance of the spirit of life that made it a unity; the parts now fall out as separate "individuals," and the organism has become a heap. And the center —the headquarters, as it were—from which this whole destructive revolution began, the relationship of man to God, shows most clearly our abnormal, pathological situation: godlessness. But it is not as if all this described our real, present condition. It is rather the other, the negative pole, at which we would find ourselves if the positive pole, God, were not working against that complete alienation. The original will of God is working against the arbitrary legalism of this godless world. This is the second basic fact: the living God, who in the grandiose vision of Ezekiel pours his spirit of life into the world of death in order to bring it back to its original life. The living, active God, who as the totally "other," the factor beyond causality, time, and space, breaks into the world of our experiences, overcomes its "autonomy," transcends its own fatally analytic tendencies through the organic and synthetic power of life of the "Spirit," of love, of "eternal life." There is a divine history that runs alongside and permeates world history. At every point where it breaks out of the beyond into this world it transcends the dependence on nature and the relativity of the ordinary course of history and brings the Absolute into the relative, the timeless into the temporal, the divine-human into the all-too-human, the transhistorical into the merely historical. And the goal of this cosmic event is the return to the beginning, to the homeland, to God. In this way, and only in this way, is it possible to speak of "re-demption," of "re-storation," of healing and reconciliation. It is only within this total cosmic, eschatological concept that the main thoughts of the Bible get their due. The "eschatological," the divine history, is for Paul, as well as for the writers of the Synoptic Gospels and the prophets, the essential matter, and not an appendix which can be added *ad libitum*. The older theology which presented the Bible only as divine doctrine without divine history is just as much a distortion of the gospel as the newer theology, which, though it brought us much history, suppressed the divine history.

But it is only thus that the realism of the Bible, and of the Letter to the Romans, can be understood. Paul, indeed the whole Bible, does not merely give us a new and better view or interpretation of the world. It does not teach us merely an ideal concept of reality nor demand from us merely a new attitude. It is not moral idealism, but it confronts us with new facts. When, for example, Bousset in *Religion in Geschichte und Gegenwart,* from the point of view of his superior, subjective idealism, criticizes Paul's "theology of facts," he is showing very clearly the chief difference between modern idealism and the realism of Paul and of the Bible. For Paul it is not a question of reading something of God into the natural and historical world, but of becoming witnesses of a real intervention of real, new, creative factors into the natural course of history. Paul thus stands in radical opposition to all "as-if" philosophy, and also to that unphilosophical, "pious" "trust in God" that regards the whole state of the world and the course of history *sub specie aeternitatis* and, reducing everything to one level, regards it all wholesale as an expression of the divine will. In this way, the difference which the Bible, and particularly Paul, stresses between divine and non-divine facts is eliminated. This is the heathen world speaking in Christian terms. On the basis of this relativism, the effort of modern research into the life of Jesus is understandable, the effort to understand Jesus entirely in terms of what is under our control. The Bible, however, and particularly Paul, places the emphasis on Christ's origin in the "beyond" and does not wish to know him "after the flesh." This results in that (unconscious) impudence with which the moderns with no hesitation apply everything that Paul says about the Spirit of God to "moral religious consciousness," while Paul clearly contrasts the two. Thus the newer theology (not only that of the professional theologians!) is forced, in order to do anything at all with Paul, to dull the edge of all his thoughts, and ends up with nothing left except the platitudes of liberalism. In addition, in recent years a curio case has been set up for specialities and absurdities determined by the limitations of their age, and it is displayed to those in the know with especial pride as an evidence of historical understanding. Barth resolutely turns his back on this aesthetic dallying with admiration of Paul and this pedantic correction of Paul. It is not a "lack of historical thought and historical insight resulting from the limitations of the times," but superior, divine insight that enables Paul to show the heathen world in Romans 1 as having fallen away from God. It is not merely the self-righteousness and the statutory character of Pharisaic moralism that Paul "actually means" in his destruction of the moral standpoint in Romans 2, but Paul really "means" that he sees an opposition in principle between "moral consciousness" and the Spirit of God. The contrast of Adam and Christ in Romans 5 is not the strange whim of Paul the Jew, who "with genuine rabbinical sophistry" "gives theological account for his simple

experience of Christ." (Exhibit 1 in the curio case!) Rather this is
the foundation and the supporting beam without which the whole
highly esteemed eighth chapter, with its "magnificent trust in God"
and its "pure spirituality," would be hanging in the air.

All this, however, is not simply stated on the basis of an uninspired
dogma of inspiration—by "tried and true" orthodox patterns, but it
is developed with a steady, unexpressed appeal to that divine reservoir
in us and understood through the basic knowledge of the living God in
Christ. The "other-worldly" presupposition is laid bare, this subterranean rock structure supporting the visible surface, as it were, and
without which the surface cannot be understood. Many who learned
from Ritschl the opposition of faith and metaphysics may feel quite
strange when it develops that for Paul (as for the Bible in general)
"metaphysics" is that which deals with what is "beyond" empirical
knowledge, beyond all psychic experiences. But this is not, as it was in
the older idealism, metaphysics of logical thought, but metaphysics of
divine activity seen by men. Visible, historical reality is not—as historicism claims it is—the content and norm of knowledge of God, but
only the transparency that shows the "other-worldly" reality that lies
behind it. The world of empirical knowledge is, as it were, a horizontal
plane which is cut by the vertical stream of the light of divine history.
The points of intersection, the divine-earthly facts, the acts of God,
cannot be recognized through what lies to right and left of them on the
horizontal plane, but only through what lies behind and before them
in the vertical plane, in the stream of *divine* events. The empirical
world takes part in the divine occurrences; but the latter are to be
understood not in terms of it, but in terms of the "beginning" in God
and of the "end" in God, in terms of the past and future which lie in
the eternity which is "beyond." That is the metaphysics of Paul and
of the Bible.

This "other-worldliness" is decisive as opposed to psychic experience. All modern religious thought is, to use Barth's expression, more
or less "pietistic." It depends on experiential knowledge, on "personal
experience." The patron saint of modern theology and the representative of modern piety is Schleiermacher, who endeavored to recon-
struct the content of faith out of the experience of the faithful.
Religious psychology is the trump card, and with its fine psychological
methods the temperature and degree of saturation of the religious
consciousness are determined. Even the preacher has to be a psychologist above all else. And yet these psychological factors fall outside
that which Paul and the entire Bible understand as faith. For Paul
"faith" is the apprehension of something objective, and the mode of

apprehension is not considered. Where it is really a matter of this apprehension—not only in thoughts or in imagination—it is always the same, and all psychological variants are related only to subjective peripheral circumstances. Faith is "absolute." This is the insight which Luther brought to light again after it had been so long forgotten, the insight through which alone the *sola fide* can be understood, but which was too soon lost again in the intellectualistic misunderstanding of orthodoxy or in the emotionalistic misunderstanding of pietism. Today it is still forgotten or misunderstood. The way we speak of faith today as the "personal experience," of a "powerful" or "ingenious" or "living" religious "personality," would be plainly appraised by both Paul and Luther as work-righteousness. It is dependence on inner works (which Luther in his "Sermon on Good Works" distinguished with marvelous clarity from the timeless work of faith), on the intensity, force, warmth, and persistence of the inner experience. These are all measurements which miss the essence of faith just as much as, for example, measurements of attentiveness miss the act of thinking as such.

I regard it as one of Barth's greatest achievements that he has dared to, and been able to, bring this timeless, supra-psychological, "absolute" nature of faith to light again, and that he manfully withstood all temptations to psychologize, temptations which are so strong for modern man. This psychological subjectivism found in—to name only the best—a Johannes Müller or a Rittelmeyer, had to be overcome, no matter what valuable services it had rendered in freeing us from a sterile dogmatism. It, like its partner, religious historical positivism, is only a transitional stage in the direction toward the truth, and he who remains in it is in mortal danger. It is not merely a question of "theories" *about* faith, but it concerns the practical and real religious life as it has been formed under the influence of the modern spirit. Theologies reflect rather than produce. Barth deals with this in the two very significant chapters: "Romanticism" and "Pietism." Here, too, it is only a question of giving God his rights over against (inner) works; a question of divine objectivity over against subjective feelings and activities, of the divine "Spirit" over against a purely human "religious-moral consciousness"; a question—in the struggle of Paul and of Luther—of one thing: God or the world; of the God who will not let himself be confused with the "world" but who as the one he is, as God, will make his influence felt also in the innermost realm of his creation, in the human heart. Even justification by faith alone, the *soli deo gloria*, can be completely understood only from the point of view of metaphysical-eschatological realism, which takes into account a piercing of the divine world through all that is relative and arbitrary in the natural and human. This "other-worldly" reality of "laying hold as one who has been laid hold upon" (Barth), orientation to the divine, immovable evaluation of man instead of to unsteady experiences, understanding everything in terms of this saving divine movement instead of the viewpoints of this world, and asserting these "impractical," paradoxical, and "absurd" positions determinedly against all temptations of natural, human thought and will—that is the faith that "justifies" and at the same time redeems. That is the act through which man is grafted into the divine tree of life and taken up into its own organic life movement. It is through this that the common will, socialism, love growing out of an ideal and a demand, become self-evident expression and fact. In this event—wholly timeless and supra-psychological—the Kingdom of God wins, as it were, a new foothold in the empirical world. Therefore it is no more possible to speak of a world-renouncing heavenly joy than to speak of a this-worldly, "religious-moral" cultural optimism. Salvation consists in being transplanted into the cosmic movement of the Kingdom of God— "we are saved in hope"—and therefore in feeling for the first time as our own distress and shame the deep contrast between the unredeemed world and the Kingdom of God. Individual blessedness would be— godless.

The same realism, however, which abolishes the separations of individuals from one another—the members of a body—also invalidates the separations of time. There is not merely an analogy or an ideational similarity between our faith and Paul's. We plunge into the same stream and are carried and made alive by it, the same stream with the same movement and direction. We do not need a complicated apparatus of research and investigation into religious history and the history of ancient times to make the "strange" thoughts of the Letter to the Romans "somewhat understandable." We too can and must see what Paul saw. If his truths are strange to us, the fault lies not in their being "conditioned by the antique world," but in our eye, which has forgotten how to see in the third dimension—how to look into the depths of the world beyond. Thus we do not need any arts of modernization in order to apply the Letter to the Romans to our present-day spiritual and religious situation. That which lay for Paul straight ahead, or to the left or the right of the straight road, lies in the same place for us. The Letter to the Romans applies itself as soon as it is understood, as soon as one has pushed through from a mere outward understanding of the words—for which modern science offers us splendid means—to an understanding of the content.

There will be dispute as to how far Barth has succeeded in achieving this in detail. The exploration of a newly discovered land is always a work of several generations. The decisive factor, however, is that someone has finally noticed again that there is a third dimension, and indeed someone who is equipped to tell us what is to be seen there. He has assumed the responsibility for finally leaving aside all the various matters of modern investigation and making the central thought of the Bible really the central point that influences everything else. This is the knowledge of the supra-worldly movement of the Kingdom of God, which in Jesus came from hiding into clear sight and which reveals in him its goal: Immanuel.

A MODERN INTERPRETER OF PAUL*

Adolf Jülicher

Karl Barth, the Swiss pastor who is well known to our readers and is now in Safenwil, published in 1919 at G. A. Bäschlin in Berne, an extensive work (438 pp.) which bears the title: *The Epistle to the Romans*. In the Foreword the author stresses that he wrote the book in the joy of discovery, and indicates that he has now understood the Apostle Paul, the Paul who as prophet and apostle of the Kingdom of God speaks to all men in all ages, while the critical historical method of biblical research teaches us to understand him only provisionally as a child of his time speaking to his contemporaries. He hopes that we are now entering a period in which we will take a position of objective commitment alongside Paul and no longer a position of passive detachment as observers. If Barth should deceive himself in the cheerful hope for a joint new research and quest for the biblical message, then this book has time to—wait; the Letter to the Romans itself is still waiting.

If the Foreword were not there—I hope Barth's book will have many readers who for the time being will skip that presumptuous Foreword—and one began reading perhaps the compact paraphrase of Romans 1:1-7 and the two pages of explanation that go with it, or some other section, for example, p. 195, Romans 7:7-13 "The Law and Romanticism," and p. 204, Romans 7:14-25 "The Law and Pietism," or the highly original survey of the contents, pp. 437 f., which gives precisely the impression of a work of art, then one might believe he had gotten hold of a "practical" exposition of the Letter to the Romans, which, without losing itself in the details of scholarly exegesis, reproduces the basic thoughts of that letter in the language of our time, indeed recast in the conceptual world of today, and shows its own value in steady confrontation with the religious and moral problems of the present day. The author has at his disposal superb gifts for attaining this goal. With passionate commitment he stands in the middle of the struggle with the problems. He did not inherit his position in the battle, but won it for himself, earnestly sought it by various solutions. He knows how to speak penetratingly, at times charmingly, and always with colorful vividness. He is able to use the technical expressions of philosophical terminology, including even

---

* From *Die Christliche Welt*, XXXIV (1920), issue 29, columns 453-457.

"meon," without running the danger of losing sight of his readers. He enlivens the work with an adroit use of quotations from poetry and prose, spiritual and secular; not only Zündel, Schlatter, and Rieger, but Calvin and Luther as well; Schiller, in particular, somewhat more often than the interest of the Pauline text seems to require.

Barth forced me point-blank to make a decision about the question of the significance of practical exegesis of Scripture compared to strictly scientific exegesis. His *Epistle to the Romans* is well suited to showing its necessity, especially when it reaches the heights it does in this book. It is not a handy collection of material for sermons on Pauline pericopes, but a stimulus for the direction which thought must take if it is to keep Paul alive and arouse the spirits of present-day men. The reader will frequently object to what Barth states; it will often call forth even the sharpest opposition, particularly as the author likes to present his opinions in the most pointed way possible. All politics, like the struggle for power and the diabolic art of winning a majority, is dirty. Even the noblest, purest attitude of those who exercise it does not change the ungodliness of its essence in the slightest. Whether it is Gustavus Adolphus or Napoleon, whether it is Cromwell or Fredrick the Great, whether it is Windthorse or Bebel, it is "a nasty song, faugh, a political song" which any "honorable man" had better not listen to, not to mention join in singing. It is not worthwhile determining why then Jakob Burckhardt is introduced as chief witness with the sentence: "The earliest content of the State, its attitude, its task, yes, its pathos, is essentially the enslavement of the subjugated." To be sure, Barth fails to mention that Burckhardt says this only of the earliest content of the State, and most certainly is not thinking like Barth of the present State, which has taken the place of the original godly State which is to be renewed in Christ.

It is to the credit of this form of exegesis that, for the sake of practical applications, considerations are ascribed to Paul that do not fit in his situation, as for example when the comment is made in connection with Romans 15:30-33 about the "anxious, gray-streaked net that awaits me in the citadel of the church among the obstinate—and probably also among the saints." Paul had no dread of the obstinate in the church in Jerusalem, and most certainly could not have been concerned with any "vague anxiety" with which the Romans could think of the unpleasant and dangerous things that awaited him there. The practical exegete may take such liberties, as when he considers the church in the role of Israel in Romans 9 and 11, if and insofar as the errors of the old Israel are repeated in it. Only after longer occupation with the new commentary is the impression gained that the several favorite concepts of the author recur much too often, that he cannot cope with the splendid multiplicity of the thoughts of the apostle. Moreover, the reader gets the impression that even if he had wanted to close the door so tight against the last century, as to keep out any critical historical chaff, he would have done well to let the old exegetes of the Pauline text (naturally not only scholarly commentators, but also preachers, and why not systematicians as well?) stimulate him more strongly and with greater variety. Still, over against such wishes it must be said that the better is the foe of the good, and Barth's *Epistle to the Romans* is to be thankfully recognized as contributing much that is useful and good, and even as a model for further progress in this field of edifying exegesis.

But Barth intends to do more than give applications for the present day. He believes he has a larger task; first of all he has completely understood the Letter to the Romans down to its foundation, and his commentary is the revelation of this essentially final understanding. Is it desirable, is it even possible, to impart this understanding in the form of a thoroughgoing detailed exposition of a Pauline letter? The other letters of the apostle appear in this commentary on Romans even more seldom than in any other of which I know. But is a Paul really to be understood completely by *one* of his letters, as an Augustine perhaps by the conclusion of his *Confessions*? Does not an interpreter of Paul who leaves out of consideration what is by far the greater part of the self-witness of Paul to his piety or to his gospel lay himself open to the suspicion that he does not really need the historical bases of Paul's "understanding" at all, if everything can be achieved with a small part thereof? Or perhaps the discoverer wished to prove that he had not selected only a few passages from Paul that suited his view, but that by following Paul step by step in a longer letter and devoting to each turn of thought and expression the same care, he demonstrates throughout the agreement between his "Paulinism" and that which is found in the sources, and also shows the untenability of the former "theories of Paulinism." It then must be asked, can that work succeed in a book of the arrangement, extent, and attitude of this newest *Epistle to the Romans*?

As long as it is not sufficient to reject a priori other positions, such as historical criticism or the method of the science of religion, or at best compassionately to let them serve as a preliminary step, but scarcely to present them at all to the reader for comparison, and certainly not to undertake anywhere a thorough refutation of their ideas and their apparent replies—so long will we be unable to speak of an overcoming of the "old" by this neo-Paulinist. Barth well knows that without scholarly equipment no Greek document written 1900 years ago can be properly evaluated. A few times he betrays to the reader that there is some doubt as to how the original text in Paul may have read. But he makes his decisions in such cases with remarkable haste, and one gets no information about the tremendous difficulties involved in grasping to any extent the literal meaning of passages such as Romans 3:9; 4:1; 7:24, 25. Barth translates Romans 4:1 as, "What shall we now say to the way of Abraham?"—and no manuscript of Romans gives a hint of any "way." In 3:9 he decides for "Can we find an excuse? By no means." I am of a similar opinion, but may one completely fail to mention that "find an excuse" rests only on a hypothesis? And when in Romans 16:6 Barth finds it necessary to justify in a special note his preference for the name "Mariam"—rather than "Marian," he compels his readers to assume that in his work too they will find something about the more important difficulties of transmission. These scholarly notes—they are not at all numerous—would all have been better left out, because they clash with the style of this work and offer nothing new. It would have been better for Barth to have avoided giving the impression that he had independent ability to deal with the manuscript transmission of Romans and its families of texts. Unfortunately, he relied heavily on Zahn. Where he differed—I mean, in matters of text-critical and exegetical difficulty—he chose poorly. Naturally, this was often, but by no means always, due to his viewpoint concerning the Kingdom of God. Thus, for example, when he translates Romans 12:11 as "harken to the command of the moment" and justifies it because the other reading "serve the Lord (only)" betrays by its trite flatness the hand of a correcting scribe to whom the correct text might have seemed morally suspicious because along with many successors he misread the fluidity of the Pauline "ethic." As if triteness had not been merely brought in by the choice of the word "heed" instead of "serve"—Barth rightly did not find "servant of Jesus Christ" in Romans 1:1 trite. This fluidity, this adaptation to the third dimension of the new world age, is found in Romans 12:11 only by one who has prepared the way for it by the arbitrary rendering of the preceding dative "in zeal" and "in spirit" as "when things get serious" (be untiring) and "when the Spirit moves you" (be zealous). Paul himself never knew a moment in which he was not serious, nor one in which the Spirit did not move him.

In Romans 9:5 Barth rejects the only satisfactory explanation of the latter part of the verse as praise of the almighty God and recommends a pure conjecture. In consequence of this Paul would be saying of the Jews, as the last, highest title of honor, that "they have the God who stands above all things, exalted forever, Amen." There are linguistic objections that could be raised to this text, but the simple reference to Romans 3:29 makes it impossible: "Or is God the God of Jews only? Is he not the God of Gentiles also? Yes, of Gentiles also, since God is one." For it is only in modern translation that the "have God" in 9:5 appears as a deviation from 3:29; according to Barth, Paul in 9:5 plainly asserts what he elsewhere rejects—at least he asserts it in the form of the claim to have a privilege. The possession of the patriarchs, of the law, and of the ancestry of Christ showed and was intended to show this privilege.

Of the innovations in the wording of the Letter to the Romans which we find in Barth, I should like to discuss here one other that will no doubt attract great attention. At the same time it might well bear the chief blame for Barth's feeling that he has made new discoveries in the exegesis of Paul. In the place of righteousness by faith the newest Paulinist puts justification through faithfulness, God's faithfulness. Certainly the corresponding Greek *pistis* can mean both. But can Barth be serious when in a letter in which the verb *pisteuein* occurs innumerable times, always in the sense of having faith, he dares in the same context to transfer the corresponding noun to precisely the opposite side? In a document from the Christian world, where such words as "Your faith has saved you" or "Lord, increase our faith" are always heard, can such a thing be done? Or can it be done in the Letter to the Romans where in 4:5 and 16:26 even Barth cannot avoid translating "obedience of faith," in 1:8 as "your faith," while in 1:12 he can understand the meaning only as hope for an exchange of faith between Paul and the Romans? In 1:16, where in solemn repetitiveness the revelation of the righteousness of God is proclaimed as from faith to faith, should we suddenly follow the discoverer who interprets it rather as "out of God's faithfulness to the faith of men" and then even repeats the passage from Habbakuk as "the one made righteous out of faithfulness will live"? In Romans 3:25 God presents Christ as the gift of propitiation (!) through his faithfulness shown in Christ's blood. In 3:26 the one is made righteous who is rooted in God's faithfulness shown in Jesus. Here where the word *pistis* stands without the article, with "Jesus" in the genitive, the supplying of "his" and "shown in Jesus" is an arbitrary act of the first order, an act of violence. But if we ask in 3:31, "Do we set aside the law by the faithfulness of God? No, but we are the ones who set up the law," then the view that someone could uproot the law by faithfulness—first Barth introduces the phrase "of God"—is grotesque. And in 3:30 the emotional assurance that God will justify the circumcised out of faithfulness and the uncircumcised also out of faithfulness would, moreover, betray by its triteness the hand of a scribe making insertions. Moreover, only pure caprice can mistake for a moment in 3:28 the fact that beside "without works of the law"—Barth falsely and lamely: "quite apart from the activity to which the law exhorts"—a justification of man through *pistis* must mean not "God's faithfulness," which is precisely what could help me to deeds in accord with the law, but only a performance, a *habitus* of man, and thus faith. The *non plus ultra*, however, surpassing even 1:16, is found in 14:23. "A man is sentenced to death . . . because his deeds then do not come from faith. For everything that does not come from the faithfulness of God is sin." The author, who is innocent of all exercise of power in this world, perceived that a word that had just stood for "faith" could not be understood in the next line, when reproduced as "faithfulness." In order to force the reader to his view he simply inserted, as so often, the decisive words "of God" and thereby destroyed the grandiose thought of Paul, who proclaims the unlimited autonomy of the conscience of the believer. It is reasonable to inquire why Paul here (as elsewhere) did not use the word he so frequently chose, "grace," instead of the terms "faithfulness" or "mercy" interpreted this way, and thereby eliminate all ambiguity. The thought which Barth has brought into the final sentence, verse 23*b*, is, however, taken generally, after all not false in the sense of unPauline; but to trace the "offenses" and the agitations of superstition back to the faithfulness of God, indeed to justify them as coming directly from it, can hardly have been the intention of the apostle.

And the author bypasses in almost total silence such a fundamental question of Pauline interpretation as that concerning *pistis*. He nowhere informs his public of the various possibilities, much less takes the field with counterarguments against the almost unanimous opposition of all other exegetes. When he then consistently imparts his own opinion exclusively, and does not give the impression by occasional references to other readings, interpretations, and relationships that he is seriously concerned with dealing with other opinions, then we must take this lack of consideration as a peculiarity of this age, in which the interpretation of Scripture has again become the exclusive concern of pneumatics and of the bearers of revelation, and Mark 4:11 f. applies to all others. But the one who looks deeper perceives Barth's dependence on mere scholarly research, on Zahn, Lietzmann, Calvin; he himself does not wish to hide it. But why then does he not deal more thoroughly with other opinions, as the seriousness of the questions demands?

The riddle of this dichotomy can be solved. Karl Barth is a man of two worlds; in his breast two souls are struggling. One of these knows that the interpretation of a very difficult text in a foreign language from ancient times, whatever subject matter the text may deal with, is a task that can be fulfilled only with all the aids of a multi-branched science, with as great commitment as possible in the always-instructive course of its development, and that in this interpretation both defects in the transmission of the text and obscurities in the presentation, perhaps even inconsistencies and contradictions in the thoughts of the author, must be taken into consideration. And for the other, the understanding of a book of the Bible is restricted to the citizens of the new world, e.g., Barth; for them it is absurd, for example, to write a book about the Christian and sin, since there is room only for the Christian and grace; for the Kingdom of God, which was destroyed by the Fall, has now been restored in the risen Christ in its fullest purity through the faithfulness of God. Barth formulates his standpoint as one superior to that of historical criticism and that of the doctrine of inspiration in that he hopes to look beyond and through the historical "into the spirit of the Bible, which is the eternal Spirit." By this he is saying that those before him have attained only to the historical. He does not oppose the historical, but passes through it to the Spirit. This is exactly the standpoint of Origen, except that Barth declares the former's spirit to be an unspirit; it is exactly the standpoint of the Gnostics, except that they, to be sure, were not at all concerned with the historical. One of them, however, who though not the greatest in spirit is yet the most congenial, Marcion, about A.D. 150 in Rome, held the same position as Karl Barth in his exegesis of Paul. He proceeded with the same sovereign arbitrariness and assurance of victory, with the same one-sided dualistic approach of enmity to all that comes from the world, culture, or tradition, and never tired of tossing a few pet ideas in front of us. And this has the same effect—that when we give ourselves to these tones without interruption we finally hear only them and nothing else.

In issue 25 of the *Die Christliche Welt*, I characterized the anonymous author of "Augustinus Redivivus" as a representative of a modern Gnosticism. In issue 24 Friedrich Gogarten uses precisely this designation for himself; our *Epistle to the Romans* belongs in the same category. Naturally these are three very different types of Gnosticism; there perhaps we have one of the Elchasaites, who based their teachings on the successive revelations from the first fathers on through Abraham and Moses down to the mysterious book "Elchasai," and were then proud of possessing the whole truth. In Gogarten we have a Basilides who wanders between the aeons, or a new Valentinus, who out of the planet of Achamoth, writhing in pain, stretches out his arms toward the blessed pleroma above. In Barth we have the half-Gnostic Marcion with his radical dualism of all or nothing and his wrath against those who take only half—wrath where Redivivus has scorn, where Valentinus-Gogarten feels tender compassion for those men of the former generation who do not realize they are dead, for us who are today old.

However differently these men think and feel among themselves, what they have in common is that they are not susceptible to our counterarguments. When has a pneumatic ever let himself be instructed by a psychic or a hylic? They need no further witness for themselves. As for Redivivus the seal of truth is the absolute assurance that it gives—to him!—so for Gogarten and Barth there is nothing more sure than that there is no more progress in history, that development is forever at an end, and that no optimism in the interest of culture moves us anymore. Thus it is not really to be expected that they can do justice to men of the distant past. Gogarten no longer even tries; he "rejoices in the decline, for no one likes to live among corpses." Barth does not go that far. Like Marcion, he wishes to save his Paul from such a decline. Indeed, in some sections he has powerfully renewed Paul, most successfully it seems to me, in the irrational excesses of the Pauline spirit. The "much more," which has abandoned all logic, Romans 5:15 (and 16, 17) finds an enthusiastic echo in Barth. The allegedly biblical figure of the Abraham who believed in Christ two thousand years before there was a Christ seems to our interpreter to be almost as necessary for salvation as Christ himself. The contrasts of flesh and spirit, God and world, mankind since Adam's fall and mankind in Christ, are heightened rather than diminished. Less obvious is their agreement in Christology, the view of hell and Satan, of reconciliation and redemption, of predestination and the possibility of falling again from faith. Since the interpreter here is the deadly foe of anything that smacks of system, philosophy, or theory, and avoids clear positions, in opposing, for example, the systems of other interpreters, even though they be Luther, Calvin, and Bengel, and retreats always to his renewed Kingdom of God, it might be that it is unjust to charge him with deviating from his master.

But in another place the difference, the opposition even, becomes as great as that between Paul, who praised righteousness as the end of the ways of God, and Marcion, who introduced a duality of gods in Paul—a lower one who is barely righteous, and a higher one, the good God, the God of love. Barth can never tire of outlawing the remnants of the world of the Fall, such as dogmatics and ethics, speculation and religion, church—and even Christendom. He still demands on the last page that we be blind, stupid, without understanding for theories, modes, and undertakings that have come into being without God, that we have no organs to perceive that which is fundamentally nothing. Soon after the beginning the reader learns what Barth means by theories that are fundamentally nothing. He does not know where anyone —anyone who preaches blindness, thus without having practice in the art of distinguishing the spirits, and, I think, without practicing it to the end of life—gets the right to this absolute condemnation of everything that does not suit him. When Barth so frequently repeats the rather fantastic remark of Goethe that the whole history of the church is nothing but a "hodgepodge of error and force" to support his interpretation of Paul's term "Israel" as meaning the "church," he flatly contradicts the spirit of Paul, as a glance at Romans 9:1-5 shows. Paul cannot even enumerate the gifts of God to Israel, such as law, worship, promises, and, in 3:1 ff., circumcision, without being overcome by grateful awe. Involuntarily he feels that he too is still distinguished and highly privileged by these benefactions. In Barth there remains no room for the impulse of even a limited respect for what the gospel has accomplished in the 1900 years before the Letter to the Romans was discovered again. Even the Reformation is not excepted; it was all not of God. That is actual denial of history, while Gogarten only resolves on a denial. And this lack of reverence toward that which was great in the past is what is specifically Gnostic, and it makes it impossible for even the most ardent admirer of Paul in the no longer Christian Christendom to explain Paul impartially and aright.

At the end I return again to the beginning with a word concerning the real value of this commentary on the Letter to the Romans. The great gifts of the author make it possible for him to evoke a strong impression with his transferal of the Pauline world of ideas into the present. Because he knows so precisely how it concerns him, and what the whole of truth means for him, and because he has learned to control the spirits, he forces all of Paul into his own course. He believes he has placed himself on the side of Paul, while we others are content merely to observe him. He does not want to notice that he often enough places himself ahead of Paul, or that, exactly as did all his predecessors, in order to be able to speak about Paul he partially produces, partially uses, theology, theory, religion, science, dogma, and morals. His entrance into the new Kingdom of God has altered nothing essential in that. He theologizes as before, and if he concerns himself less with proof, that does not serve his final purpose. His work will win for Paul only those souls whom he has previously won for himself. The success of this effort will be less significant for the history of interpretation, in which one must earnestly participate—as Luther did in his day—if he wishes to influence it, than for that of Christendom. The Barthian Paulinism is a landmark on the road of church history, and the value of these observations throughout is for the history of the *church*—and yet his protest is not able to release the author out of that hodgepodge. Much, perhaps even very much, may someday be learned from this book for the understanding of our age, but scarcely anything new for the understanding of the "historical" Paul. Why the results are so meager at the decisive point is made clearer by the observations of others who share his opinions than by those of Barth himself. He who despises the past because only he who is alive is right cannot gain anything from the past. He who in holy egoism thinks only of his own problems and chides the dead, who can no longer answer him, can surely not demand that a product of the past—as the Letter to the Romans most surely still is—should become alive for him. I hear—from the past—besides my own questions, the questions which the men of the past ask of me, and because I do not limit the duty to love my neighbor as myself to my neighbors living and future, my conscience compels me to answer their questions, or at least to attempt to do so. My own questions I answer as well as I can in the privacy of my own room. I do not pretend to anyone that as one who does historical research I can give an answer to his questions. And I act as a scientific exegete in dealing with the books of the Bible just as with those of Marcion, Augustine, or Luther. And because I am what I am only on the basis of what those who were before me have been, and would long since have starved if I had not been able to nourish myself on what they have provided, I am still acting in my own interest when I strive to come even closer to them, and to discover even finer nourishment. When I declare that I am outside that old world I am not a whit further away from them than those who do not sense any development at all. The ostensible woes of a new age have already existed and have already been overcome.

Without doubt we have now to reckon with a period in the history of culture that is not historically oriented—as always when deep causes for discontent with what has developed appear—but the occasion does not suffice to give rise to concern that what has been achieved through faithful work in the past might perish. Even if Europe perishes, the "church," Christendom, religion, will not perish, and the letters of Paul will not die. Karl Barth's *Epistle to the Romans* reveals how greatly even one of the most determined representatives of the new, despite all joy of discovery, remains dependent on what was there before him. The Letter to the Romans does not need to wait.

THE HOLY EGOISM OF THE CHRISTIAN:

An Answer to Jülicher's Essay: "A Modern Interpreter of Paul"*

Friedrich Gogarten

I do not know if agreement is possible between Adolf Jülicher and us. (Moreover, I can speak only of Karl Barth and myself, and that only on my own responsibility. I know nothing about the "Augustinus Redivivus.") This is not because, as Jülicher thinks, pneumatics will not let themselves be taught by a psychic or even a hylic, but because our situation is a basically different one from Jülicher's. Jülicher's situation, that of a scholarly historian, is known to everyone. Still, according to his own description, it is somewhat distinctive. This results from his characterizing it as a position of a scholar motivated by love for his neighbor, in contrast to us egoistic searchers. Thus we get the remarkable picture of such ancients as Paul and Luther having left their questions behind for the historical scholars, who seek to answer them out of neighborly love, and who modestly push their own questions into the background. Still, the sense of the picture is clear, that is, to make very plain the contrast to the "holy egoism" of those who "always are thinking only of their own problems." Our situation is then indeed presented quite well in contrast to that of Jülicher.

And I feel that in this we have said nothing extraordinary, but only given the inner situation of every, in the emphatic sense of the word, living man. Until now I have never doubted for a moment that even in this objective and scientific age every scholar wishes to answer his own questions, whatever distant objective detours he must make in order to do so. This leaves open the question of whether he remains true to that original intention.

I am even sure Jülicher will agree when I say that he does not solve the problems of historical research out of neighborly love for the long-dead ancients, but in order to find a decisive answer to the difficult, burdensome problems of the spiritual crisis in which we are living. Whether this can be found in the path of historical research is of course the question which, as far as I know, has accompanied historical research since its beginning and which has not been definitely answered.

Anyone who answers this question in the negative has not thereby given up all relationship to the past. Jülicher presents the mat-

---

* From *Die Christliche Welt*, XXXIV (1920), issue 35, columns 546-550.

ter as if both Karl Barth and I had totally denied history; Karl Barth in actuality, and I only in resolve. Now we both certainly (I believe I can include Barth here) do not have that specifically modern historical respect for the whole sweep of history. We therefore do not equate Christendom with its historical expression. Still, to be quite precise and eliminate misunderstandings as far as possible, I must insert here that Barth's usage, following the usage of Kutter, is such that he says *Christendom* for this broad historical expression and development of Christendom, in order to distinguish it sharply from the eternal, temporal-supratemporal deed through which God in Christ redeems the world.

We are convinced that Christendom (I am not following Barth's usage here), as the eternal, original deed of God, of course transcends history and continues to do so, and that everything depends on its not being mixed and confused with its historical effects. Thus, to take an example, the Reformation cannot simply be included in it. For it is indeed in its broad historical appearance a "hodgepodge of error and force." And if in considering it we confine ourselves to Luther, and then too, to his central work, there is no doubt for even a moment whose side of the question Luther would take. He would most certainly not deny his own achievement, the meaning of which was precisely making God's original deed free again and keeping it free from all human appendages and adjustments.

Luther (I may still appeal to him, despite the fact that as an assumed Gnostic I am said to be disrespectful to him, and not to want to learn anything from him) had the following opinion of respect for the great men of the past:

Yes, they say we must honor the saints and belittle ourselves and act humbly toward them. Answer: In this, not humility is of value when it concerns God's grace, but pride. Thou shouldst be humble in thy own cause and being, for thou art nothing but a bag of worms. But thou canst never be proud enough of Christ's goodness and must say, Were I ten times as filthy, I still have the blood that makes me clean and holy, and it cost Christ as much to redeem me as to redeem St. Peter. They were just as low as we, and we are just as high as they, so that none has more than I except they were stronger in the faith, but the cost and the benefit are not greater (WA 24, 484).

If someone objects that this word of Luther concerns only the ultimate, innermost relation to God and therefore has no validity in the context in which I am speaking, then I will answer that it is precisely of this ultimate, innermost relation to God that Barth and I wish to speak. One may criticize how far we have succeeded, or if at all.

But not even so learned and respectable a scholar as Jülicher has the right to charge us with egoism and lack of piety.

A person will have one relation to history when he regards the whole span of its development as the proper revelation of God, and he will have another when he sees the proper revelation in God's original action which does not enter into its own effects and consequences and is not modified by and recognizable in them, but which must be grasped ever and again in its pure original nature beyond its historical effects and forms, however important these may be.

In each case a different method will be needed in order to recognize the revelation of God in history. In the former case, historical research must be taken as an aid in order to establish first of all the actual historical facts. And since this involves a historical process the results and conclusions are to be sought in the area of probabilities and endless approximations. This means that we are never finished and cannot attain even penultimate results. We must turn first to the systematicians in order to find at least provisional results from this endless series which is not concluded and never will be. Or, as Jülicher expresses it, we must withdraw into the privacy of our own meditations with these questions for which finally a subjective decision must give the results. And beyond that the scholar is concerned that his work move one step further on that interminable and endless road toward historical probability. In our case, the step is a mere factor in the history of the scholarly interpretation of the Letter to the Romans.

In the other case one will of necessity not travel at all this endless road of historical approximation and probability, because the goal, God's original deed, does not lie there. But if it is at a given place, that is, where it made its historical appearance, and is for us, the latecomers, tied to the historical record which brings us its message by that unending passage of time, then there remains for us only the "leap" out of the endless mediacy of history to the place where it is located. But this leap is no greater and no harder for us than it was for the apostles, who lived and walked with Christ. If they had not made the leap, and if they had wanted to have exact historical knowledge of the revelation, even today they would still be at the unending task of trying to acquire it.

Luther thought as follows about the importance of development in matters of faith. "Then see how boldly the Old Testament speaks of things. It is written there that Adam was a Christian even such a long time before Christ's birth. For he had the same faith in Christ that we have. For time makes no difference to faith" (WA 24, 99).

Even here we are then not in such bad company when we hold the opinion that in matters of faith we must place ourselves directly beside the great possessors of faith, and that it is necessary to push through the historical to the spirit of the Bible, which, since it is the Spirit of God, cannot be the spirit of historical probability and therefore is not an object of scholarly, historical research.

If Jülicher reads contempt and lack of respect for the greatness of the past in my essay, it is possible for him to do so only because he holds the position which I reject there, and which, as a panhistorical position, includes all events which occur on earth as a part of human, historical development and is convinced that it can grasp all that is essential in these events through scholarly research. When in reference to this position I say that it makes everything that happens on earth into the work of man, it is not possible to refute me by simply making me into a Basilides who wanders among the aeons and to reproach me with contempt toward all that is "great in the past." It could even be that my intention was to free what is "great in the past" from the humanizing and belittling that is implied by that panhistoric inclusion in general development and the pervasive dependence on development. To be sure, this would presuppose a very thorough distinction among the various great things in the past. It would be necessary to carry out very strictly the distinction of which I have already spoken between the original, eternal deed of God, and its historical consequences and expressions. One would then also know that the hour in which the work of man finally collapses, because the men who built it and who used it for this and that have lost their power, could be the hour in which the eternal significance, which was imprisoned by human wisdom, human anxiety, and human selfishness, becomes free for new expression. But it becomes free only if the men who are then at work are able to allow that which wants to become new to be free and unmolested by their own purposes, their own anxieties, their own programs.

I believe I realize that this is no easy task, but also that this halt, this rethinking, is the only absolutely necessary task today.

Moreover I am comforted here again by the agreement of Luther, who thinks basically as follows about active work on a development:

I have done nothing. The Word has performed and arranged everything. If I had wanted to proceed with toil, I would have brought Germany such a shedding of blood that the emperor would not have been safe. But what would that have been? It would have been a game for fools. I have done nothing; I have let the Word act. Do you know what the Devil thinks when someone wants to do something by popular opinion? He sits in hell and thinks, O, aren't the fools going to have a fine game! But it gives him pain when we use the Word alone and let it work alone. It is almighty, it captures the hearts, and when they are captive, then the work must fall of itself (WA 10, Abt. 3, 18 f.) .

At the end of his article, Jülicher expresses his view that the situation does not call for concern that what has been established concerning the past, through faithful work, might perish. "Even if Europe perishes, the 'church,' Christendom, religion, will not perish, and the letters of Paul will not die."

That may well be. This dull, undecided condition in which the world has now long lived in divine matters may even continue to exist for us for an indefinite time. Decline and death cannot be equated with each other in this case either. The way one thinks about this will be determined by what one holds life to be. It will also depend on how far and how intensively "one in holy egoism thinks of only his own problems." If Jülicher comments that a product of the past could never come alive for a person who holds such a view, I would like to establish by way of answer the simple fact (probably I may do it also for Karl Barth) that just here the great men of the past have led me to determine to have the courage to seek answers to my own questions, and not to questions which the past poses. And the longer I associate with Luther, for example, the clearer it becomes to me that this courage is a duty and was never more a duty than it is today, and that only he who concentrates so constantly on his own questions that it seems to him "as if he and God were alone in heaven and on earth, and God were dealing with no one but him" (WA 7, 566) can get a decisive answer!

He who sees in this intensive "subjectivism" (the context will make clear enough how the word is meant)* the sign of real life, life under the eyes of God, will not see any too much life in the "church," in Christendom, in religion, and will not think that the letters of Paul are alive for the men of today. And he will attach little importance to the results of faithful research into the past, because, in the aspect of this research which we are considering here, it is by nature totally disinterested and objective. He will be unable to avoid seeing in all this the signs of decline. He will not be concerned with delaying the

---

* I would like to use this opportunity to refer to a small book by A. Albers, recently published by C. H. Beck Verlag, Munich, "Der Untergang des Abendlandes" und der Christ. Under the influence of Kierkegaard he attempts to show how only intensive, religious subjectivity (this reminds us of Kierkegaard's category of the "moment" and of the "individual") can lead us out of the great crisis of culture.

decline, or, if he wants to avoid this word "decline," which is becoming rather disagreeable, he will not be concerned with prolonging this situation or this development, for there is no static situation on this earth.

But he will not cease to regard this decline, or this development, as a sign that behind, under, and in this something novel is struggling to be born, which he can with confidence equate with the primordial and for which he can prepare. And he will know that if it drives him out of the confusion of history to the pure, original deed of God, then this which is new and thoroughly different has already been realized in him; and that he, if he holds it fast and commits himself to it, can accomplish more for his age than he could with the greatest activity, and that in any case here he can win for his work in time a significance beyond time.

That would then be "Barth's renewed Kingdom of God" which Jülicher so often refers to with friendly, superior mockery.

FOREWORD TO THE SECOND EDITION

Karl Barth

οὐδὲ ἀπῆλθον εἰς Ἱεροσόλυμα
... ἀλλὰ ἀπῆλθον εἰς Ἀραβίαν

Gal. 1:17

In the Foreword to the first edition I called this book a "preliminary work." If this allusion has attracted as much attention as that almost notorious last sentence ("This book can wait . . ."), I do not need to justify myself today when I present the book in a new revision in which no stone from the first work has remained on another. It has performed its "certain limited service" as I then dared and yet scarcely could hope it would, of attracting to Paul, and to the Bible in general, the attention of some who formerly paid no attention to it. Today with its merits and errors it can disappear from the scene. I have continued the work I began there and now present a further preliminary result. The position I took then has been moved to points further forward, and there it has been set up and fortified afresh. It offers now an entirely different view. The unity of the historical object and the matter itself have seen to the continuity between here and there, and will do the same for the reader if he will take the trouble to join also in this second "preliminary work." For this second edition too is preliminary work and only that, but by so saying I am not promising a third and, above all, in no case a final work. All human work is *only* preliminary work, and this is true of a theological book more than of any other! I say all this in the hope that those who saw the specter of a new orthodoxy arising in my *Epistle to the Romans* will not now, in complete but not hopeless (insofar as I know a part of the public) misunderstanding of the state of affairs, bring against me the opposite accusation of all too great flexibility.

Detailed information about the relationship of this second edition to the first must be given by the book itself, and that for the most part tacitly. I am surprised that the real weakness of the first edition was, so to speak, not seen at all by the public critics, but I have no intention whatsoever of providing here for the readers, and especially not the reviewers, the formula for what could and should have been said in almost devastating manner.* Here I shall only say that there were

---

* At the last minute I have seen the essay by Ph. Bachmann in the *Neue kirchliche Zeitschrift* (October 1921). Here objections which I must recognize as correct and relevant are raised in a very considerate manner. The author will note that they have in the meantime been my concern too.

chiefly four factors involved in the now completed further development and advance of the front line. *First,* and above all, the continued involvement with Paul. In my method of work this could be extended to only a few further fragments of the Pauline literature, but at every step it brought me new light on the Letter to the Romans. *Second,* Overbeck. Together with Eduard Thurneysen I have made detailed reference elsewhere to his warning to all theologians. I have first of all applied it to myself, and only then turned it against the enemy. Concerning the success or lack of success of my attempt in this second edition of the *Epistle to the Romans* to come to terms with this extremely remarkable and quite pious man, I shall accept judgments only from those who have shown that they have seen the real riddle (and truly not only the biographical, psychological one!) posed by Overbeck for all time, and that they have at least attempted to find its solution, and thus not, for example, from Eberhard Vischer! *Third,* better instruction concerning the real orientation of the thoughts of Plato and Kant, for which I am indebted to the writings of my brother Heinrich Barth, and the increased attention to what is to be gained from Kierkegaard and Dostoevsky for the understanding of the New Testament. Here the hints of Eduard Thurneysen have been particularly enlightening. *Fourth,* a close pursuit of the reception which was given my first edition. In this connection I must note that the favorable discussions which it received were more useful for self-criticism than the others in that I am so dismayed by some expressions of praise that I could no longer avoid the necessity of expressing things differently and of undertaking a vigorous change of position. I say all this in order at least to put on the right track all those who cannot help inquiring everywhere about influences. Does not everything in the world have its own circumstances and course?

More important for me are certain basic matters that concern both the editions.

This book does not intend to be anything else but a part of the conversation of a theologian with theologians. Jülicher's and Eberhard Vischer's triumphant discovery that I am also a theologian is quite superfluous. I have never intended to practice anything else but theology. The only question is, what kind of theology! I consider the view that today the most important thing is to shake off theology and to think, and above all to say and write, something anyone can understand to be a thoroughly hysterical and rash view. My question is rather whether those who attempt to address such speaking and writing to everyone would not do well first to come to a better understanding among themselves over their theme than is the case today. I shall permit myself to reject the speedy accusation of Ragaz and his followers that this is an undertaking of obdurate theological pride. If anyone really feels for a moment that my question is an idle one, he may go his own way in peace. The rest of us are of the opinion that the question about the "what" is a very important question, particularly in the times when apparently everything points to sounding an alarm in the streets. I make no secret of the fact that it is simply theology that awaits the reader here. If, in spite of this warning, non-theologians should also take up this book, and I know some who would understand what it contains better than many theologians, that will give me great pleasure. For I am thoroughly of the opinion that its content concerns everyone, because the question is everyone's question. But I could not make the thoughts any easier than I felt I should, and a few quotations in foreign languages which would have lost their force in translation, and occasionally a little theological, philosophical abracadabra must be taken as part of the bargain. If I am not mistaken—and here I must contradict Artur Bonus—we theologians have the interest of the "laity" most at heart when we are least inclined to turn to them expressly and intentionally, but simply live for our own work as every respectable craftsman does.

One of Ragaz' circle has thought to finish me off with the word of the elder Blumhardt, "Simplicity is the mark of the godly!" To this I answer that I have no idea that what I am saying or writing is "godly." As far as I know the "godly" is not contained in books. Should the task for us who are not the elder Blumhardt consist of *seeking* for the godly, then the simplicity through which man with God's help understands the Bible and much else stands not at the beginning but at the end of our ways. Thirty years from now let us talk about simplicity, but now let us talk about truth! For us, neither the letter of Paul to the Romans, nor the present situation in theology, nor the present situation of the world, nor the situation of man in relation to God is at all simple. Anyone who in this situation is concerned with the truth must muster the courage now for once *not* to be simple. In every aspect the life of man today is difficult and complicated. If we should talk at all about the thanks of the people, they would thank us last of all for out-of-breath, pseudo-simplicities. I really wonder, though, whether the cry for "simplicity" is anything other than that in itself very understandable concern, shared also by most theologians, for a direct, non-paradoxical, not merely believable truth. I remember the experiences which I had with so earnest and genuine a man as Wernle. If I make the "bare and simple" statement "Christ is risen!" he complains in the name of his modern man, who is offended in his holiest of holies, about great eschatological sayings and the violence done to the difficult, difficult problems of thought. But if I set out to say the same thing in the language of thought, that is, dialectically, then at once in the name of the plain and simple Christian he sighs about the oddness, ingenuity, and difficulty of such teaching. How shall I answer him? Is it not obvious that I could satisfy him only if I determined to give up the broken line of faith and to say that which is well-known, moderate, direct, non-paradoxical, which in the kingdom of truth, the kingdom of the totally childlike and the totally unchildlike, would be the third inadmissible category? Certainly I also long to be able to speak simply about that which is the concern of the Letter to the Romans. If someone appears who can do that, then it is all over for me; I will not insist on my book and my theology. But until now I have met among those who speak "simply" only such as spoke simply of something else, and who thus cannot convert me to *their* simplicity.

I want to consider another matter. I have been called the "declared foe of historical criticism." Instead of such excited words, why not rather merely state what the issue is. As a matter of fact, I have raised objections to the newer commentaries on Romans—not merely against the so-called critical historical ones, but also against those of Zahn and Kühl. I do not reproach them for their historical criticism, the justification and necessity for which I to the contrary do specifically recognize, but for their contentment with an explanation of the text which I cannot regard as any explanation at all, but only as the first primitive attempt at one: the establishing of "what is there" by means of translation and paraphrasing the Greek words and phrases in the corresponding modern language by means of philological, archaeological exposition of the results so achieved, and by means of a more or less plausible ordering of the individual elements according to historical and psychological pragmatism. *How* uncertain, *how* very dependent the historians are on the often questionable assumptions even in this establishment of "what is there," Jülicher and Lietzmann know better than I. This primitive attempt at an exposition is also not exact science. An exact science of the Letter to the Romans would have to limit itself to the deciphering of the manuscripts and the compilation of a concordance. But the historians rightly do not want to limit themselves to that. Rather, even Jülicher's and Lietzmann's commentaries, not to speak of the "positive" scholars, show numerous traces of the authors' intention to press beyond this primitive attempt and to try to *understand* Paul, that is, to discover not only how what is there can somehow be repeated in Greek or German, but how it can be *rethought,* and what it may perhaps *mean.* And it is here, and not with the obvious use of historical criticism in reference to the work which must be done before, that the dissension begins.

While I follow the historians attentively and thankfully as long as they are occupied with that primitive attempt at explanation, while I have never dreamed of doing anything else in the field of establishing "what is there" than to sit attentively at the feet of such scholars as Jülicher, Lietzmann, Zahn, Kühl, and their predecessors Tholuck, Meyer, B. Weiss, and Lipsius, I am always astonished at the modesty of their claims when I consider their attempts to press forward to a real understanding and explanation. I call real understanding and explanation that activity which Luther practiced in his expositions with intuitive sureness, which Calvin obviously and systematically set as the goal of his exegesis, and which has at least been clearly attempted by the more recent writers such as Hofmann, J. T. Beck, Godet, and Schlatter. Compare Jülicher, for example, with Calvin. How energetically the latter goes to work after he has conscientiously established "what is there" to think the thoughts of the text after it, that is, to come to terms with it until the wall between the first and sixteenth centuries becomes transparent, until Paul speaks there and the man of the sixteenth century hears here, until the conversation between document and reader is concentrated entirely on the *matter* (which *cannot* be different here and there!). Truly, anyone who thinks he can eliminate Calvin's method with the cliché, now so well worn, about the "restriction of the doctrine of inspiration," proves only that in *this* direction he has not yet really *worked* at all. Conversely, how near Jülicher (I mention him only as an example!) stays to the runic symbols of the words, as little understood afterward as before; how quickly he is ready to credit to some singular view and teaching of Paul this and that exegetical raw material, scarcely touched by any scholarly reflection as to the meaning; how quickly ready, by means of a few rather too banal categories of his own religious thought (feeling, experience, conscience, conviction), to *have* already understood and explained him then and there; but how quickly he is ready, if all this cannot be done in the twinkling of an eye, to save himself from the Pauline ship with a clever leap, and to ascribe responsibility for the meaning of the text to the "personality" of Paul, to the "Damascus experience" (which evidently can explain the most incredible things), to Late Judaism, to Hellenism, to the ancient world in general, and to some other demigods. The "positively" oriented exegetes are better off in this respect than their "liberal" colleagues, in that the more or less powerful orthodoxy or other historical form of Christianity to which they customarily withdraw is always a somewhat more stately haven of refuge than cultural Protestantism's religion of conscience. Strictly speaking, this means only that they have been more successful in concealing the lack of will to understand and explain.

In contrast to all this, I intend now for this first primitive attempt at paraphrase and what belongs with it to constitute only the starting point for a dialectic movement as inexorable as it is elastic, using all the crowbars and wrecking tools needed to achieve *relevant* treatment of the text. The historical critics must be *more critical* to suit me! For how "what is there" is to be understood cannot be established by an appreciation of the words and phrases of the text, strewn in from time to time from some fortuitous standpoint of the exegete, but only through an entering, as freely and eagerly as practicable, into the inner tension of the concepts presented by the text with more or less clarity. Κρίνειν means for me, in reference to a historical document, the measuring of all the words and phrases contained in it by the matter of which it, unless everything is deceptive, is clearly speaking, and the relating to the questions it unmistakably poses all the answers given, and relating these again to the cardinal question, which contains all questions, the question of the meaning of everything that it says in the light of that which is all that *can* be said, and therefore really is all that *is* said. As little as possible should be left over of those blocks of merely historical, merely given, merely accidental concepts; as far as possible the connection of the words to the Word in the words must be disclosed. As one who would understand, I must press forward to the point where insofar as possible I confront the riddle of the *subject matter* and no longer merely the riddle of the *document* as such, where I can almost forget that I am not the author, where I have almost understood him so well that I let him speak in my name, and can myself speak in his name. I know that these sentences will bring me another severe reprimand but I cannot help myself. What then do we call "understanding" and "explanation"—has Lietzmann, for example, ever seriously asked himself this question?—when one scarcely makes the slightest attempt to at least concern oneself in this direction (I too can do no more than this), but rather, in contrast to so much astonishing diligence in another direction, takes *no* pains, is content with the most meager results, and sees in this the triumph of a true scientific attitude? Or are these historians, whom I truly respect as scholars, quite unaware that there is a content, a cardinal question, a Word in the words? That there are texts, e.g., those of the New Testament, which to make speak, cost what it may, can be termed an ultimate and profound concern of culture? That through the ecclesiastical future of their students a question is posed which is truly not only a practical but a highly material one? I know what it means to have to go into the pulpit year in and year out, obliged to understand and explain, and wishing to do so, yet being unable to do it because we were given almost nothing at the university except the famous "respect for history," which despite the beautiful expression means simply the renunciation of earnest, respectful understanding and explanation. Do the historians then really think that by so doing they have fulfilled their duty to human society, that with a beautiful gesture they have imparted the Word by adding a supplementary volume to their commentary series containing a practical commentary by Niebergall? Yes, to be sure, it was out of the needs of my task as pastor that I came to have a greater desire to understand and explain the Bible, but can those in the camp of the members of the New Testament guild really think that this is just the concern of "practical theology," as Jülicher, in opposition to me, has pronounced with the old exorbitant assurance? I am no "pneumatic" as he has termed me. I am no "declared enemy of historical criticism." I know that the problem is not simple. But only when the problem is seen from the other side and is therefore spoken of somewhat more penitently will I be able to consider coming to an agreement about the difficulties and dangers, not unknown to me, of what I call critical theology, and its expedient avoidance of the issues. But not until then.

But what do I mean when I say that the *inner dialectic of the subject matter* and the recognition of it in the wording of the text is the decisive factor in understanding and in exposition? I am told (a Swiss reviewer has said this in a particularly blunt manner) that by this naturally I can only mean my "system." The suspicion that here more is read in than is read out is really the most relevant thing they can say about my whole undertaking. To this I have the following comment. If I have a "system," then it consists in my keeping in mind as constantly as possible what Kierkegaard called the "infinite qualitative difference" between time and eternity, in its negative and its positive meaning. "God is in heaven, and thou on earth." The relationship of *this* God to *this* man, the relationship of *this* man to *this* God, is for me the theme of the Bible and the sum of philosophy in one. The philosophers call this crisis of human knowing the source. At this crossroads the Bible sees Jesus Christ. When I now approach a text like the Letter to the Romans, I do it with the provisional assumption that when Paul formed his concepts he had the both plain and immeasurable meaning of that relationship at least as clearly in mind as I have when I now busy myself with the attentive rethinking of his concepts, just as another exegete approaches the text with certain provisional assumptions of more pragmatic nature, e.g., with the assumption that the Letter to the Romans was really written by Paul in the first century.

Whether such presuppositions can be maintained can be shown, as with all presuppositions, only in using them, that is, in this case, in the exact investigation and consideration of the text verse by verse. Naturally this verification can be only a relative, more or less certain verification, and of course my presupposition also is subject to this rule. If I now proceed provisionally on the assumption that in Romans Paul was really speaking of Jesus Christ and not of something else, it is to begin with an assumption as good or as bad as any of the provisional assumptions of the historians. The exposition alone can decide whether and to what extent I have succeeded in carrying through my assumption. If it is false, and Paul has really spoken of something other than the permanent crisis of time and eternity, why then in the course of dealing with the text I myself will carry it *ad absurdum.* If someone should ask me further, on what ground I approach the Letter to the Romans with just this assumption, I would answer with the counterquestion of whether an earnest man can approach a text which is not patently frivolous with any other assumption than this—that God is God? And if anyone should persist in complaining about what violence I do to Paul with this assumption, then I must raise the countercomplaint that it is doing violence to Paul to let him speak apparently of Jesus Christ but in reality of a truly anthroposophic chaos of absolute relativities and relative absolutes, of precisely the chaos for which in all his letters he has only expressions of the most angry disgust. Even though I can by no means claim to have explained everything satisfactorily, I have found no reason for abandoning my assumption. Paul knows something about God which we as a rule do not know, but which we too could know well. That I know Paul knew this is my "system," my "dogmatic presupposition," my "Alexandrianism," and whatever other names people want to give to it. I have found that, even considered from the point of view of historical criticism, this is relatively more effective. For the modern pictures of Paul are for me and a number of others no longer at all believable even historically. The numerous allusions to contemporary conditions and problems have only the significance of illustrations. My intention was not to say this or that about a passage, but to understand and to explain the Letter to the Romans. It is consistent with my principle of exposition that I cannot see how the contemporary parallels which in other commentaries are about all there is, should be more instructive for this purpose than the events of which we ourselves are witnesses.

And now, some in praise, some in censure, call this position of mine in relation to the text *Biblicism.* I can also accept this comparison which I did not make, on the condition that I am allowed to interpret it myself. With a certain bitterness Wernle writes, "There is absolutely no point in the thought of Paul that he finds disagreeable . . . no remnant conditioned by the history of the times, however modest, is left over," and then he lists what should have been "left over" as "disagreeable points" and "remnants conditioned by the history of the times," namely: the Pauline "belittling" of the earthly lifework of Jesus, Christ as the Son of God, reconciliation through the blood of Christ, Christ and Adam, Pauline scriptural proofs, the so-called "baptism sacramentalism," double predestination, and Paul's relation to the magistrate. Let us imagine a commentary on Romans in which these eight little points remain unexplained, that is, are declared to be "disagreeable points" which are "left over" under a scrollwork of contemporary parallels! How could that be called a "commentary"? In contrast to this agreeably ignoring disagreeable points, my Biblicism consists in my having thought through these "offenses to the modern consciousness" until I feel in part that I have discovered in them the most excellent insights; and in any case am able to speak of them and explain them to some extent. How far I have explained them correctly is a question in itself. Now as before, there are passages in Romans that are also hard for me to explain. I could go even further and admit to Wernle that my calculation does not come out as exact in any single verse, that I (and the attentive reader with me) sense more or less clearly in the background a "remnant" that is not understood and not explained and which awaits working out. But it awaits *working out*—not being left over. The view that unexplained historical crumbs should in themselves be the seal of true research is something that I as a so-called "Biblicist" and Alexandrian cannot get through my head. Moreover, I do not hide the fact that I would use my "Biblicist" method—the formula of which is simply "think deliberately"—also on Lao-Tzu or Goethe if it were my job to explain Lao-Tzu or Goethe, and that on the other hand there are some books of the Bible to which I would have difficulty applying it. Taken exactly, all the "Biblicism" which I can be shown to have consists in my having the prejudice that the Bible is a good book, and that it is worthwhile to take its thoughts at least as seriously as one takes his own.

As for the content of this present commentary on Romans, I admit that now just as three years ago, I am more concerned with the *true* gospel than with the so-called *whole* gospel, because I can see no road to the whole gospel other than by grasping the true, which has never revealed itself to anyone in its entirety. The customary idle speaking and writing about the whole gospel, which includes faith, love, and hope, heaven, earth, and hell equally in beautiful proportions, I do not find very edifying. I will blame no one who in the name of Christendom wants to say something different from what is said here. At most, I would ask how he has passed by what is said here. Paulinism has always found itself on the edge of heresy, and we must really marvel what harmless and inoffensive books most commentaries on Romans and other books about Paul are. Why not? It is probably because in them the "disagreeable points" are handled according to Wernle's formula. I should like this time to anticipate Wernle and myself exhort the theological children, I mean naturally the students, to read the book very carefully, not too quickly, not without checking my progress against the Greek text and other commentaries, and, please, preferably not "enthusiastically"! It is a matter of earnest and, in the pregnant sense, critical work that is to be done here. K. Müller of Erlangen has rightly said that the book can have a very fatal effect on immature spirits. If anyone would bring this complaint against me, let him consider whether in dealing with what is most dangerous in Christendom we have not always put our light under a bushel, whether Spengler may not have been right when he said that we are about to enter an "iron age," and whether if this be the case theology and theologians can escape its influence?

When I was in the midst of the work, Harnack's book on *Marcion* appeared. Anyone who is acquainted with it and who only leafs through my book will know at once why I must mention it. Certain striking parallels also startled me when I looked at the first reviews of that work. I would like, however, to ask the reader to look carefully both here and there and not to praise or to condemn me too quickly as a Marcionite. In the decisive points we simply do not agree. Even before the appearance of Harnack's book, Jülicher placed me with Marcion, Harnack himself with Thomas Münzer, and Walther Koehler, if I am not mistaken, with Kaspar Schwenkfeld. I might take this occasion to raise the question of whether this favorite pastime of the theological historians of passing out old and even ancient heretical labels should have taken place before they came to more agreement among themselves? Perhaps it will be to my credit, as the one labeled this time, if I am amazed at how varied the nominations of the three scholars are.

One word more about a specific matter. The translation of πίστις as "the faithfulness of God" has been ascribed an importance which it did not at all have for me. Jülicher even expressed the opinion that it was for this reason that I felt that "joy of discovery" of which my first Foreword spoke somewhat romantically. Above all I must admit that Rudolf Liechtenhan is the spiritual father of this innovation. While he was alive he mentioned the possibility of this translation to me in a

letter, and later advanced the view in public. Because of the general
protest I have somewhat reduced the number of passages in which I
give preference to this translation (its opponents will find them in
disagreeable frequency now only in chapter 3), and for the rest I can
only protest that by so translating I only wanted to draw attention to
the shifting meaning of the concept, which effect can obviously be
achieved as little through the customary monotonous reproduction of
"faith" as if I were to pedantically use the occasional "faithfulness"
everywhere. That the concept does actually shift surely no one will
wish to or be able to dispute in the light of Romans 3, or of the well-
known variants to Habakkuk 2 in the LXX, and of the analogical situation of the related concepts, ἀγάπη, γνῶσις, ἐλπίς, χάρις, δικαιοσύνη,
εἰρήνη, etc.

This time, for various reasons, I have decided to omit a compilation of the related literature. One thing should be put to rights. The
commentary on Romans by C. H. Rieger (1726-1791) in his *Betracht-
ungen über das N. T. 1828*, mentioned in the first edition, remarkably
agrees word for word from chapter 3 on with the exposition of Fr. Chr.
Steinhofer (1706-1761), edited in 1851. The plagiarism cannot in any
case be laid at the door of the worthy Rieger. Perhaps a Württemberg
specialist may be able to cast light on this dark matter. Concerning
textual notes, which Jülicher in his zeal to turn me out into the quiet
pastures of practical theology wished I had omitted entirely, it may
be said that I introduced them in those places where I felt I had to
deviate from the text of Nestle, which I assumed to be in the hands
of most of my theological readers. I do not intend to intervene in matters in which I am notoriously incompetent. Yet I could not simply for
that reason entirely decline to give a brief explanation of why I prefer
other readings in passages, not all of which are unimportant, though I
am always ready to be corrected.

If I could, I would like to urge certain reviewers to notice that this
time it is even more dangerous than the first time to write quickly
something enthusiastic or morose about the book, and I would advise
them to reflect on what it means to answer here with Yes *or* No, but
also what it means to answer here with a friendly mixture of Yes *and*
No. But it is not in my power to tell them this in a way that they
would have to hear.

It remains for me to thank my friends Eduard Thurneysen in St.
Gallen, Rudolf Pestalozzi in Zürich, and Georg Merz in Munich for
their faithful help in correcting the manuscript. The first-named has
even read the whole manuscript while it was in the process of being
written, given his opinions, and in a very selfless manner erected a hid-

den monument by the insertion of numerous corollaries that deepen, clarify, and sharpen, and which I for the most part took over unaltered. No specialist will be able to determine where in this continuation of our teamwork the thoughts of the one begin and those of the other stop. The completion of this second edition of the *Epistle to the Romans* comes at the same time as my departure from the congregation in Safenwil. My fellow members of the congregation have often in the last year found their pastor only in his study, and have also experienced all sorts of disconcerting things with him in matters that were closely connected with his research in Romans. The patience, at least in part, very understanding, with which they have borne this situation merits their being gratefully mentioned here. No one of the friends of this book who is himself a pastor should feel easy over the fact that he is unable, not only for himself, but also for his congregation, to make it easy. To greet all these friends, the known and the unknown, the old and the new, the Swiss and the Germans, in the pressure of all their so different ways, is a duty and a joy for me in the moment in which I myself have a long road behind me and another longer one before me.

KARL BARTH'S *EPISTLE TO THE ROMANS* IN ITS SECOND EDITION*

Rudolf Bultmann

THE FRAMING OF THE QUESTION

Karl Barth's *Epistle to the Romans* may be characterized by one sentence, the phraseology of which he would disagree with, but which would still be valid in terms of the usage that has been prevalent in the present time: The book attempts to prove *the independence and the absolute nature of religion*. It thus takes its place, even though it is in the form of a commentary, in the same line with such works as Schleiermacher's *On Religion* and Otto's *The Idea of the Holy*, with modern attempts to demonstrate a religious a priori, and finally with the Letter to the Romans itself, which, with its radical contrast of works and faith, basically has no other intention than this. However different all these attempts may be in detail, they seek to give verbal expression to the consciousness of the uniqueness and absoluteness of religion.

It is natural that such an undertaking is always determined by the times to the extent that the front line of the battle is constantly determined by the intellectual situation of the time, and the undertaking basically demands the author's coming to grips with the situation. As Paul fought for faith against the law of works, so Schleiermacher fought against the "Enlightenment," and Otto against a rationalizing and ethicizing concept of religion that had held wide sway in the school of Ritschl. And on what front is Barth fighting? Against the psychologizing and historicizing concept of religion, which not only plays or has played a role in the historical (so-called liberal) theology, but in theology and modern intellectual life in general. He is fighting against all cults of "experience" (wherein experience is understood as a psychic factor or a psychic action), against every concept which sees in religion an interesting phenomenon of culture, which wishes to understand religion in the context of psychic historical life. He is fighting also against many other things, but that fight gives his book its distinctive character.

To be sure, Barth does not speak of "religion" in this sense, for this expression is for him only the designation of a psychic historical re-

* From *Die Christliche Welt*, XXXVI (1922), issue 18, columns 320-323; issue 19, columns 330-334; issue 20, columns 358-361; and issue 21, columns 369-373.

ality. But we should not be concerned with a quarrel about words, and in order to come to grips with Barth we are glad to concede to him the use of his own terminology. The question would then go like this: In what does the essence of faith consist?

FAITH AND "EXPERIENCE"

"Nowhere is it [faith] identical with the historical and psychological empiricality of the religious experience" (p. 126).* "Even your impression of revelation, your emotion, your experience, your enthusiasm, is flesh, is of this world" (p. 72). "When faith happens, the warmth of feeling, the power of conviction, the attained stage of conviction and morality, are always only auxiliary, this-worldly, and therefore unimportant signs of the actual occurrence . . . For this reason, faith is never identical with 'piety,' even if it were the purest and finest" (pp. 39 f.). "What can become visible psychically and historically as the advantage of one man over another is only the 'person,' the form, the mask, the role assumed in a drama . . . It has its worth in itself, but does not signify an *eternal* distinction, nor one that extends beyond the crisis involving all that is perishable with the imperishable" (p. 63; cf. 108-110, 239). Faith is no "return to direct living" (p. 168), no "blessed, happy feeling" (p. 151). Religious excitement is, for example, different from the need for sleep only in degree (p. 235). The message of faith therefore does not serve for the satisfying of so-called religious needs (p. 37).

For psychological consideration, faith thus is not at all visible, it is a nothing (Barth: a "vacuum"); thus it is also not visible for historical science, inasmuch as the latter wishes to describe the evident reality of human life in time. There is no history of faith (p. 126). "All history of religion and of the church takes place entirely in the world" (p. 57). Faith is "only faith insofar as it does *not* lay claim to historical and psychic reality, but is inexpressible divine reality" (p. 58; cf. 85).

A religious a priori, a religious "drive," is always nothing but a part of the world, and has nothing to do with faith, if the latter really has to do with God. If this is not recognized, the theories arise in which "now the human or animal processes are elevated to experiences of God, now the being and work of God are 'experienced' as human or animal experience. That which is solid in this fog is the delusion that a unity or even the possibility of a compact between God and man could exist without the miracle (vertically from above), without the

---

* Quoted material is our translation. Page numbers refer to Barth's *The Epistle to the Romans* (London: Oxford University Press, 1933), translated by Edwyn C. Hoskyns from the 6th edition of *Der Römerbrief.*

annulling of all that is given, apart from *the* truth which lies beyond
birth and death. Religious experience, at whatever stage it takes place,
insofar as it claims to be more than a vacuum, to be content, possession,
and enjoyment of God, is the shameless and unsuccessful anticipation
of that which can be and become true only from the side of the unknown God. It is in its historicalness, reality, and concreteness always
betrayal of God" (p. 50).

Thus far Barth is original (in the relative sense, which is all the
word can have here) not in his thoughts, but in their clear and powerful formulation. Materially speaking, he stands throughout in the context of the modern polemic against "historicism" and "psychologism."
I do not say this in order "to understand him historically," but in order
to grasp the substance; much less do I say it to pass judgment on
Barth, since the clarity and radicalism of Barth in each case reaches
far beyond the usual polemics; much less since with him it is basically
not a question of a modern fashionable trend, a reaction, a mere negation, but here speaks the self-confidence which has always belonged to
living faith. No one in our time has proclaimed with this self-confidence the uniqueness and absoluteness of "religion" (of faith!) with
more clarity than Wilhelm Herrmann, with whom Barth is in complete
agreement.*

How little Barth may be taken simply as a symptom of modern
moods is shown by his clear rejection of all mysticism. In this it is a
question only of an apparent flight from the world; to be sure, it seeks
to escape "historicism," but religion here remains nonetheless a psychic
event, an "experience." In it a new work-righteousness takes the place
of the old, where "being still before God himself (if, e.g., the sayings
of Angelus Silesius were intended as psychological recipes, or should
be read as such!)" is conceived of "as the most clever stroke of human
piety, and remaining in the 'moment' (which is not a moment in
which one can remain) as the highest extreme of human experience."
"So there could appear as the triumph of Pharisaism, the *New* Pharisaism, more fearful than the former, and capable of achieving the result
of being not merely 'self-righteous' but, in addition, humble! Human
righteousness is capable of anything, of self-exaltation and self-extinc-
tion, when it is necessary (Buddhism, mysticism, pietism) . . . He who
once boasts of himself, who once as a man wants to be in the right
before men and before God, will boast even of the deepest sinking into
the non-ego and non-being (where possible, of his unsureness and his

---

* What Herrmann called "experience" is not that against which Barth polemizes.
And Herrmann's polemic against the philosophy and psychology of religion as
opposed to mysticism was no less radical than that of Barth.

brokenness) and—as a man (only as a man!) stand there vindicating himself" (pp. 109 f.; cf. 59 f.). Faith is absolutely different from all myth and all mysticism. "It is not concerned with one of those exaltations, abasements, and enrichments of this world through the Beyond of an 'inner' or even 'higher' world, not with one of those cosmic, meta-physical doublings, triplings, or sevenfold multiplyings of the given condition of our life and existence, but with the ultimate and unique, because unsurpassable, contrast of life to death, of death to life, of be-ing to non-being, of non-being to being. The life and existence in the Beyond is for it what can only be called, from the point of view of the life and existence in this world, death and non-being; and again, the life and existence in this world is what, from the viewpoint of the life and existence in the Beyond, can only be called death and non-existence" (p. 141). No "method" can lead to God (pp. 57, 110, 137). Grace is not to be grasped with the mystic attitude of passivity, else it would be a "human possibility" (p. 214).

What has been said yields two results. First, *the renunciation of all pantheism,* of all veneration of a god in nature, all belief in imma-nence, all attempts to grasp God in natural occurrences or in psychic and historical occurrences. God is neither a natural nor a psychic power (p. 36). "God as the highest affirmation of the being and the state of the world and of men: this is the unbearable, this is the non-god, despite the highest attributes with which we passionately bedeck it" (p. 40). Anyone who wants to attain to God—without first having heard God's No pronounced over him and the world—attains only to a Beyond that is in truth an improved this-world (p. 108; cf. 50, 82, 89 f.). "Only in that which *restricts* things in their independence and validity . . . only *sub specie mortis* does the splendor of the Creator shine in them" (p. 169). "We must lose the awe of pseudo-life which we are able to grasp, this awe through which we precisely do *not* become related to the divine secret of the cosmos" (p. 308). "To wish to grasp the world in its unity with God is either punishable religious arrogance or a final insight into that which is true beyond birth and death, insight from God" (p. 37). "Moreover it is sentimental liberal self-deception to think that from nature and history, from art, morality, science, or even religion, direct roads lead to the impossible possibility of God" (p. 337). Naturally all this does not lead to a metaphysical dualism; it is not a matter of a "balance between two situations," but of a "dialectic" contrast between God and the world, of a "duality which is established only in being transcended, and the transcendence of which is its establishment!" (p. 165; cf. 178, 188).

With this, the other matter becomes clear, that is, that any kind

of *flight from the world is folly,* that no asceticism, no self-chosen
martyrdom determines the way to God (pp. 161, 324, 368, 63). The
"resurrection" of which faith knows is "the negation of all this-worldly
positions *and* negations" (p. 462). And even though we are standing
"deeper in the No than in the Yes," if "the 'abasement' of our chance
situation in life" has relatively more "witness value" than the heights
(pp. 462-464), then we would still sink only deeper into sin if we
wanted to flee from the world of our intellectual, historical life. Thus
there can be no contempt for art and science! no cult of the "irrational"! no flight from religion and church as the evident historical
spheres in which we move! All radicalism of anti-religious polemic is
only sham radicalism (p. 241; cf. 221 f.). "No one should want to
escape the ambiguous historical reality of religion—and care has been
taken that no one can escape it. Grace is grace where the religious
possibility, taken quite earnestly, and standing in full power and development, is sacrificed. Only there!" (p. 186; cf. 238). "For the true
crisis in which religion finds itself consists in that it not only *can*not
be shaken off by man 'as long as he lives,' but also that it *should* not
be shaken off, because it is so characteristic of man as man (of *this*
man!)"; "precisely because in it the human possibilities are limited
by the divine, and because we, in our consciousness that God is *not*
here and that we cannot take a single *further* step, must stop and
remain here with this human possibility in order that, beyond the
boundary which it indicates, God may meet us" (p. 242).

Thus there is very little fashionable polemic here against "historicism" or "psychologism" or "rationalism," and therefore so little
fanaticism or Gnosticism. It is the simple—Pauline—radicalism, which
is clear about what faith means, and what grace means.

FAITH AS A MIRACLE

What then is the significance of the denial of the world that
takes place in faith? This significance can be grasped only from the
point of view of faith itself. It is only from it that the concept "world"
can be inferred at all, a concept which can be understood in its radical
significance only from the Beyond—we have here a dialectic antithesis!
—so that no inner-worldly critique, no pessimism, can come close to
it; but rather the difference between "pessimism" and "optimism"
becomes a matter of total indifference (pp. 154, 309). "He who says
humanity, says unredeemed humanity. He who says history, says
finiteness and perishability. He who says I, says judgment" (p. 85).
"World is what our whole existence as it now, conditioned by sin,
becomes and is" (p. 168).

From such a position in relation to the world, faith in God arises. "The revealing of non-meaning is also the revelation of meaning" (p. 77). "The most primitive and the most advanced self-reflection of the human spirit will always be . . . found in the realization of our limitedness and in the looking out at that which limits us, which is the negation of our limitedness" (p. 45). "No relativity which in its lost-unlosable relationship does not point back to the absolute from which it really has its life, no appearance of death which is not the witness of our participation in the life of God, the witness of the relationship of *God to us* which is not broken by sin" (p. 170). "The recognition of complete bondage is also the recognition of freedom; revulsion at corruptibility is also the hope for incorruptibility" (p. 309). — How is this to be understood? It can very easily be misunderstood. Is it a matter of a simple logical inference by means of which we assume, out of the limitations of the world of which we are aware, the one who limits, that is, God? Is it a matter of our pronouncing a No to the world, in recognition of the questionable nature of our existence, and of now realizing that a No always exists only in relationship to a Yes, and of our now drawing the conclusion that this Yes is the non-world, is God? With the result, then, that we would have a sort of ontological proof of God, the inference drawn from the concept of his existence? It seems almost to be thus. "The place from which the whole closed circle as such is to be seen cannot lie inside the circle. The possibility of grasping what is humanly possible as such in its limitation is obviously . . . a totally unheard of new possibility. . . . With the question about the Whence of our knowledge of ourselves, characterized by the insight into our absolute sinfulness and mortality, we confront directly the existence of the *new* man who stands over against *this* man" (pp. 271 f.; cf. 91 f.).

A lack of clarity adheres to such formulations, as though faith were still a matter of a process of consciousness in which a first and a second element were distinguished: first the No, then the Yes. By means of a logical inference one comes from the first to the second. But this is not Barth's real meaning; for "even saying No, insight into the paradox of life, bowing under God's judgment, *are all not it,* even waiting on God, even the 'being broken,' even the attitude of the 'biblical man' *are not it,* insofar as they intend to be attitude, standpoint, method, system, matter" (p. 56). No, this negation of the world is no standpoint, but *the experiencing of divine judgment.* That No is not the presupposition in a logical inference; rather, if it is a *real* No, it contains the Yes in itself. It is also not a matter of a before and an after in the consciousness. In the *consciousness* of the one who believes (I believe I am able to say this in Barth's meaning) the Yes can even be the primary element; to dispute this would be to fall back into psychologism. This can be so because the No that is spoken over the world is not the inner-worldly criticism of a defiant, resigned, or despairing pessimism (Schopenhauer, Spitteler), that is, a No that always proceeds only from man, who would like to have the world different from what it is, so that in truth it proceeds only from a *human* Yes. But the No which is decisive for faith is that which is spoken by *God*. "He who recognizes the limits of the world through a contradicting truth, the limits of his own self through a contradicting will, *he who therefore confesses he belongs to this contradiction* and undertakes to base his life on it, he has faith" (p. 39).

This contradiction is not a standpoint; it is a *crisis* into which we are placed by God. That man "awakens to the consciousness of this situation, that he is aware of the crisis and recognizes it as a divine crisis, that he in this crisis chooses the fear of the Lord, that he hears and understands the No of God, because it is God's No—that is his faith" (p. 123). "We must take upon ourselves the full paradoxicality of the situation of human life. If we come at all to a consciousness of ourselves and our situation in the world, this paradoxicality consists in our being led step by step by the holy demand of God which meets us in the recognized problematic of our existence to the final possibility in which we, looking, perishing, pleading, crying out of deep need, stretch out our arms toward the great unknown, toward the Yes which stands unperceivable over against the No in which we are imprisoned —and that we then must recognize that even such life, destruction, pleas, and cries do *not* justify, do *not* redeem, do *not* save, that by all this we have only confirmed and sealed the fact—that we are men" (p. 256). Man must stand "naked" before God (pp. 68, 111, 408 f.); only so can he be "judged, and thereby also made right" (p. 95).

Only so can it be truth and not a mere inference, even when it is presented in the form of one. "Only from redemption can man grasp that he is unredeemed. Only from righteousness, that he is a sinner. Only from life, that he is dead. It is only on *God* that man can be so shattered. If man were not free beyond *all* human possibilities, how would he be able to recognize the boundary, the significance, the reality, of the *highest* human possibility as imprisonment?" (p. 286; cf. 284, 363). The recognition of the crisis, the taking the crisis upon oneself, is faith, or is possible only in faith. "There *is* a claim to deliverance from the wrath of God, there where all claim is given up and beaten down by God himself, there where God's No is recognized as final, God's wrath as inescapable, God as God" (p. 76). "The barrier is also the escape. The No that confronts us is God's No. What we are lacking is also that which helps us . . . That which negates all worldly wisdom is also its foundation. Precisely because God's No is complete, his Yes is also" (p. 38). "This No is therefore not the No of unbelief, which, while it strikes against God's wrath, does not strike through to the hidden truth of God, but only shatters itself on fate, matter, all, chance, *ananke*" (p. 43). Faith is bowing under the No of God. "Those who take on themselves the burden of the divine No are carried by the greater divine Yes. The weary and heavy-laden are refreshed. Those who do not avoid the contradiction are hidden in God. Those who uprightly let themselves be brought into a time of waiting recognize God's faithfulness in that they may, should, and can wait. Those who have respect for God and observe the distance live with God" (p. 41). Therefore "the final bowing under God's wrath is faith in his righteousness" (p. 78). Faith is the progress of the soul to the "King of the dark chamber" (Tagore).

Now it is clear what the often-repeated expression *"Faith is a vacuum"* means (e.g., p. 42, "The faith of man is the awe which is content with this No, the will for vacuum, the agitated waiting in negation"). It is, namely, not that faith is a vessel waiting to be filled, a human organ for the revelation of God, but that it is only a "crater" formed by the explosion of a shell, through which revelation makes itself observable within the realm of historical perceptibility (p. 29) and in which the message of faith presents itself (p. 36). The last remnant of psychic historical perceptibility, the last remnant of the character of work, is to be taken from faith through this negative designation. Admittedly the expression is not attractive and not even appropriate, because from the standpoint of historical perceptibility, faith not only cannot be perceived as a vacuum, but cannot be perceived at all. No, if faith is to be described in terms of our consciousness, it cannot be described otherwise than as *obedience*, as submission, as commitment (e.g., pp. 83, 88, 405 f.). We who believe stand in the place "where only God can support us . . . where all else except God himself, God alone, drops out of consideration," in the place that is no place at all, but only the moment when man is moved by God, the true God, who is the Creator of man and all that is human, his Redeemer, when man *gives up to him* all of himself and all that is human (p. 110). "To believe means to bow beneath the judgment, which inescapably points to the general situation between God and man" (p. 367).

But it is clear that this submission can be neither resignation, nor human despair, nor an inner attitude that can be achieved methodically; faith can be understood only *as a miracle,* that is, it is not at all "understandable." "Faith *is* a miracle, or it is not faith" (p. 366); it is the "absolute, vertical miracle" (p. 60; cf. 59, 102). The knowledge which is gained in faith, the divine Yes in the divine No, is no perceptible possibility, but lies beyond the boundaries of humanity (p. 231). *Credo quia absurdum* (p. 112). Faith is the "breaking in of God himself" (p. 75). "In relation to man, God is always beyond, new, far, strange, superior, never within his reach nor in his possession; whoever says 'God,' always says 'miracle.' God indeed stands as the either-or before the soul of man; there is therefore a human choice or rejection, affirmation or negation, awakening or sleeping, understanding or mistaking, in reference to God. But what is possible, probable, perceptible, and conceivable is always only to reject, negate, be asleep to, and mistake God, not seeing what is not perceptible, not conceiving what is inconceivable—as surely as man has no organs to perceive a miracle, so certainly all human experience and understanding ends just there, where it begins—in God. Insofar as from man's side it comes to an affirmation and understanding of God, insofar as the psychic occurrence receives from God its direction toward God, its being conditioned by God, and takes on the form of faith, to that extent the impossible, the miracle, the paradox, occurs" (pp. 120 f.). Thus it is again only a figurative expression, an attempt to describe what is obscure in terms of what is perceptible, when faith is described as a venture, as a leap into the void (e.g., pp. 98, 99, 107, 149 f., 202). This venture is no "work," but it is taking on one's self the divine No, which in itself is already a miracle (p. 41).

From the point of view of God, faith can be described as a beginning, as creation (pp. 229, 499), but as a constantly new beginning, a new creation. "This walk is a continuous self-repeal, self-renunciation, an untiring, incorruptible *desire* to decline, renounce, descend, and die; a continuously renewed departure from naked, neutral humanity in all its poverty and questionableness" (p. 132). "Faith is therefore never something finished, given, assured; it is, from the point of view of psychology, again and again the leap into the uncertain, into the dark, into the empty air. Flesh and blood does not reveal *that* to us (Matt. 16:17); no one can say it to another, no one can say it to himself. What I heard yesterday, I must hear anew again today, and I shall have to hear it anew tomorrow; always the one who reveals is Jesus' Father in heaven, only he" (p. 98).

The new "I," the one who has been justified, is not "perceptible" as a psychic historical element, so that the one having faith would now be distinguished from the unbeliever to our knowledge and our consciousness. " 'Our' righteousness is real and remains real only as God's righteousness" (p. 102). Perhaps faith is real precisely in such persons who stand outside of "religion"! "In their serene creatureliness and worldliness, in the simple, modest factualness of their actions, they are recognized by God, and they recognize him; they are not without insight into the transience of all that is human, not without a view of the silver rim of redemption and forgiveness which bounds the dark cloud of our existence, not without respect for that No, which separates the creation from the Creator, and for that Yes, which makes them creatures of the Creator. . . . Perhaps ultimate, terrible skepticism, complete inaccessibility for all that is 'higher,' complete incapacity to be impressed by anything at all—but perhaps precisely for that reason and in that way *real* brokenness, a mind for God, for God himself! Grumbling restlessness perhaps, protest and inner dissatisfaction that find fault with everything; but precisely therefore and therein the allusion to the peace of God, which is higher than all reason" (pp. 66 f.; cf. the frequent references to Dostoevsky's characters).

The one justified is "the inward, the imperceptible man, who is called into being through God's creative Word, the man, who *he is not*, who in the perishing of *this* man is renewed from day to day" (p. 126). "The grace of creation, like the grace of redemption, is nowhere present as a given condition among other given conditions. It is the imperceptible relation in which all given conditions stand, and knowledge of it is always and everywhere dialectic" (p. 135). That I am justified through faith is a paradox. *"Not I* is the subject, insofar as it, as subject, as that which it is, is absolutely in the Beyond, is the radically other in relation to what I am. And—*I am* this subject, insofar as what it does, its predicate, faith, consists just in the establishing of the identity between it and me" (p. 148). "The truth that *we are* new men, consists for us always and everywhere only in its starting point" (p. 150). We can never be certain that we believe, but only believe that we believe (p. 150). Once more, faith is not a "blessed, happy feeling" (p. 151), but brings man into the greatest inner unrest. Perhaps a word from Heinrich Hesse's *Demian* can make this faith that one believes clearer: "The life of every man is a way to himself, the attempt at a way, the suggestion of a path. No man has ever been entirely and completely himself. Yet each still strives to become it, one dully, another more lightly, each as he can."

In continually new expressions Barth describes *the great paradox of faith, the identification of the perceptible with the imperceptible "I,"* of the unredeemed man with the justified. It is a paradox, an "impossible possibility," for the justified person is "the imperceptible subject, newly constituted beyond all continuity with the psychologically perceptible human subject" (p. 158). "Therefore the fact which establishes the new man stands in contrast to all content of human life in basic superiority and priority. It was never the content of our life and never will be, because it is in its own essence the critical negation of all *content* of life" (p. 160; cf. 163 f., 198 f., 202, 205 f., 297). "Though it is a thousand times unavoidable that I, as the one that I am, in my perceptible being, knowledge, and activity, make myself guilty of sin; as the one who has received grace, placed in relation to that which I am not, to the new man, I cannot even reckon with the possibility of this which is unavoidable" (pp. 200 f.; cf. 207 f.). "We may then, as it is proper, *also* stand under the law—and yet stand much more under grace. We are then 'devout'—as if we were not so. We live—bypassing our experiences, or rather, passing through them" (p. 239; cf. 240, 284, 313 f.; esp. 291 f.).

FAITH AND CONSCIOUSNESS

It is clear that this radicalism, which does not shy away from paradox, or even from the appearance of blasphemy, is always seeking only to give expression to the fact that faith and justification are absolute miracles. But is not the paradox overdrawn? Is faith, when it is divorced from every psychic occurrence, when it is *beyond consciousness*, then anything at all real? Is not all talk of this faith only speculation and at that an absurd one? What is the meaning of the talk about my "ego" that is not my ego? What is the point of this faith of which I am not conscious and of which I can at most believe that I have it? Is not this alleged identity between my perceptible and imperceptible ego not in reality a speculation that is Gnostic or anthroposophic in nature? For these also talk of the relationship of my ego to higher worlds, relations that are really beyond my consciousness and in truth are matters of total indifference to me! — "Certainly, even faith always has its 'legal' side; it is *also* procedure and circumstance. But even on this, its legal, perceptible, psychic historical side, even as conceivable procedure and attainable situation, even as possible possibility, faith is clearly without its proper dynamic, and it establishes no certainty. It is 'emptied' . . . Faith establishes certainty insofar as it is the eternal step into total imperceptibility and is itself also imperceptible. Every perceptible procedure and situation, every temporal road, every describable method with its accompanying pragmatism, is also its negation" (p. 134).

This seems to be the answer to our questions. But it seems to me

—even though basically I believe I am one with Barth—that there is still some lack of clarity here. Certainly our justification is not an experience (in the Barthian meaning: as a psychic occurrence), not an occurrence in the consciousness. It is present with God, even without our knowing about it. And of *it* we can only say that we believe it. But that we can only believe that we *believe* is at least not the view of Paul, for whom faith is rather the conscious acceptance of the message of salvation, the conscious obedience under God's new saving ordinance. And that corresponds quite well with the subject matter. A faith beyond consciousness* is most certainly not the "impossible possibility," but in every sense an absurdity. Surely the sentence just quoted is right in that the proper dynamic of faith does not lie in its perceptibility as a conscious occurrence. But does it follow from this that faith is not the perception of that identity of the perceptible with the imperceptible subject?

Perhaps the lack of clarity lies in Barth's concept of the "perceptible." His polemic against faith as the content of consciousness rests on his understanding of consciousness always as only a psychic process, not as intellectual content, which in such a process becomes "perceptible." It is nevertheless remarkable that in the previously cited sentence (p. 134) scientific thought, moral will, artistic formulation, can be substituted everywhere for "faith" without the sentence's losing its meaning. For, in fact, the contents of our consciousness have meaning and validity apart from their being perceptible in the consciousness as a process (understandable psychically and historically), without their having for that reason an existence beyond consciousness. Thus faith does not lose its dynamic by being the content of consciousness; indeed it is faith only insofar as it is such. To be sure, however, consciousness is not understood here as a psychic process nor as reflection. For as little as the laws of this relationship are or must be conscious in scientific thought, in moral will, or in artistic formulation, so little is there necessarily present in believing a reflection on one's faith. Faith is throughout a peculiar definite quality of the contents of our consciousness. In Paul's meaning, it would be simple to distinguish between justification and faith; justification is God's pre- or supra-temporal deed; faith is the paradoxical fact of the appropriation of justification by man (*this* man) in his consciousness. (This concept of faith comes then very close to the Barthian concept "impact of revelation," an equally paradoxical, "impossible" concept.) Perhaps it is also possible to cast light on the problem of faith and conscious-

---

* Editor's note: Bultmann has written me that he would now replace here "consciousness" with "concrete existence." J. R.

ness by making it clear that faith is not without *confession* (cf. Rom. 10:9 ff.) , and this confession does not need to be confession in thoughts or words, but can just as well find its expression in deeds, in the attitude of men. Even my trust of other men, my love, my gratitude, are not only "perceptive" occurrences, and do not have their significance in being psychic processes, and I do not need to "know" anything about them. They are however not at all outside my consciousness, and they are not without "confession."

As strongly as Barth (with full right!) has separated faith from every psychic process, as much as he (with full right!) stresses its nature as creation, its constantly "being at the beginning," so clearly must faith still be distinguished from the object of any speculation. Perhaps I possess all sorts of astral or other bodies of which I know nothing. They are to me a matter of total indifference, and a speculation which asserts the identity of my "perceptible" ego with such astral bodies either leaves me completely cold, or seems comic. My justification and my faith, however, are not some sort of pseudo otherworldly factors, but my faith is something definite and precise in my consciousness. And this then means that faith cannot be without confession, but what faith is as confession seems to me to be treated too briefly by Barth.

FAITH AND LOGOS

This is closely related to the fact that Barth strictly delimits faith in reference to *psychic historical* occurrences, but not in reference to our *mental life,* insofar as the latter is more than psychic processes, that is, in reference to the content of our mental life. This is shown again by that sentence on page 134, in which I would again like to substitute for faith, scientific knowledge (or moral will, artistic formulation). Scientific knowledge too always has its "legal" side (and is also psychologically understandable as a psychic occurrence); it too is procedure and situation.

But even on this legal, perceptible, psychic historical side, precisely as a conceivable procedure and attainable situation, precisely as a possible possibility, scientific knowledge is obviously without its peculiar dynamic; it does not form the basis of certainty. It is "emptied," that is, the difference between true and false is given up, since false knowledge, as a psychic act, is just as understandable as the true. In addition, we should consider what Barth says on pages 140 f. and 146 about the meaning of history. History as a perceptible process is, according to him, a mere struggle for existence (p. 77; cf. 86 f.) . It receives meaning only from the imperceptible, non-historical, and supra-historical Logos. "Apart from this unhistorical element, the past remains silent and the present deaf." Naturally! And this Logos is also known to the rational idealistic view of history, which regards history as "within the limits of humanity"; it too knows that only the unhistorical and the supra-historical can bring the present to hear and the past to speak; and yet it knows nothing of that "revelation," but moves completely within the "world." Thus it is then rather surprising in Barth when (pp. 467 f.) the ethos of grace is depicted entirely in terms of the idealistic (Kantian) ethic: "It is the transcendental (never appearing anywhere as 'purity'!) purification of activity from all biological, emotional, erotic elements." "An action is ethical insofar as it, approved by the imperceptible one in all, is regarded as a control on the perceptible action of the many," therefore a paraphrase of the "categorical imperative" (whereby, moreover, Barth admits the contact with Kant). But how then is faith distinguished from the theoretical and practical Logos? What Barth says of the contrast of world and God is also largely applicable to the contrast of nature and intellectual life (culture), though both nature and culture, from God's point of view, are "world." It is not possible to do justice to the problem of culture by regarding it, as Barth does, simply as a product of nature. Basically, by so doing, a bit of the radicalism of the concept of faith is broken off, insofar as what is basically valid for culture, and cannot be regarded as nature (thereby eliminating culture), is said of God, and thereby God is made a part of the world. And the concept of world and man in the light of the dialectic opposition of No and Yes threatens to break down into transcendental philosophy. At this point Wilhelm Herrmann saw more sharply.

THE WAY TO FAITH

At another point, however, Barth marks progress beyond Herrmann, that is, in the question: How do I come to faith? In an address,* Heitmüller once made clear accurately and relevantly wherein Luther's progress over Paul consists, namely, in the question: How do *I* get a gracious God? Paul demands obedience for the message of faith, and the question of how I can be obedient does not come into view for him. Obedience consists in the acknowledgment of the proclaimed facts of salvation as the new saving ordinance of God. For Luther, as a true son of the church, this acknowledgment was self-evident, but he saw that obedience did not really consist in *that,* and that such obedience was dead if it were not at the same time the personal appropriation of the message, the inner submission to the revelation. Following Ritschl, Herrmann consistently advocated this

* Wilhelm Heitmüller, *Luthers Stellung in der Religionsgeschichte des Christentums* (Marburg: Elwert, 1917).

view with great emphasis. Obedience remains a "work" as long as it
does not signify the inner conviction of revelation. It is not genuine
as long as the reality of God does not show itself to be reality in my
life. Obedience as an act of the will would be a "work"; real obedience
can only be "free self-commitment" under the compelling and transforming (creative) impression of revelation. And for this reason, the
question of how I come to faith, that is, how I succeed in subjecting myself to the revelation with inner veracity, assumes decisive significance.

Now, to be sure, Herrmann—not exclusively, but yet with strong
emphasis—answered this question by reference to a psychologically
understandable "experience," to a process, a psychic historical procedure, and in this he was not free from a trace of pietism. His answer
consists in the well-known theory of rationally grounded obedience
under the moral law, of the despair which is the end of this road, of
the intervention of the forgiving grace of God, revealed in Jesus, for
which this is the preparation. To ask and to answer the question of
the way to faith in this sense is false—Barth was right here. Even
Herrmann's students were often not fully satisfied with this schema,
which does not fit Paul at all.* And indeed this schema dulls the edge
of the miracle of faith, or at least endangers it. In another sense, however, the question of how I come to faith has its necessary significance
if faith is to be honorable, true obedience.

It is only evading the question to speak—as is now so popular—of
subjugation to the "objective." For as surely as God is not the
symbolization of subjective "experiences," but the objective, so surely
can the "objective" be the reality before which I bow only when it
becomes reality *for me*. It becomes this only when it destroys, kills my
old self—the perceptible man. By wanting to use the talk about the
"objective" to gain support for dogmas of old or new provenience,
one makes faith into a work and God into an idol, and in truth,
empties the objective of its character. And how many messages calling
upon us to believe in them offer us the "objective"! How many mes-
siahs are preached! Where is the objective to which I should bow?
Thus there remains the question of how I come to faith. And to
answer *here*—as is now often done—with the secret of predestination,
is dodging the issue, not really a serious answer. For at this point the
concept of predestination can be only speculation which is intended
to explain something. The concept of predestination takes on meaning
only in the moment of faith.

The question "Where is the objective to which I must bow?" must

---

* Cf. Wilhelm Heitmüller, "Die Bekehrung des Paulus," *ZThK*, XXVII, 1917
(Festgabe für Herrmann), pp. 136-152.

rather be stated as "Where is the objective to which I *can* bow?" And with this insight the question of how I come to faith gains its simple and clear meaning. It can only be answered by showing what faith *means*. For in that the meaning of that which is called faith is made clear; faith is protected from every misinterpretation as a psychic process and is severed from every "method." It becomes clear that the possibility of bowing becomes the necessity of bowing, and that the man who is confronted with the question "How do I come to faith?" can find his answer only by taking thought whether and where in his life he meets the reality which he can absolutely bow to and must bow to. Inner veracity is the only "way" to faith, veracity which does not avoid the ultimate question of the meaning of human existence, veracity which is ready to sacrifice its own self, which is ready for the path to the "King of the dark chamber." That veracity can never be made "perceptible," and the decision must be made by every man for himself. Others can only help him in that they try to say what faith means.

THE CHRIST

Or is there nonetheless a bit of reality which can enter the life of every man, and which is "perceptible" as the *revelation of God*? Herrmann would answer, Jesus! The inner life of Jesus, that which perceived from the Gospel tradition grasps the observer as reality, as the living embodiment of holiness and love, overcomes, transforms, redeems him. Barth rejects this answer, not only because he knows that New Testament research has generally led to the concession that we can know little, or almost nothing of the inner life of Jesus, but because Jesus as a man belongs to the psychic historical reality, to the "world," and we cannot be helped by such psychic historical perceptibleness. Barth's answer rather runs, "The Christ is the revelation of God." And here I confess that I simply do not understand him. Here I can discover only contradictions.

According to Barth there is a line at which the two planes of God and the world intersect. (Can this be spoken of in earnest, when the contrast between God and the world is a purely dialectic one? But let us first hear Barth further!) "The point of the line of intersection, where it is to be seen and is seen, is Jesus, Jesus of Nazareth, the 'historical' Jesus, 'descended from David according to the flesh.' 'Jesus' as a historical designation signifies the point of the break between the world which is known to us and an unknown one. At this point of the world that is known to us, time, things, and men are not superior to other times, things, and men, but yet they are superior insofar as they delimit that point which lets the hidden line of intersection between time and eternity, things and origin, man and God, become visible. Therefore the years 1 to 30 are a time of revelation, a time of discovery" (p. 29). To be sure, every other time can also become a time of revelation and discovery, but that is a possibility which is given only by that basic time of revelation (p. 29). For here we really meet, at *one* point of time, the truth of another order, of a divine answer (p. 96).

And to what extent does the divine world now become perceptible in Jesus? "The life of Jesus . . . is complete obedience to the will of the true God. As a sinner he joins the sinful. He places himself totally under the judgment under which the world stands. He places himself where God can be present only as the question about God. He takes the form of a servant. He goes to the cross, to death . . . 'Therefore God has highly exalted him,' " etc. (p. 97). We see here a paraphrase of Philippians 2:6 ff., the Pauline Christ myth, and nothing of the life of Jesus, of the historical Jesus. These sentences take on meaning only if one already has a definite opinion of their subject (of this "he") ; this, however, cannot be gained from psychic historical perceptibleness, for it is intepreted by the latter. To what extent therefore is revelation contained in the life of Jesus? Other statements of Barth may be compared here (e.g., pp. 105 ff., 178, 202 f., 276 ff., 327 f.). They all come to the same thing.

Alongside this are statements such as that in the life and death of Jesus as an act of obedience, it is not an individual, a personality, one person, that is illustrated, but the individual, the personality, the person (p. 182). "Neither the personality of Jesus nor the Christ concept, neither his Sermon on the Mount nor his healing of the sick, neither his trust in God nor his brotherly love, neither his call to repentance nor his message of forgiveness, neither his struggle against traditional religion nor his exhortation to follow him in poverty, neither the social nor the individual, neither the indirect nor the eschatological side of his gospel" constitutes the meaning of the "Christ," but only his death on the cross, in the light of which all those possibilities appear as merely human; the death in which the "imperceptible" life becomes "perceptible"; his death, which means dying *for us*, "insofar as in this death the imperceptible God becomes perceptible for us" (pp. 159 f.; cf. 202 f.). So in the Son of God we recognize ourselves again, and see in him the existential nature of the new man who is alive in God (p. 282), and are ourselves "sons of God" (p. 296). As "I myself am the one crucified, who appears to me in the mirror image of the death of Christ" (p. 198), so "we believe in our identity with the imperceptible new man who appears beyond the death of the cross" (p. 202). Thus also, Jesus' resurrection is "no event of historical extent *beside* the other events of his life and death, but the 'unhistoric' relationship of his *whole* historic life to its origin in God" (p. 195). If the resurrection were itself in any sense a fact of history, then no assertion however strong, and no deliberation however refined, would be able to prevent it from appearing to be drawn into that see-saw of Yes *and* No, of life *and* death, of God *and* man, which is characteristic of the historical superficiality" (p. 204).

Good. But cannot this also be said of the "life of Jesus" in general? And what meaning would it then have to speak of the years 1 to 30 as the time of revelation? Is not the "historical Jesus" in truth completely ignored? "Jesus Christ, however, is the new man beyond the humanly possible man, especially the pious man. He is the abrogation of *this* man in his totality. He is the man who has come from death into life. He is—not I, my existential I, I as I am in God, in the freedom of God" (p. 269). I can understand all this only to mean that *the historical Jesus has become a symbol*. This does not mean he has become an idea (Barth rightly rejects this, p. 160), and neither does it mean an illuminating or aesthetically fascinating illustration of a general truth (of reason), but a symbol as living, present power—not the power of any sort of magic, but simply as *verbum visibile* (cf. Barth, p. 529; Jesus Christ authentically "interprets" God to us as he meets us in the reality of our life!). The Word speaks and is heard, and is therefore a living, present reality in connection with which it is completely unimportant how the historical Jesus of Nazareth is to be included in the context of psychic historical occurrences. The Christ speaks through Grünewald's painting of the crucifixion, of which Barth likes so much to speak, just as much as through the Synoptic Gospels. And what does he say? He is, as the crucified and risen one, the most powerful sermon of God concerning God's judgment, in which his No becomes his Yes, and embodies "God's existentiality, illumined by his uniqueness" (p. 276). "God is personality, unique, alone, peerless, and as such the eternal and almighty, and nothing else. The proof of this is Jesus, the human, historical Jesus. But Jesus is the *Christ*. This is God's uniqueness illumined by his existentiality. Therefore despite all believing and unbelieving historicism and psychologism, the *skandalon* of an eternal revelation in Jesus, a revelation of that which truly Abraham and Plato also had already seen" (pp. 276 f.; cf. 381 ff.).

I do not know if I understand Barth correctly, but I can interpret his statements only thus: that Jesus is a symbol for the truth (preaching of the truth), that God's revelation is neither a psychic historical fact or form as such, so that it would be possible to read off directly the divine reality in the methodically conceived, "perceptible" history —perhaps in its "high points"—nor something that would be at all immanent for all "perceptible" occurrences. As a result, the attempts of a certain liberalism to have revelation immediately in the historical person of Jesus are just as false as all pantheistic talk of the revelation of the "God-nature" in the All. Therefore he is a symbol for the fact that God's revelation is present always unhistorically and supra-historically, always unnaturally and supra-naturally, always only in a definite now, in a definite man. The symbol for this is the "Christ," and that not as an idea (all rational considerations are eliminated), but as *verbum visibile*, as living, present power.

How I can get beyond this, I do not see, even though I exert myself to follow the Barthian thought patterns and reflect on the meaning of faith and revelation. "Christ" is thus just as much a "sign" as baptism "in its paradoxical uniqueness" is for Barth (p. 192), or as Adam, in whom the imperceptible No of God becomes perceptible; in this connection Barth expressly declares the historicity of Adam a matter of indifference (p. 171). In reality, Barth makes Adam and Jesus parallel in this sense: "In the one man Adam the imperceptible becomes perceptible, that God says No to us . . . In the one Jesus Christ the imperceptible becomes perceptible, that God does not cease to say Yes to us" (p. 178).

THE RELATIONSHIP TO THE TEXT

With my references and critical comments I have not exhausted this book, which despite all its one-sidedness is a rich one. I also intentionally declined to go into the relationship of the new edition to the first one, and hope that someone else will undertake this task. I must confess, however, that the new edition made a much deeper impression on me than the first did. I have also refrained from regarding the book as a commentary on the Letter to the Romans, for the sake of the clarity of the issue with which it basically deals. But precisely because of the issue it seems to me that in conclusion a word is necessary about the relationship of Barth to the text. In the understanding of the task of explaining the text as Barth develops it in the Foreword, I am quite in agreement with him. As it is self-evident for him that the philological historical explanation of the text is a necessary side of exegesis, it is self-evident for me that a text can be explained only when one has an inner relationship to the matter with which the text deals. And I agree also when Barth formulates the high point of exegetical understanding as follows: "As one who would understand, I must press forward to the point where insofar as possible I confront the riddle of the *subject matter* and no longer merely the riddle of the *document* as such, where I can almost forget that I am not the author, where I have almost understood him so well that I let him speak in my name, and can myself speak in his name." In other words, a paraphrase, truly the greatest art of exegesis, is the best commentary.

But I must reproach Barth for having let this ideal become a schema by means of which he does violence to the Letter to the Romans and to Paul. Before I go into the matter, I would like to confess once again that Barth has grasped Paul's view of faith in its depths, and likewise that through his exegesis many details have become more alive for me. But I must express the verdict that his "commentary" does violence to the individual life of the Letter to the Romans and to the richness of Paul. It is not at all a matter of a more or less correct or complete presentation of psychic historical perceptibleness, but of the understanding of the subject matter.* The measuring "by the subject matter of all words and phrases contained" in the document to be explained, which Barth justifiably demands in the Foreword, cannot, if one is in earnest, occur without criticism. And this criticism is much more radical than philological historical criticism; nor is it criticism from a standpoint taken outside the text and its subject matter, which Barth correctly rejects for exegesis (p. 10), even though it may be justified in other contexts. Rather it is the consistent carrying out of the basic principle, which it is agreed is correct, of understanding the text on the basis of the subject matter. One must measure by the subject matter to what extent in all the words and sentences of the text the subject matter has really found adequate expression, for what else can be meant by "measuring"? In Barth, however, I find nothing of such measuring and of the radical criticism based on it. It is impossible to assume that everywhere in the Letter to the Romans the subject matter must have found adequate expression, unless one intends to establish a modern dogma of inspiration, and something like this seems to stand behind Barth's exegesis—to the detriment of the clarity of the subject matter itself.

It would not be doing Barth a favor to leave the book uncriticized; for example, to ignore to what degree neo-Kantian (Cohenian) terminology often has influenced the words and concepts, or not to consider that many antitheses are based on the origin of the author in the

---

* Barth will in part take from what is said here and in part will say to himself that, in that which involves the philological historical explanation and in what concerns the evaluation of the content of Romans and of Paul, I largely follow what Jülicher said in this journal [*Die Christliche Welt*], 1920, issues 29 and 30, concerning the first edition.

land of psychoanalysis, that many formulations are obviously determined by the works he happened to be reading at the moment (and in a new edition will probably share the fate of corresponding expressions in the first edition, that is, to disappear) —in short, to forget that the subject matter is greater than the word which interprets it. And I believe it is from no lack of respect when I say that the same is true of Paul and his Letter to the Romans. When I discover in my exegesis of Romans tensions and contradictions, heights and depths, when I endeavor to show where Paul is dependent on Jewish theology or on popular Christianity, on Hellenistic enlightenment or Hellenistic sacramental beliefs, then I am thereby practicing not only philological historical criticism (at least not if I do not consider my task as an exegete mechanical) , but I am doing it from the point of view of showing where and how the subject matter is expressed, in order to grasp the subject matter, which is greater even than Paul. I believe that such criticism can only serve to clarify the subject matter, for the more strongly I feel that in this matter it is a question of saying the unsayable (and Barth knows this very well) , the more clearly I perceive also the relativity of the word and as an exegete stress it. It is not merely a question of the relativity of the word, but also of the fact that no man—not even Paul—can always speak only from the subject matter itself. In him there are other spirits speaking besides the *pneuma Christou*. And therefore criticism can never be radical enough. Such criticism therefore is—it follows from Barth's own basic premise of "measuring by the subject matter"—inseparable from exegesis and real history. Only in such criticism can the historical work attain its final goal, in which it meets the systematic theology which has traveled on another road—reflection on the motives and forces, on the bases of our life.

KARL BARTH'S *EPISTLE TO THE ROMANS**
Adolf Schlatter

"The author to the readers." These are the words which Barth placed over Romans 1:1-7. These words repulse anyone who has learned to know Paul. Paul an "author" who had nothing but "readers" in mind—but how were things done in those days? After his letter arrived in Rome, it was read aloud to the Christian community there. Paul is here giving instruction to hearers, and these hearers were not sitting isolated, each in his study busily reading; they were a congregation gathered with one accord before God, and they then and subsequently carried out their common worship by letting Paul speak to them. Does it have no consequences for the reproduction of the letter if the apostle is turned into an "author" and the community that listens to him into "readers"?

This apparently incidental little heading is a product of Barth's intention which supports his entire undertaking and which created the total material of his extensive book. Paul is to speak to us; are we not isolated, lonely "readers" who have long since forgotten that we are members of the church, and for that reason do not stand in any inner relationship to Paul? In contrast to those commentaries which offer only preparatory helps to understanding, Barth conceives of the work of the exegete as the responsibility for repeating the word of Paul to himself and his readers in such a way that it becomes a component part of their own inner being. Barth seeks to achieve this by bringing the Pauline word out of the situation in which it arose. The exegete is not to repeat once more a word directed to men who were once alive, but the word should encounter us free from all restrictions of time, and loosed from all historical conditions, "vertically from above."

In saying this I have indicated the power of the book, which moved many to listen and made them grateful. His presupposition is an earnest, unbroken affirmation of God, of the God who is present for us when we see Jesus. Therefore the Letter to the Romans is for Barth a timeless, entirely modern, entirely contemporary word. All that is human, all that is historical, sinks away. What is Rome, what is the early Roman Christian community, what is Paul? Nothing that should keep our eyes from God. The plight of finiteness and corruptibility, of "being thus and so" rests upon them; therefore let the veil

---

* From *Die Furche*, XII (1922), issue 6, columns 228-232.

of oblivion cover them! They stand beside us, not above us, on the same plane of conditioned life as we; life which, when it becomes religious, creates the "non-god." The exegete of the divine Word should not be a historian, because the historian allegedly speaks only human words.

By this, Barth joins the long list of exegetes of the early church and the Reformation who read the Letter to the Romans under the domination of the then-current theory of inspiration. This theory affirmed that God speaks here; therefore let man sink from sight! Because, however, he cannot entirely disappear, everything that belonged to the history of a New Testament document stood in the old commentaries only in the "introduction," only in the foreword. After such matters are quickly dealt with as mere preparatory knowledge, the real work of the exegete begins; now God speaks to him.

But no postulate, no theory, can succeed in making the God-given ordinance of our lives powerless. Barth too knows this, and he says powerfully that our attempts to escape the activity of God which shapes us are childish. It remains a fact that history gives us our life with its entire intellectual content. Since the exegete does not wish to say anything to us about the history of Roman Christendom, of Israel, of Paul and Jesus, what is he then going to talk to us about? He becomes the exegete of his own life and the interpreter of his own heart; it is done not by placing before us what is his own, for that would be the refutation of the Letter to the Romans, which negates our whole work and shows us the righteousness and grace in all that is divine; but it is done by his own life situation and that of his contemporaries providing the content of the Pauline words, which would otherwise remain empty. It was this way with the old exegetes, and it is this way also with Barth.

Does the word of Paul still come to us in this way? In the first two chapters of his letter Paul said what it was that sank the Greek and the Jew into guilt and death. It is undeniable that these verdicts show us a significant part of the Pauline lifework, but neither can it be seriously questioned that the struggle of Paul with Greeks and Jews belongs to the deepest and most exciting of all human events and forms an achievement that is worthy of our attention in the highest degree. But in the exposition of chapters one and two we hear nothing of the Greek religion and its devastating effects, of the synagogue and its religious failure, of the law, which at that time ordered by its very concrete norms the conduct of all who looked to God. You, the reader, are the Greek; you are also the Jew; and your sole concern must be that the word of Paul reaches you and shows you the divine wrath, which sinks you with all your piety into nothingness. But are we still hearing Paul when the Greek and the Jew have disappeared from the Letter to the Romans?

Paul showed the Roman congregation divine justice not only in the way in which God brings each individual into his grace, but also in the dying and rising again of Israel, chapters 9-11, and we could easily come to the insight that how a Pauline congregation related itself to Israel's fate was a question of life and death. But in Barth's opinion these events tell us nothing. We are living, to be sure, "in the church"; as a result, Israel disappears, and without hesitation the "church" is spoken of in chapters 9-11. Has the word of Paul still remained unharmed? Was Paul really speaking of Christendom in chapters 9-11?

The instruction which Paul gave the congregation on the nature of righteousness is closely related to that which the congregation for its part treasured as its possession and toward which it strove as its goal. This is shown, even if we reject every deeper consideration, in that the letter often becomes a dialogue and specifically mentions the objections which it will refute. Should not the question as to which needs of the community Paul was meeting in this manner have a claim to our attention? This rule, too, that the exegete should make clear the convictions and concerns of that Christian community to which Paul is speaking, is not regarded as significant. In its place there appears as the fully adequate basis for explanation the view of the religious chaos of the present.

Where does this quarrel between the exegete and the apostle come from? In the fullest sense of the word, Paul is writing a "letter to the Romans"; to the men for whom he is working he gives his penetrating observation and his unbroken love. Their religious situation, their guilt, their corruption, the gift of God granted to them, go to his heart. In the message of Jesus he shows them the saving power of God, and by showing it to them he shows it also to us. In the hands of the exegete, on the contrary, the Letter to the Romans ceases to be a letter to the Romans. Why? For Paul and for his exegete the concept of God is the presupposition for all their judgments; the concept of God of the exegete, however, remains different from that of Paul, and rejects it.

Barth's God is "the Other," who is other than we are and other than the world is. From this arises the powerful No which he places over against the entire state of the world, including the highest and purest in human life. All that we are, possess, and achieve is therefore judged, for it is not God, not divine, and therefore stands under the law of condemnation and negation. In Paul, too, every refusal to honor God falls under absolute condemnation, and he sees in every religious attitude which places man beside God and makes God dependent on human resolution and on human activity, on our willing and working, the perversion of religion. But that is not all Paul has to say about God, not the statement which he places in our souls, at Jesus' instruction, with praise of the righteousness and grace of God. For this reverts to the pre-Christian state of the knowledge of God, since it is the relationship of the unreconciled man to God.

A negation can never stand by itself alone. It always gains its basis and support only through the affirmation which upholds it. Therefore Barth, too, did not fail to hear the affirmation granted to man in the gospel of Paul. It spreads into the world through the presence of Christ. Here the God who gives it to us becomes visible, the one who makes of us his work, or as Barth says, "will make." For "I saw a new heaven and a new earth"; and only then will God be revealed. Therefore the declaration of war against our whole body and against the whole context which unites our life with nature, and against the world, inclusive of everything, even the Christian bonds of community, retains its undiminished force. But this is no longer the Letter to the Romans. Paul too, like every messenger of Jesus, gives us a glimpse of the majesty of God, which will make the world new, and the Barthian Letter to the Romans can remind us of the greatness of the apostolic goal, which lifts us entirely above the present. But Paul wrote his letter precisely so that the congregation would have not only a hope, but would recognize the work of God which took place for it and in it, and preserve the gift given it by using it according to God's will.

The "No" which Barth places on our entire life situation falls with devastating force on the act of thinking. In that God is the unattainably distant, the "Other," every thought directed to God breaks down; every religious statement, every theology, becomes basically folly, for they can speak only in perpetual self-contradictions. With Barth it is always a question of "impossible possibilities" and "possible impossibilities." This puts an end also to the consideration that the formulae of Paul might not possess a clearly thought-out, quite definite content. In its exposition the church has earnestly endeavored to determine clearly and comprehensively what the Pauline expressions are. But this exposition rejects participation in this work. What good would it do? The religious words are after all only a covering for what is entirely incomprehensible.

If the act of thinking is shattered, faith does not remain untouched, since it needs a content that is accessible to our perception, and can be appropriated by us by means of solid judgment. It gets this content through Christ. That is the statement that comes from Paul. Nonetheless, for Barth faith remains "a leap into the void," and in this a deep gap between his exposition and the Letter to the Romans opens up. Paul did not leap into the void, but joined himself to Jesus.

Barth's reproduction of the Letter to the Romans can be an aid to the one who must first awake because the enticing call of the senses enchains him and the clamor of the busy world has made him deaf, for it restrains one from the attempt to satisfy himself with that which belongs to the flesh, and turns the secret revulsion over our situation into a strongly resounding accusation. By this that "vacuum" of which Barth so often speaks can come into being. It is not yet faith, but makes a place in us for faith. Thus our hearing can be awakened, so that we are able to hear not only the expositor, but also the apostle, and this is the splendid, the only desirable goal of all exposition.

FOREWORD TO THE THIRD EDITION

Karl Barth

The third edition is an essentially unaltered reprinting of the second. It is to be feared, or to be hoped, that one day it might be necessary to say everything once again in an entirely different manner. Today we live remarkably fast. Who will say whether that is a sign of decadence or a sign that we are approaching great intellectual decisions? But it is so that the situation changes from day to day, the conversation goes further, one teaches and is taught, one says something and notices that it finds such a lively echo that one would rather not say it a second time for fear that because of all the echo it might turn into its opposite; new, useful contradiction comes on the scene and demands, along with new, dangerous applause, careful reflection. "We cannot step into the same river twice, for it is always dispersing and gathering itself again, flowing to and fro." How could such a lively and responsible enterprise as the explanation of the Letter to the Romans remain fixed for any length of time? But for the moment I do not yet feel that necessity and therefore can only affirm the content of what I produced a year ago. The Foreword to the second edition I have let be reprinted, because it can scarcely be dispensed with for the understanding of *this* book, although particularly the polemic it contains is one of those things it does not suit me to repeat.

The most remarkable thing that has happened to the book since then is surely the fact that Bultmann received it in its essentials in friendly manner, and that Schlatter rejected it in its essentials in equally friendly manner. I take the first as a gratifying confirmation that the lament about the Diocletian persecution of critical historical theology, with which it was first received, was not necessary, and the second as an indication that in reference to positive theology, to which I feel fundamentally closer and more akin, I have traveled my own way. I have provisionally taken note attentively and gratefully of the old and new hesitations and concerns set forth by Schlatter and Bultmann as well as by Kolfhaus.

Because it concerns methodology, one point, in supplement to what was said in the second Foreword about "historical criticism," "dialectic of the subject matter," and "Biblicism," should be discussed briefly here. Bultmann raised the objection that I was not radical enough for him. The criticism on the basis of the subject matter, which was spoken of there, would of necessity have to be directed also against certain positions of Paul, because Paul himself did not always speak "from the subject matter itself." "In him there are other spirits speaking besides the *pneuma Christou.*" I will certainly not argue with Bultmann which of us is the more radical, but I must still really go a little further than he does and say that what speaks in the Letter to the Romans is nothing but the "others," the various "spirits" which he adduces, such as the Jewish, the popular Christian, the Hellenistic, and others. Or, at what place could one point his finger with the observation that *there* assuredly the *pneuma Christou* speaks? Or to turn the matter around, is the Spirit of Christ perhaps a spirit which can be presented as competing *along with* other spirits? Therefore my conclusion is that in no case can it be a question of playing off the Spirit of Christ, the "subject matter," in such a way against the "other spirits," that in the name of the former certain passages are praised, but certain others, where Paul is not speaking "from the subject matter" are belittled. Rather it is a question of seeing and making clear how the "Spirit of Christ" is the crisis in which the whole finds itself. *Everything* is *litera,* the voice of "other" spirits, and whether and in how far *everything* can be understood also in the context of the "subject matter" as the voice of the *spiritus* (of Christ) is the question by which the *litera* must be studied.

The exegete stands before the either-or, whether or not he, knowing himself what is at stake and entering into a relationship of faithfulness to the author, intends to read him with the hypothesis that the author also knew with more or less clarity down to the last word (for where should the limit be set—surely not through the discovery of relationships of historical dependence?) what is at stake. He will then not write his commentary *about* Paul, but, certainly not without frequent sighs and shaking of the head, as well as he can, down to the last word, write it *with* Paul. The quantity of the "Spirit of Christ" which he thereby discovers in Paul and can make perceptible in his rendering will certainly not be equally great everywhere, but will be a "more or less." He feels, however, that he is responsible in this matter. He never lets himself be entirely bluffed by the voice of the "other" spirits who often make the dominant notes of the "Spirit of Christ" almost inaudible. He always looks first for the lack of understanding in himself and not in Paul. He spares no pains to see and to show to what degree what is scattered is still paradoxically part of the context of the subject matter, and how all the "other" spirits really are somehow subject to the *pneuma Christou.*

Naturally the exegete can also approach Paul without that hypothesis, and refuse to trust him. Perhaps he himself does not know, or does not know clearly enough, what might be at stake in such a writing as the Letter to the Romans. Or perhaps he has despaired of the task of discerning, in the chorus of the "other" spirits which rings out from all lines of his text, the voice of that knowledge. He will then write his commentary *about* Paul, and at the most only occasionally *with* Paul, when Paul chances to say something that is clear to him. The quantity of the Spirit of Christ in Paul will appear to him, if he is at all willing to designate in this way what is clear to him, under the formula "in part—in part." He stands as an irresponsible observer *beside* the conglomeration of Spirit and spirits, which is what the text means for him. He does not know that concern for the meaning of the text, because he does not know that relation of faithfulness to it, because, even when under certain conditions he travels a little way beside it, he is still by no means determined to stand and to fall with it. I hold that it is impossible for anyone to do justice to any writer, to be able really to bring any writer to speak again, if he does not dare to assume that hypothesis, does not enter into that relationship of faithfulness to him. To speak *about* someone seems to me to be hopelessly condemned to speak *past* him, and to seal his grave tighter.

I understand that we must in despair travel this road from time to time. There are truly enough phenomena that seem to permit us only to talk *about* them, although in this there is always the question whether what is enigmatic and puzzling is to be sought for more on their side, or more on the side of us who observe them. But what I cannot understand is the invitation which Bultmann issues to me to mix fire and water, to think and to write *with* Paul, that is, first of all in the entirely foreign language of his Jewish-popular-Christian-Hellenistic thought-world, and then suddenly, when this may get to be too much for me—as if something struck me as especially strange where everything is strange!—to speak "critically" about and against Paul. Does Bultmann not perceive that, even considered only from the point of view of purity of style, this will not do; that, as I see it, this would be a matter of bad taste, a falling back into the method of the "temporally conditioned remnants" and "disagreeable points"?

He hints that here in my work a "modern dogma of inspiration" must be in the background. To this I answer that from the first edition on I have not denied the certain analogy between my procedure and the old teaching of verbal inspiration (Schlatter also expressed disapproval of this). This doctrine, in the form in which *Calvin* presented it, seems to me at least very ingenious and worthy of discussion. I believe I have already shown to what degree I have adopted it. I cannot understand how there could be any other way to the spirit of a writing (whatever it is) than the hypothetical expectation that its spirit would speak to our spirit precisely through the letter. The unavoidable critique of the letter by the spirit is not at all abandoned by this. On the contrary, faithfulness to the text necessarily demands that the ideas in the individual words of the text be expanded or contracted (either tacitly or explicitly), while formal, verbal consistency results in an obvious suppression of what should, and indeed must, be expressed.

Calvin practiced *this* type of criticism in a masterful manner, without neglecting the discipline which must certainly be exercised in this connection. I have not avoided the necessity of *this* type of criticism, as the perceptive reader will notice at once, hopefully without succumbing unrestrainedly to the accompanying danger that is bound up with it. I have, however, intentionally not directed it against Paul, and do not intend to let myself be tempted to do so. The *pneuma Christou* is not a position on which one can take a stand, and then from there more or less play the schoolmaster to Paul. Let it suffice us, not entirely forsaken by him, to place ourselves, learning and teaching, beside Paul, despite the "other" spirits, ready to grasp spritually things that are meant spiritually, and ready to recognize that even our own voice, with which we pass on what we have perceived, is from the first entirely the voice of "other" spirits.

I believe I have the same opinion as Bultmann and all reasonable persons concerning the relativity of all human words, even those of Paul. But what does relativity mean? *Question*ableness? Certainly, but, if it is necessary, how can I better demonstrate this than by bending all my efforts to work out its question*ableness*? Has not what is problematical in Paulinism become clear to more than one reader precisely in my book? I have no objection to raise against this. Certainly, we must learn also to see *beyond* Paul. But we can achieve this only by assuming that relationship of faithfulness and exerting ourselves to see *into* him earnestly without regard for the consequences.

In regard to the specific content of my second exposition of the Letter to the Romans, I would like to send the book on the road with the following word from Calvin's commentary on Hebrews 11:1 to accompany it.

Grace is not without the appearance of contradiction. Faith is the groundwork, that is, the support and possession on which we can set our feet. But possession of what things? Not things that are present, which, far distant, exceed even the power of the imagination of our spirits to bring under our feet. The same is the case when faith is called a proof of the things that do not appear. For proof means reference to things that appear and can only be applied to what is accessible to our senses. So these two apparently conflict with each other, and are best united when it is a case of faith. The Spirit of God shows us hidden things, the knowledge of which is not accessible to our senses. He promises us eternal life, us who are dead. He speaks to us of the blessed resurrection, to us who are surrounded by corruption. We are called righteous, and sin dwells in us. We learn that we are saved; in the meantime we are crushed by endless misery. Abundance of all goods is promised to us, and we are rich only in hunger and thirst. God calls that he will be with us at once, but seems to be deaf to all our cries. What would become of us if we were not *strong in hope*, if our hearts were not hurrying over the world in the midst of darkness on the road that is lighted by God's Word and Spirit?

This time also I want to express my thanks for faithful help. Georg Merz has read the proofs and made the index, and Lukas Christ in Pratteln gave his services for the very necessary polishing of my style in numerous places.

3

The Debate on
the Concept of Paradox

CRITICAL AND POSITIVE PARADOX:
A Discussion with Karl Barth and Friedrich Gogarten
> *Paul Tillich*

THE PARADOXICAL NATURE OF THE
"POSITIVE PARADOX":
Answers and Questions to Paul Tillich
> *Karl Barth*

ANSWER TO KARL BARTH
> *Paul Tillich*

THE INTELLECTUAL SITUATION OF THE THEOLOGIAN:
Another Answer to Paul Tillich
> *Friedrich Gogarten*

CRITICAL AND POSITIVE PARADOX:

A Discussion with Karl Barth and Friedrich Gogarten*

Paul Tillich

I am reluctant to comply with the invitation of the editors of the *Theologische Blätter* to enter into a discussion on the ideas of Karl Barth, Friedrich Gogarten, and their friends. For every criticism of their criticism runs the risk of lessening the disquiet which it has aroused, and of giving the impression that the cutting edge of their radical criticism should be dulled. Nothing would be more fatal than that. Rather, everything must be done to make the cutting edge of this criticism felt in wide circles inside and outside the church. But just for this reason we must prevent opponents from using incidental weaknesses of this standpoint in order to make what is more than standpoint invisible and harmless. And this danger already exists. With the comment that one "cannot always be suspended in negations and paradoxes," one eases his conscience for all the things that by rights are brought under the judgment of crisis and paradox. And the name of "heretic," which is better avoided, takes one step forward. Thus I would like to venture the attempt at a discussion which, while acknowledging critical negation, seeks to demonstrate the position on the basis of which negation first becomes possible.

In dealing with a dialectic such as that practiced by Barth and particularly by Gogarten, it is necessary to use dialectic oneself. The rejection of their thoughts because they are dialectic lies beneath the level of the dialectical and is out of the question as a serious refutation. Whoever sees the relationship of the unconditioned and the conditioned undialectically does not see it at all; he has no idea of the force of that which is meant by the concept of the unconditioned. Therefore we must resolutely take the side of Barth, and in this connection that means the side of Kierkegaard and Pascal, of Luther and Augustine, of John and Paul. A direct, unparadoxical relationship to the unconditioned which does not pass through the constant radical No is a relationship not to the unconditioned, but to a conditioned which makes the claim to be unconditioned, that is, to an idol. And it is just those things and words that should express paradox, such as religion and Bible, Christ and God—especially God—that are in con-

---

* From *Theologische Blätter*, II (1923), pp. 263-269.

stant danger of receiving this idolatrous-undialectic character, and of becoming objectified and therefore conditioned. The crisis which proceeds from the unconditioned is therefore not to be gone through once, but constantly. And it is at least deceptive to make the theology of crisis into a temporal point through which to pass, and then to wish to be led out beyond it. Where to? In any case not to a "theology of synthesis between the absolute and the relative" as Arnold Hein desires (*Theologische Blätter*, 1923, No. 10, pp. 246 ff.). For this synthesis is a combining of two things that are conditioned, one of which is an illusion. But we must ask, however, whether in the theology of crisis there does not lurk a presupposition that itself is not a further crisis.

Barth and Gogarten frequently emphasize that their own position also stands under the crisis, and that they ascribe meaning to the undialectic attitude only insofar as it is a reference to something else. That is consistent, but the necessary conclusions are not drawn from it. The dialectic transcending of dialectic remains dialectic, and if this dialectic which has been transcended dialectically is again transcended, then that too remains dialectic on and on without end. The completely endless row of self-transcendings, however, is not transcended. It is the position on which the dialectician stands, but it is itself no longer dialectic. The same thing can be demonstrated for the concept, so characteristic of Barth, of humor in contrast to all that is theoretically and practically problematic within the world. Here too humor is admitted over against humor's own position, but it is not realized that this endless line of humor against humor presupposes an element of seriousness which cannot in its turn be subjected to humor. It is on this point that humor rests, and only for this reason is it humor and not a game, just as is the case for dialectic. There is thus a positive, a serious something that makes criticism and humor possible. Everything depends, however, on the determination of this point. Here it is decided whether the theology of crisis still acknowledges an absoluteness that it itself forbids, or whether it is willing to recognize the positive form of paradox which is presupposed in the critical.

The opinion could be held—and certain observations of Gogarten's doctrine of revelation support this understanding (I think it is a misunderstanding)—that the position of the dialectic which transcends itself to infinity could be posited absolutely, that the constant crisis, the constant linking with the "difference between God and man" could be made into a law, into an absolute religion. If that, however, is not the case—and it would be the destruction of the entire position if it were the case—then a real transcending (and not an inner-dialectic one) of the dialectic position must be sought from the starting point of the unconditioned. The dialectician must perceive that as a dialectician he has one position among others which does not cease through any dialectic self-transcendence to be a position, and he must, as he is prepared to do—despite his conviction of the truth of his position—submit to the No, and concede to the other positions—despite the No which he pronounces on them—the same Yes which he concedes to himself. He must include himself with them in the unity of No and Yes. That is not relativism. It does not mean that the conviction of the superiority of the dialectic position *under* the Yes and No must therefore be given up, but it is the awareness of the non-transcending position which is contained even in the proclamation of the crisis; it is the comprehension of the Yes which is the presupposition of the No; it is the step back from the critical to the positive paradox.

But once this presupposition of the critical position, that it is a position, is recognized, our view has been freed for every position, for this cosmos and this earth and this people, for these spiritual forms and this history and this religion, for this man in this place and in this present day. All of these are of course elements of the dialectic position. Without them there would be no dialectician and no believer. But for this reason they all partake of the No and the Yes which stand above the dialectic position. They all stand under the unity of judgment and grace, as does the dialectician, provided he claims his proclamation is truth. And to partake of the truth—not to have the truth, for that would be unparadoxical, idolatrous—means to stand under grace. To be sure, grace is not perceptible, not something given. We cannot say of it, here and there it is or is not; we can say that of grace as little as we can of judgment. Both grace and judgment are non-objective, accessible only to faith, and neither can be isolated from the other. It is not permissible to ascribe judgment to this world and grace to the other world. Then no position, not even that of the one who believes, would be possible. But it is possible, even though as an unfixable, "imperceptible," "impossible possibility." And only because it is possible and real is judgment possible. Only through grace does judgment become judgment. Only there where love is revealed is wrath revealed as wrath. Without its unity with grace, judgment is merely a natural process.

These basic thoughts are now to be tested in a threefold respect: in the relationship of God and nature, of God and spirit, of God and history. Barth and Gogarten manifest a definite disinclination toward the religious use of the concept of creation. It would be better not to speak here of the ordinance of creation; it has been made unrecognizable through sin. That which the heathen could have gained of knowledge of God from nature would have been knowledge of judgment, and even natural science presses deeper and deeper into the irrationality of the created world.

Here at the start it must be said dialectically that as soon as one speaks of the world or nature or life, in which judgment, irrationality, or death is revealed, the corresponding positions—namely, the world as unity of form, nature as unity of configuration, life as reality—are presupposed. For the negative can reveal itself only in terms of the positive, not of the negative. Further, it must be said that the irrationality of nature, as it comes to inimitably powerful expression in the book of Job, is by no means only the desperate situation of the world, but reveals the abyss in the creator God just as much as it does the infinite majesty of God as the object of worship. Finally it should be said that to see the "birds of the air and the lilies of the field" is by no means to see only judgment, but also the grace which creates life; and that Psalm 104 and the song of the angels in the Prologue to Goethe's *Faust* are nearer to this position than to the one which sees judgment without grace. To be sure, both judgment and grace are paradoxical and show themselves only to the eyes of faith, and then in their paradoxical unity. It is idolatrous idealism to want to see grace without judgment, to grasp immediately and unparadoxically the unity of the unconditioned and the conditioned in nature. And it is demonic realism to see the destruction of the conditioned in nature as a natural process without paradoxical unity with grace. The one is as impossible as the other, and demonic realism does not stand any closer to revelation than idolatrous idealism does.

Christian dogmatics has set up the statement that the works of the Trinity are not divided externally, that they always proceed equally from Father, Son, and Spirit, and the New Testament regarded the Son as the agent of creation. That means, however, that the order of creation and the order of redemption belong together; that it is the one, indivisible act of grace which is presented in creation and redemption; that creation is directed toward redemption; that redemption is planned in creation. Neither is an objective, perceptible judgment, but a paradoxical, imperceptible one. Both can be comprehended only in faith.

The human spirit and its form also belong to creation. As a result it is significant when Gogarten carries out radically the negative crisis even in relation to the spirit. In his discussion with Emanuel Hirsch about ethics and in his continual battle against autonomy (cf. the journal *Zwischen den Zeiten,* published by Chr. Kaiser in Munich) his position becomes very clear. Not only the customary work-righteousness, but also the absolutizing of conscience, as it appears in Hirsch, is combated, and the attack (unfortunately not made with the necessary desire for understanding) is intensified to the point that it is stated that not the conscience but Christ is the place of revelation. Now it is clear that Hirsch in undialectic and unparadoxical manner makes ethical, personalistic piety absolute and therefore has no understanding of the dialectic position. But it is just as evident that the dialectic position as a position can make itself absolute in the same manner, and in the quarrel between Gogarten and Hirsch it appears with the gesture of absoluteness. Again it must be asked, what is the position which lies at the basis of crisis? And the answer must be, faith in the unity of judgment and revelation, even in the human spirit. Either the dialectic position is truth—in that case the spirit which can proclaim this truth is the site of revelation, imperceptible of course, not given, not fixable, under judgment—and therefore also right against truths that are not formulated dialectically. Or, the dialectic position stands only under judgment, is only expression of human untruthfulness—then the pathos of the struggle against other human untruthfulness is, to say the least, superfluous. Even the concept of autonomy is seen here in another light; if autonomy were in and of itself opposed to God, the Fall, and revolt, then each word and each concept which Gogarten uses in his dialectic would be fall and revolt, for these words and concepts are creations of the autonomous process of the mind. It is not autonomy in itself that is opposed to God, but the autonomy which is demonically composed and misused. Autonomy in itself is obedience to the eternal demand in the theoretical as in the practical and stands against arbitrariness and demonism, both the consecrated and the unconsecrated. But of course autonomy is empty, and if the content of revelation does not fill it, it becomes the prey of the demonic. Therefore not autonomy, but demonically distorted autonomy, is to be opposed. Law, however, to which autonomy belongs, is good, is truth and justice.

Intellectual life is also supported by the unity of grace and judgment. There is no autonomy that stands by itself; there is always revelation and always concealment, always something godly and something demonic in it. And the struggle of the godly and the demonic, of the holy and the unholy spirit, of the creative and the destructive principles, is the deepest, most hidden content of intellectual history, which by this gains a seriousness that permits humor only as a relative, superficial consideration, and forces one in every moment and in every question to take sides for the godly or for the demonic. There is no neutrality—it is already taking sides, and not for the godly. It is not only the

conscience that is the site of this contradiction, the site of revelation—
and of judgment—and it is not only dialectic, and with it all philosophy, that is the site of judgment—and of revelation—but art as well,
and critical historical science, community and law and the State, yes,
and even religion. It is the greatest service of the theology of crisis that
it vigorously led the struggle against the unparadoxical claim of religion to be absolute, and every word on this subject, particularly in Karl
Barth's *Epistle to the Romans,* is destruction of idols. But it is again forgotten that no dialectic self-transcendence can transcend the religious
position which forms the basis of this negation. The religion of faith
is religion, just as dialectic autonomy is autonomy. With this insight
the way becomes free again for religion with its "profundity and its
splendor." Barth does not use the words just cited in order to caricature. He attests his awe for the heights and depths of the spirit, but ultimately he intends to rob them of value. "Profundity" is not revelation, and thus not truth. But there is no profundity that does not see
into the depths of the eternal source of things, that is, there is no profundity that is not faith. Everything that does not signify this depth is
superficiality, and it then really becomes a caricature if it is called profundity. In all religion and all secular culture there are phenomena
which make visible the source on which they stand, the revelation of
grace and of judgment in terms of faith. There are powerfully symbolic
phenomena in religion and culture which are nevertheless under the
No, but the context and the consideration of them make possible a
metaphysics of history, a symbolic, paradoxical salvation history. This
is sensitivity to the depths, and where it becomes conscious it is the
profundity of culture and religion. This sensitivity to the depths is not
to be viewed objectively or immediately, but paradoxically, by faith
and in the unity of Yes and No.

And this holds also for mysticism, a main target of Gogarten's
polemic. It is entirely right that the word of Heiler concerning the
"healthy degree of mysticism" is to be rejected, for in the relationship
to the unconditioned the category of degrees is not valid, least of all
that of "healthy degrees." A mysticism which has a healthy and an un-
healthy degree is really something conditioned that has no right to
claim to be revelation of the unconditioned. But it is not possible to
do justice to true mysticism in this way. It has traces of unconditioned-
ness, the "infinite degree" which characterizes its object. It knows how
to speak of the paradoxicality of the source. It knows the abyss of grace
and judgment, and in this it is believing. It is an indication of the
hybris of the standpoint of faith if it overlooks the root of faith of the
mystical standpoint. In this way it becomes deaf to the mystic tone

which accompanies every word of faith, even the dialectic, and which no dialectic has succeeded in concealing in Romans 8, for example. For the word of mysticism is, God is present. And the standpoint of faith can attack this word only when it is meant as direct, objective, as mere feeling or artificiality, and not paradoxically, having passed through the judgment, as faithful. But is the standpoint of faith guarded against being made into an object? Cannot it, for all its true dialectic, become immediate, unparadoxical, unbelieving, merely a work of the intellect? This is not the place to speak of the contrast of standpoints and of the undoubted superiority of the standpoint of faith. But it was necessary to show that mysticism also in its essence (not in its technical hardening) is believing, and lives from revelation, from the unity of grace and judgment. It had to be shown that a "boasting" on the basis of the standpoint of faith would not only be dialectically, but also really, impossible.

With this we come to the last of the problems in which the positive root of the critical paradox must show itself—history. It contradicts the meaning of paradox to posit unconditionally a historical reality, to admit an objective, perceptible historical metaphysics or salvation history. This basic proposition is carried out by Barth and Gogarten with great emphasis and full justification in reference to the supernaturalistic as well as the critical historical conception of salvation history. Critical paradox makes the dissolution of salvation history into secular history impossible in the same way it does for its dissolution into miraculous history. All history is marked by a negative warning sign. But this negative warning remains the only sign. History is the scene of a false resemblance of man to God and is subject to wrath just as nature and spirit are.

This judgment of crisis also is possible only on the basis of a position which is itself not subject to this judgment. Nowhere is the positive root of negative paradox more evident than here, for the proclamation of the crisis is itself history, and its content is historical content. The place where this message is proclaimed is a site of revelation in the midst of history. It is not that a place in history is cut out and grasped objectively. The revelation which takes place itself in history and sustains history is imperceptible, but it is not unreal. Barth and Gogarten reject this thought. They overlook the positive root of their theology of crisis, but yet are forced to seek a position in history on which the proclamation of crisis can be based. This place of revelation is Christ. In Christology the contrast of positive and critical paradox becomes a decisive issue. The formulations of Gogarten here are particularly instructive. They delimit in history a unique historical occurrence in which history is transcended and something absolutely new is set up. What happened in Christ happened completely beyond humanity, yet it occurred in the historical man, Jesus of Nazareth. It occurred as "merely objective historical fact," it occurred once, and it occurred once for all. "Only here is the No not valid for that in which it appears." "O contradiction of all human knowledge of God."

These statements show that in its search for a foundation for its criticism the theology of critical paradox ends as a theology of the positive absurd. In this, however, it has abandoned its own presupposition. The imperceptible, non-objective character of faith is broken down. There is a point at which the direction of faith is bound by an objective historical factor. The recognition of an empirical fact has been accepted into the act of faith. Into this opening, however, heteronomy, law, and absolutistic religion break in unhindered. *Heteronomy*: for, to take an example, critical historical science, which might possibly be able—speaking dialectically—to make the non-existence of this factor probable, or to cast doubt on "every deed, every word, every gesture" of Jesus of Nazareth or to interpret them in the opposite direction, would be broken in this its autonomous work, that is, in its obedience to the truth. *Law*: for if through the absolute crisis of what is human every presupposition for the act of faith is taken away, then this act is a deed of intellectual asceticism which is no less work and law than is the practical asceticism of the mystic. *Absolutistic religion*: for the community of those who proclaim and practice this work would have toward all other communities the same absolutism as does absolute finitude, in which they believe over against all other finitude. If Gogarten wishes to escape these consequences, he must recognize the imperceptibleness of even the revelation in Christ. He must recognize that the empirical fact is a reference to the unconditioned, which becomes revealed in it non-objectively. But then the contrast of the absolute relative to what is relatively relative is transcended and with it heteronomy, law, and absolutistic religion. Historical criticism, for example, can, without disturbing the imperceptible revelation in Christ, make the perceptible relations discernible to the point of the possible transcending of their givenness as such. Faith is not a work of the affirmation of the absurd, but it has grown up on the ground of the imperceptible history of revelation, which passes in hidden manner through history and has found in Christ its complete expression. And the congregation of the faithful is imperceptible and cuts through all communities of the history of culture and religion. In all this it is not a question of positing something human as divine. Every pantheism, every idealism, every synthesis of relative and absolute, is overcome through the proclamation of judgment which is contained in the positive as well as in the critical paradox.

The theology of crisis is right, completely right, in its struggle against every unparadoxical, immediate, objective understanding of the unconditioned. It is no transition, but something permanent, an element in the essence of theology. But it has a presupposition which is itself no longer crisis, but creation and grace. It can be spoken of only by passing through the crisis, only paradoxically, but it must be spoken of thus, everywhere, in nature and spirit, in culture and religion. It can be spoken of in a threefold manner: as eternal source, the ground, and the abyss, which is evident to faith imperceptibly and ungiven through all that is real in Yes and No; and as eternal redemption, itself imperceptible and ungiven, which is evident only to faith, and runs through history and its creations as hidden salvation history, which presents itself in Christ with complete symbolic power; and as eternal consummation, as imperceptible promise, in which the ambiguity of the source and the struggle of the godly and the demonic are transcended in the eternal unity in God. In creation, redemption, and consummation the meaning of paradox is presented to faith. The theology of critical paradox, which submits not only dialectically but really to paradox, thereby becomes the theology of positive paradox.

THE PARADOXICAL NATURE OF
THE "POSITIVE PARADOX":

Answers and Questions to Paul Tillich*

Karl Barth

I feel the same way Tillich does. I too am reluctant to be drawn into the public conversation desired by the editors of the *Theologische Blätter*. In any case, the wording of his article seems to be more directed toward my friend Gogarten than toward me, and the content seems to indicate it expects an answer from him more than from me.† It also gives me little pleasure to spread out before the eyes of those smug persons who are not involved in our joint concerns, my differences with a man like Tillich who, even across various appreciable gaps yet stands so close to me, and I begrudge them this spectacle. In addition, I must confess, the instructional and edifying value of such an exchange of shots in print (not in vain called an *Aus-Einander-Setzung*—"putting away from one another") is, in my experience, after all, somewhat doubtful. And finally (second public confession) I feel technically so foreign in the thought-world of Tillich that by coming to grips with his statements and making mine public beside them I certainly run the danger, more than is usually the case among us theologians, of looking past and speaking past the things which he really desires of "us." I would have preferred, until I could perhaps understand him better, to have left the matter with the assertion of the "somehow" present subterranean community of work, which was not more closely defined. But now since he has, although "reluctantly," written about and to, for and against us; since my reaction to this is requested; and since I do not have any compelling reason to ask permission to remain silent, so let it be.

Tillich's intention is to demonstrate a "position" on the basis of which "critical negation" would for the first time be possible at all, an "element of seriousness," without which "humor" could not exist, a presupposition of "crisis" which is itself not crisis, but rather the "transcending of the dialectic position." I think I understand what Tillich means. But then I am at once put off by the fact that Tillich is obviously of the opinion that by this he has called our attention to something of which we previously had heard as little as had those

---

* From *Theologische Blätter*, II (1923), pp. 287-296.

† I have no desire to encroach here, it should be said at once, even when in the following I often speak in the first person plural.

disciples of John the Baptist of whether there was a Holy Spirit. If this is his serious opinion (and the whole tenor of his essay leaves no doubt about it), then to clarify the situation let us first establish that Tillich basically agrees with that judgment held about us by a part of the theological public that is quantitatively not insignificant, according to which what we are doing with the "dialectic," "crisis," "paradox" (all astonishingly supplied with the designation "negative") is understood as essential and exhaustive. Must I cite quotations or page numbers or opinions of reviewers to show that what Tillich presents to our eyes as something new and unheard of has for some years now not been entirely unknown to us, at least as a concept? How does he really picture our mental and intellectual situation if he thinks otherwise? It should be understood that I am also of the opinion that nothing less than *all* depends on the exact and thorough determination of the positive point which is here in question, and I am not of the opinion that the determinations which we have given until now or could give even today would be even approximately satisfactory. Tillich had full right to bring our previous attempts in this direction under his magnifying glass, to criticize and correct them. But he had no possible reason for proceeding from the presupposition "they overlook the positive root of their theology of crisis"; as if we had had to wait for his explanations in order now at last to discover that the whole time we had been talking about *something,* that our theological thought was not turning around *nothing.*

The first comment I would like to make is that I do not find any cause for asking the solemn question whether the "theology of crisis" was willing to "acknowledge" the positive form of the paradox presupposed in its critical form. Or am I deceiving myself when I think I understand what Tillich means? Is it possible that he sees at the conscious, positive point something so entirely other from what I see, that he, by an optical illusion, believes he perceives in me at the same point an empty spot? With respect to this possibility I must then vary my first answer (dialectically!) as follows: yes, they are quite right, Tillich and the others, when they succeed in discerning clearly at this point, on the determination of which everything depends, only a hole in our thinking. It seems that way to us also; our whole "theology of crisis" seems to us also as only a see-saw of "negations," as the result of a very inappropriate "humor," as an empty "dialectic," as a system of relationships that are related to nothing, as soon as even for a moment we conceive of it as a part—perhaps even the most impressive part— of a philosophy of culture, as soon as we fail to stick to the matter at hand and let theology be theology. And we run the whole risk unavoidably bound up with it (without prejudice against philosophy, perhaps precisely in its interest, when it is well understood) of having to call μωρία σοφία in as far as our "science" has neither a negative nor a positive root, but no "root" at all. If the judgment of Tillich and the others on what we are lacking proceeds from that—not from the approach of theology, but from the approach, as such quite justified, of a philosophy of culture—then the protest which I have just raised is naturally irrelevant. Then Tillich obviously means something different from what we mean when he speaks of the "dialectic position," and something really different when he speaks of its "beyond," or its "transcending." Then we could very well do him the favor of taking his side with the warranted amazement of the non-theologian in the face of that "hole"; we could, with him and the others, miss the "positive" in our teaching and make suggestions about the removal of this notoriously evil state of affairs, in which even the "ethical religion of conscience" and similar not undiscussable possibilities would have to be present! We are really to a large extent ourselves non-theologians, and the objection which is to be raised continuously from outside against theology is also our objection in as far as we continuously also stand outside. Tillich can reject my protest against the presupposition with which he wrote his article, but only on the condition that he admit that his presupposition is the characteristically non-theological one, against which it would not even occur to me to protest because it is obviously possible.

If I now attempt to understand Tillich's essay better than he understands it himself, less presumptuously but quite simply, as an undertaking which seeks to examine and improve our previous observations about the "positive paradox" (of which we have really not been unaware until now), an undertaking in which he has my undivided attention, I am at once confronted by his objection that "we" probably also knew something of a "transcending of dialectic," but that this transcending (he probably will have found in what I have just said a new example of this way of ours!) is for us again merely dialectic, in that in our work it issues in an endless line of "self-transcendings," and this endless line is now the no-longer dialectic position on which the dialectician "stands," the "forbidden absoluteness" which he and we have worked for secretly or openly. Concerning this line of thought (have I understood it correctly?), I would like to make the following observation. I first of all examined Tillich's essay for elucidation of this reproach against a "forbidden" absolutizing of our "dialectic position," but could find nothing except the complaint about the "gesture of absoluteness" which Gogarten is said to display in his conflict with Hirsch. I may therefore probably assume that Tillich's objection is ultimately based on observations of this type. He sees us break out from time to time, on paper or even in life-size, in categorical manner, now to the right, now to the left, into a decisive Yes or No to the point where we are suspected of impenitence, as if we were not confined, together with all other "positions," within the unity of No and Yes. In such moments he then thinks he is on the trail of the canker of the "theology of crisis." To which I ask, by what dialectic right does Tillich wish to forbid precisely the "gesture of absoluteness"? What endlessly boring, truly Schleiermacherian heaven of peace does he confront us with in such a prohibition? Should not this "gesture" be allowed at the right hour, even demanded, in the light of the "positive paradox," and be filled with "theonomous content," to speak in Tillich's language? What if Gogarten's quarrel with Hirsch were *kairos,* and the "gesture of absolutism" were there very appropriate and in place? I am only supposing, but how does Tillich know that it is not so? Let Tillich, or whoever it may be, call to us in such moments that they are *critical* moments, that we as little as anyone else can persevere in such a "gesture," without exposing ourselves in most dangerous fashion, that one can only pronounce such an (almost!) "absolute" Yes or No in order then in remembrance of the frailty of all earthly things (and under the same crisis!) to be silent with equal eloquence. But "crisis" surely does not mean in itself negation, and therefore "prohibition," but in any case *warning,* or perhaps also *exhortation.* Then why should it not in certain cases be able to signify position and command for the "dialectician" as for other mortals, who may even, and that is the clear meaning of the crisis in which they stand, in some cases know what they are doing? How can Tillich on the basis of observations of this sort (the details of which we would certainly not wish to refuse to discuss) arrive at the suspicion that we were "standing" on our dialectic, on—horrible thought!—the endless line of our self-transcendings? Certainly the dialectic transcending of dialectic (as a position) is, and remains, dialectic. In reality it runs into that unending line of humor, which becomes more humorous the more humorously it takes itself. I do not dispute the prospect of this sea serpent which needlessly bites its own tail. But it would be valid to frighten us with this monster only if Tillich could show us, first, that we are maintaining and defending our dialectic attitude as a position at all, and second, that we seek to accomplish this by manipulating this (the dialectic) transcendence. It seems to me now that he who has ears to hear must allow that we wished and do wish with this really dialectic "transcendence" nothing else than to warn against a forgetting of the crisis, to which even our attitude, the dialectic one, is subject. In what other form could this intention (which in relation especially to innovations is surely not inappropriate) be carried out except (as *ultima ratio* of the dialectic) in the form of such a "self-transcending" of the dialectician? In this then perhaps, if nothing was of avail, the terrible glimpse of the sea serpent which appears here would say to the still uninstructed person *which* transcendence is intended (not carried out) by this self-transcending and all other previous transcendings; even this to be sure only perhaps, for how should even the terrible glimpse of the sea serpent instruct the one who is not already instructed that the "transcendence" signified by our *ultima ratio* can, as an intellectual act, never—not only not dialectically, but never at all—be carried out? By this we would then have come to the foot of the mountain which, speaking in Tillich's language, I would term the "real transcendence." To conclude the question before us I thus say, why should the "dialectic transcendence of dialectic" which Tillich perceives in us be of necessity always the "position" on which we "stand"? Why could it not be allusion (not to *an* Other, but to *the* Other) to the "real transcendence"? Before Tillich proves this *must* and this *cannot* I really do not see that I have anything to learn from the attempt to knock us out by use of this point which is really not even central.

Now we must speak of Tillich's "positive paradox," the demonstration of which is clearly the purpose of his whole essay. I wonder if I am the only one of his readers who wished that here, in his determination of the point on which everything depends, he might have demonstrated in somewhat more detail what it *is*, and above all, how he comes to (he indeed speaks promisingly of "making aware of") what he at this point contrasts to our alleged "proclamation of crisis," or rather, what he wishes to insert into it as its meaning which only now becomes apparent. He passes much too fast for me ("but once this presupposition . . . is recognized") over the critical point and goes on to his order of the day, to which we, however tempting it is, cannot commit ourselves before he gives us further information about the point on which everything depends. To begin with, only the concept "real transcending on the basis of the unconditioned" is understandable to me in itself. But in my opinion it is precisely around this concept that the questions gather which disquiet me in Tillich's following arguments.

Transcending: who transcends here? Is it an intellectual act of the philosophical theologians? If so, in what does it then consist? How do I accomplish this transcending of something "really" and in addition "on the basis of the unconditioned"? Are we not confronted here with a philosophical story in the style of Baron von Münchhausen? If not (i.e., if "transcendence" by means of some kind of divine act), how do I recognize such a transcendence coming from such a different quarter? To what extent is my knowledge of it not dialectic all over again? Is not the concept "transcendence" an unfortunate choice for the promised entity beyond Yes and No?

Real: until I am better instructed, I understand that word as our forefathers did, in contrast to "ideal." It would however interest me to learn whether in Tillich's opinion the marks of uniqueness and contingency are indispensable in the determination of the concept of the real. And then I am stopped short by the fact that in any case the knowledge of this "real" can hardly be the promised "recognition" of a position that is untranscendable and secure against all dialectic. Would not the concept of the "existential," in the meaning given it by Kierkegaard, have been comparatively more suitable for what Tillich apparently wanted to say here? "On the basis of the unconditioned." You have spoken a great word . . . ! Is it God that is spoken of here? Why this hide-and-seek with the frosty monster "the unconditioned"? If then the presupposition of the "positive paradox" (which even according to Tillich is of benefit to religion) is "once recognized," and the fear of the possible "idolization" of the word "God" seen as justified but also as invalid, why not then with all good and bad Christians name God "God"? Or is there perhaps also a "prohibition" here? A prohibition which might not rather be a command for the theologian? Is not the old simple word "God" in the mouth of a theologian who does not want to be anything else but a theologian safer in the end against dialectic, in the face of which I do not regard "the unconditioned" as weatherproof either?

But I am even more concerned here with another question: By means of what philosophical reflection does Tillich really come to set this up "on the basis of the unconditioned," to lay claim to nature, mind, and history on this basis, and finally to develop not only a doctrine of science, but a whole doctrine of the Trinity? I think I can understand what this x, in which we apparently have to perceive the Tillichian "positive paradox," is intended to represent. But I do not understand the stroke—and it impresses me as so rebellious—with which Tillich (in all his utterances with which I am acquainted, and here also, at the latest on the second page or column) makes himself master of the situation by a clever pointing, the laying of a basis in which the subject matter itself is identical with what used to be called "metaphysics"; only the old metaphysicians among the theologians as far as I know practiced this rather as a sideline, while with Tillich, unless everything deceives me, the matter is exactly reversed. Is the answer to the question about the presupposition of the crisis which is itself not crisis to be provided so simply, namely, by setting up a new concept which says everything or nothing, or which is an old one in new dress? How does one succeed, I would like to ask my honorable partner in the conversation, in *beginning* with such things as "theonomous spiritual situation," "prophetic attitude," "action that is aware of the *kairos*," etc., and then even with "transcending on the basis of the unconditioned" his theological offerings without so much as a by-your-leave, as if this—that is, as if the overcoming of human godlessness—were a matter of course? Where is the paradoxicality of the "positive paradox" if it is possible to apply this quantity at will at the decisive point in any direction as something given, and on the ground thus laid, now, if you please, no longer dialectically broken, but quite unbroken, straightforward, and confident, to throw up against the clouds the house of true gnosis? Is the promised supracritical "element of seriousness" really the positive paradox if its "demonstration" consists (instead of in asking and answering, seeking and finding, falling and rising again; instead of in the presentation of a history between the known and the knower, between man and God) in the dogmatic (without the dignity of a dogma) establishment of a first principle for the comprehension of which the church and the Holy Spirit, the Scripture and Christ, are basically superfluous (at most they come into consideration later as symbols of that which exists without them), and in the subsequent development of which along well-known patterns, everything follows of itself if one is only able to think logically enough to feel at home in the manifold arrangements of the discoverer. It is this *method* above all which is always strange and incomprehensible to me even at the first step in Tillich's temples of thought, and its point of departure makes his conclusions, however often I rejoice in the agreement with him in the subject matter, as a whole so improbable as theology.

After these candid statements, Tillich will not be surprised that I cannot at all go along with the transmigration of his concept of God through nature, spirit, and history. All (cosmos, earth, nation, intellectual forms, history, etc.) take part in the Yes and No. "They *all stand* under the unity of judgment and grace." Judgment and grace are equally true in nature, and both are equally true in the human spirit. "Autonomy in itself *is* obedience"; "the struggle of the godly and the demonic . . . *is* the . . . content of intellectual history." Conscience, dialectic, philosophy, art, science, community, law, state, religion, are sites of judgment and of revelation, of revelation and of judgment, "*there is* no profundity . . . that is not faith," "*there are* phenomena which make visible the revelation," "*there are* powerfully symbolic phenomena," mysticism *knows* the abyss of grace and of judgment, it "in its essence" (!) *is* belief, and *lives* from revelation. "Where this message is proclaimed *is* a site of revelation in the midst of history," "the imperceptible history of revelation . . . *has* found in Christ its complete expression."

There are three things which I reject in these statements. First, all the verbs in the indicative, which refer to those many *un*paradoxical statements of the relationship of God and world, or God and man, unless, as is my opinion, the concept of the theologically understood paradox is by no means exhaustively characterized by the mark of "imperceptibility," etc. Anyone who really speaks of that relationship in reference to the "positive paradox" could hardly let so many *it is*'s and *there are*'s and *they stand*'s flow from his pen, and least of all with the occasional betraying comment that "sense for the depths" becomes real "profundity" just "where it comes *to consciousness*"! He would know that in faith it can by *no* means be a case of a profundity which "is there." Second is the continual, confident reversal of the concepts "judgment" and "grace" (or revelation). In this is seems to me that a debasement of Christian thought and speech is revealed, which I regard as just as bad as the use of the word "God," despised by Tillich as idolatrous. Anyone who, in reference to the "positive paradox," speaks of judgment and grace should first be clear himself that in this he is dealing with things of which one may not dispose now this way, now that, as if it were as obvious as broad daylight, simply because one naturally has at hand all the time the logical possibility of doing this, over against those who are defenseless. And in the third place, this generalizing which Tillich does so generously, this asserting of relationships between God and one and all, between heaven and earth, this broad, general steamroller of faith and revelation, which, when I read Tillich, I cannot help seeing affecting everything and nothing as it rolls over houses, men, and beasts as if it were self-evident that everywhere, everywhere, judgment and grace reigned, that everything, simply everything, "is" drawn into the strife and peace of the "positive paradox," which being so well in hand, is, with all its "imperceptibility," really no longer a paradox at all, which bears no similarity to the God of Luther and Kierkegaard, but a striking similarity to the God of Schleiermacher and Hegel. If Tillich is serious about the paradoxical nature of the positive paradox, then he cannot be serious about either the directness of the relationships he asserts between God and world, or the logical agility with which he thinks he can manipulate the positive and negative sides of these relationships, or with the generosity with which he believes he is authorized to distribute such relationships to the various higher and lower dignitaries of this aeon. One does not talk this way of the "positive paradox" if he knows that as a theologian he is dealing with the *divine* paradox, that is, not with this "imperceptible," but with what is real *and* knowable really only on the basis of God's own free will, only by laying aside his majesty, or what is the same thing, only out of love and in love in the world and for man, with the revelation which is by no means a relationship to be designated with a general "there is" or "there are," or to be discovered merely by man; not some secret given, but something very special, made known only by God, and only, in that we are known by him, an *occurrence* to be known, an *event* from person to person, a *communication*, a *gift* in the strictest sense of the word, and therefore both the subject matter *and* knowledge of it.

Here it is, if I see correctly, that Tillich's road and "ours" separate in earnest. Therefore, it is my impression that it is not so much in the more or less positive or negative light in which we see earthly things (a question which we who find ourselves inside the dialectic could certainly come to an understanding of) as it is much more in the understanding of that which he and we think we see *beyond* all Yes and No. I miss in Tillich's "positive paradox" that which would make it into a *divine* paradox, and thereby into an object (the older writers would have said here, more profoundly, "subject") of theological science; that is, its designation as free, personal *action*, its unambiguous character as *pneuma*, through which it would be removed just as much from that simple, intellectual grip which would deal with it as with a credit balance, as from that uninhibited directness which proclaims its "imperceptible" presence, and from that dexterity which deals all too skillfully with its abysses, and from that all too cheap universalism through which it becomes one with that paradoxicality which is the predicate of the universe. It could well be, as I suggested at the beginning, that at the point on which all depends, Tillich and "we" really see something *different*, something *so very* different that he would be justified in forming the opinion that he must instruct us that there is no hole there.

The point where this contrast comes to expression could indeed be Christology. For "us" Christ is *the* salvation history, the salvation history *itself*—*Christ* is the "positive paradox." For Tillich he is the presentation of a salvation history which more or less occurs always and everywhere with completely symbolic power. This means, as

Tillich himself states, two things. Against the path on which he sees us setting out he raises the objection that through such "singling out" and "objective grasping" of *one* "place in history" the imperceptible, non-objective character of faith would be "broken through." To this I answer that this objection shows the revenge that Tillich's incomplete definition of the paradoxicality of the "positive paradox" takes. Inflexibly directed toward the admittedly quite earnest sign of "imperceptibleness," he loses sight of divine freedom and love, and runs the great danger of letting the justified polemic against the *"man-god,"* once waged by Kierkegaard and Dostoevsky, be converted into its opposite, the polemic against the *God-man.*

The following detailed remarks should be made: Where revelation is spoken of, it is not in any sense a matter of rebellious intellectual activities such as the well-known "singling out" and "grasping." Such undertakings would rather be identical with denial of revelation. On the contrary, it is a matter of affirming that we are by no means intellectual monads wandering lost in space, by no means relying on ourselves in the authority of free speculation, in the unambiguity of our relation to God and its interpretation, but are *baptized Christians,* and that for us as such (and thus also for us as Christian theologians!) "there is," according to the testimony of Scripture and the confession of the church, a history which qualifies as *the* site of *the* salvation history, yes, "there is"—"positive paradox," that is, imperceptible; not only imperceptible, however, but above all God's special, personal, real (not to be understood without the marks of uniqueness and contingency) act of freedom and love. Because it is *God's* freedom and love —therefore we say "imperceptible"; because it is God's *freedom* and *love*—therefore this special imperceptibleness at that time (inseparably connected to something at that time perceptible). According to us this would then be the "positive paradox." Therefore it is obvious that the revelation in Christ is "imperceptible" and "non-objective" in the sense that the qualification of *this* history as *salvation* history (as the history of God's becoming man) is concealed all along the line by the view of perceptible historical relations which "are" in themselves nothing else than possibilities of *offense.* No "empirical fact" *is* in itself the revelation. No "recognition" of such a fact *is* in itself faith. The whole historical "life of Jesus," for example, divorced from the testimony of those who encountered the majesty in this abasement, is in itself nothing else than the possibility, the great probability, of *offense,* and the hypothetical "non-existence of this factor" might, without being of particular importance in principle, push this probability to the limit. But the witness of the apostles is beyond a doubt related to that "em-

pirical fact," and even if all is myth, then in any case the myth describes the revelation as inseparably bound to an "empirical fact." And
if the Christian church, taking up the testimony of the apostles, speaks
of revelation in Christ and of faith in him, it neither can nor will
abstract anything from that concealing, offense-giving "is," at the risk
of the danger of misunderstanding, as if the revelation were *directly*
identical with the empirical fact, with what was then perceptible (and
of course it is not identical!). It neither can nor wants to abstract it, not
because it cannot speak without symbols, but because the revelation,
while it is the revelation of *majesty,* is throughout the revelation of
majesty in the *lowliness* of this which is empirical, of that time, and
subject to misunderstanding, and only as such is it the "positive paradox" in the serious meaning of this concept. And thus all Christian
speaking of Christ, all Christ*ology,* remains necessarily dialectic. In
order to protect the "positive paradox," it must continually take into
account the possibility of offense, which is given through the historical
in the apostolic testimony. Yes, it must be and remain so dialectic that,
if it recognizes the Christ in *Jesus* and Jesus in the *Christ* by continual
reminder that these are two different things (it should be noted in
passing that I am here speaking of *Reformed* Christology) it calls
attention to the possibility of offense, and keeps alive the knowledge
that here it is a matter of spirit, faith, and revelation.

Christology must not, however—and now I return to my partner
in this conversation—confuse itself with its object. It must not sabotage
the "positive paradox" which is given through the witness to Jesus
Christ by not merely distinguishing, but even, with the help of a theory
of symbols, separating the "eternal redemption" from "Jesus of Nazareth." It can make all sorts of concessions to the historians. If it takes
itself seriously, it can only be pleased when through the historical fray-
ing of the "empirical fact" its own question and answer—This was the
Son of God!—is brought all the more clearly to light in its character
as *divine* question and answer. It may not, however, retreat before an
opponent who cannot even meet it on its own ground. It may not let
itself be misled into disputing the singular qualification of *this* history
by revelation, or, what comes to the same thing, into maintaining the
qualification of *all* history by revelation. What is "absurd" from the
Christian or *theological* point of view is not at all what Tillich so desig-
nates the "once and once for all" which it is rather simply our theological duty to affirm. What is "absurd" is all unreflecting, unclassical,
disrespectful deviation from the formula of the Council of Chalcedon,
for to hold quietly to this confession would still indicate, *mutatis
mutandis,* good insight even today.

In reference to the "heteronomy" which Tillich discerns as a consequence of such Christology, and which threatens critical historical science, I can only remark again that under no circumstances may anyone deny the historians the right, even in the area which is the "holy land" of Christendom, to do whatever they wish and must, and that we as theologians even have an interest in seeing that this really happens. But that in all this the autonomy of *theological* science is not at all considered, that so many "theologians" who are very reputable historians in all good faith do not have the faintest idea of a task of theology as such, that their work on the Bible is today almost nothing but an involvement in the possibility of finding offense; this I regard as a situation which can no longer be endured. If Protestant theology is to recover once more from its emaciation, and it is by no means certain that it will, then let our Old and New Testament scholars, without prejudice to what they do as historians (as an avocation!), be *theological* exegetes, and as such really *also* work in obedience to "the truth."

If Tillich further fears that "law" will break in here, I answer that in my opinion it is a judgment on theology and the church if today through mere lack of law they stand without knowledge and without will in a time when they and everyone need both very much, and that a bit of "intellectual asceticism" ("work and law" are on both sides— it is not a question of that!) would do no harm to our already questionable, degenerate intellectual life. And if Tillich is finally afraid of the third and worst thing, of the breaking in of an "absolute religion," then I can only ask with astonishment what he was actually thinking of in this warning. It is really a μετάβασις εἰς ἄλλο γένος (I would say that of all three of Tillich's threats) in a serious conversation about Christ suddenly to treat Christianity as a religion among others, to demand of the church and theology (which truly do not need such exhortation!) that they should not take themselves so seriously as to think that in contrast to other communities they represent the truth. What is he getting at? Precisely if the church is what she should be, proclaimer of the positive paradox, precisely if she places herself under and within this severest crisis, she will not lose courage, but gain enough to challenge the crowd with a resounding "Thus saith the Lord!" Has not Tillich here once again fallen victim to the fatal confusion of "crisis" with "prohibition"? In any case, I must say of myself that when I spoke of the "crisis" to which everything human, and not least of all Christianity, is subject, I never dreamed of setting up such lists of prohibitions (which strike me as being so very pedantic!), and thereby providing business for modern relativism. Quite the contrary!

I hurry to the conclusion, and only assert once more that Tillich as a theologian, and therefore also his criticism of "us," is a riddle to me. Provisionally I make sense of it to myself by the assumption that he is still engaged (without perceiving the dialectic of this matter) in the frontal attack of modern man against the "Grand Inquisitor." There is no doubt about how it will end. By persisting in his anti-orthodox resentment he cannot possibly do justice to the "positive paradox" which has the task of protecting Christian theology, and therefore, on the lower plane, he cannot do justice to "our" efforts either. In general he wrote in a friendly and appreciative manner about us, and I wish I had been able to return him like for like. But the correction which he would introduce in reference to the so-called "theology of crisis" is an attack on the decisive things that we want to say. The replacement of what we think we see at the point on which all depends with what he sees there would transform "our" intention into its opposite, however related his melody seems at first to be to ours. I do not wish to have anything to do with a Tower of Babel theology. We definitely do *not* want a theology free of presuppositions, in which each according to his free, blissful, Protestant arbitrariness and inventions would be turned loose to think and talk as his own spirit suggested— even if this occurred under the banner of "theonomy"! Not only God, not only Christianity, but the church, by which I mean the "one holy catholic church," and to a lesser degree also the individual churches to which we belong, are the presuppositions of theology. The "positive paradox" cannot be dissolved and juggled away in this form either, any more than it can in the scandalous historicity and factuality of revelation. Not that we assume the "standpoint of faith," for not "Gogarten's dogma of revelation," not the "theology of crisis," is the point on which we clash with Tillich, but rather our reference to the indissoluble correlation of the theological concept of truth with the concepts "church," "canon," "*Holy* Spirit." It is quite clear to me how much I myself still have to learn in this as in other respects. The altars before which Tillich worships are really not entirely unknown to me. Perhaps just for that reason my rebuttal of his statements must turn out to be rather lively. He will perhaps understand the *paradoxicality* of the positive paradox which I am thinking of, at least for a moment or two (or will he raise the lament that I am obviously in full retreat in the direction of quite obscure regions?), when in conclusion I quote Augustine—he can and should really take it as a word of peace—*In ecclesia non valet: hoc ego dico, hoc tu dicis, hoc ille dicit, sed: haec dicit Dominus* ("In the church it is not significant that I say this, you say this, he says this, but rather that the Lord says thus").

ANSWER TO KARL BARTH*
Paul Tillich

My answer should be quick and brief. Therefore not only must I refrain from entering into a detailed discussion of the content, but also from going into various expressions of Barth's in which his temperament and zeal for battle carry him beyond the limits of an appropriate analysis. My pleasure in our conversation, the goal of which I regard always as the "with one another" rather than the "apart from one another," far outweighs the little defensive impulses directed toward formulations carrying ironic or pedagogic overtones.

On the other hand, I would like to follow up Barth when near the end he raises the question of the "intellectual situation" on the basis of which my thoughts are to be understood. It is a fact that I see a very close connection between my philosophical, theological work, including my positive and negative criticism of Barth and Gogarten, and our present scene and intellectual situation. The concept of *kairos* means for me that it is not possible to say and do just anything at any given time, but that each time has its task of creating anew the eternal meaning of all time out of its life and in its words.

Barth is justified in asking whether the defense against the "Grand Inquisitor" with his insignia of heteronomy and law is an essential determining factor in my position. It is and it must be. Liberation from the alternatives, loss of salvation or the shattering of veracity, alternatives into which orthodoxy and pietism, and indeed liberal theology as well, have repeatedly thrust each new generation, must be accomplished by an ultimate radicalism, which in the name of religion abrogates every, truly every, religious heteronomy of cognition. But because it occurred in the name of religion, it was no negation, but the positing of the unconditioned even over against every work of cognition. It was a breakthrough of certainty that there can be a justification of the "irreligious" and of the "atheist" and of the one who "blasphemes the Son of Man," if only the spirit of truth is not blasphemed. This was the carrying through of the Protestant crisis of works even in respect to the theoretical work of requiring a certain content of faith as a precondition of salvation (irrespective of whether that content was God or Christ or Jesus). And where this breakthrough was

---

* From *Theologische Blätter*, (1923), pp. 296-299.

perceived and proclaimed it had a liberating effect, liberating not only from the burden of the intellectual law, but also from resentment against it. It had the effect, which is precisely the effect of genuine crisis, of making what is objectified, solidified, codified, and therefore arouses enmity, visible in its symbolical, allusive, questionable, and at the same time, revelatory character. It is not surprising that everyone who has followed through with this development jealously guards the purity of faith against every new intellectual work-righteousness. And this attentiveness is directed not only toward the orthodox, but even more toward the liberal, and also toward the critical dialectic work of the intellect, the true goal of which is precisely this—proclaiming the paradox itself.

This is one side of the intellectual situation on the basis of which I should be understood. And now the other. Barth says that the presuppositions of theology and its concept of truth are canon, church, and Holy Spirit. As a general statement that is doubtless correct. But the question is precisely what this general statement can mean in our intellectual situation. And here I see above all the following: It is impossible at present to speak as though the words in which Scripture and church refer to the unconditioned could directly achieve that which is their essential meaning. This is the fault of the Grand Inquisitor, of the law, of heteronomy, and of objectification. And all of us, theologians and non-theologians alike, share this same fate. For example, it is impossible for the one who is aware of this situation to speak of God as if this word could directly convey to him its essential richness. Therefore we must speak of the *unconditioned*. Not that this is a substitute expression; it is rather a key to open for oneself and for others the closed door to the holy of holies of the name "God." Then the key should be thrown away. Precisely here it seems to me that the idea of any direct access to God and the assumption that one can obviously speak of God are forbidden.

It is equally impossible to speak so directly and immediately of Jesus Christ as the positive paradox in the way Gogarten's teaching of revelation does. It is not to avoid the genuine offense that one must speak differently here, but to avoid that offense that brings guilt not on the one who takes offense, but on the one who gives it. Even the name of Jesus Christ can be misused to give this false offense. If the Spirit of Christ were one with the name of Jesus Christ then the blasphemer of the name would be damned and the Grand Inquisitor would be right. But the Spirit of Christ, the positive paradox, is not exhausted in its empirical manifestation. Even theology has never asserted the absolute contingency of the positive paradox. It has rather spoken of the Logos, which by revealing itself in Jewish and in heathen history leads to the complete revelation. Theology should not be forbidden to travel this road and make visible what is even at present revealed of the Logos among heathen and Jews, that is, in the creations and crises of autonomous culture. It is surely not kneeling before false altars or building a Tower of Babel if the positive paradox is so proclaimed that in the creations and ruins of culture the traces of the divine Yes and No are made imperceptibly perceptible. Thus our attention is directed beyond all these allusions to where there is *only* allusion, where the Yes and No shine in perfect brightness. This may be called philosophy of culture because the allusion to this ultimate is not expressed in the words of the Scripture and of the church. For our situation forces us, *as* theologians, to be *not* theologians but philosophers of culture. One may call the spirit which is at work in these allusions to the ultimate allusion something other than Holy Spirit. Then theology must, for the sake of the spirit of truth and of love, wait for the Holy Spirit, or better, it must explain that the Holy Spirit cannot breathe on us wherever it will, and that the Spirit of Christ, the Spirit of the concrete paradox, *can* blow on us from the splendor and the wilting of the flowers of the field, from the creative power and the despair of a work of art, from the profundity and the self-transcendence of logic, more strongly—even than can offense in the true sense of the word—than from words, tales, and pictures, which always still bear the seal of the Grand Inquisitor for our consciousness.

That is the situation, on the basis of which I should be understood. That is the situation which we as theologians must take upon ourselves and to which we dare not be untrue. There is, however, a way of speaking of culture and a leap into absolute contingency which is faithless to our situation, and which above all condemns itself by breaking community with those who in all areas of culture struggle for the revelation of the positive paradox, for a glimpse of the Spirit of Christ, and by making unbridgeable the chasm between them and those who, emptied of culture and religion, stand in the struggle against the forms of culture and religion responsible for their fate of having become mass and nothing but mass. Here too the spirit of truth and love decides against the "holy" spirit, which is bound to canon and church in the concrete sense. It would be fatal if the direct, unmeditated proclamation of the concrete paradox, as it is present in Kierkegaard and Gogarten, would, for all of us who are in the situation sketched above, if not block off, then at least make extremely difficult the access to the complete vision of the paradox in Christ, thus rendering impossible a real sharing of burdens and sufferings.

This has been said by way of explaining the intellectual attitude with which I think and work and construct concepts which perhaps seem strange when they are not seen in this light. And now, two more words to Barth. It is my fear that the way in which he and Gogarten use dialectic will unintentionally lead on beyond the dialectic position to a very positive and very undialectic supernaturalism, and that the Yes and No of the relationship of God and world which is essential to every dialectic will become a simple No to the world, the fate of which is always to remain unattainable in practice, and at some point unexpectedly to be transformed into a Yes that is all the more positive and undialectic. I believe I see this point in the doctrine of revelation, in the doctrine of absolute contingency, and the like. Therefore it was incumbent on me to show that the radical No can be carried out only in unity with the Yes, also in relation to the world. This does not mean relativity in reference to conviction. I hope that the presentation of my own conviction nowhere sounds relativistic. Rather it signifies a crisis in reference to the unconditioned certainty, the certainty of salvation, which may by no means rely on anything empirical, not even on its own creative conviction.

And the second thing. Barth rightly appeals to Reformed theology. The dualism between the profane and the holy spheres attained significance for world history through the influence of Reformed theology. The profanization and emptying of cultural life as a whole, on the one hand, and the reduction of religious life to a subcultural level, on the other, are visible consequences of this attitude, which is undoubtedly far removed from the original intentions of the Reformers. I cannot regard it as a gain, but rather feel it as a contradiction of our position when the profanization of culture is held to be necessary. In contrast to this I consciously place myself in the German Lutheran tradition, the significance of which for intellectual history consists in its producing ever new attempts to overcome profane autonomy through a filled, theonomous autonomy. In this line stand Schleiermacher and Hegel. While I very clearly differ from them insofar as they attempt to obliterate paradox in favor of dialectic identity, I emphatically place myself beside them when it is a question of making the reference to paradox perceptible in the forms of the logical and ethical, of transcending profane autonomy with theonomy.

THE INTELLECTUAL SITUATION OF THE THEOLOGIAN:

Another Answer to Paul Tillich*

Friedrich Gogarten

Since public discussion has in fact begun, I believe that for my part I also have no right to keep silent. To be sure, I can entirely subscribe to the answer which Karl Barth made to Tillich, and would have nothing to add to it. But I may be permitted to make a brief observation on Tillich's answer, not, as I wish to state explicitly, in order to show my disagreements with him, though of course not to reach agreement with him in the sense of trying to show that we basically mean the same thing—which I think we do not, in spite of our being very close to each other. Rather, I wish to present to him my concern with the same clarity with which he presented to me his concern in his answer to Barth. I believe I am very close to the intellectual situation in terms of which Tillich would like to be understood, and that I have an understanding of it derived from my own similar situation. But from this situation I draw a different conclusion from Til-

* From *Theologische Blätter*, III (1924), pp. 6-8.

EDITOR'S NOTE: To what extent the discussion continued here by Gogarten defines the theological situation can be seen not only in the various small observations one can make here and there (e.g., the report on "new editions in theology" in the previous issue), but above all in the articles that have appeared in the recent issues of journals dealing with systematic theology. Five issues of the journal *Zwischen den Zeiten* (Munich: Chr. Kaiser), edited by Merz, under the joint editorship of Barth, Gogarten, and Thurneysen, have already appeared. In the fifth issue of *Zeitschrift für Theologie und Kirche* (Tübingen: J. C. B. Mohr), edited by Stephan in cooperation with Bornhausen, Heim, and Steinmann, Wünsch continues the discussion of the problem of ethics ("Ethic of Wrath and Ethic of Grace"), which was carried on between Gogarten and Hirsch in the second and third issues of ZZ. In the same issue of ZThK, Fr. W. Schmidt contributed a critical report of periodical literature and discussed the relationship of Barth and Gogarten to Tillich. An extensive contact with Tillich's *kairos* is evident in Siegfried's essay on "Futuristic and Present Eschatology." Although the direct discussion between the persons involved is not in the foreground, the two sizable issues to appear thus far of the quarterly *Zeitschrift für systematische Theologie* (Gütersloh: C. Bertelsmann), under the leadership of Althaus, Hirsch, and Wehrung, and edited by Stange, show how much these questions are the focus of discussion. Both issues contain well-documented studies on Kierkegaard. Hirsch's position is best shown by his article on "God's Judgment" in the second issue. Concerning the discussions and responses carried out concisely in *Theologische Blätter*, Tillich limited himself essentially to the description of the "intellectual situation," and Gogarten has addressed himself to this point. In addition to this, Tillich still owes us a discussion dealing with the real matter and substance of the questions which he raised and Barth answered. (Karl Ludwig Schmidt)

lich's. I would not be able to say with Tillich that this situation could force us *as* theologians not to be theologians but rather philosophers of culture. I could agree with him, in spite of certain misgivings of which I shall speak presently, if he said that our situation could force us no longer to be theologians under any circumstances but to be philosophers of culture instead. And naturally such a philosopher would be extremely careful to cleanse philosophy from traces of *any* theology, which could only hinder it from performing its particular task. How little what I refer to here is a mere possibility is shown by recalling Nietzsche. But this reminder shows at once to what dangers such an undertaking is exposed, precisely in our intellectual situation, of which the most dangerous deficiency, it seems to me, is the lack of a thorough and honest theology concerned with its object and *only* with its own object. Be that as it may, I could understand it if someone resolutely turned his back on all theology, but in addition also on all theology camouflaged as philosophy or philosophy of culture. There-fore it seems to me to be a half measure, and more than that, a fateful error, if Tillich thinks that by speaking of the unconditioned instead of speaking of God he can decisively avoid the idea of any direct access to God and the assumption that one can obviously speak of God, which he rightly rejects in discussing the name "God." Here it is no help at all to use another term for the same thing, but the only help is to determine resolutely to speak of another "thing." For it is not at all a question of protecting the word from the idea of a direct access to God and the assumption that one can obviously speak of God, pro-tecting the "thing"; only so we can avoid making it into an object. This determination to concern oneself resolutely with another "thing" seems to be present where one resolutely turns his back on *all* theology, even the disguised one of a philosophy that speaks of an unconditioned.

This other "thing" with which one would then deal can be nothing else than the reality of our life, the reality of man. It would be a matter of investigating it, and giving it form, all under the passionate and sober rejection of every thought of God, or of an unconditioned or absolute that resembles God, or of whatever other term might be used. And here at last it would be a question of the deadly serious attempt to justify not what is called "irreligious," but what truly is irreligious, the atheist and the blasphemer of the Son of Man. In order to avoid an extensive presentation I would here refer once again to Nietzsche, who probably made the only attempt of this kind that is to be taken seriously. Naturally in this way one ceases being a theologian. In *this* way one cannot *as* a theologian *not* be a theologian.

To be sure, I am convinced that every attempt of this sort must fail. The reason is that for us there is no reality outside that of the God who was revealed in the man Jesus Christ. I say this explicitly, say it as a theologian, and see no possibility of saying differently what should be said here. It is precisely by means of *this* direct and unmediated statement that I know I am guarded from *that* directness and unmediatedness which Tillich rightly rejects. For by means of this statement, provided I know what I am saying, and I think the same holds for the attentive hearer, I am referred directly and unmediatedly to the reality of my life, to what is "existential" for me. And here surely the highest directness and unmediatedness is obligatory. On the other hand, it seems to me that nowhere but here, in the talk of Jesus Christ that is direct and unmediated in *this* way, is this reference to the "existential," here unavoidable because of its directness, to be found. But it is more than a reference. For such direct talk excludes all revelation that is symbolic, referential, revelatory (in the sense in which Tillich uses this word). For only when the symbolic is totally razed—precisely what Tillich misses in our decisive statements—is, on the one hand, every objectification of revelation, even its objectification as dialectic, made impossible; and, on the other, the danger eliminated that our own life and the reality of the world might be reduced to a symbol, to a reference. I do not see how Tillich can escape doing this if he makes revelation into the "Spirit of Christ." Insofar as I understand what he says of *kairos,* I am afraid that he is busying himself with this reduction.

I fully realize, and sense painfully that, at least to a large extent, we do indeed destroy, as Tillich says, "the community with those who in all areas of culture struggle for the revelation of paradox, for a glimpse of the Spirit of Christ." But I can by no means concede to him that this is a betrayal of our situation. On the contrary, I am convinced that precisely faithfulness to our situation as theologians—and I gladly confess to Tillich that my *homeland* is *over there,* and that I left home and went abroad when after long hesitation I entered a theological lecture hall for the first time, and that his talk strikes my ears like a call from home—calls upon us to carry through the painful renunciation of this community, in order to perform the service which we have to render them as theologians.

I do not need to assure Tillich that I do not think I stand anywhere else than at the first beginning of this task. I know well that speaking of the revelation of God in that man Jesus Christ should be of even sharper directness, so that it can confront speakers and hearers much more bluntly with their own humanity and their own "existential" reality, and give them with much more urgency the recognition of their own being and of the being of this world. Nevertheless, I intend to say in the continuation of my work everything that I can say about it, and to say it as clearly as I can. Therefore it is not a question here of defending the individual results of my work against Tillich, but only of demonstrating its starting point and direction, which runs diametrically opposite to his own. And in order to formulate this concisely, I would say that I—and I believe that here I can also speak in the name of Barth—am seeking in terms of Jesus Christ, yes, more precisely, in Jesus Christ, the reality of the world and of life and the knowledge of it, while Tillich seeks for the knowledge of Jesus Christ, or, as he so characteristically says, of the Spirit of Christ, in the knowledge of the world and of life.

4

The Debate on the Critical Historical Method:
Correspondence Between Adolf von Harnack and Karl Barth

FIFTEEN QUESTIONS TO THOSE AMONG THE
THEOLOGIANS WHO ARE CONTEMPTUOUS OF THE
SCIENTIFIC THEOLOGY
> *Adolf von Harnack*

FIFTEEN ANSWERS TO PROFESSOR VON HARNACK
> *Karl Barth*

AN OPEN LETTER TO PROFESSOR KARL BARTH
> *Adolf von Harnack*

AN ANSWER TO PROFESSOR VON HARNACK'S
OPEN LETTER
> *Karl Barth*

POSTSCRIPT TO MY OPEN LETTER TO
PROFESSOR KARL BARTH
> *Adolf von Harnack*

FIFTEEN QUESTIONS TO THOSE AMONG THE THEOLOGIANS WHO ARE CONTEMPTUOUS OF THE SCIENTIFIC THEOLOGY*

Adolf von Harnack

1. Is the religion of the Bible, or are the revelations in the Bible, something so unequivocal that in reference to faith, worship, and life it is permissible to speak simply of the "Bible"? But if they are not, can the determining of the content of the gospel be left entirely to subjective "experience," or to the "experiences" of the individual, or are not historical knowledge and critical reflection necessary here?

2. Is the religion of the Bible, or are the revelations in the Bible, something so evident and clear that no historical knowledge and no critical reflection are needed to understand their meaning aright? Or on the contrary are they something so inconceivable and indescribable that one must simply wait until they shine forth in the heart, because no human mental or intellectual faculty can attain to them? Or is it not rather that both these assumptions are false, and that one needs, in order to understand the Bible, in addition to an inner openness, historical knowledge and critical reflection?

3. Is religious experience different from, or identical with, the awakening of faith? If it is different from it, how is it distinguished from uncontrollable fanaticism? If it is identical with it, how can it come about except through the preaching of the gospel, and how can there be such preaching without historical knowledge and critical reflection?

4. If religious experience is contrary to or disparate from all other experience, how can the necessity of radical flight from the world be avoided, or how can the sophistry be escaped that one must still remain in the world, because even flight from the world rests on a decision of one's own will, and is thus something worldly?

5. If God and world (life in God and worldly life) are absolute contrasts, how are we to understand the close connection, even equating, of love for God and love for one's neighbor which constitutes the heart of the gospel? How is this equation possible without a high regard for morality?

6. If God and world (life in God and worldly life) are absolute contrasts, how can we lead people to God, that is, to what is good?

---

* The correspondence appeared in *Die Christliche Welt* (1923).

How is such nurture possible without historical knowledge and a high regard for morality?

7. If God is definitely not all that is said of him in the development of culture and its knowledge and morality, how is it possible to protect this culture and one's self in the long run against atheism?

8. If the pantheism of Goethe, or Kant's concept of God, or similar things are simply contrasts to the true statements about God, how can we avoid abandoning these statements to barbarism?

9. If however the opposite is correct—that here, as in all physical and intellectual development, contrasts are at the same time steps, and steps are likewise contrasts—how can one grasp and develop this basic insight without historical knowledge and critical reflection?

10. If the insight "God is love" is the highest and final knowledge of God, and love, joy, and peace are his spheres, how is it permissible to remain always in the sad fix of making the transitional points of Christian experience independent and wishing to prolong the duration of their terrors?

11. If the liberating exhortation is still valid, "Whatever is true, whatever is honorable, whatever is just . . . whatever is gracious, if there is any excellence, if there is anything worthy of praise, think about these things," how is it permissible to erect a dividing wall between experience of God and the good, true, and beautiful, instead of uniting them with the experience of God through historical knowledge and critical reflection?

12. If all sin is nothing but lack of respect and love, how can one put an end to this lack other than through the preaching of God's holy majesty and of God's love? How can one dare to mix in with it all possible paradoxes and arbitrariness?

13. If it is certain that everything that is subconscious, nonrational, fascinating, numinous, etc., remains subhuman as long as it is not apprehended, understood, and purified by reason and protected in its proper character, how is it possible to wish to belittle, even reject, reason? And what can one expect if this destructive work is completed? Is there not already a Gnostic occultism arising on the ruins?

14. If the person of Jesus Christ stands in the center of the gospel, how can the basis for a reliable and common knowledge of this person be gained other than through critical historical study, lest we exchange the real Christ for one we have imagined? But how else can this study be accomplished than by scientific theology?

15. Is there—admitting sloth, shortsightedness, and numerous ills—really any other theology than that which has a firm connection and blood relationship to science? And if there be such a one, what power to convince and what value does it have?

FIFTEEN ANSWERS TO PROFESSOR VON HARNACK
Karl Barth

Concerning the title: One who makes a criticism of the form of Protestant scientific theology which since the days of pietism and the Enlightenment, and in particular in the past fifty years in Germany, has established itself as normative, is not therefore necessarily "contemptuous" of "the scientific theology." The point of the criticism is that this theology may have moved further than is good from its theme (first clearly stated by the Reformation).

1. Beyond the "religion" and the "revelations" of the Bible, the *one revelation of God* should be taken into consideration as the theme of theology. "Historical knowledge" could then of course say to us that the communication of the "content of the gospel" can, at least according to its own statements, take place only through an action of this "content" *itself*. But "critical reflection" could lead to the result that this statement of the gospel is grounded in the essence of the subject matter (the relationship between God and man) and is therefore to be properly respected. The "scientific nature" of theology would then be its dependence on the remembrance that its object had *previously* been the subject, and must become this again and again, something that has nothing *at all* to do with "experience" and "experiences."

2. "Inner openness"—experience, experiences, heart, and similar things—on the one hand and "historical knowledge" and "critical reflection" on the other hand are possibilities which, for the *"understanding"* of the Bible, could equally well be useful, indifferent, or a hindrance. The Bible is "understood" neither through this nor that "mental or intellectual faculty," but by the power of *the* Spirit, who is the *same* as its content, and that in *faith*.

3. Therefore the so-called "religious experience" is as different from the awakening of faith by God as earth is from heaven, and *in fact* is not distinguished from "uncontrollable fanaticism." Why therefore should it not be possible for it to be the more or less clear symptom and witness of the awakening of faith? Faith, however, comes indeed from preaching, but preaching (whatever may be the state of the preacher's "historical knowledge" and "critical reflection") "by the word of Christ." The task of theology is the same as that of preaching. It consists in taking up and passing on the word of Christ. In this why could not "historical knowledge" and "critical reflection" serve by way of preparation?

4. The faith which is awakened by God will never be able fully to avoid the necessity of a more or less "radical" protest against *this* world, inasmuch as it is a hope for that which is promised but unseen. A theology that would lose understanding for the basic distance of faith from *this* world would of necessity also be equally unmindful of the knowledge of God the *Creator*. Because the "absolute contrast" of God and world, the *cross* is the only means by which we as men can conceive of the original and final unity of Creator and creation. Sophistry is not the insight that not even our protest against the world can justify us in the sight of God, but rather the usual attempt to bypass the cross by the help of a trite concept of creation.

5. It is precisely the bringing together in the gospel of love for God and love for our neighbor that is the clearest indication that the relationship between our "life in the world" and our "life in God" is that of an "absolute contrast" which can be overcome only by the miracle of the eternal God himself. Or is there anything more strange, more incomprehensible, any fact in the world more in need of the revelation of God, than that of "neighbor"? "High regard for morality," yes, but do we love our neighbor, or can we love him? And if we do not love him, what is the state of our love of God? Does anything show more clearly than this "heart" (not of the gospel, but of the Law), that God does not make alive unless he first slays?

6. "No one can come to me unless the Father who sent me draws him; and I will raise him up at the last day."

7. The statements about God which are derived from "the development of culture and its knowledge and morality" (e.g., the statements of the war theologians of all lands) may have their significance and value as expressions of particular "religious experiences" (e.g., one's experiences during a war) alongside those of primitive peoples who do not yet know such higher values. As the "preaching of the gospel" (3) *these* statements in any case do *not* come into consideration, and whether they *"protect"* culture and the individual "from atheism," rather than, derived as they are from polytheism, *plant* atheism, may be in each case an open question.

8. "True statements about God" can only be made at all where one knows he is placed not on some height of culture or of religion, but before revelation and thereby under judgment, under which, together with all human statements on this subject, those of Goethe and Kant also stand. Schleiermacher's intimidation by "barbarism" is to be rejected as unreal and irrelevant, because the gospel has as much and as little to do with "barbarism" as it has to do with culture.

9. Although within human statements about God *among themselves,* it may be that "as in all physical and intellectual development"

"contrasts are at the same time steps and steps are likewise contrasts," even then (and it is more urgent, at least for *theology*, to "grasp" and "develop" *this* insight!) between the truth of God (which *can* indeed also be expressed in a human statement) and our truth there exists only contradiction, only either-or. For humility, longing, and petition will always be for our part the end, as they were the beginning. The road from the old to the new world is not one of stages, not development in any sense, but a being born anew.

10. If the insight "God is love" is the *highest* and *final knowledge* of God, how do we dare to continue to act as though we were in possession of it? Is not the "transitional point" precisely as long as time? Is *our* belief not always also disbelief? Or should we believe in our *faith*? Does it not live by being faith in God's *promise*? Are we perhaps saved other than in *hope*?

11. ". . . the peace of God, which passes all understanding . . ." (Philippians 4:7). The "dividing wall" indicated by this "passes" is basic and insurmountable. If "the peace of God . . . will keep your hearts and your minds in Christ Jesus" and make the exhortation in Philippians 4:8 ("whatever is true . . .") *possible*, then it is peace of a kind that *passes* all understanding. There *is* a connection between it and that which *we* call good, true, and beautiful, but the connection is precisely the "dividing wall," the divine *crisis*, which is the only basis on which it is possible to speak seriously of the good, true, and beautiful.

12. If sin is perhaps something more than "lack of respect and love," that is, a falling away of man from God and being lost in a likeness to God, the end of which is death, then preaching (theology) God's holy majesty and love is a task which seems not to be able to spare our human thinking and speaking from going on unexpected paths. Spectator theology may then speak of "all possible paradoxes and arbitrariness." Anyone who is in a position where he can show a simpler solution for the same (the *same*!) task, should show how it is done. Historical knowledge tells us that Paul and Luther were not in this position.

13. After all, which theological tradition is it which, starting from the apotheosis of "feeling," seems to have had a happy landing in the fearsome quagmire of the psychology of the subconscious? Who is it that apart from critical reason thought he could open a particular "religious" source of knowledge? And *ad vocem* "Gnostic occultism": which theology is it that is notoriously in danger every moment of losing its most gifted followers to Dr. Steiner?*

---

* Translator's note: Rudolf Steiner, founder of Anthroposophy, a school of theosophical Neo-Buddhism.

14. The reliability and common nature of the knowledge of the person of Jesus Christ as the midpoint of the gospel can be no other than that of a *faith* awakened by God. Critical historical study signifies the deserved and necessary end of the "bases" of this knowledge, which are not really bases, because they were not laid by God himself. He who still does not know (and we all still do not know it) that we no longer know Christ according to the flesh may let himself be told this by critical biblical science; the more radically he is terrified the better it is for him and for the subject matter. And this may well be the service which "historical knowledge" can render to the real task of theology.

15. If theology regained the courage to be objective, the courage to become a witness of the *word* of revelation, of judgment, and of the love of *God,* then it could also be that "science" in general would have to look out for its "firm connection and blood relationship" to theology, rather than the other way around. For it would perhaps also be better for the jurists, physicians, and philosophers if they knew what the theologians should know. Or should today's accidental *opinio communis* of the others really be the norm from which we must gain the "power to convince" and the "value" in our activity?

AN OPEN LETTER TO PROFESSOR KARL BARTH

Adolf von Harnack

Highly Honored Colleague!

I thank you for dealing with my "Fifteen Questions." They were addressed to you, particularly to you.

Through your "Answers" some things have become clearer to me, but precisely thereby the contrast which exists here between us has become all the clearer; I shall attempt to formulate this in what follows. To be sure, other things have remained completely obscure, or rather have become so; above all your answer to my first question. Despite strenuous efforts it is totally unintelligible to me. Since, however, very much depends on this basic question, an important matter remains here under the burden of an oppressive fog, that is, your concept of "revelation."

In reference to the title of my questions and to question 15: You see in the scientific theology of the present an unstable and perishable product, which has been formed since the days of pietism and the Enlightenment, and which possesses only the value of a fortuitous *communis opinio*. I see in this scientific theology the only possible way of mastering an object through knowledge, a way that is both new and old at once—new because it has come to greater clarity and maturity only since the eighteenth century; old because it began when there were first thinking men. You say, "The task of theology is the same as that of preaching." I answer that the task of theology is the same as the tasks of science in general, but the task of preaching is the pure presentation of the task of the Christian as a witness to Christ. You transform the theological professor's chair into a pulpit (and wish to divide up what is called "theology" among the secular disciplines). I predict to you on the basis of the course of all of church history that this undertaking will not lead to edification but to dissolution. Or is it intended that your proclamation should work only as a "ferment"? Surely no one would intend that, and it is certainly not your intention. And yet, I acknowledge the ferment: courage to be relevant, courage to bear testimony.

On questions 2 and 3: I cannot understand what in your opinion remains if one is obliged, in reference to the understanding of the religion of the Bible, as a matter of principle to make a *tabula rasa* of "inner openness," "experience," "experiences," "heart," "historical

knowledge," "critical reflection." To be sure, you say, the religion
of the Bible is only understood "by the power of *the* Spirit, who is the
same as its content, and that in *faith*." But since you continue, "Therefore the so-called 'religious experience' is as different from the awakening of faith by God as earth is from heaven, and *in fact* is not distinguished from 'uncontrollable fanaticism,' " the "therefore" is just as
obscure to me as the justification of the figure of speech you use and
as your designation of the relationship between religious experience
and faith. However, I am not able to speak about things I do not
understand. I am glad that you subscribe to the thesis "Faith comes
by preaching through the word of Christ." Yet, just as the "of Christ"
instead of "of Jesus Christ" already appeared to me to be fatal because
of reminiscences from church history, so my mistrust is strengthened
in reference to the context in which you (on question 14) make use of
the Pauline words "we no longer know Christ according to the flesh."
Thus we no longer know the Jesus Christ of the Gospels, the historical
Jesus Christ? How am I to understand that? On the basis of the theory
of the exclusive inner word? Or on the basis of one of the many other
subjective theories?

On question 4: It pains me that you have given only a very hurt
answer to this question, "The faith which is awakened by God will
never be able fully [!] to avoid the necessity of a more or less [!] 'radical'
protest against *this* world, inasmuch as it is a hope for that which is
promised but unseen." Have you perhaps not yet made up your own
mind on this point? Then it would have been better to postpone the
answer. It sounds so indecisive that it lacks either insight or the courage
to testify.

On question 5: You answer my question in reference to love for
God and for one's neighbor with the problematical nature of the concepts "neighbor" and "love for neighbor" which is especially characteristic of your theology but not of the gospel, which does not see
any problems here at all. In your statement I see the greatest contrast
to the simple gospel.

On question 6 (the possibility of leading a person to God): You
simply answer with John 6:44. If that is all that you have to say here
you condemn all Christian education and, like Marcion, sever every
link between faith and what is human. According to my understanding
of the matter, you have the example of Jesus against you here.

On questions 7-9: You comment that in each individual case it is
an open question whether the knowledge of God which has developed
in human history apart from revelation protects from atheism or plants
it. That is only half an answer to my question of whether God is

decidedly not all that is said of him on the basis of the development of culture and its insights and morality. Or should I assume that you join me in rejecting such an observation? Scarcely! For your statement that "the gospel has as much and as little to do with 'barbarism' as it has to do with culture" can be understood only as a radical denial of every valuable insight concerning God within the history of human thought and morality. And your standpoint becomes thoroughly clear through the statement "between the truth of God . . . and our truth there exists only contradiction, only either-or. . . . The road from the old to the new world is not one of stages, not development in any sense, but a being born anew." But is it not contradictory to perceive the foundation of one's own status as a Christian in this way, and yet to acknowledge that God has let it come to be in stages in the process of which eternal values are given? You should recall how Augustine tells of the development of his status as a Christian!

To questions 10 and 11: The answers which you give to the questions posed here are, in my opinion, those which as a result of the problematical situation into which you bring Christian faith, are furtherest removed from evangelical Christianity. The "transition point" from godlessness to God should last for each Christian as long as "time"; *our* faith is always also disbelief; we are saved only in hope; a connection between what *we* call good, true, and beautiful and the peace of God exists only to the extent that a dividing wall connects, etc. By giving these answers to my questions you use what is incomplete in Christianity, of which we are all aware, to destroy the possession itself, and to make an illusion of the confidence in which we are privileged to live, and frivolity of the joy which should fill our life. You will deny this, but what you put in its place is the description of a frame of mind which at best can be felt by only a few to be the "peace of God," and which can by no means be the necessary presupposition for all Christian humility.

On this basis your answer to question 12 is also understandable. The simple gospel out of which Jesus spoke his easily intelligible and comforting parables for the salvation of souls does not suit you; but rather, Christian preaching cannot "spare our human thinking and speaking from going on unexpected paths." Will there be anyone who can understand you at all when you are entirely involved in extremely sublime psychology and metaphysics? And if you then surprisingly leap over to Paul and Luther, I have no doubt that even today every Christian would find it easier to imitate the preaching and life of these Christians than to follow your message. Yet—are Paul and Luther examples for us to imitate? Can we dress ourselves in their armor?

Must we lesser ones torment ourselves in trying to experience what they experienced? It is—permit me once more to speak "problematically"—at one and the same time our power and our fate that we have experienced Paul and Luther. Against this fate nothing helps except the word of comfort which they themselves call out to us, "I believe in the forgiveness of sins."

You did not answer question 13, but contented yourself with a reference to the fact that the dominant theology or one of its lines has led into the quagmire of the psychology of the subconscious, and into occultism. Since my question was not addressed to your theology but was aimed in an entirely different direction, I will remain silent there, but must still comment that by divine ordinance all contempt of reason and science is punished with occultism, and that each age possesses only one science.

I also miss a full answer to question 14. Does the awakening of faith take place insofar as it includes the knowledge of the person of Jesus Christ as the midpoint of the gospel, without reference to his historical person? If this question must be answered in the negative, can faith dispense with historical knowledge of this person? If such knowledge is necessary, can critical historical study thereof be irrelevant to faith, or is it not rather absolutely necessary? What you indicate in this connection in reference to biblical science can well be reduced to the formula: The most radical biblical science is always correct; thank God that it is so, for in this way we are rid of it. This standpoint, known to us all too well from recent second-rate church history, gives carte blanche to every conceivable fantasy and to every theological dictatorship that dissolves the historical element in our religion and seeks to torture the consciences of others with its own experience.

I sincerely regret that your answers to my questions only show the size of the chasm that separates us, but what is important is neither my theology nor yours, only that the gospel is taught aright. But if your method should gain the ascendency, it will not be taught any more at all, but exclusively handed over to revival preachers, who freely create their understanding of the Bible and who set up their own dominance.

In highest esteem,

VON HARNACK

AN ANSWER TO PROFESSOR VON HARNACK'S OPEN LETTER

Karl Barth

My Highly Esteemed Doctor:

It is not necessary to say that I regard as an honor the detailed discussion which you gave to my answers to your questions, and that I am very grateful to you for it. In spite of this, it is with hesitation that I approach the task which the editor thought it was obvious I should take—that of giving to you on the basis of your letter further information about my theological thought. You yourself state that my answers have shown you only the *chasm* that separates us. Is it not useless and vexatious for me to present to you and most of the other readers of *Die Christliche Welt* merely more riddles? My position is awkward in another way as well. The first time you posed real questions, to which I, as one of those involved, could and must answer, as well or as poorly as I might. In your letter, however, you oppose me—and here I would not wish to dispute your right to do so as my honored former teacher—as the one who has arrived and is knowledgeable and who, on the basis of the experience and the reflection of a full and rich life, no longer has the time and the ear not only for answers other than those he himself would give, but also for questions other than his own. Is there anything left to be said to your observations? Is not the conversation ended? But since you would say to me that my answers are not those which you possessed when you asked your questions—which I would not doubt—I still owe it to you and our hearers to confess that on my part I regard my answers as very questionable, and that I reserve everything further for the future and for the possibility of being better instructed, and also that your objections will not disturb me from seeking further, first of all in the direction of my answers. Let me also, but this time somewhat by way of recapitulation, take up each point separately. For the proper understanding of my continuing disagreement I must refer you—as you in a similar situation would certainly also do—to my detailed published writings and those of my friends Gogarten and Thurneysen (for the other group of those envisaged by you I take no responsibility at all!). Speaking less to you than to the public I may permit myself the observation that it will not be possible to refute us effectively for very long without having read us seriously.

You see in what you term "scientific theology" "the only possible way of mastering an object through knowledge," and call it "new because it has come to greater clarity and maturity only since the eighteenth century; old because it began when there were first thinking men." I hope I am not attributing anything inappropriate to you when I assume in this definition, made clear by reference to the eighteenth century, that for you among the Reformers, Luther and Calvin (together with all that annoying tribe of "revival preachers"), although perhaps not Zwingli and Melanchthon, are probably *excluded* from the "scientific theologians," and that it would be quite foreign to your thought to consider seriously regarding the Apostle Paul (besides whatever else he was) as such. But be that as it may, I think I know "thinking men" in ancient and modern centuries who as theologians have traveled very different roads from those regarded as normal since the eighteenth century, and the dismissal of whose "science" (if science is intended to mean "relevance to the subject matter") seems to me highly questionable. If one appeals to the theology of Paul or Luther, you can only explain it to yourself as a presumptuous attempt at imitation. On this side of the "chasm" the procedure appears to us simply as one in which the superior relevance of these and other older theologians, however little they fit into the present theological clique, has forced itself so irresistibly on us that neither by the protest of the modern spirit (which must perhaps first learn to understand itself!) nor by faith in the forgiveness of sins (!) to which you appeal, can we feel ourselves freed from the duty of taking into consideration the possible validity of their basic approach more earnestly than has been done, especially in the most recent epoch of theology, despite all research in Paul and enthusiasm for Luther. Basically it cannot be here a question of repristination. To be sure, it is my private opinion that the practice of repristinating a classic train of thought in theology, the practice which was called "theology" in the Middle Ages and the period of Protestant scholasticism, was probably more instructive than the chaotic activity of theological schools of our day, for whom the concept of an authoritative *object* has become foreign and monstrous because of the sheer authoritativeness of *method*. But I also think I know that the *same* thing neither can nor should return, and that we are to think *in* our day *for* our day. Therefore it is really not specifically a question of removing from theological study the critical historical method of biblical and historical research developed in recent centuries, but of a meaningful way of incorporating it into theology and of sharpening the questions which result from it. I think I said this in my answers 2, 3, and 14, and may be permitted to express surprise that you continue to charge me with regarding critical biblical science as something "irrelevant," with wanting to be "rid" of it, and with needing to be threatened, because of contempt for reason and science, with the penalty of occultism, which is "by divine ordinance" determined for such a misdemeanor. What I must defend myself against is not historical criticism, but rather the matter-of-course way in which one, still today, *empties* theology's task: Instead of that which our predecessors called *"the Word"* (the correlation of "Scripture" and "Spirit") one has placed this and that which have been dug up by historical criticism *beyond* the "Scripture" and *apart from* the "Spirit," which one calls the "simple gospel," a gospel that can be called "word of God" only as a figure of speech, because it is in fact at best a human impression thereof. The sentence which was so repugnant to you and to others, that the task of theology is the same as the task of preaching, is unavoidable for me as a *programmatic* statement (in the carrying out of which, of course, many things must still be considered). In this I assume it is conceded that the preacher by rights is also to proclaim "the word" and not his own experience or experiences, maxims, and reflections. You have conceded that "through the word of Christ" (the definite article is not important to me)* comes the truth of preaching and faith. If, however, it is the task of the preacher to reproduce this "word," then it is also the task of the theologian (who finds himself at least in virtual personal union with him). The tactical and practical differences of execution are obvious, as is also the fact that some things which belong in the lecture hall can be omitted in the pulpit, and vice versa. The *theme* of the theologian, however, which he *investigates* in history, and which he must strive to express in a manner relevant to his own situation, cannot be a second truth distinct from the truth which he is obliged to present as a preacher. This is what was obvious in the beginnings of Protestant theology (I think particularly of Zürich and Geneva). I cannot see, however, how the subsequent abstract separation of "scholarly" and "edifying" thinking and speaking can be based on the nature of the subject matter. But if this unity of the task of the theologian and the preacher is justified, what they both must abandon as their theme is, along with everything that is merely human impression and not word of God, the "simple gospel" that is left over in the Bible as an alleged "revelation" after the adequate basis of knowledge of all revelation given in the correlation of "Scripture" and "Spirit" has been completely eliminated.

---

* Translator's note: The German reads, "das Wort des Christus," literally, "the word of *the* Christ."

But here we come to your categorical declaration that my *"concept of revelation"* is *"totally* (italics yours!) unintelligible" to you. You had asked (question 1) how it is possible to arrive at a "determining of the content of the gospel" without historical knowledge and critical reflection. To this I answered: 1. *Historical knowledge:* the gospel itself affirms that this determination occurs exclusively through an activity (through an acting and speaking) of this "content" (of God, or Christ, or the Spirit). You will surely not require of me specific proof texts for this thesis. 2. *Critical reflection* (!): it cannot be proper to reverse this order and make out of "thus saith the Lord" a "thus heareth man." If there is a road to *this* "content," then the content itself must be the road, the speaking voice must also be the hearing ear. All other roads do not lead to this goal; all other ears do not hear this voice. The fact that just as God himself is alone the goal, so he alone is the way, is —as I gladly concede to you—to *me* as to you, *"totally* unintelligible" not only "fog," but, to speak with Luther, darkness. If you would say to me that one cannot "believe" in a road from God *to us,* to which there is apparently no corresponding road from us *to God* (for it is always quite exclusively the road from God *to us),* then I can only answer you that in my innermost heart I agree precisely. But is it not included, quite apart from that which the Bible says about it on all sides, in the *concept* of revelation (and really not only in *my* concept!) that it is not possible to "believe" in it? If "revelation" were only the designation for the highest or deepest but always *possible human* discovery, would it not be better to renounce this high-sounding word? Or should not we theologians, if we do not wish to do this, muster the courage to let our theology begin with the perhaps basically skeptical, but in any case clear, reminder of the witness, which is of course *"totally* unintelligible," unheard-of, unbelievable, and of course offensive, that God himself has said and done something—indeed something new outside of the correlation of all human words and things—yet brought *as* this new something *into* this correlation, *a* word and thing alongside others, yet *this* word and *this* thing? I am not now speaking of the possibility of accepting this witness; I am only asking whether we should not first of all quite soberly *reckon* with the fact that so-called Christianity so far as we can tell began with this witness. This witness, which can never be analyzed enough by historical criticism, but which will not for that reason cease being *this* witness, is what I term in its totality the "Scripture." In this the question of the delimitation of "Scripture" in reference to other writings seems to me to be a secondary one. Should a non-canonical writing contain this (but really *this)* witness to a noteworthy degree, there can be no a priori impossibility of letting this witness also speak through *it;* on the contrary. From this conclusion to the canonization of, for instance, *Faust* is a long road, which a sensible church will *not* enter on.

Thus Scripture bears witness to revelation. It is not necessary to believe it; indeed one *cannot* believe it. But neither should one undermine the fact that it witnesses to revelation, and indeed *genuine* revelation, not a more or less veiled religious human possibility, but God's possibility, that *he* has acted under the form of a human possibility— and this as *reality.* The witness relates that the word became *flesh,* God himself became human, historical *reality,* and that this occurred in the *person of Jesus Christ.*

From this it by no means follows for me that this event can also be an object of human, historical *knowledge,* but that precisely this is excluded because and insofar as it deals with *this* reality. The existence of some Jesus of Nazareth, for example, which can of course be known historically, is not *this* reality. Moreover, a "simple gospel," historically knowable because humanly convincing, which provides no offense and is thus in your meaning a "simple gospel," a word or a deed of this Jesus, which really would be nothing but the realization of a human possibility, would not be *this* reality. I of course doubt that it is possible at any significant point, even considered only historically, to loose a word or a deed of Jesus from the background of *this* reality, that is, from the Scripture which witnesses to revelation and thus also to the offense, and to regard it as "simple gospel" in your sense. Why, for example, I regard this as impossible in reference to the command to love God and one's neighbor, I have indicated previously in my answer 5, and for this I was chastised by you, but not refuted. I can now only in passing enter protest against your designation of the parables of Jesus as "easily intelligible and comforting" parables, and hope in both cases to have at least a *few* historians on my side. But even if you should succeed in claiming one point or another from the tradition for your viewpoint, it would only mean that this point is *not,* or *is* only in context with other points, the object of the testimony, the kerygma, which is no doubt also in your opinion the sole point of the writing of the New Testament. But the object of the *witness* was designated so clearly by the apostles and evangelists themselves as *revelation,* as the activity of God himself, it was placed in such complicated concealment, so *protected* against all desire to understand it directly, that not only all obvious references to this "central point of the gospel," as they are brought together for example in the second article of the creed in a suspiciously threatening bundle, but assuredly also the "Sermon on the Mount," the parables and disputes of Jesus, the passion account, allow on careful consideration only the verdict that it is impossible to say that the historical *reality* (of the revelation!) claimed here is knowable directly and historically. All that is knowable is that other which constitutes the historical context of the alleged revelation.

Beyond this other the barrier falls, and the offense, the fable—or the miracle—threatens. The historical reality of Christ (as reality of revelation, or of the "central point of the gospel") is not the "historical Jesus," whom an all too zealous historical research had wanted to lay hold of while bypassing those warnings erected in the sources themselves (only to come upon a banality which is now and will continue to be vainly proclaimed as something precious), of course not, as you said, an "imagined" Christ, but rather the *Risen One,* or let us say— holding back because of our little faith—the Christ witnessed to as risen. *That* is the "evangelical, the historic Jesus Christ," and otherwise, that is, apart from this testimony to him, apart from the revelation which must here be believed, "we know him no longer." In this sense I believe I can legitimately appeal to 2 Corinthians 5:16. Hence at the decisive point, that is, in answering the question what makes Jesus the Christ, the reference to *the resurrection,* there remains from the human point of view indeed only your *"totally* unintelligible." And I shall gladly confess to you that I would a hundred times rather take the side of the No, the refusal to believe which you proclaim on the basis of this state of affairs, than the artifices of a "positive" theology which end up by letting what is incomprehensible appear under control again as entirely comprehensible and evident; this is an emptying and a denial of the revelation, which with its apparent witness to the revelation, is worse than the bitterest and worst refusal to believe, which has at least the advantage of being suited to the subject matter. It is in this sense also that my declaration of sympathy for the "most radical" biblical science is meant. The theology of the Reformation did not need this negative discipline because it still had the courage *not* to avoid the offense of revelation and therefore did not raise at all the question of a historically knowable middle point of the gospel. *We need* it because in our flight from the offense we have fallen into this impossible question. I see the theological function, especially of historical criticism, as being that of making clear to us a posteriori that this *cannot be done,* that in the Bible we are dealing with testimonies, and always *only* with testimonies. And I maintain that this is the function which, in its way, it has actually splendidly *fulfilled* among us since the days of David Friedrich Strauss, even though largely not understood, and above all not itself knowing what it did.

The *acceptance* of these incredible testimonies of the Scripture I call *faith*. Here I once again cannot admit that this is a discovery of *my* theology, but ask, aside from sentimentalities, what else faith could be than the obedience which I give, as if it were God's Word, to a human word which it testified to as God's Word directed to me. Let no one deceive himself here concerning the fact that this is an unheard-of occurrence, that the Holy Spirit must now be spoken of; otherwise all the objections which Herrmann hammered home against "holding as true" historical events apart from this basis of knowledge would be valid. I therefore distinguish between faith as *God's work* on us (for only God can say to us in a way that we will hear it, what *we* can*not* hear, 1 Cor. 2:9), and all known and unknown human organs and functions, including all our so-called "religious experiences." Is that such an unheard-of innovation? Must I, as Reformed, raise the question of whether Luther's explanation of the third article in the small catechism is really valid or not? And are you unable to perceive that it is through the rash abandoning of this concept of faith for the mess of pottage of a less paradoxical one that all doors are opened to the anthroposophic *tohuwabohu* of faith and occult "capabilities" of man, confronted with which official theology stands in total confusion?

It must be the case that everything that can be said against the possibility of revelation may also be said with the same weight against the possibility of faith. And now as the *second* excluded possibility *this* must remain, that the *God* who according to the witness of the Scripture has spoken "the word of Christ" now speaks it *through* the witness of the Scripture, through the power of the *testimonium spiritus sancti internum*, also to *me*, that I *hear* it and by hearing it, *believe*. Is this then the "theory of the exclusive inner word" or one of the "many other subjective theories"? In question 3, you yourself spoke of the *awakening* of faith. I agree, but in the sense that as in the "intelligible and comforting parable" of the Lost Son, Luke 15:32, it is a matter of the awakening of one who is *dead*, and, just as in the case of revelation, of God's *miracle*. In any case, I have no confidence in any other objectivity than the one outlined here or through the correlate concepts of "Scripture" and "Spirit," least of all in the papacy of a science that would first have to demonstrate through its results its absolute superiority to the subjectivistic activity of the "revival preachers."

But now you also, highly honored Doctor, have conjured up against me the shadow of Marcion with the claim that I "sever every link between faith and what is human." May I inquire what basis you find for this in my second and third answers? Have I really made *tabula rasa* of those human organs, functions, and experiences? In any case it is not my intention to do this. I think I also really know that man, believing or disbelieving, lives on as man, in time, in the world of things, from his point of view exclusively dependent on his own human possibilities. I think I also know that man's faith is at any moment entirely determinable as "inner openness," "experience," "experiences," "religion," "historical knowledge," "critical reflection," etc., just as the witness of revelation *can* be entirely interpreted, yes, *must* be interpreted (insofar as God himself does not interfere!) as a bit of disagreeably obscure human intellectual and cultural history. Neither here nor there would I "sever" (that would be a completely senseless undertaking!), but rather say that what is human is only relative, witness, parable, and therefore is not, as would at least be a consistent inference from your statements, on some peaks or heights of development, *itself* the absolute! Rather the human is the pointer (understood or not understood) to the absolute. According to this then, that which is historically and psychologically comprehensible, that which we know in ourselves and others as "faith," would be witness and symptom of that work and miracle of God in us, of faith, which, created by "the Word" and absorbed in "the Word," to speak with Luther, is our righteousness before God himself. In the same way then, the religions of the Bible, which were the starting point for your first question, would be witnesses and symptoms of the historical reality of the incarnation of God. The basis for knowing both justifying faith and revelation would be God's activity through his Word to us. Do I really not make myself clear to you?

But, and here I think I strike the nerve of all your objections, I am indeed *satisfied* with regarding only as witness all that which occurs here and there in time and by human activity, and I *reject* specifically the possibility, somehow and somewhere, be it in history or in ourselves, of making something relative absolute, or, to speak in Kierkegaard's terms, of passing from witness to "direct communication." If I do not completely misunderstand the Bible and the Reformation, the latter is and must remain, in the most exclusive meaning, God's affair. But solely as Word and work of God, as the activity of the Trinity itself, which can be witnessed to and believed only as revealed, is it true that eternity becomes time, the absolute relative, and God man (and thereby—only thereby—each time the opposite also occurs!), that the reality corresponds to the sign and only thereby the sign to the reality, as Luther, with ultimate insight, remarked in his teaching on the Lord's Supper, though not far from the natural titanic arrogance of the *homo religiosus*. It can never become true as a historical psychological reality that becomes directly knowable somewhere in our religious experience, in the movements of our conscience, in the relationships between man and man, nor, even though they were the purest, in the ideas of God of Goethe and Kant, or whatever heights of human resemblance to God you might name. If it does become knowable here or there, then the miracle has occurred, which we do not *deny* but with which we may not *reckon* as with a possibility or even a general truth, which we, when it is *present* (present as the miracle of *God*), are to worship. My rejoinder to your reproof of "severing," which I do not regard as justified, is to the effect that through the continuity which you claim exists between the "human" and faith you rob faith of content just as in the continuity which you claim between history and revelation you rob revelation of content. I do not sever, but I do contest any continuity from the one to the other. I maintain a dialectic *relationship* which points to an *identity* which cannot be carried out and therefore also is not to be asserted. Therefore the pointers visible on the stages of life's way are to be ascribed value only as *parables*—such pointers as those provided by "Christian" *biography* of all ages (which despite Augustine, or rather precisely in reference to him, is to be designated as an undertaking both promising and ambiguous). Value only as parables is to be ascribed to the struggles and successes of "Christian" pedagogy, which truly and for good reason has never become rid of heathenism, and which is honored rather than dishonored when it is placed under the hope and under the judgment of John 6:44. Value only as parables is also to be ascribed to all "Christian" protest against the world, which as human undertaking (why do you insist on drawing the inference that I am here irresponsible? —I repeat in due form my "devious" answer) can surely only be a more or less "radical" protest, a "half-breed," little protest, a demonstration, a gesture, but can never hope to anticipate and actualize the passing away of this world and the coming of the Kingdom. All "becoming" can be parable, only parable, in contrast to the birth that moves from death to life through which we alone—but only on the way which God himself travels and is—come from the truth of man to the truth of God.

You would like (always in connection with the charge of Marcionism) a "full" answer from me to the question: "whether God is *decidedly not* all that is said of him on the basis of the development of culture and its insights and morality." All right. But then let me ask you really to listen to my *full* answer: *No*, God is "*decidedly not* all that," as surely as the Creator is not the creature or even the creation of the creature. But precisely in this No, which can be spoken with full sharpness only in faith in revelation, the creature recognizes itself as the work and the possession of the Creator; precisely in this No, God is known as *God,* as the source and the goal even of the *thoughts* which man, in the darkness of his culture and lack of culture, is accustomed to form of God; precisely this No definitively established by revelation is not without "the deep, secret Yes under and above the No," which we should "grasp and hold to with firm faith in God's Word," "and confess God is right in his sentence on us, so that we then have won." And thus it is with this No: "Nothing but Yes is in it, but deep and secretly, and it seems to be nothing but No." What "contrast-greedy" person may have said that? Kierkegaard or Dostoevsky? No, Luther! (EA, 11, 120). Is Luther perhaps to be suspected of Marcionism? According to Zwingli, yes, but I think that you join me in understanding him better than that, and why should you not at the same time understand *me* a little better? Should what is human really become meaningless because in faith in revelation its *crisis* dawns, which makes really impossible all identifications between here and there—always with the exception of the one identification which it does not become us to express (the end of all things foreseen in 1 Cor. 15:28)? Does it not really become full of meaning and promise, for the first time important and possible, by moving from the twilight of supposed fulfillment into the light of real *hope?* Is it really *not* enough for *us* to have and behold in the perishable the parable of the imperishable, to live in it and work for it, to rejoice as men that we have at least the *parable,* and as men to suffer from the fact that it is *only* parable— *without* anticipating the "swallowing up of death in victory" by a spurious consciousness of eternity, precisely *because* the great temporal pointer applies to the greater eternal Is and not to something other? Have I really made a *"tabula rasa"?*

Yes, you say it, highly honored Doctor, and you must know *why* you say it, although you cannot base it on my statements. I fear that here, *precisely* here, you *necessarily* misunderstand me, even if we could agree concerning revelation and faith. How does it come that just here where it is a matter of the existential question of our relation to God and the world, of the confirmation in *hope* of faith in revelation, that you quite unambiguously exchange the role of defender of *science* for that of defender of the so-called Christian "possession"? What is the meaning of the complaint about the "sublimity" of my metaphysics and psychology, as if now suddenly *general intelligibility* were for you the measure of correct theology? What is the meaning of measuring the distances which, sometimes more, sometimes less, are said to separate me from so-called "evangelical Christianity," as if in our conversation it were suddenly a question of the *Christianness* of my theology? What is the meaning of the reproach for "commending" a "frame of mind" that is disagreeable to you, when it was your scientific misgivings that pointed to the fact that for me neither revelation nor faith is made understandable in the familiar "simple" way as a frame of mind, and hence the topic "frame of mind" was obviously introduced into the debate by you? What is the meaning of all the strong words "illusion," "frivolity," "greedy for contrast," etc., where you have certainly not demonstrated the right to draw from my perhaps unsatisfactory, but in any case cautious answers such tumultuous conclusions and accusations? How am I to explain to myself this transition from teaching to chastising? How shall I answer it? You can certainly guess that I too have angry thoughts about the connection between the *scientific* character of your theology, which makes it necessary for you to reject what I (and not only I) call revelation and faith, and its *Christianness,* which comes to expression by casting suspicion on the Pauline expression "saved in hope" as "problematical." I too would be in a position, where the misunderstanding between us seems hopeless, to announce strong scruples and to utter very sharp words. But what would I accomplish by that except on my side also to put a seal on this hopelessness, and that should not be done. It will also be better in every respect if I stop here.

Let me repeat: I do not intend to be obdurate in the positions in which I have revealed myself to you, highly honored Doctor, and to our voluntary-involuntary audience in this conversation; first because I know how shatteringly relative *everything* is which can be *said* about the great object which occupies you and me. I know that it will be necessary to speak of it quite differently from the way which corresponds to my present understanding, and in the future I would also like to be able to listen attentively to what comes from *you.* But that with your questions and answers you have driven me from the field, though I will gladly endure it when it really *happens,* I cannot this time admit.

With highest respect,
Yours,
KARL BARTH

POSTSCRIPT TO MY OPEN LETTER
TO PROFESSOR KARL BARTH

Adolf von Harnack

Professor Barth has given a very detailed answer to my open letter. I thank him for the rich content of his presentation. I regret, however, that I am unable at this time and in this journal to continue the discussions, since the number and the weight of the problems are too great to be dealt with briefly and in this place. But there are two things I would not like to leave unsaid.

1. Paul and Luther are for me not primarily subjects but objects of scientific theology, and so also are my colleague Barth and all those who as preachers express their Christianity as prophets and witnesses, whether they do this in biblical commentaries or in dogmatic writings, etc. In life, of course, scientific theology and witnessing are often enough united, but neither of them can remain sound if the requirement that they be held separate is not enforced. Both are "relevant" —not just bearing witness, as it might appear on the basis of Professor Barth's exposition—but the type of relevance is in each case very different. A scientific theological presentation can also inspire and edify, thanks to its object, but the scientific theologian who is bent on inspiration and edification brings strange fire upon his altar, for as there is only one scientific method, so there is also only one scientific task—the pure knowledge of its object. Success that comes to science in addition to this fruit is an unexpected gift.

2. The concept of *revelation* is not a scientific concept. Science is unable to bring the God-consciousness and the paradoxical preaching of the founders of religions and prophets (as is true of religious experiences in general) together under one category, or to explain them as "revelation." It is however completely futile to attempt to take a "word" of this sort as something so purely "objective" that the influence of human speech, hearing, perception, and understanding can be eliminated. I have the impression that Professor Barth seeks to do something like this, and in so doing calls for assistance on a dialectic which leads us to an invisible point between absolute religious skepticism and naïve biblicism—a most tormenting explanation of Christian experiences and of Christian faith! But since for centuries it has again and again been presented in new guises, it is probably individually justified and must therefore be treated with respect. But is it

able to build a community, and are the wild blows justified with which it beats down everything else that appears as Christian experience? And if he who perceives Christian faith in this way and never otherwise is able to find footing on its glacier bridge, is there room on it for even his children and friends? Would he too not do better, instead of setting up a strict either-or, to recognize that he plays *his* instrument, but that God has yet other instruments?

In Barth's answer at a few points a certain sensitiveness appears which is magnified even to the assertion that my responses sounded like "chastisement." I cannot be judge in my own case, and I am therefore all the happier to say that in my letter I was moved by no other intention than that of attaining clarity in reference to a theologian friend.

5
The Beginnings of Barthianism

MARGINAL GLOSSES ON BARTHIANISM
Paul Schempp

MARGINAL GLOSSES ON BARTHIANISM*
Paul Schempp

Even on the basis of a detailed knowledge of the literature, it would be impossible for a commentary on the controversy surrounding Barth to achieve sufficient distance not merely to prolong the debate, interesting as it would be useless, by evaluating the most important of the all-too-numerous sallies and sorties around his theology, nor to provide just another concise and informative lexicon article—a theological survey in the style of Kattenbusch, characterized by wide reading, tolerance, and brevity. But it is clear that such a commentary would neither justify Barth's theology nor, with the drunkenness of victory, herald his elimination from the field, because Barth, unfortunately, has still not found a really dangerous opponent, and therefore passing judgment would not be difficult. It is surely the curse of present-day theology that it knows neither community nor genuine divisions, and this curse makes for loneliness. It forces one to be neutral, or to attempt to take up alone the struggle against everyone.

It seems that Barth is just as much alone today as he was ten years ago, despite the great success of his theology, and that most of the literature about him either neglects the matter with which he is concerned, or else speaks of it from presuppositions quite different from his. Since a conflict in theology between the Word of God and the Spirit of God cannot be maintained, this is evidence only of a difference in understanding and applying the subject matter, whether it is Barth, the Barthians, or the anti-Barthians who are now speaking correctly of it. It is not a question here of only such differences in speech as might be compared to the differences in the Synoptic, Pauline, and Johannine traditions; that is, of the always variable personal disposition and intention of the witnesses, which do not in the least hinder unity in the spirit but are rather proof of the freedom that reigns in the service of Christ. It is clearly evident, however, that this unity in the spirit—whether it is God's spirit or man's that speaks here—is definitely not present. It is possible that there could be theologians whose dogmatics could look very different from Barth's, and who could still stand in the same church with him and believe the same gospel, but the talk which is heard for and against Barth in all

* From *Zwischen den Zeiten*, VI (1928), issue 4, pp. 529-539.

the literature about him does not bear witness to such community. *Barth and the literature about Barth are mutually exclusive,* not in principle of course, for there can be writings and words that clearly show intellectual community with Barth, and here is not the place to pass judgment as to whether that is also community with Christ. This is a judgment of faith which has as its presupposition and as content of its hope justification by God alone. It is therefore merely a statement of experience and does not imply taking sides with Barth, or canonizing Barth; that would a priori be blasphemy. Barth's *Dogmatics* is not a confessional statement of the Christian church, but a confession of Barth's deliberations on faith in this church, deliberations that can be false, even if some empirical church would be so foolish as to let itself be Barthianized. Barth should not dominate any more than a church should.

When one places what Barth has written alongside what has been written or imagined about Barth, one can discern, along with the misunderstandings, numerous influences and here and there even a completely correct reproduction of Barth's theological position (e.g., Metzger), but even so, as far as I know, Barth is universally first placed in the frame of a more or less fortunate photograph and then praised or reproved, corrected, improved, or corrupted—a preliminary procedure thoroughly justified theologically; but they remain stuck here in the discussion of Barth's theology, as if theology were as harmless and peaceable an undertaking as determining the year-end balance of a well-financed business. Barth flourishes, his books sell, and the competitors exert themselves. But this does not prevent that whole branch of production—church and theology—from being included among the luxury items; it must deliver very interesting products if the public is to keep on buying. It is not the wares, the seller, the packaging, the advertising, and above all the respectability of the firm that bring the results. The success: a few significant theologians, preservation of the enterprise by government subsidy, preservation of market outlets, satisfaction of the religious needs of the middle class, slow modernization. Within the science, culture, mentality, and religiosity of the twentieth century, theology and church maintain their traditional little place, the market fluctuates, but the enterprise is more secure than the peace of Europe. All this is justified by theology itself, not in so coarse and unbelievable a manner as to give it out as the work and will of God; no, in much finer and imposing manner, by bringing the wrath of God over it all, by storming and threatening against the godlessness of the church and the unfruitfulness and the lack of spirit in theology.

The existing order is supported more effectively today by self-accusation than by simple piety and the feeling for pious traditions. Barth has a following because his theology corresponds better to the present intellectual climate than do other theologies, because the sacrifice of intellect is a pleasure for those who here have little to sacrifice, because paradox seems profound, because the critique of the morbid counts as an accomplishment for weaklings, because through him theology has become once again interesting, problematical, worth having, an asylum for doubters and believers and the whole crowd of religious stages in between. Everywhere, and thus also in relation to theology itself, progress is all too fast from accusation to justification; and all along the line there dominates instead of war, diplomacy, instead of division, compromise, instead of the Yes *or* No of faith, the Yes *and* No of theological speculation, and because of the wide radius of Barth's theology, it would be a miracle if almost every theologian could not count off a few points at which he could triumphantly say, "That is what I have already 'advocated' for a long time." Thus, for example, Wobbermin believes himself to be several years ahead of Barth in the fight against psychologizing. Or, "Barth is entirely right when he," etc. It would also be a miracle if each one could not also think he finds in Barth his own foe, and a miracle if there did not crop up on every side the attempt to show Barth that he is not consistent enough on one side or the other, that he would do well to develop a little more, or on the contrary to reduce certain radical ideas to a point where they would be tolerable, or to eliminate a few atavisms. One could almost say that the discussion of Barth is gradually beginning to be as boring and comfortable as a theological retreat. A few defensive measures and a few alterations in one's thinking apparatus and Barth has been made suitable for church, seminary, and parlor. One can speak about him so splendidly, object to everything, defend everything, and be somewhat vexed that the chameleon is always changing color. A few examples chosen at random may show how the new star on the German theological stage is received by the spectators.

Messer has insisted on interpreting Barth's theology in terms of Kant and Fichte and, by eliminating the question about God, on evaluating it ethically as a noteworthy accomplishment of the "religion of renunciation" with the humane wish that it might soon recover from Bolshevism and conclude a harmonious marriage with the "religion of consecration," a useful philosophy of values serving as the justice of the peace. Although neither Barth nor Messer will be guilty of this, many Barthians will probably fulfill this wish in order to take the wind out of the sails of the competition from Catholic philosophy.

Oepke has established by the study of family trees that Barth is a radical mystic, and Oepke does not quote falsely. To be sure, according to Oepke, Barth is also half a theologian of faith. He has his mission, is a passionate revivalist like all great mystics. We must be thankful to him, but go further and continue the old fight between gospel and Asia against him as well. Concerning the strategy in this struggle, Oepke should come to terms with W. Bruhn. And yet Barth is also said to assert in extreme manner the exclusive transcendence of God. *Dörries* even protests in the name of God against Barth, that in this world he sees only the absence of the beyond and proclaims in the national pathos of a Prussian Lutheran the near God of love, one might almost say the most splendid, useful, and lovable example of a God who "creates nothing complete" and lives with the world in the best conceivable division of labor, a gospel that, *horribile dictu,* is also law, a love that simply loves in all directions, an optimism hostile to reflection, which confuses about everything that there is in theology to confuse, and wants to be still more paradoxical and dialectic than the allegedly so pessimistic Barth. One can only envy Dörries, and would like to warn him against reading Luther lest he be overcome by hate and by the blasphemy against God, which, according to Luther, the whole of Scripture testifies to be strong in a holy man, and lest the alleged relationship of man to God become questionable for him.

According to *Harnack,* Barth is contemptuous of scientific theology, and it has already been observed that Barth is suitable for the pulpit but not for theology. Should it not be recommended that Barth and Dörries be allowed to preach one after the other? The gloomy No would precede the blessed Yes in dialectic tension. "Great thoughts," as Dörries desires, would be introduced to the people—Dörries should certainly know how dangerous great thoughts are for the people— and salt and light would be distributed appropriately. Pastors could escape from studying, for in the pulpit anything is permitted. Karlstadt may lay aside the doctoral hood, for the Holy Spirit has room even under a cap. Theology is only for those who already have one before they study, or who do not need any. Either the flesh already understands God's Word—according to Dörries faith is present before one knows what he believes in—or the Spirit works "vertically from above" and consciousness and reflection can be dispensed with a priori. (Despite this Dörries cries, "To work, theologians!" but does not say what work—perhaps that of correcting his own Bible quotations?)

Is Barth a spiritualist, a fanatic, or an idealist? Again and again, not only in Heinzelmann, one reads the reproach that Barth no longer has a religious subject. The glorification of God always takes place only through slaying man; the Kingdom of God is the destruction of the world with its pious and godless culture. Therefore they say Barth also has no ethics. Mere criticism, pessimism, odor of corpses, instead of insight into the real connection and transformation of humanity with and by God. God in us *and* God above us! Both must be retained instead of the exclusiveness with which Barth says only the one. At this point quite startling agreement may be observed between Catholic critics (Przywara and Adam) and those of the liberal *and* pietistic side. One time the godliness of the creation, the next the inner-worldly and strictly human reality of redemption is brought into play, but behind this there stands, explicitly or unconsciously, the teaching of the *analogia entis,* through which God becomes an object placed in relation to the natural or the converted man. On reading Wobbermin in his newest interpretation of Luther's "God and faith belong together" and in his lecture in Meissen on dialectic theology, in which, for Luther's sake, one would gladly do without the appeal to Luther, one can see to what a naïve theology of experience and to what a false critique this leads if the consequences are not prevented by a firm church dogma or a robust Biblicism.

After *Traub,* in consistent loyalty to the impossibility of logical contradiction within theology—thus in the neat severing of thought and being—has solved the Christological problem through the interpretation of impressions on the conscience which force one to a verdict of trust, Barth necessarily appears to him as a woolly-headed theologian, who is always sawing off the branches on which he wants to sit, and finally ends up helpless with only the *assensus fidei,* the orthodox belief in authority, while ignoring in a stiff-necked manner the question of a material standard for dogmatics.

Barth is, furthermore, a rationalist; he continuously mixes his philosophical presuppositions, taken from the Marburg school, with the contents of Scripture; he is the secret prisoner of his mortal foe, Idealism; besides this he is a scholastic, and according to *Otto Ritschl* his theology ends in Averroism, in the statement of twofold truth.

It is not a happy sign that the objections to Barth can almost invariably be predicted before you read the article if you know the name or the tendency of the theologian who is reporting on him. What else should there be in *Licht und Leben* except the reference to the lack of recognition of the love of God and a lack of holding to the historical deeds of salvation precisely as historical facts, of insight into the Christian's positive life of sanctification, of victorious certainty of salvation? What can *Gustav Krüger* reject if not Barth's Biblicism and his ignoring of the world of revelation in the history of religion? One could continue in this way and eventually all objections would so confront each other that they would be mutually annihilated. But that would be an apologetic for Barth's theology, and therefore not appropriate. Barth's friends are already seeing to it that Barthianism holds its own and goes forward in the life of the congregation and in theology, and it is greatly to be wished that their writings (e.g., Strauch, Burckhardt, Haitjema) were less in the nature of recommendations, because the heavy pronouncement of judgment and grace gradually has such a comforting and soothing effect. One should bear in mind that Otto Ritschl (who far surpasses Barth in his knowledge of the history of dogma and in the anchoring of his theology in the nineteenth century), in observing that in Barth's theology talkativeness is one of the main attributes of God, has of course confused Barth and Barthianism with God, yet the possibility of such confusion urges caution, even though at this point Ritschl would have done better to turn to the churches with the request for a limit on official talkativeness. It should be said that the literature *for* Barth is almost entirely (exceptions are Metzger and Kolfhaus, within the limitations imposed by the attempt at popularization) no better than that *against* Barth. The many lectures which seek to respond to the interest in Barth show this even more clearly than does the literature. They are either "Yes . . . But" theology in the worst sense, or student exercises that often remind one of juvenile enthusiasm for Nietzsche.

But what is the case with Barth and the other dialecticians? Are not Brunner, Gogarten, and Bultmann representatives of the same "direction," Barth's comrades in arms? And are not many dialectic tones heard in Althaus and Heim? Indeed, is there still a course or seminar in systematic theology where there is not an earnest coming to grips with dialectics? Yes, there is a front of dialecticians, and the student encounters it directly or indirectly in every seminary and university. Barth has given the theological task new directions and questions, has brought into the student's study struggles of awe-inspiring seriousness. But despite this each wages his own fight with books and paper, and for each the distinctions from the others become more and more important. One theology stands alone and solitary beside another, one teacher beside another. Individualism and virtuosity begin to reign in all attempts at coming to terms with one another or at cross-fertilization. The student has been sacrificed to the academic freedom of the scholars. He must be the student of a master or he will go to his first pastorate with only a confused mixture of knowledge in his school satchel. He then preaches a certain theology and the congregation remains hungry, or he adapts himself to the congregation and it remains satiated. Will not the student who has run through all the courses and departments sigh in confusion over the many parts which lack the bond of intellectual unity? What good does it do him to have memorized the systems of ten masters? And is he not all the poorer if he is sworn to one of them?

If among the teachers only books transmit thoughts and each one sets up his theological edifice only in speculative synthesis or in speculative distinction to the other, each of them objective, ecclesiastical, scriptural, each also in personal faithfulness to himself, each out of the sovereignty and protection of his academic office transforming letter into spirit and spirit into letter; if knowledge and knowing much are surpassed at best by speculation, and the movement of thought is only away from the being of the thinker—life and teaching must, however much according to Luther they are to be kept apart like heaven and earth, come together in the person of the teacher—then of course science can flourish and the libraries can grow. But just as the rich and profound Catholic scholarship today does not overturn a single holy water vessel, so Protestant theology is on the dump heap of the merely reflective interpretation of the Scripture and the Reformation. A decisive turn toward biblical freedom and submission to the divine law would have to bring a real crisis in theology, and would have as its first consequence extensive regroupings in the universities (theological department and professor, theological department and other departments, theological department and church, theological department and State, theological department and specialization, theological department and examinations.) There would be widespread regulations on the distribution of rights and duties, while the primacy of the theology, which according to Luther is necessary for salvation, would be increasingly abandoned. The community of church teachers and servants would be dependent almost solely on chance, option, and the exigencies of examinations; too little severity of law—how little the student today knows what he should study—and too little evangelical sovereignty—how dependent theology is on the ordinances of this world, above all on that representative "they"!

The contemporary exegetical judgments of Barth already show that reaching an understanding, whether it results from agreement or contradiction, is always an act of violence, violence to the word or spirit of the one being exegeted, and violence to the exegete through concealment of his own words or his own spirit with the mask of a protagonist or antagonist. The problem of reaching an understanding is the problem of faith and knowledge. Attempts at understanding from without, that is, by the path of science, must be inexorably made and

carried forward to the point at which it becomes evident that community and a parting of the ways can be genuine only if they have
their basis not only in more or less scientifically grounded theses and
antitheses, but in the attitude of the two partners in the discussion
before God; and this attitude itself can only be a response to God's attitude to them, which, without intermediate stages, is only that of
wrath or of grace. The law of the scientific method may not be broken,
but theologically, before God, and not *humana ratione,* this law leads
to hypocrisy, to hypocritical community, and to false separations.
Preserving unity in spirit and the parting of spirits is law and cannot
be fulfilled through theological work. And this inachievable quality of
the demand of total community before God or of complete parting
before God becomes clear in the discussion about Barth: Premature
conclusion of peace—as though one could carry on theology like an
exchange of wares and did not have to discover in himself the mortal
enemy of all theology (Luther: *"qui dicit se legem diligere mentitur et
nescit, quid dicat"*—He who says he loves the law is lying and does not
know what he is saying); and premature attacks—as though the opponent were not also justified by his clinging to Christ rather than by
his theological position.

     Knowledge is law; faith is gospel. Both law and gospel are accord-
ing to Luther, *"re ipsa diversissima, longissime distincta, plus quam
contraria, alterum infernus, alterum coelum"* (in the matter itself most
diverse, furthest distinguished from each other, more than contraries,
the one inferno, the other heaven), but *"in corde, in affectu,"* they are
"conjungenda" and *"conjunctissima." "Speculative conjunguntur
facillime, sed practice ea conjungere est omnium dificillimum"* (They
are easily joined in speculation, but to join them in practice is the most
difficult thing of all), and it is impossible without *"experientia"* and
"tentatio." This struggle between heaven and hell, which is decided
only through the *"quotidianus adventus Christi"* (daily advent of
Christ), is hampered in the theological discussion of the present day by
a constant confusion of Christian and Stoic love. To wish to fulfill the
law of scientific research must necessarily lead to a community of guilt,
which completely excludes any personal ambition, all desire to be in
the right; and faith, the yielding up of thinking and being to their
complete justification through Christ, would have to lead to a struggle
in which a severing would occur that would of necessity reach not only
into a person's standing in society, but also into families, a struggle
more dangerous, deeper, more thoroughgoing than any Bolshevism;
richer, more fruitful, more liberating than all general justification of
creation through theological penetration and hope. There is nothing in

all the social relationships of the present and in all efforts to improve them that has not so far waited in vain for an active, renewing answer through the church. The pastors want to help, but, hampered by their theological training, they all attempt it with the μηδὲν ἄγαν—"not too much"—by mediation and reconciliation and consolation. The half-heartedness in dissension and half-heartedness in fellowship, characteristic of theology, continues in the pastorate, and all the sighs of the young theology students perish in resignation, which is confused with faith.

The layman has a right to ask the theologian, On what may I ground my activity, thought, and being so that it takes place in God and to God's glory? And it is the duty of the student who here must later give an account to insist ruthlessly on this question until his teachers, alone or together, but not in a general synthesis of the present state of theological science nor through well-intentioned delimitation and moderation, but with the extravagance of the divine authority bestowed on them by their office, give an answer which may unite or divide, but which does not leave him neutral. Else it were better for them to display the naïve, honorable humor which a peasant showed when he said to his neighbor about the heretic-hunting sermon of his pastor, "i müeßt aber lache, wenn jetzt mir da falsche Glaube hättet" (I would really have to laugh if we turned out to be heretics). But perhaps it would be still more advisable to practice theology even more radically until it can no longer be done without blessings or cursings, but with both, and against oneself and one's neighbor without respect of persons. One would then swallow fewer camels and strain at fewer gnats, and would progress from the theologies a step further in the direction of theology, from the churches a step further in the direction of the church, which in the midst of its foes is upheld by God through his Word, having died through law to the law, through theology to theology.

BIBLIOGRAPHY

Metzger, W. "Der Angriff Karl Barths als Kampf um die Sache." *Monatsschrift für Pastoraltheologie* (1925), 1-3.
Messer, A., in Gemmer-Messer. *Sören Kierkegaard und Karl Barth.* Stuttgart, 1925.
Oepke, A. *Karl Barth und die Mystik.* Leipzig, 1928.
Bruhn, W. *Vom Gott im Menschen,* 1926; cf. *Zwischen den Zeiten* (1927), p. 33.
Dörries, B. *Der ferne und der nahe Gott.* Gotha, 1927.
Heinzelmann. "Das Prinzip der Dialektik in der Theologie Karl Barths." *NKZ,* XXXV, 12, pp. 532-556.
Schmidt-Japing. "Die christologischen Anschauungen der dialektischen Theologie." *Apologetisches Jahrbuch* (1925).
Przywara, E. "Gott in uns oder Gott über uns." *StZ,* LIII, 11 (1923), pp. 343-362.

Adam, K. "Die Theologie der Krisis." *Hochland*, XXIII, 9, pp. 271-286.
Wobbermin. "Der Kampf um die dialektische Theologie." *ChW* (1928), No. 3-4;
    "Gott und der Glaube gehören zu Haufe." *ZThK* (1928), No. 1, pp. 51 ff. Cf.
    (1927), 4, pp. 251 ff.
Traub, Fr. "Karl Barths Dogmatik." *MPTh* (1928).
Knappe, W. "Karl Barth und der Pietismus." *Licht und Leben*, XXXIX, No. 30-34.
Krüger, Gustav. "The Theology of Crisis." *HThR* (1926).
Strauch. *Die Theologie Karl Barths*. München.
Burckhardt, P. *Was sagt uns die Theologie Karl Barths und seiner Freunde?* Basel,
    1927.
Haitjema, Th. L. *Karl Barths "kritische" Theologie*. Wageningen, 1926.
Ritschl, O. *ThLZ*, LIII, 10 (May 12, 1928).
Kolfhaus, W. *Die Botschaft des Karl Barth*. 1927.
RGG, 2nd ed., I, Col. 1914 (includes a bibliography).
Heim, Karl. *Glaube und Leben*, 2nd ed. Berlin, Furche Verlag (foreword).
Kattenbusch, F. *Die deutsche evangelische Theologie seit Schleiermacher*, 5th ed.
    Giessen, 1926.

PART II

Christianity and Culture

1

Rudolf Bultmann

RELIGION AND CULTURE

ETHICAL AND MYSTICAL RELIGION
IN PRIMITIVE CHRISTIANITY

THE PROBLEM OF A THEOLOGICAL EXEGESIS
OF THE NEW TESTAMENT

THE QUESTION OF "DIALECTIC" THEOLOGY:
A DISCUSSION WITH PETERSON

RELIGION AND CULTURE*

Rudolf Bultmann

In political controversies the significance of "religion as a cultural factor" is sometimes sharply contested and sometimes even more sharply asserted. The evidence of history seems to speak in favor of its cultural significance; the important developments of culture had their origins in religion, or at least were very closely connected with it. The same is certainly true for the history of science. All primitive explanations of the world are religious; the schemes of the religious imagination answer the questions of the awakening reason about cosmic processes and the remarkable processes of human life. An understandable explanation of the world is inseparably bound to the answers given by the religious imagination to such questions as what thunder and lightning are, how things grow, where sleep and sickness come from, and what birth and death mean. Science was originally the prerogative of the priestly caste; theology, as well as astronomy, originated in their circles; and the reckoning of time and the establishment of the calendar are traced back to them. Systematic-scientific motifs came into existence at the instigation of the cult. Primitive mathematics, as well as medicine, had religious origins; the origin of literature would have to be located in religious circles; the beginnings of historical work arose in the gathering of ancient traditions in sacred documents. The Middle Ages of our own culture, seen in the clearer light of history, offer the same picture, in principle, as the rise of ancient culture. One hardly needs to be reminded of how medieval culture grew under the protection of the church. Philosophy and the discipline of history arose within the framework of theology; universities and schools were born for ecclesiastical purposes and were nurtured by the spirit of the church.

It is no different in the history of art. Primitive ornamentation was religious in its design to keep away the evil spirits or secure healing powers. Veneration of the dead and the cultic sites were the occasion for artistic display; temples and representations of the deities emerged. Thus, when we think of ancient art, it is natural that works of religious art come most readily to mind. It is the same with Byzantine or medieval art. The cult with its dances and songs, and war—whose original function was religious in character—with its martial tunes,

* From *Die Christliche Welt*, XXXIV (1920), issue 27, columns 417-421; issue 28, columns 435-439; issue 29, columns 450-453.

were both important in the origin of music. The practice of music was also an exercise of the priestly caste; one has only to think of the Levites in the Old Testament. Oratorios and masses by such composers as Bach, Handel, Bruckner, and Reger remind us of the significance of church music for modern compositions. What the rest of ancient literature contains for us demonstrates a religious character almost throughout. A primitive poetic art originated in the formulas of the cult and incantation. The Old Testament Psalms show how lyric grows out of cult, just as is true for Greek lyric. Greek drama was born out of the cult of Dionysius, and remember how important that is! Every new beginning of drama in the Middle Ages was fostered by the ecclesiastical sphere; the mystery play has its roots in this realm. Need names be given again? "Aeschylus will live in eternity as one of the most exalted religious poets" (Wilamowitz); without ecclesiastical culture Dante is unthinkable, as is Wolfram von Eschenbach, and even Goethe's *Faust*.

Finally, the history of morality. In primitive peoples the concepts "good" and "evil" were very closely connected with the religious concepts "pure" and "impure." Rite and holy law played such a role in the development of moral consciousness that on a more developed cultural level they are often irredeemably confused with moral concepts. And even where the characteristic features of moral consciousness began to make themselves felt, God still remained the Giver and Protector of moral law; Holy Scriptures were the code of justice, and "morally good" and "pious" were often considered identical. The moral movement of prophecy was born out of religious experience and belief. Medieval Catholicism performed its cultural work of moral education in the form of religious-ecclesiastical tutelage.

It would be wrong, however, to judge the relation of religion and culture on the basis of history as such, for history also teaches us that the emancipation of culture from religion occurs in all areas of intellectual life. Consider the history of science. The real flowering of science in our cultural sphere occurred in Ionia; when the Ionians left their native soil, the close tie between their intellectual life and their religion was loosened or cut. Subsequently Greek natural science and philosophy originated and scientific prose emerged. And in the narrower circle of our modern culture, science always flowers where it knows itself emancipated from the church and self-sufficient: mathematical natural science, the philosophy of the Enlightenment, and German Idealism all stemmed from the great intellectual movements of Humanism and the Enlightenment. The role played by pagan antiquity in this development is characteristic. And how entirely free modern science, as well as medicine and technology, is from religious-ecclesiastical motivations and tendencies needs no further comment.

The development of art is again parallel. Even if we acknowledge the pictorial art of antiquity as essentially religious, further reflection shows this to be merely external, a matter of origin; in its essence it was secular. The forms of the deities in classical Greek art lost their divinity; God became a beautified man. High Renaissance art, which furnished the motifs for the ecclesiastical sphere, demonstrates the same thing. In Realism also, where representation of man as beautiful triumphed over the stylization of Byzantine and early Italian art, the object of art became man, in his worldly feeling for life and his functional existence. Impressionism, which dominates the scene to our day, makes very clear how this is correspondingly valid for modern pictorial art. And even if religious motifs do appear in the most recent development of expressionism, one still cannot say this art serves religious or, in any sense, cultic purposes; this art is not judged by its religious content, but by its sense of form. One needs no protracted arguments to show how modern music has become secular in opera and song, as well as in instrumental music, and also to show that the concert hall and not the church is the main place of musical enjoyment. Ionia offers the classical example in poetic art of the emancipation of poetry, as well as science, from religion. In Homeric poetry the forms of pious belief have become the forms of aesthetic drama; true, lyric poetry and drama originated in the cult, but their laws and meaning were discovered in the representations or self-representations of man. It is no different in modern poetry.

Though morality was perhaps most closely associated with religion, it also has become emancipated. With the feeling for a secular national and working community which appeared in the ancient cultures alongside the feeling for cultic solidarity, there grew up among the people a treasury of secular wisdom that had no connection with the rules of holy rite. The ancient Orient demonstrates this process, as well as antiquity (again Ionian), from which comes the "Sayings of the Seven Sages." With the rise of the secular state there developed, alongside the unsystematic popular morality, a consciousness of the laws of good intentions and secular law with its secular demands for justice. The issue finds its clearest expression in the conflict which arose between moral and religious thinking in this development. The Old Testament manifestation of this conflict is found in the matter of retaliation: The behavior of the deity (and man must indeed view his earthly destiny as governed by deity) does not conform to the demands of moral consciousness, of justice. Just as the conflict achieves its peculiar Israelite form in the book of Job, so it reaches its peculiar Hellenistic form with the Greek tragedians, Aeschylus and Euripides—it is the struggle with the inhumane demands and ideas of a long-standing belief in God, or the protest against these demands and ideas from the standpoint of humanistic morality. This inner conflict has assumed its most powerful form in Aeschylus' *Orestes*. In modern culture, with the exception, perhaps, of the Protestant Reformation, the emancipation of morality from religion was accomplished without such a conflict. In any case, in the Enlightenment, in Kant, and in the life of modern law and the State, the secular ethic has more and more achieved the upper hand.

Thus the autonomy of intellectual culture has been one of the consequences of historical development. Science is autonomous; that is, its statements are guided by its own laws of scientific thinking and not by a sacred revelation or tradition. It is without presuppositions. Naturally, that does not mean it is unmethodical—its methodology is basic to its work; it means rather that science has not allowed itself to accept presuppositions for its mode of operation and its results from an entity outside itself (in our context, religion). Although many individual researchers are dependent on or influenced by the ecclesiastical or religious tradition, the statements of science are not validated by such associations, but only by being grounded in the scientific system of thought. Thus, the secular and autonomous character of science is evident in the fact that it counts on natural explanation and historical investigation without supernatural factors. And art is autonomous; that is, its representations are to be measured by the laws of artistic form, not by extra-artistic purposes. Morality is autonomous; after Kant, there was nothing more to be said; but so much confusion developed in the conflict over the relation of church and State that morality required religion, or whatever other discipline would claim it, to give grounding to moral education. The legislation of morality is engendered by the rational will itself. God is not the giver of moral law; what then would be the criterion for the knowledge of God's will? Tradition perhaps? That would be only the expression of the moral insights of earlier generations, and since it is used only selectively and critically, the last resort would still be one's own moral judgment. Perhaps revelation? But which one? The individual conscience? That would be nothing but the self-legislation of the rational will, and thus not a religious insight, but an entirely secular one. The pious man may trace his rational endowment back to God in this respect as well as in all others; but that does not alter the fact that in man's use of his reason, it is not God who speaks to him. However, the view which makes God into the protector of moral law, needed by religion for the motivation of moral behavior, has not yet attained the concept of the moral sphere at all, as the following indicates: "I do not wish to decide whether in this connection the most contempt is directed against law and morality, which need such a support, or against religion, which should support them" (pp. 18 f.).[1] ". . . for I must only admit that I do not believe the situation is so hopeless concerning the unjust dealings, which it [religion] hinders, and moral dealings, which it is said to engender" (p. 21). The primary influence in the formation of the will is not religion, but the development of moral judgment, and primarily the training in communal life.

One may even reverse the assertion that religion is a force for the fostering of culture. Religion has not infrequently hindered the development of intellectual culture. The relation of primitive Christianity to antique culture is well known. The early church was a historical entity rich enough and complex enough to sustain many aspects in the continuity of culture; but primitive Christianity was essentially alien to culture and obstructed it not only in the area of science and art but also in law and morality. One cannot overemphasize the fact that primitive Christianity was a specifically religious movement, not an ethical one. It brought with it no new ethical ideal; the Christian commandment to love, insofar as it is an ethical demand and not a rule of communal religious life, brought nothing new, nothing which could not have been expressed in the ethic of antiquity at its best. Primitive Christianity had no organ for dealing with the specifically ethical problems, such as law, social community (the slavery question), the relation of the sexes, and so on. It is Stoicism which deserves the credit for having dealt with all these problems and having made them a part of the life of Western culture. One could think of the religious demands of the vendetta (Orestes), of excommunication (1 Sam. 15), of religious wars and the persecution of heretics, of the denominational divisions in our modern cultural life, and of the serious hindrance these divisions constitute to the development of education, art, law, and the State.

The contrast is seen most clearly in a consideration of the essence of culture and religion. Culture is the methodical unfolding of human reason in its three realms—the theoretical, the practical, and the aesthetic. Thus the activity of the human spirit is essential for culture; it is this spirit which builds the three worlds of culture: science, law and morality, and art. The development of culture continues on methodically; that is, all its manifestations have the character of necessity and general validity. It may be true that the contingent and personal aspect, the moment of inspiration, intuition, and such, play as great a role in the history of culture as the psychic dimension from which the forms of culture emerge. But it is not through the association with their psychic source that these contingent and personal aspects establish their rights as cultural entities; it is in their connection with what is rational and predictable. The Pythagorean theorem bears the name of its founder, but its accuracy is guaranteed not by the authority or character of Pythagoras, but only by its conformity to mathematical laws. The sculpture of ancient classical art is effective, even without our knowing the least bit about its creators, because the language of its form convinces our aesthetic judgment. A good deed is considered good not because of the psychic condition that infused it with life, but solely on the basis of the idea of the good. Thus, the essence of culture has a supra-individualistic character; the individual figures only as a point of transition into the self-unfolding of the supra-individual spirit. Cultural manifestations have their validity only in their content, totally apart from their actual realization.

In all three realms religion shows its contrast to culture. Following Schleiermacher, I would say religion is the feeling of absolute dependence; to avoid a psychological interpretation and misunderstanding, it is perhaps better to say it is the consciousness of absolute dependence. It all depends on proper comprehension of the notion of "absolute." We cannot speak of the dependence of the slave as absolute, because his real being, his most inward self, cannot necessarily be subjected, even by the most powerful master. Neither does "absolute" mean the thousandfold dependence of modern man, educated by natural science, who realizes that he is bound and imprisoned in his corporeal and intellectual life by the order of nature, since pure order allows no inner flexibility; it is precisely against this exacting demand that the self rebels. Absolute dependence is possible only where man encounters a power to which his inner being unfolds itself freely, into whose arms he throws himself in freedom and release, to whom he subjects himself in open self-surrender. If religion is such absolute dependence, it is the opposite of the creative-active behavior of spirit; for absolute dependence consists not of creating, but of receiving what is given (in which again, the psychic condition of the experiencing individual, very active indeed in individual experience, must remain entirely out of consideration).* It is profoundly and exquisitely expressed in the inscription on the Holy Grail in Immermann's "Merlin":

---

* One should not be led into a confusion of religion and morality by the fact that the moral injunction demands devotion, abandon, and sacrifice; it demands these as an act. Moral commitment is an act in the most exalted sense. It is entirely different from dependence in religious experience.

Ich habe mich nach eignem Recht gegründet,
Vergebens sucht ihr mich.
Der Wandrer, welcher meinen Tempel findet,
Den suchte ich!

I based my life on my own rights,
In vain ye seek me.
The wanderer who finds my temple
Was sought by me!

The knowledge and concepts of religion are not universally valid
or necessary concepts, but have only individual validity. According
to Schleiermacher, the origin of religion must always be provided
by a "legend" (p. 230). It would be folly to claim that, "Little by little
man should become religious, just as he becomes intelligent, understanding, and whatever else he becomes; all this should come to him
through education; nothing supernatural or strange should be included" (p. 232). "If a particular religion does not begin with a fact
(that is, with something accidental), it cannot begin at all" (p. 234).
Thus the basic difference from culture becomes clear: Religion is not
available in objective formulations as is culture, but only in being
realized; that is, in that which happens with the individual. The meaning of religion is the being, the life, of the individual.

What was previously said about the autonomy of culture is illustrated still more clearly by religion. Religion is neutral in relation
to the manifestations of culture; it is neutral in relation to science.
Science may consist of the natural correspondence of its statements,
but religion knows nothing of this. "It stays with the direct experiences
of the being [Dasein] and activity of the universe, with individual
outlooks and feelings; each religious experience is a work existing for
itself without association with other experiences or dependence on
them. It knows nothing of derivation and connection; among all the
things it encounters it strives most against this correspondence" (p.
53). "Philosophy indeed strives to bring those who wish to be informed
to a common knowledge . . . religion, however, does not strive to bring
those who believe and feel to one belief and one feeling" (p. 55). Religious instruction, which desires to educate one toward a religion or
into a religion, is therefore as senseless and impossible as a philosophy
of religion. For its legitimate subject could be only assertions, that is,
objectifications of religious experiences, but religion itself is never
such objectification.

Religion is neutral also in relation to art. Art consists of forms,
the objectifications of experience; religion is nothing but the experience itself. And no matter how powerfully the religious experience
may move the artist to attempt its formulation, what makes these

formulations into art is still only the form that corresponds to aesthetic principles. A work of art as a work of art is not religious, and neither does aesthetic pleasure lead to religion.

Religion is neutral also in relation to morality, as Schleiermacher inexhaustibly argues in the *Speeches*. "Its [religion's] feelings should possess us; we should express them, hold on to them, embody them. If, however, you wish to progress beyond this with them, they will give occasion for real deeds and move us to action. Having done this, you will find yourself in a strange area; and if you think nevertheless that this area is religion (as rational and commendable as that may appear), then you are sunk in unholy superstition. All real activity should be moral, and it can be, but religious feelings should accompany all man's actions like sacred music; he should do everything *with* religion, nothing on the basis of religion" (p. 59). "This entire misunderstanding that religion should be active can be nothing but frightful abuse, and it can end only in unwholeness and destruction wherever this activity turns. But peaceful activity, arising out of the source peculiar to religious souls—that is the goal of the pious man" (p. 60). "Who hinders the prospering of religion? Not the doubters and the scorners—although they eagerly induce a disinclination to religion, they do not disturb nature which strives to effect religion. And, contrary to opinion, neither do those who are immoral; their activity is directed against an entirely different force. It is rather the reasonable and practical men of the present day who are the counterweight to religion, and their great preponderance is the reason why it plays such a petty and insignificant role" (p. 125). "Religion knows nothing of such a partisan preference (for the moral); the moral world is not the religious universe; and what is valid only for morality cannot serve religion as a world view. In everything which belongs to human activity, in play as well as in serious matters, in small as well as in large, religion discovers and traces the activity of the world spirit" (p. 84). Indeed, this is said not only for both play and serious matters, but also for both immoral and moral actions. This relation becomes very clear when one realizes that even the "immoral" man may be a religious hero. Such persons as Augustine and Mohammed come to mind. It is also expressed in the principle involved in the location of the Grail in Immermann's "Merlin":

> Die Schelmenlist,
> Das höchste Kleinod für den Pfennig "Tugend"
> Sich zu erhandeln, hier verrufen ist,
> Auf Monsalvatsch gibts wilde, freche Jugend,
> Auf Monsalvatsch geraten kühne Sünder:
> Sigun', Amfortas, eitle Lüste suchend!

The scoundrels' cunning,
To trade the rarest jewel for the penny "Virtue,"
Is here in disrepute.
On Monsalvatsch are wild, fresh youths,
On Monsalvatsch clever sinners thrive:
Sigun', Amfortas, seeking worthless pleasure.

It is thus entirely self-evident that religion is a private matter and has nothing to do with the State. "There can be no question of whether a priestly (that is, religious) man can represent his religion with the taste and vigor due it, and at the same time faithfully and adequately carry on a secular business. Thus, why should anyone who makes priesthood his profession (precisely, the representation of the religious life), not be permitted, if he be so gifted, to be a moralist in the service of the State? There is nothing to prohibit it—only he must be both, side by side, not one in and through the other.[2] He must not bear both natures in himself simultaneously and both businesses ought not be performed in the same activity. Let the State content itself with a religious morality if it will. But religion disowns all moralizing prophets and priests; whoever wishes to preach should do it unfeignedly" (p. 173). ". . . after it [the State] has established its institution of moral education, as it must by all means do, let it allow them [the "priests"] to cultivate the essence of religion for themselves and not concern itself with the priestly tasks which are performed within its territory, since the State actually needs them for neither display nor use, unlike the other arts and sciences. Away then with any such connection between church and State!—that will be my Catonic counsel until the last or until I live to see it really demolished—away with everything which even resembles a closed association of laymen and priests, separately or together" (p. 174). The ideal is not, in fact, the institution of a well-organized church, which includes all citizens, a people's church, but rather small, active communities, free churches, above which is the one, invisible, true church, to which all the truly pious belong. Schleiermacher ascribes all evil to the state church. "You are right to wish that the hem of a priestly garment would never have touched the floor of a royal room; but let us only wish that the purple would never have kissed the dust on the altar; had the latter not happened, the former would not have followed" (p. 167). "Whenever a prince made the church into a fraternity, into a community with its own prerogatives, fit for a respectable person in the middle-class world —whenever, I say, a prince let himself be misled to this most dangerous and corrupt deed, it was then that the corruption of the church was irrevocably introduced and determined. That horrible Medusa head then forces the religious community into the mold of political existence . . . The necessary distinction between the larger, artificial community and the smaller, truer community can no longer be made . . . in such a large community, form and article of faith can no longer be altered; the views, customs, and everything else are condemned to continue just as they are. And that is not all—the members of the true church, included in this larger community, are as good as thrust out of every part of its government from now on, excluded from doing even the least bit which may still be done for it" (pp. 167 f.). Had the State consigned religious life to religion itself, then "the members of the true church would have continued to be able to undertake their priestly office amongst themselves in new and better forms. Each group would have gathered to itself those who understand it; with these people, who accepted the common method, the result would have been most effective. Instead of a monstrous organization . . . a large number of smaller and looser communities would have arisen . . . O golden age of religion, when will the upheavals of human concerns bring you about, since you have not been met on the simple path of nature! Happy are those who are then called! . . . Would that all heads of State, all political virtuosos and artists, had always remained strangers to even the remotest inkling of religion! . . . For there is the source of all our corruption!" (pp. 166 f.).

This reflection on the nature of religion and culture and their mutual relation is brought to its conclusion by a renewed glance at history. Intellectual history exists only as the history of science, morality, and art, as a presentation of the flowering of reason in the struggle with the natural and the material. In contrast, there is no history of religion. If the religious life is to be found not in objective formulations, but in individual life, there cannot be a history of religion. The moments of religious experience form no orderly correspondence, neither causally nor teleologically. They do not develop cumulatively or in a single direction, so that one generation could solve a religious problem for the next, and new problems develop organically like the statements of mathematics or law or art. In religion there are no problems in this sense, but always only one and the same "problem," which must be solved ever anew individually—to find the power in relation to which free self-devotion is possible. Religious experiences do not stand in a developmental relation to one another; either they are there or not, and they are always fundamentally the same. There can be no history of religion, just as there can be no history of such mental events as trust, friendship, and love, since their essence is not available in objectification or in representation but only in their fulfillment, in realization, in action. No man would think of writing a history of trust. One may think it possible to write a history of religion since religious experience, like all experience, leads to representations, concepts, institutions, and works of art, the history of which may in fact be written. But these objectifications are not religion; they merely are its evidence, and they form a historical continuity only within the history of culture, not as religious history. Thus, the so-called history of religion in the field of primitive anthropology is actually nothing but the history of primitive science, art, and morality; in more developed cultures it becomes the history of developing science, morality, law, politics, and art. The history of dogma and the history of the medieval church come particularly to mind. Or one could observe what a minor role religion and its life play in the usual formulations of church history; in fact, the role of religion appears only with the presentation of particular personalities—an indication that religion exists only in the existence of individual life.

If, by the term "cultural factor," one understands an intellectual force created by history and existing in the objective representations of culture, then religion is not a cultural factor, and the history of intellectual culture can be written as thematic history without regard to religion. However, if the natural force of religion is considered a cultural factor, that is, the force which sets in motion human life in general and which leads to the creation of cultural aspects, then passions such as covetousness and love are cultural factors too; thus, hunger and sickness, crime and war, also become justified as cultural factors. In fact, a few years ago, such justifications were made. Or is there some other criterion to justify religion to culture?

Man is not only a rational creature, but also a creature of nature. Intellectual culture as a whole is not only occasioned by nature, but has meaning only in relation to nature. The relation of science to nature is essential, not in the sense that science would never have arisen without the struggle for being and would cease without this struggle as a result of man's indolence, but because science would be meaningless without this relation; its meaning lies in the conquest of experience. It is possible perhaps to do mathematics without any relation to nature; but even mathematics becomes meaningful only in association with theoretical science as a whole, which has as its object the regulation of experience. Morality ceases if there is no longer a natural-material world for whose organization it prescribes the goal. All activity is related to nature, all will to resistance, and therefore, all judgment which has to do with the regularity of acts of willing is also related to nature. Similarly, art has no meaning without relation to the natural-material world. There is no pictorial art without stone or color, no music without tones of instruments or human voices, no poetry without the natural sound of words. In spite of the fact that the realization of the artistic idea in material form is inadequate, the idea always tends toward its material realization; the essence of art, that is, is to be found in the material realization of the idea.

It must be added, however, that there are individuals who experience this relation of culture and nature in themselves. We do not mean that they would not participate in culture if nature did not force them into the midst of the struggle for being, but that they can be creatures of culture only as they are creatures of nature. Just as the content of intellectual culture cannot prove its justification and truthfulness through the fact that it is realized, although it could not exist otherwise, so the individual may, or even must, not only be considered as a transition point in rational self-unfolding, but must see that something happens in him as he participates in intellectual culture—he becomes something, namely, a living self. We are not merely creatures of nature, but the stronger and more elemental our creaturely nature is, the richer is our inner life. Our being as individuals whose content is constantly determined by the tension between the poles of nature and culture becomes much deeper and richer in content (unlike the conflict in the ascetic world view, in which nature is to be overcome and destroyed). Without intellectual culture we remain like animals in the natural life of instinct. But without nature, intellectual life becomes meaningless for us; without nature, we have no tensions, no experiences, no living self.

In these tensions man experiences his destiny; or rather, his destiny is offered to him in them. For the question is whether he can make the events in which he is placed his own inner possession, whether, that is, he can acknowledge them as his destiny and see in them a unified, meaningful, dominant power, or whether they are confusing, entangling, meaningless events against which he must struggle and within which he encloses himself. If he knows moments when an abundance of life accrues to him in such a tension, then he experiences such abundance as a gift. For this life is neither nature nor a methodically created representation. In this acceptance of the gift lies the paradox in which the self renounces entirely its own strength and activity, and nevertheless feels that only in such subjection does its own life become free, that it remains honest and achieves greatness only in such submission and subjection. This experience of being able to open oneself to such a gift is the experience of absolute dependence, of free self-surrender, the hour of the birth of religion. In this respect all experience is religious; it becomes religion in the real sense when it becomes conscious of the law of life and enjoys it, when it inwardly experiences a power which desires and brings about such a destiny for the self and which the self experiences as the power over everything real. In this respect religion is the "intuition of the universe," as Schleiermacher says in his *Speeches;* the real is not grasped like a system of rationally conceived order, but a point beyond the world of experience is achieved, from which everything real appears in meaningful unity. Lagarde's dictum that "to have religion" means "to find the plan of God in one's life" says the same thing. We are not thinking here of the experiences or illusions of a childish faith in providence, such as the Jung-Stillings type, or of falsely edifying tracts, but of the ability to grasp the power in one's destiny which makes and enriches and enlivens the self, which releases it from nature and from striving after itself. To have religion can also mean a man's taking his destiny into himself, identifying himself with his destiny. It is obvious how the meaning and power of this divine life are experienced as other-worldly in relation to both nature and culture; in fact, the religious notion of other-worldly first becomes clear here. It is also obvious how natural it is that the striving for a metaphysic so easily adapts itself again and again to the religious life—obvious, too, why a metaphysic is impossible. It might be asked whether Kant's postulate that the world of experience must be determined according to the moral idea has its most profound meaning in the fact that the connection of the natural world and intellectual culture is meaningful for the individual.

Only one who stands in both worlds can have religion. It is not the level of culture which is presupposed, but participation in culture and being rooted in the life-forces of nature. The period unilaterally dominated by intellectual culture was followed by a reaction in which the elemental forces of nature, from which the self is nourished, asserted their right—more strongly put, the self, whose own original and mysterious nature threatened to perish in culture, asserted its right. Romanticism followed the Enlightenment; we notice today the setting in of a reaction against the period of modern scientific culture and historicism. This reaction is primarily in art, which reverts to the Gothic period as more congenial because it reaches out over the cultural world into a beyond which can fill the self with mysterious powers and give it a feeling for its own life.

Religion can seldom be a peaceful possession, since it represents the epitome of experience.

> Falle nicht, Gott, aus deinem Gleichgewicht.
> Auch der dich liebt, und der dein Angesicht
> erkennt im Dunkel, wenn er wie ein Licht

in deinem Atem schwankt,—besitzt dich nicht.
Und wenn dich einer in der Nacht erfaßt,
so dass du kommen mußt in sein Gebet:
        du bist der Gast,
        der wieder weitergeht.

Fall not, O God, from your serene estate.
The one who loves you, who knows your face
In darkness, when like a light
He flickers before your breath; even he does not possess you.
And in the night if one lays hold of you,
So that you come in answer to his prayer:
        You are the guest,
        Who travels on again.

These lines from Rilke hold true not only for a certain kind of "mysticism," as one would perhaps like to say disparagingly, but, in honesty, for all religious life. The peace of trust may well accompany the pious man and its warmth may pervade his entire life. But real religion is available only in the moments of experience, and we alternate between believing thoughts and operational thoughts. The greatest part of the religious life consists, nevertheless, in a yearning, in the drive which forces us beyond the reality of nature and culture, which form, admittedly, the major content of our conscious life. Consequently, religion is sometimes ascetic, at odds with nature and sometimes with culture itself. It lives always in the drive for experience, for inward fulfillment, sometimes as a desire for home and peace, for release from conflict and tension, and sometimes as a thirst for deep emotional experiences. In moments such as these the only real meaning of "living" is to be brought to nothing by the overwhelming power of the highest Lord. Instincts are the source of a constant, ardent longing—the longing to feel the justification and meaning of the self, and, as the self is neither a merely natural creature nor the subject of intellectual culture, it becomes certain of the reality of its life only in experience. Our inner life thrives on paradox; tensions are essential to it; a "perfect" man cannot have religion at all.

        Is religion a cultural factor? In the sense just described, it certainly is; it is, in fact, a cultural factor of the strongest kind. Without the force of experience, culture would be meaningless; thus, it is not really religion which is vindicated in the eyes of culture, but culture which is vindicated by religion. Man does not exist for the sake of culture, but culture for the sake of man. What makes man a man is the power of religion, the longing for experience, the power of experience, the faith to grasp reality in experience, and the faith to grow into the reality which carries one beyond all the joys and sorrows of the tension between nature and culture, the reality which enriches and enlivens the self.

The danger of all culture is that it idolizes and absolutizes one particular cultural position, and thus empties man's self. Culture becomes devoid of content and poor in experience, and it flees, as it were, from itself in order to quiet the voice of its longing; it becomes an end in itself in order to exempt itself from the question of its own meaning and purpose. It believes in humanity without men; it desires to make humanity happy by "by-passing and overstepping the individual" (Werfel). The power of religion is "the total contrast to the belief that one may help humanity over the head of man." What would it help man to gain all of culture and still corrupt his soul! Reaction to the idolizing of culture has gained profound expression in writers such as Dostoevsky and Franz Werfel. The fact of Communism urges the consideration upon us all; in its intellectual leaders, however, Communism appears to be a protest against the idolizing of culture, and the justification of Communism lies in its negation of any particular dimension of culture as absolute. In this respect it stands in sharp contrast to Social Democracy, which rejects it instinctively because Social Democracy tends toward the absolutizing of culture. The error of Communism, if I understand it correctly, lies in its misjudgment that the real meaning of culture is not a condition but a direction, an "ideal norm which exalts itself as such over every level of its development actually attained in practical experience"; it errs also in the misjudgment that culture in this sense necessarily belongs to human intellectual life, that, without culture, the self becomes just as devoid of content as if it were absolutized. From the standpoint of culture, we certainly have reason to desire continuity in culture; from the standpoint of religion, we have no such reason. If the eschatology of primitive Christianity was an expression of the unworldliness of religion, then Communism today (apart, of course, from its fellow travelers, who are interested in it only from the standpoint of economics) will be the strongest expression of the yearning for religious rebirth. It cannot be overcome through force (who knows whether it will bring the entire world into subjection?), but through recognition its inner validity. Communism can bring us to a full awareness that an absolutizing of culture destroys men; furthermore, it tells us that man, in order to gain his soul, must be ready to sacrifice not only the whole world, but all culture as well.

Only a religious rebirth can save us, can preserve us from despair over the catastrophe of our culture, can lift us above it, and give us courage for the future. We must devote our strength to an all-out effort to rebuild the State; the State cannot help us here. It can do nothing for religion but leave it to its freedom, and remain aware of its own inability to comprehend and fulfill the whole life of man. In the State all cultural work and values are actually subsumed. But there is something higher than culture for the individual; the realization of his life and happiness is not something obtained by working—it can only be received as a gift. Experiencing something is superior to creating something.

NOTES

1. Friedrich Schleiermacher, *Reden*. Quoted material is our translation. Page numbers refer to *On Religion: Speeches to Its Cultured Despisers,* translated by John Oman (New York: Harper & Brothers, 1958).

2. Cf. what Herrmann said on occasion about the alternation of belief, concepts, and operational concepts.

ETHICAL AND MYSTICAL RELIGION IN PRIMITIVE CHRISTIANITY*

Lecture held on September 29, 1920, at Wartburg

Rudolf Bultmann

I. HISTORICAL PRESENTATION

A. THE ANCIENT HISTORICAL PICTURE AND ITS DISSOLUTION

The first thorough attempt at a historical understanding of primitive Christianity was that of F. C. Baur; in spite of modifications in its details it has until recently dominated all presentations of the history of early Christianity, customarily called "New Testament theology." The dominant concern was to comprehend the history of primitive Christianity as a unified, linear development in three stages, characterized respectively by Jesus, Paul, and John. One can recognize, to be sure, many alien influences, complications, and modifications, but they all take their place on this unified line of development.

According to this approach, the spiritual content of the message of Jesus, consciously developed and formulated in Paul and continued in John, is the essence of the Christian religion. The content of the Christian religion (understood primarily as an antithesis to Judaism) is a purely spiritual, universalistic belief in God, in which all cultic and ceremonial institutions and all legal and national bonds are abolished. In this piety, God is the holy one who wills the good, the law of the good, and, at the same time, the Father of the person who affirms the good with his whole will. The pious man finds God if he desires the good; in fact, he finds God also when his conscience condemns him—then he experiences God as the forgiving power of grace (disclosed in Jesus), which judges sin and saves the sinner.

---

* From *Die Christliche Welt*, XXXIV (1920), issue 46, columns 725-736; issue 47, columns 738-743.

Man finds God in his moral will, and in his belief in God he fulfills his role as a moral personality; the love of God becomes actual and experiential in loving your neighbor. Thus, being a child of God is at once a gift and a task, and the new life is already present in love. Whether the emphasis falls more on the active side, where *doing* the will of God makes one a child of God, or on the passive side, where forgiving grace certifies one as a child of God, a concept of God and man which is essentially based upon ethical categories underlies it; Baur and Ritschl agree completely on this point, and also that the interpretation of the "Kingdom of God" in the message of Jesus corresponds to this ethical view. The central point of Paul's position, the doctrine of justification, is also understood in this way.

This view of history was already undermined to some extent by various observations, but the consequences were not immediately apparent. In examining the history of the early church it became clear that a completely different kind of factor appeared in the history of the Christian religion—Hellenism; certainly since Harnack's *History of Dogma*, everyone has been aware of this factor. Harnack once showed in an article[1] that Paul's doctrine of justification had no effect at all in the early church, and up to the time of Augustine was either misunderstood or expressed in half-understood formulas. Harnack, however, always expressed the view that the gospel of Jesus operated as the constitutive factor in the history of the early church. In contrast, Loeschcke has shown in outline form that the influence of the gospel in the early church was very slight.[2]

But when do the Hellenistic factors begin to take effect? It was recognized early that the Gospel of John in the New Testament indicates strong influences of Hellenistic piety, but this did not disturb the picture of a unified development. It is also true that here and there in Paul one can observe the influence of Hellenistic thought, mood, and forms of expression; but these too had no far-reaching consequences. Really, Wrede's *Paulus* (1905) was the first work to express a fundamentally new view. Wrede saw the uncanny, gaping rift between Jesus and Paul with intense clarity. In his presentation of Pauline theology the doctrine of justification was expelled from the center and relegated to an appendix as apologetic or polemic; the foreground was occupied by ideas of mythical and mystical character. Although Wrede's presentation met with almost complete opposition at first, it was all the more important since it was drafted at a time when research into the history of religion was only beginning to be applied to the New Testament.[3]

The new epoch begins with the energetic investigation of Hel-

lenism and its enrichment of New Testament study from the approach
of history of religion. The chief credit for this belongs to Reitzenstein
and Wendland, among the philologists, and Bousset and Heitmüller,
among the theologians; it is primarily Bousset's brilliant work *Kyrios
Christos* (1913) which allows an entirely new picture of history to
emerge. His view of the difference between Jesus and Paul is, in fact,
similar to Wrede's. But the transition in primitive Christianity is
already evident *before* Paul, at the same time that Christian preaching
moved from Palestinian to Hellenistic ground. Paul stepped into an
already existing primitive Hellenistic Christianity. This situation
(quite apart from his individuality and significance) provides the presupposition for Paul's Christianity, and his fundamental intuitions
can be understood only on the basis of this presupposition. It is almost
incomprehensible to us now how anyone (especially in the "Jesus and
Paul" debate instigated by Wrede) could have ignored the Hellenistic
congregation.

To be sure, one scholar, Jülicher, reminded us of the congregation
as a fact;[4] but it was the Palestinian congregation. Indeed it deserves
more attention than it has previously received. The analysis of the
Synoptic Gospels has shown more and more clearly (especially since
Wellhausen) how little we know for certain about Jesus and to what
extent the Gospels are primarily the testimony of the Palestinian
congregation. Above all one should not compare persons, but congregations—primitive Palestinian and Hellenistic Christian.

I must here pass over methodological considerations as merely
preliminary and partial questions, and will present the problem only
in terms of four examples.

B. The Status of the Historical Problem

The Narration of the Life of Jesus

Separate fragments such as words and conversations of Jesus
and stories of miracles were handed down in the Palestinian congregation. Jesus appears in them as the eschatological preacher of repentance and the prophet of the coming rule of God, as a teacher of
wisdom and a rabbi. On Palestinian soil, there were collections (catechism fashion) of individual fragments, but not of a unified "life of
Jesus." Such a unity was first created by the Christ myth of the Hellenistic congregation, for whom the life of Jesus was the epiphany of
the heavenly Son of God and thus a unity. The first known attempt
at such a presentation using Palestinian materials is the Gospel of
Mark. It is true that the life of Jesus appears here against the back-

ground of myth, but the myth has also created separate new fragments, such as the stories of the baptism and transfiguration, and Matthew 11:27, among others. Finally, in the Gospel of John, the Palestinian material is almost completely supplanted; Jesus appears as the God-man; his earthly life is the revelation of the heavenly Logos for those who are able to discern it. Outside the New Testament, the Odes of Solomon are a characteristic example of how the myth of lordship has prevailed in the figure of Jesus. One must clarify how, even until recent times, it was not the historical Jesus, the "religion of Jesus," which was operative in the church, but essentially the Christ myth—as modern piety, in part, prefers, in opposition to the historical Jesus of "liberal theology." That myth is a creation of Hellenistic Christianity, whereas "liberal theology" reaches back to the Palestinian tradition.

The Kyrios Cult

The cultic Christ is very closely connected with the Christ of myth. The Palestinian congregation as yet knew no such thing as a cult; they knew no such name as "Lord" for Christ, since they had created no cult whatsoever. For them Jesus was prophet and teacher and, above all, the soon-to-come "Son of Man." In the Hellenistic congregations, however, a new cult soon arose, the cult of Kyrios Christos. It became the center of congregational piety; each separate individual was related to the Kyrios and all the individuals combined into the "Body of Christ." The cult distributed the powers at work in individuals and the congregation—the powers supplied by the sacraments. The picture of the eschatological Son of Man and of the eschatological rule of God faded.

The Conversion of Paul

The earlier attempts to understand Paul's conversion psychologically (from Holsten to Weinel) offered Romans 7 as the primary basis; that is, since they saw the seminal point of Paul's view in his doctrine of justification, they conceived of his conversion as the result of a moral development. In connection with that, the tradition of the Palestinian congregation and the words and person of Jesus mediated through it were usually considered an essential factor. All three presuppositions are false; the doctrine of justification does not stand at the center of Paul's understanding; Romans 7 is not a presentation of Paul's inner development;[5] and one cannot speak of a significant influence of the Palestinian tradition on Paul. Consequently, the conversion of Paul appears in a totally new light; it is the ecstatic experience of a Hellenistic Jew, which drew him under the sway of the Kyrios cult of the Hellenistic congregation. His inner disposition must therefore have been totally different from what it was formerly considered to be.

The Sociological Structure of Primitive Christianity

In his great work on the social teachings of the Christian churches and groups (1912), Troeltsch characterized the Christian church as follows: It is not a worldly, operational community with a program of reform or culture, but a purely religious community with a supra-worldly goal and center of force. It is indifferent to worldly order; but this indifference can nevertheless lead to a conservatism with regard to the order ordained by God, as well as a disdain of and revolt against the demonic obstructions to the Kingdom of God. This attitude of the Christian church until the beginning of modern times was rooted in primitive Christianity, indeed, ultimately, in the message of Jesus. But Troeltsch came to his view of history by interpreting Jesus according to Paul and John, under the influence of the old concept of the unity of primitive Christian history. He ingenuously carries Pauline terminology (self-deliverance, the summons into God's community, cooperating in the work of God, etc.) into the message of Jesus. However, Jesus is not to be understood in terms of the subsequent Hellenistic development, but only on the basis of the earlier Jewish development. Troeltsch describes the moral ideal and sociological structure of the Hellenistic congregations quite correctly as follows: A specifically religion-oriented ethic was present, the ethic of a religious individualism, which created the drive and goal of moral activity from the experience of fulfillment with the Divine Spirit and mystical union with the Kyrios. The goal is a transcendent one, and the formula "God and the human soul, which achieves infinite worth in communion with him" is justified if God is also represented by the Kyrios. The souls entering into communion with the Kyrios are intermingled in a community of love, which is found in the cultic congregation. The act entails man's sanctifying himself for this communion and enlisting new members as co-workers with God for the community of love. It is entirely different with Jesus, who does not acknowledge such a supra-worldly, mystical goal of conduct. For Jesus, God is not the goal with whom those sanctifying themselves are bound in mystical communion, thus achieving infinite worth and intertwining in a community of love. For Jesus, God is primarily the holy will, demanding a good will from man; and the relation to God is one of obedience and trust. In contrast to Judaism, Jesus demands not works, but genuine feelings, truthfulness, and unconditional obedience to the good. This, not some sort of mystical view, is the meaning of the commandment to love. With Jesus the idea of God does not determine the content and motive of the moral demand; the reverse is true—the idea of God receives its content through the consciousness of the moral demand. This was also true for the great prophets of Israel, whose achievement was the purification of the popular notion of God by the consciousness of the moral demand of law and justice. Since Troeltsch completely ignores Jesus' message as the antithesis to the legal ethic of Judaism, he does not see that Jesus concludes and fulfills the history of Judaism, that something new begins with Paul and the Hellenistic congregation. The difference between Paul and Jesus can be most clearly observed in their attitude toward the law. Paul does not argue, like Jesus, from the moral demand of goodness, truthfulness, and unconditionality in relation to the law; for Paul, the law is annulled through the institution of God's salvation, and moral activity is not viewed primarily as obedience to the demand of the good, but as the working of the Spirit in the redeemed child of God.

The examples will have demonstrated to some extent that primitive Palestinian Christianity can be characterized as an ethical religion. God acts according to his own will in the tradition of the Old Testament and Judaism; and the good serves primarily as his will. He demands that man will the good and that alone; the person who does so is counted among the saved, who will share in the coming rule of God. The Father is gracious to the meek in the land and to the repentant sinner; and this same Father spurns those who follow stereotyped piety and seek salvation by works. In contrast, Hellenistic Christianity is characterized as a mystical cultic religion. Here, God is not, at least primarily, the holy one who wills the good, the reality grasped in obedience to the good, but the supra-worldly Essence, Spirit, Life, Light, "Truth," and Incorruptibility, in contrast to the material, sinister, dead nature of the "world." Hellenistic piety is dualistic, as is most mysticism. Therefore, it does not see the divine reality in its activity in the world and in destiny, nor look for it in the tasks and fortunes of life; but it seeks it, rather, in miraculous experiences which transport the devotee out of this world in an ecstatic and miraculous vision of God, in spiritual experiences and cultic "expressions" which are not at all to be compared with everyday experiences. This mysticism is primarily cultic. The Kyrios, present in the cult, distributes the gifts, the "Spirit," of the supra-natural world; the Kyrios is himself the "Spirit." His portrait is the symbol and source of divine powers, and in the mystical cultic community one is transformed with the Kyrios into the essence of the heavenly world—is "transfigured."

Consequently, the result of all this is that Jesus and primitive Palestinian Christianity are seen as manifestations within Judaism; they represent a Jewish sect, if you please. From the viewpoint of the historian the judgment must be made that "Christianity" as a self-sufficient, historical entity, a religious community with its own forms of myth and cult and communal life, begins with primitive Hellenistic Christianity.

Primitive Palestinian Christianity must be considered a more unified entity than the primitive Hellenistic form. In any case, one finds all sorts of nuances in the latter. Its forms of expression may be more intellectual or they may be more crude. And although the mystic cult is the most important factor, it is not the only one. I cannot go into the abundance of nuances in this regard, nor can I linger over the various influences which assert themselves. To make the new view of history comprehensible, however, I must at least comment on a few points of the problem to show how primitive Palestinian and Hellenistic Christianity can present a coherent historical movement at all.

1. The cultic deity of primitive Hellenistic Christianity is not a purely mystical figure. It is identified with the historical person Jesus of Nazareth, whom the Palestinian congregation worshiped as prophet and teacher and awaited as the coming Son of Man. This connection between the Palestinian and Hellenistic congregations is represented in the Gospels of Mark and John, each in its own way.

2. The new community took its origin as an eschatological movement from the message of Jesus, and felt itself to be the congregation at the end of time. The gospel was carried into the Hellenistic world as an eschatological message. Paul, too, was convinced that time was short and that the gospel had to be proclaimed throughout the world with the utmost urgency. To expect the coming of the Lord was one of the first lessons learned by the Hellenistic congregations. Though the eschatology of the Hellenistic congregations differed from other current syncretistic views of time, this was its connection with the Palestinian congregation. And even though the emphasis on eschatology decreased, it provided them at the beginning with a feeling of community.

3. The Old Testament was then accepted by the Hellenistic congregations. Apart from the fact that a part of its content operated alongside the mystical cult (eschatology, in fact, and then moralism, among other aspects), this acceptance as such produced a consciousness of historical continuity with Israel and thus with the Palestinian congregation. Each member felt himself to be the true Israel; he called Abraham his father, he associated himself with the promises, he utilized an abundance of material from the Old Testament for apologetic and

other purposes. The Palestinian tradition of Jesus was also taken over. Thus, even if its spiritual content is not fully operative, a tradition assumes a momentum, making itself felt particularly in the self-consciousness of the community, and constituting an extremely powerful bond.

4. The first Hellenistic missionaries were Jewish Christians; to be sure, Hellenized Jewish Christians, who had been driven from the Palestinian congregation. With their converts (such as Paul), they were the first bearers of the gospel to the Hellenistic world; and, even though Hellenized, they were still Jews, for whom the tie with Israel, with Jerusalem, was taken for granted. The fact that Jewish Christians as a rule formed a certain percentage of the first Hellenistic congregations also operated as a binding force. Then, too, the Hellenistic congregations took over certain forms of the Hellenistic synagogues, especially prayer and preaching, so that alongside the Kyrios cult was the service of the Word of God.

Paul must be mentioned as one of the most influential persons in this regard, especially in the significance of the tendencies just mentioned. As was evident earlier, Paul's importance is not to be seen primarily in his struggle for freedom from the law in Hellenistic Christianity. Freedom from the law was effected before Paul. Others were working on this problem alongside him in different ways, and Hellenistic Judaism had preceded him in this task. Paul's importance lay much more in his ability to maintain the link with Jerusalem and the Palestinian congregation and in his conscious cultivation of this tie in spite of freedom from the law. Herein also lies the importance of the so-called assembly of Apostles, which played such a special role in Baur's construction—the question was not the freedom of the Gentile Christians—that would have carried at the assembly even without Paul and his triumph—the real problem was the tie with Jerusalem, which was retained. Thus, the most important result of the assembly is the least obvious—the collection for the congregation at Jerusalem. The continued concern of Paul for this collection is a part of his most important work.

But Paul's importance goes much further. It lies primarily in the fact that his letters became the literature of Hellenistic Christianity and that a particular combination of ethical and mystical religion is present in these letters. Paul's personal piety, in fact, contains elements of both. First, he differs in a basic respect from Jesus through his polemic against legalism, which, while similar to Jesus' polemic, has a different base. Paul's view bases salvation not on good intent and God's goodness, but on the act of salvation of which the Christ myth speaks. He bases it on the faith which accepts these acts of salvation and subjects itself to them. If, however, one asks where Paul understands God to be present (always the decisive question for religion), and this is the inner experience assuring him of salvation, the answer is not in the events of salvation, for the incarnation, death, and resurrection of Christ cannot be the object of inner experience in any sense. The interpretation of these facts as revelations of God, which subject man and overcome him, plays no part for Paul. (Compare with Luther and Ritschl.) It is much more the "Spirit," which assures Paul of being a child of God; the certainty of God's grace grows in spiritual experience. To the extent that salvation can be experienced now, it is the community of Christ; but regarding what is still in the future, it is the "being with Christ." Mysticism therefore reaches into the center of Pauline piety. Nevertheless, the "Spirit" is also an ethical force and demonstrates its fruits in moral change; Christ, therefore, not only symbolizes (in the cult) mystical-spiritual powers, but also the power which rules in Paul's professional life; Paul is aware of this abundant power which his inner life achieves in conflict and suffering; he experiences it in his inner history as moral personality, in the destiny which is his task. For Paul, God is not the peace and quiet of the mystical God, but the Old Testament God of will who rules the history and destiny of man and the world. The peculiar combining of ethical and mystical religion in Paul finds its expression in the duality of divine forms; mystical experience is related primarily to the Kyrios-Spirit, whereas events in time and the world are directed by God, who has called that Spirit to its task.

II. THE TASKS OF SELF-REFLECTION ON THE BASIS OF HISTORICAL KNOWLEDGE

A. THE CRITIQUE OF CRITICAL HISTORICAL WORK IN MODERN PIETY

I shall pass over the question of whether the juxtaposition of ethical and mystical religion in Paul is to be characterized as organic and to what extent this particular duality became operative in the further development of Christian thought, and now turn from the historical presentation to the question of what history teaches us about the present.

Critical historical work is falling into disrepute in modern times. I can understand the disappointed or hostile complaints that this work is religiously and ecclesiastically unfruitful. I certainly believe it had, and still has, a lesson for the churches, though it is not the most important lesson, nor the one least subject to misunderstanding and danger. The modern direction of piety, in its turning away from historical work, has been characterized as Gnosticism. This is correct to the extent that piety wishes to tear the connection with historical forces into shreds, and completely reinterprets history as myth, as appears to me to be the case in Barth's *Epistle to the Romans;* it is also correct to the extent that modern piety is mystical. There is, however, another trend, impressively represented by Gogarten, which seems different. Gogarten says: "Religion is so little to be conceived without historical experience that one can almost say that it is itself the experiencing (not the knowing) of history. In any case, it is shot through and through with historical experience."[6] However, one should not misunderstand this bond with history: "One does not desire to be bound to a past time and its limitations (in spite of all personal breadth and significance) in order to be freed from the fetters and dilemmas of his own spatial-temporal being. Religion is concerned with eternity, and it allows no temporal period to capture it, not even the most important period on earth. . . . It is absolutely not the business of religion to find a revelation of eternity in some past period and to venerate it; religion desires to find eternity in its present." Such piety rebels against the view that our connection with history has to rest upon the most exact knowledge of history possible, which is precisely the critical historical task. And it rightly resists it. Furthermore, it boggles at the opinion that one epoch or one person of the past, even classical ones, can serve as a normative foundation for a religious community. Only in entities which exalt themselves above time and history—i.e., myth and cult—could the inexhaustible, ever-changing content of religion come to expression. There is some justification in this also.

Two objections, therefore, are raised against critical historical work, or, as one ordinarily says, against "liberal theology" (within which I count myself): (1) Generally, that critical historical work becomes the presupposition of piety; (2) specifically, that a particular period of history and a particular person, the "historical Jesus," are viewed as normative.

B. The Significance of This Critique

The first objection has some objective validity; to what extent it is valid for the individual representatives of "liberal theology" remains undecided. In any case, the task of critical historical theology (indeed, of all theology) can never be to establish piety, but only to lead to reflection, to help clarify and purify the intellectual consistency of consciousness. If, in this task of reflection, it happens that the intellectual content is small, one should not blame those who do the work of reflection, but lament the weakness of the community, a weakness of which theology is always a symptom or exponent. Our present situation and the historical consideration already employed demonstrate how very much this is the case and how very much the task of theology is that of reflection. The difference between primitive Palestinian and Hellenistic Christianity parallels the movement in modern piety which turns away from an ethically or morally established view of Protestant Christianity, specifically, of the Ritschlian brand, and demonstrates a strong inclination to mystical tendencies. To what extent the insights of research, its capacity to analyze manifestations in the history of religion, and its being the agent of Hellenistic mysticism itself, can be considered as causal factors in the inclination toward the new piety, or to what extent they are the consequences of this inclination, must remain undetermined. In either case, it is enough that they are symptoms of the transformation of the general outlook of our era. And thus their work contributes to the explanation of this outlook. This brings us to the second reproach.

"Liberal theology" would have made the "historical Jesus" and his religion the foundation of piety and put a limited, historical individual in the place of myth and cult, which, nevertheless, could be only the expression of the living, eternal, supra-historical aspects of religion. In fact, at first "liberal theology" itself protested against viewing a limited, historical form of Christianity as normative; we refer to Pauline Christianity in its ecclesiastical, dogmatic form. In reaction, "liberal theology" has set up the message of Jesus, the religion of Jesus, as the normative form of Christianity.

We see now what that means: for one thing, the decision for Palestinian Christianity in preference to Hellenistic Christianity; but above all, that a historical manifestation was accepted as the normative form of Christianity, a manifestation which from the standpoint of history is not at all to be characterized as Christianity. Christianity exists as a self-sufficient, religious congregation only where it has created its own sociological form, where it has created its own myth and cult. Jesus was a Jew and the Palestinian congregation was a Jewish sect. Judaism was the only historical form of religion in which the intellectual content of the message of Jesus could exist. Without Judaism the message of Jesus would not have been possible at all, or perhaps only in a compromised form—that is, within a different ecclesiastical community, whose skeleton (cult, myth, etc.) would have been of a different origin. One would think "liberal theology" has existed only in the framework of a transmitted religiosity. If "liberal theology" does not succeed in finding its own new forms for the religious community, cult, and myth, then it will be just another episode in the history of the church, much as Rationalism was an episode (in spite of all its achievements in many areas for the church), and not essentially an epoch, because it had no organ for dealing with cult and myth and was not able to find new forms of religious community life.

C. The Significance of Cult and Myth for the Religious Community

What are the consequences? The consequence of deciding for the other alternative, for primitive Hellenistic Christianity, would lead to an impossible situation. The assertion that a historically conditioned form of the past cannot be normative is equally valid for that alternative. The artificiality of a Catholic repristination of the early cult, such as an orthodox transfiguration of Pauline myth and ecclesiastical dogma, is doomed from the outset. That is true also for the enthusiastic renewal of Pauline myth in Barth's construction. As much as I welcome the religious critique of culture in Barth's *Epistle to the Romans*,[7] I can see in the positive aspects he introduces little else than an arbitrary adaptation of the Pauline Christ myth. The judgment pronounced by Barth on "liberal theology" refers equally to him. It is impossible to renew an old cult and myth or artificially create a new one. What can be done, before priestly or prophetic impulses can reorganize, is simply to begin with the present historical situation, and develop it by ruthlessly cutting off what is obsolete and untrue and adding what is most urgent. But there is no bargaining in this process; in fact, the task of reflection leads one step further.

Cult and myth are not religion, but the necessary forms for the existence of a religious community. The Christ myth and the Kyrios cult were once the forms of primitive Hellenistic Christianity. One may perhaps say that mystical religion has a more intimate relation to the cult than ethical religion; actually, however, both require such forms; but the question cannot be one of form. It must be: Which religion do we feel alive in us? Do we confess to an ethical religion, as was alive in Jesus and in the Palestinian congregation of Judaism? Or do we confess to a mysticism, as was dominant in a similarly historically conditioned form in Hellenistic Christianity? The way the question is put shows the embroilment and helplessness of our present state. The difficulty is that we cannot point with clarity and certainty to what God's revelation is for us. A better and more profound phrasing of the question would be: What is really valid for us as God's reality? Where do we look for him or experience him? Where does he reveal himself to us?

D. Religious Moralism and Ethical Religion

The most serious error of "liberal theology," in my opinion, was the confusion of a religiously colored moralism with ethical religion. Only on this basis could one ascribe such a religious-moral significance to the historical Jesus; for what is really religious plays a relatively minor role in his meaning for us. Jesus' belief in God appears in many of his statements as a childish belief in providence and a naïve optimism, the sort of belief at work in the Psalms and Wisdom Literature of Israel as well as in the naïve popular belief of different times and cultures. In other statements his view of God is the mythical view of eschatology. One can scarcely characterize either view as really religious. The salvation for which Jesus hoped, the rule of God, when sin and suffering are extirpated from the world and God's will is fulfilled on earth, is a realization in which moral ideals unite with worldly hopes and pious reverence, but is not specifically religious. In Jesus' most characteristic statements the idea of God receives its determinative quality through the idea of the good. As previously asserted, God's will demands the good. That is not a particularly religious idea of God, but, as is always peculiar to naïve thinking, the binding power of the good appears under the mythical representation of a god who demands and punishes, pardons and rewards.

This expression of belief does not become a religion through the fact that particular psychic conditions of emotion or enthusiasm accompany it, but only by achieving a new content. It becomes a religion when man experiences an inner history in his act of bowing to the demand of the good; he must be able to grasp a reality which is more than a moral ideal; it must be a reality of life by which he feels that he can rise, one to which he feels himself entirely subjected and by which he feels sustained. It becomes a religion when one who is obedient to the good experiences a destiny in his obedience, a destiny which transforms him. It becomes a religion when, through experiences which lead him through heights and depths—experiences which are called "sin" and "grace" in religious language—he reaches not only the fulfillment of the moral demand, but the fulfillment of his very being. In religion we are dealing not with activity, but with being, not with opinions conforming to the goal of the good, but with the experience of mortality before the reality of God; religion has to do with the reality of receiving oneself through divine grace, with being transformed, with being created anew to a nature whose activity is not the fulfillment of a demand but the presentation of its being. I do not wish to quarrel about how far we can perceive such actual religious experience in Jesus, which Paul has expressed so beautifully; in any case, the characteristics which generally appear in the picture of Jesus presented in "liberal theology" are religious moralism. Otto has succinctly characterized the reality of religion as the "wholly other." The world of the good is not the "wholly other," but the creation of our own moral reason. The "wholly other" of ethical religion is not the demand of the good, but God, who encounters man in his experiences in obedience to the good. Such a man knows that if he feels himself to be a sinner, it is not the law of the good, not, that is, his own moral conscience, which judges him most deeply; it is the "wholly other" before which he is impure. Similarly, when he feels blessed, it is not because he is ennobled by the worth of his moral thinking; it is in the stillness of the "wholly other" that he can find purity and his very self again. He knows that if an inner life accrues to him through conflict and toil, he should be grateful not to the idea of the good, but to the mysterious power of the "wholly other," which holds his destiny in sway and undergirds his life.[8]

E. The Contemporary Summons to Mysticism

Protestantism should not get stuck in a religious moralism, and neither should it preach only the sentimental ethic of Jesus; for this is not religion. It must recognize the specific aspect of religious life and bring it to consciousness; it must be able to speak of God's revelation and find expression for it in myth and cult. But that would still not solve the problem of borrowing the aesthetic and charming forms of mysticism in order to engender emotional moods. The contemporary summons to mysticism is understandable. Frequently, it does not in the least mean a desire for mysticism as such, but simply for religious life in general. One must be clear about the essence of mysticism. The God of mysticism is not the God of will, who controls destiny and is worshiped in obedience to the good and experienced as a gracious Father. On the contrary, the mystics believe they see God beyond history and the world. Mysticism is connected either with pessimistic dualism, which cannot perceive the rule of God in destiny and in the world but considers the event of the world as a deceptive appearance or a diabolical game—or with pantheistic naturalism, which looks for God in the eternal recurrence of the life of nature, a life without history. The mystic does not experience God in an inner history of struggle and growth in obedience to the good, but through the vanishing of all struggle and activity, the vanishing even of the good, as he sinks into silence or ecstasy.

I am not judging the correctness or incorrectness of ethical or mystical religion. Neither am I asking whether either type of religion finds its way to a higher unity; that would conceal the primary question of religion, the question of reflection. But I well know that, regardless of the opposition of pure forms, one finds in individual cases transitions from one form to another and combinations of forms, and that both types of religion can demonstrate great affinity in their assertions. Ethical, as well as mystical, religion knows quiet and meditation. The God of will, of destiny, contains a quietness in which all haste and struggle find eternal rest. But that does not make him the God of mysticism.

F. CONCLUSION

What is decisive for religion is neither the cultic and mythical means of expression, nor the psychic conditions in which the pious experience God, but only a religion's spiritual content, the reality which it characterizes as God. The psychic forms of dread and excitement, terror and joy, can be a part of every genuine religion, just as they are present without religion. It is not whether man experiences particular psychic conditions or whether he participates in a cult or "believes" a myth that makes him pious, but only whether he can speak of a revelation of God, whether he has found God as a reality which subdues and blesses him, a reality in which he finds the meaning of his life. In mysticism, there is peace and rest, the empty state of "being," in which the soul glides in self-forgetfulness; in ethical religion, there is the creating of life-will, allowing us to reach the mature destiny of those who struggle in obedience to the good, and thus fulfilling our inner life.

NOTES

1. *Zeitschrift für Theologie und Kirche* I (1891), 82-178.
2. Gerhard Loeschcke, *Zwei kirchengeschichtliche Entwürfe* (1913).
3. Apart from such exceptions as Otto Pfleiderer.
4. Adolf Jülicher, *Paulus und Jesus* (1907).
5. Cf. Wilhelm Heitmüller, "Die Bekehrung des Paulus," *Zeitschrift für Theologie und Kirche* XXVII (1917), 136-153.
6. Friedrich Gogarten, *Religion weither*, 677.
7. Cf. *Religion und Kultur* by the same author, 11 ff.
8. I heartily agree with what Gogarten has said about such experience in his wonderful little book *Religion weither,* and even more profoundly in his lecture at Eisenach.

THE PROBLEM OF A THEOLOGICAL EXEGESIS OF THE NEW TESTAMENT*

Rudolf Bultmann

Orthodox Lutheran exegesis regards the Bible as a book of doctrines, directly related to me, the reader. They are not designed to enrich my theoretical knowledge, but to offer illumination about my true nature and to determine the course of my life. Insofar as these authoritative doctrines are regarded as general truths, earlier Rationalism was only drawing the conclusion of this concept of Scripture when it took the teachings of Scripture seriously as general truths. For if they are, they are rational truths, since reason is the court of appeal in deciding the universal validity of statements. What appears non-rational in Scripture is then re-interpreted or explained as accommodation to, or limitation of the times in which it was written. But the study of the elements that are unique, or determined by the times, became an end in itself, because it permitted a differentiation among the separate writings and groups of writers, and thus gave rise to a historical presentation. The transition then occurred within Rationalism which produced the modern interpretation in terms of historical conditioning. This resulted in the loss of the original contrast between those things limited by the times and the eternal rational truths. The individual elements came to be understood as expressions of the general regularity which establishes the unity of history.

This regularity can be variously conceived. In the Idealist, specifically the Hegelian, concept of history, which attained a lasting domination of New Testament exegesis through the Tübingen school, it is teleologically determined. The forces which move history are ideas, which constitute the moments of the unfolding of absolute spirit, but which have their reality only in the concrete process occurring in individual manifestations, the process in which absolute spirit comes to self-realization.

Into the place of, or parallel to, the Idealist concept of man which underlies this view of history, there came gradually a different concept of man, the naturalistic. In this concept, man is the product of circumstances, and the regularity of history, accordingly, is conceived of as causally determined. The ideas, ideals, and institutions of an epoch or an individual are explained completely as the results of a develop-

* From *Zwischen den Zeiten*, III (1925), issue 4, pp. 334-357.

mental process. Even though the factor of personality (the irrational aspect) is taken into account, its underlying concept is still explained naturalistically. The irrational element taken into account here is no different from that of historical geology, which is unable to explain why certain rock types were formed one way rather than another. And the irrational element, the x, is basically the admission that the being of persons cannot be seen in that which determines the essence of history.

The causal factors which determine history can be variously conceived. Man can be viewed biologically, as invested with varying capacities of thinking and feeling, moral will, etc.—history then consists of the development of these capacities. Since this view does not lead to chronological history, but only to a natural history of mankind, the drives which lie in economic, social, and political necessities are claimed for the realization of historical movement. Indeed, these drives alone may dominate the picture, and the history of Christianity then is turned into sociology. On the other hand, the biological view of man may be carried over from the individual to humanity as a species, and the entire movement of history be presented as a biologically understood morphology.

Similarly, since man is viewed more or less psychologically, the psychological point of view may become dominant, with the danger that our ability to understand historical movement is lost again in the process and our interpretation becomes a psychological analysis of individuals and groups. As a rule the danger is not recognized, since in the absence of fundamental clarity all other interpretations of man and history are included under psychology. In essence, however, the psychological point of view dominates the exegesis of the so-called history of religion school; it gives itself away immediately when it allows the "doctrines" of Scripture to be obscured by and reduced to experiences and moods, and turns "piety" into a theme for the historian. Cult and myth receive particular attention; institutions are explained, as far as possible, through their genesis in primitive conditions (psychologically understood). The conclusions are drawn from an approach characterized (unjustly, in my opinion) as phenomenological; it is an approach which consciously rejects the viewpoint of historical causality and passes off a refurbished psychology as phenomenology.

In reaction to the causal and psychological concepts of man and history, another approach to the New Testament is represented by men such as Gundolf, Bertram, and Reinhardt. Man is viewed as "Gestalt," that is, he is seen from the aesthetic viewpoint. A creative reservoir, a center of power, is assumed, from which the Gestalt develops in a primordial experience and in continuing experiences formed through the powers radiating from the center of the personality. This could scarcely result in a historical movement in the sense of developmental history, unless nations and cultures are also considered Gestalts, in which case the biological viewpoint would once again prevail, as is the case from the outset in this Romantic approach, in emulation of Goethe.

In all these cases the original position, in which the text lays its claim upon the reader, is surrendered—the view that it is there not to be inspected, but to determine the existence of the reader. In all the cases mentioned, the text is viewed at a distance, in the desire to see "what is there," with the presupposition that what can be perceived is perceived *only* without reference to one's own position and that it is possible to interpret the text without, at the same time, interpreting its subject matter. From texts so interpreted, the attempt is made to understand history without asking whether there are perhaps fundamental realities in history which may be grasped only by giving up a detached position, only by being ready to take a stand. To be sure, New Testament exegesis does not say that what is there is of no ultimate concern to a person. However, exegesis itself is not determined by this *tua res agitur* (your interest is at stake), but proceeds on the basis of the expectant, neutral attitude of the exegete. Historical and psychological exegesis establish primarily that this or that has been thought, said, or done at a particular time and under such and such historical circumstances and psychological conditions, without reflecting on the meaning and demands of what is said. For these views, to the extent that a particular aspect has a significance beyond the moment, that significance is only from the viewpoint of the regularity (mostly causal) of events, and thus history becomes a great relational connection in which every particular manifestation is only relative. This may result in the enterprise of reconstructing lost history. If it is correctly reconstructed, such history has equal footing for the viewer with history based on available sources.

It does not help here or elsewhere to demand a return to the Idealist writing of history. History only appears to be different in Idealism; that is, it only appears that the Idealist reads the text from the viewpoint of *tua res agitur*. This impression is created through the fact that individual historical manifestations are understood as objectifications of spirit in its historical movement, in which, indeed, the interpreting subject participates. In this process the interpreter achieves clarity concerning the nature of spirit and thus of himself. Here the interpreting subject is coordinated with history, whereas in the other case they stand alongside each other. Nevertheless, even here the distance of the viewer from history is not overcome, for the exegete sees himself from the same perspective that he sees history; that is, he views himself only as a particular case of man in general and thinks of everything individual as an expression of the laws of development. That means that the connection of the existing [existentiell] subject with history does not take place at all—or only if the existence of man does not lie in the sphere of the universal or rational, but in the individual, in the concrete moment of the here and now. For the Idealist, there is nothing in history which places demands on the individual in the sense that something new is said which is not already potentially his, which is not at his disposal by virtue of his participation in universal reason. He finds nothing which encounters him as authoritative; he finds only himself in history; this he does by reducing the content of history to the movement of the ideas impressed on man's reason. He thus controls all possible historical occurrences from the outset. Here also, then, the enterprise of reconstructing lost history may appear meaningful.

But the decisive question is whether we confront history in such a way that we acknowledge its claim upon us, its claim to say something new to us. When we give up a neutral attitude toward the text, the question of truth can dominate the exegesis. In the final analysis then the exegete is not interested in the question "What was the meaning of what is said (purely as something said) in its contemporary situation, its contemporary context?" He asks instead: "What is the content of what is said, and to what kind of reality does it lead?" Since this question is concerned not with explaining nature but with understanding history, to which we ourselves belong, it implies: What does it mean for me and how am I to understand it on its objective ground? Thus, at this stage the context in which the above two questions form the task of the exegete remains a problem. Can one be answered without the other, and if so, to what extent? The intent of such reflection is not at all to dispose of all the old methods in favor of a new one, but only to ask how far the old methods can carry us in our concern for the reality of history.

Provisionally it may be put in this way: Historical exegesis asks: "What is said?" We ask: "What is meant?" In a certain sense, of course, historical exegesis also asks about meaning, but in such a way that all history is sketched on one plane, one map; and then, a certain field or point on this map is identified by means of the most comprehensive knowledge possible of the surrounding area. All the light shed by the history of the period is concentrated on the point to be identified. Objective exegesis, on the other hand, considers this map of history as transparent and seeks to perceive the light which shines through from beyond the surface, believing that this is the only way to understand what is meant. The picture, of course, is incomplete, for psychology could describe its work in history in a similar way. Yet, by so doing psychology moves even further from what the text intends, because, from the very beginning, it interprets all statements as expressions of a particular, regularly unfolding, psychic life, whereas the point of objective exegesis is to know what *objects* are intended by the textual statements. The writer who speaks through the text did not desire to make a statement whose meaning is exhausted in the fixable, relative moment, but wished to deal with the issue lying beyond the relational connections. To interpret, for example, Paul's doctrine of justification by statements about Paul's conversion experience, brings out perhaps what Paul said, but certainly not what he meant. If someone interprets Paul's view that a Christian should no longer sin on the basis of Paul's fervor, that is, on the basis of his psychic understanding of inspiration, in which he thought it self-evident that the Christian can do only the good, and if he still uses, say, the traditional concepts of absolution in the messianic age, then he necessarily interprets Paul's statements as events in the developmental process of a Jew susceptible to psychic influences. But this approach could never get at what Paul really meant or what he wanted to direct our attention to. Whoever makes Paul's "religious life" or his "feeling for life" the theme of an interpretation of Paul obviously is interpreting something which did not interest Paul in the least; he is interpreting a psychic phenomenon or a phenomenon conditioned by the times. And with that I leave the question open as to whether and to what extent such interpretations are capable of doing the spadework needed to approach the real issue.

It can be said that historical (and psychological) exegesis wishes to interpret the word of the text, just as objective exegesis does. But it is accustomed to understanding the word as a priori the necessary expression of a speaking individual (who may also be a sociological entity). It makes little difference whether the individual is viewed as the subject of psychic complexes and functions; as an aesthetic, idealistic personality, character, or form; or in terms of naturalistic evolution, as the exponent of a particular, historical situation. In each of these cases the word of the text is unable to speak in any real sense to the interpreter, since the interpreter is a priori thoroughly in control of all the possibilities which may be expressed, by means of the principles of his approach. However, the original and genuine meaning of the word "word" is that it intends to refer to something outside the speaker, to disclose this to the hearer, and by so doing to become an event for him. The potential objection raised by Idealist exegesis, which insists that it does not exclude such a definition, rests on the fact that it does not conceive the speaking individual as a psychically or historically determined subject and can therefore interpret his statements as references to transsubjective matters. But such matters are not intended here, since they cannot become events for the hearer. Rather, since their content is the system of reason, the essence of the spirit of rationalism, such matters include only that which the interpreter as a rational subject controls a priori. Objective exegesis seeks to deal responsibly with the original and genuine meaning of "word" by understanding it as a reference to the subject matter.

The character of this objective exegesis is even more exactly determined by the fact that an objective critique of it is both possible and necessary. This critique distinguishes between what is said and what is meant and measures what is said by its meaning. To the extent that historical exegesis determines that some textual assertions are perhaps primitive or crude, unclear or contradictory, it also appears to practice objective criticism. But in historical exegesis the standard is formal logic or immanental development, not the object of which the text speaks. It only seems to be otherwise when the text is criticized from the standpoint of modern consciousness, a standpoint which plays a large part, for example, in Baumgarten's interpretation of John's first letter in the Göttingen commentary series. Since, on the basis of their own presuppositions, both historical and psychological exegesis can claim only relative validity for their assertions, this type of criticism is a naïve incongruity and basically says nothing at all. One can only be very astonished that it can even interpret a text for anyone except readers with antiquarian interests, since it always knows more than the text does. Why does it point the reader to the New Testament at all? The objective criticism called for in objective exegesis can establish its standard only through the object opened up by the text, over which it has no prior control. The "position" achieved in such objective criticism, therefore, has nothing to do with "value judgments," subsequently leveled against the historical material. Objective exegesis stands, then, in a peculiarly ambiguous and even contradictory situation, since it comes to what is meant only through what is said, and yet measures what is said by what is meant. That means, however, that it never establishes universally valid statements as "results," but always remains in motion.*

---

* It scarcely needs to be said that such exegesis has nothing to do with intuition.

The distinction between the questions of what is said and what is meant has been only roughly and provisionally formulated. But the intended difference can now be clarified if we inquire into the basis of the presuppositions for the question "What is meant?"; or when we inquire about the realm of that which is meant and about its availability to the exegete. If what is meant is nothing more than a historical fact, these two questions clearly cannot be separated. Certainly, insofar as historical facts (such as the death of Jesus or Paul's missionary journeys) are not reported for their own sake, but with a particular intention, the question of what is meant comes up in a different sense. And that surely does not mean asking about the subjective intention and view of the informant, so that instead of the one historical fact only another fact would be presented.

The distinction between these questions becomes a factor whenever the potential of what is meant exceeds the bare, historical (or psychic) factuality of what is said. In general it can be said that the realm of what is meant reaches as far as the potential of man. What is available to the interpreter depends on how responsive he is to the range of human possibility. So ultimately the question of the possibility of understanding a text depends on the openness of the exegete to the possibilities of his own human existence; what sort of interpretation, that is, the exegete has of himself as a man.

But if one has taken the question this far, he suddenly sees that the initial distinction of a neutral exegesis from one that takes a position —a contemplative exegesis over against one that grasps the demand of the text—is only rough and inadequate. It was occasioned by the false understanding modern exegetes have of their task. Actually, there is no neutral exegesis. There is no bare interpretation of "what is there," but in some way (a specific way, in fact, for each case) the interpretation of the text always goes hand in hand with the exegete's interpretation of himself. We do not encounter history in the same way that we do nature; we can assume a distance from nature; but we stand in history and are a part of it. Therefore, every word we utter about history is necessarily a word about ourselves; that is, it discloses how we interpret our own existence; it shows what sort of openness we have to the possibilities of our existence as humans. The question put to the text by the Idealist concerns the stage of development in which the text's assertions stand in the process of the unfolding of spirit, or the meaning they exhibit when they are measured against the ideal content of spirit; he questions the character which the assertions possess as knowledge in the scientific or ethical sphere. With these questions, the Idealist shows that the real meaning of man presents itself in reason, in ideas. The Romanticist knows man only as form, as personality, ultimately as a mechanism, as molded material. For him the really human mode of existence is to observe and to mold aesthetically. For the psychologist, man is the subject of psychic complexes and processes; to be really human means existing in psychic conditions, moods, and experiences.

Insofar as a specific self-interpretation underlies every exegesis, no exegesis is neutral; it can also be said that all exegesis acknowledges a claim of the text, because in each case the claim of one of the possible interpretations is recognized. Thus, the distinction between the questions of what is said and of what is meant proves inadequate, because, in fact, no exegesis is able to simply reproduce the wording of the text, but tries somehow to say what is meant. Nevertheless, the distinction indicates an actual, basic difference because one thing remains certain —all those possibilities of exegesis proceed from the assumption that the exegete is basically in control of what is said or what is meant, that the word of the text does not become an event (a temporal event) for him, and thus that the text does not authoritatively confront him and has essentially nothing new to say to him.* But that means that all these possibilities are based on the idea of human existence as controllable and certain.

Against these views stands objective exegesis, which rests on a fundamentally different concept of human existence. Here human existence is not viewed in general terms and man is approached not as a member of a species, but in his individual life, operating within time with its moments which are unique and do not recur, and with its events and decisions. That means that we are not in control of our existence and not certain of it; it is uncertain and problematic, and so we are ready to hear words as words, to hear questions which require us to decide, and to hear the authoritative claim of the text as it demands a decision.

It is entirely clear then that the concept of man as Gestalt will not satisfy the demand to view human existence in its particularity rather than in general. An interpretation which looks upon the inner form of the Gestalt ignores the concrete existence of man; it sees the concrete here and now as an example of the universal; the only difference is that here the universal is not the regulated thought process of comprehension, but the individual law of the corresponding Gestalt. One can interpret his existence in this manner only if he confronts it as timeless, or better, as belonging to the past, and that means he cannot

---

* Indeed, this is made into an explicit principle, if the exegete is required to be "congenial" to the spirit of the text.

interpret it if he accepts his here and now as moments of decision which lead to an entirely different future. The interpretation of man as Gestalt is always possible only in retrospect, that is, only if one's entire life is seen as already concluded. That means the denial of the importance of time for man's existence. And it is no different if one looks at the formation of the Gestalt from a developmental viewpoint. For the movement in question here does not contain the moment of temporality; it is eliminated as a real moment and serves only as a scheme for classifying. In the formation of the development, being disintegrates into its separate moments, but in such a way that its totality is present as an idea at every stage. The individual moments, then, bring nothing new; that is, they are not involved in decision-making. This is classically expressed in Goethe's words (Δαίμων):

"Wie an dem Tag, der dich der Welt verliehen,
die Sonne stand zum Gruße der Planeten,
bist alsobald und fort und fort gediehen,
nach dem Gesetz, wonach du angetreten.
So mußt du sein, dir kannst du nicht entfliehen,
so sagten schon Sibyllen und Propheten;
und keine Zeit und keine Macht zerstückelt
geprägte Form, die lebend sich entwickelt."

"As on the day that gave you to the world
The sun stood still to hear the planets' greeting,
You flourished then at once, and flourish still,
According to the law that governs you.
You must be so, you can't escape yourself,
The Sibyls and the prophets have decreed.
There is no time nor might can ever shatter
A form that's fixed, and living still evolves."

It is also possible to escape conclusively the reproach of subjectivism. Naturally, every exegesis, as something which a subject undertakes, is subjective. For the usual modern exegesis in its various strains, the possibility of breaking out of this primitive subjectivism is offered through its method. True, it falls into a new subjectivism through this method, since the method is merely an approach that is the consequence of the underlying interpretation of human existence. Anyone who accepts a specific interpretation of human existence in common with others, and thereby has a specific method at his disposal, may explain this posture "objectively." But if one rejects any connection with such an interpretation of human existence, especially in its aspect of being at one's disposal and subject to observation, he thereby forfeits the method and further forfeits the claim to objective results of interpretation. But that does not mean he lands in complete subjectivism, since he does acknowledge the claim and authority of the text. The sole guarantee of the "objectivity" of exegesis, i.e., that the reality of history comes to expression in exegesis, is precisely that the text bears in upon the exegete himself as reality. The presupposition for this is that the exegete has no prior control over the possibilities of what is said or what is meant; that is, he gives up the possibility of establishing by means of any method what historical reality is. In short, the possibility of an "objective" exegesis is guaranteed solely by the capacity of history itself for the subject at hand. And this is given expression only where the exegete is ready to allow the text to speak with authority. This does not mean that it reflects history as if it were a lifeless mirror or that it takes a photograph of history, but that it is existentially alive. The naïveté with which psychological exegesis, for example, regularly rejects every objective claim of the text clearly shows that the exegete in that case is not inwardly alive and that his existence poses no problems for him. Thus he can never penetrate history's capacity for the subject at hand. In contrast, the person who desires to hear the word of the text speak to him as a word admits that the possibilities of human existence are not marked off beforehand and not determined in the concrete situation through the use of reason, character, or psychic and historical conditions, but rather, that they are open, that new ones open up in every concrete situation; he admits that human life is characterized by its being led through decisions. The word, which enters his situation anew, requires the exegete to decide, and in this way it becomes an event for him. It is not an event in which the word is to be considered objectively, but an event only for the hearer who is existentially alive. If it is clear that historical interpretation is also self-interpretation, then it will also be clear that, unless exegesis is explicitly guided by the question of self-interpretation, it will fall into subjectivism.

Before pursuing this thought any further, however, we should illustrate what has been said with a few examples.

H. J. Holtzmann interprets Jesus' belief in God as a particularly high stage in the development of man's faith.[1] For Jesus, God means the "representation of the possibility of being as a power of love." Whereas the primitive picture of God based on personification of natural forces gradually disappears behind the infinity of causal connection, it achieves a "capacity for resistance and a consistency" as it assumes more and more "a firm position in connection with the claims and needs of the personal spirit and becomes an indecipherable co-efficient of the fulfillment of moral processes in self-consciousness."

Does one need proof here that the interpreter views the real existence of man in rational self-consciousness of spirit with an imitative Idealism or Rationalism? Is this neutral exegesis or does it rest on a previously given principle which controls the possibilities of the text?

When Holtzmann naïvely interprets Paul's view of the sinlessness of Christians as the formula for a "heaven-storming Idealism,"[2] he falsely attributes his own Idealistic concept of man to the text. Together with other exegetes he consistently interprets the sinlessness of which Paul speaks only as the realization of an ideal (a concept totally alien to Paul) or as the movement toward this ideal.

The essence of καινὴ ἐντολή (new commandment—1 John 2:8) is also naïvely interpreted by Holtzmann in the following Idealist manner: "new needs and new tasks of love appear constantly." There is no indication that the text itself gives the hint that "new" should be understood in an eschatological sense, because on the basis of this understanding of man, insight into the meaning of eschatology is completely excluded.

Holtzmann interprets 1 John 3:14 in a similar Idealist fashion. The text reads: "We know that we have passed out of death into life, because we love the brethren." Holtzmann explains: "Love is proof that one partakes of life; dead spirits know nothing of love; their being 'creeps feebly and sleepily away' (Rothe), because it does not reach the height of true, personal life. Who does not love . . . remains as one controlled by inertia, in death, in the grave of natural life." Rothe's comments, quoted by Baumgarten in the passage under consideration, are typical: "Only as the individual steps out of his narrow limits, thus sharing himself with others and taking others into himself and enriching and expanding his own limited being through the fullness of the being of the others as they share with him, will the individual human essence become aware of the fact that it lives." In the text, love must be understood as something other than the unfolding of the spiritual life of personality, since the possibility of love, which is indeed a new commandment, is seen as associated with the reality of revelation.

Baumgarten characterizes (in the Göttingen commentary) the content of 1 John 1:1-4 as abstract at first, but thinks it gains clarity when one notices that it is permeated by a full, warm feeling. He deals therefore with readers who are open toward the feeling with which a text is presented, readers whose motive in turning to history is to be filled with a "warm feeling." Interpreting 1 John 1:10 ("If we say we have no sin, we deceive ourselves, and the truth is not in us"), the writer explicitly rejects an interpretation of the passage from the standpoint of revelation; rather, it is to be understood through *sensi-*

tivity. As Baumgarten says: "in sensitivity, the dominant concern is to reproach those who boast of having sat in the secret council of God with the charge that they make him a liar . . ."

Especially characteristic is Baumgarten's explanation of 1 John 2:9 ("He who says he is in the light and hates his brother is in the darkness still"): It should not be admitted that every lack of love is actually hate; the writer could not seriously have meant that. Indeed, in "real life," there are so many stages and intermediate shades! Similarly, he comments on 1 John 3:14 that one could be indifferent toward the brother. Naturally! If man is viewed merely as a psychic subject, if love and hate are taken as psychic manifestations, then there is no either-or for man, but only stages and nuances. The text, however, may have a different reality in mind than the "real life" of which the exegete speaks; it may speak of the reality which Bengal expressed this way in his laconic exegesis: *"Ubi non est amor, odium est.*[3] *Cor non est vacuum"* (Where there is no love, there is enmity. The heart is not a vacuum). Bengal speaks of love and hate, therefore, not as conditions of a psychic subject which encounter each other in passing through all possible intermediate stages of neutrality, but as existential possibilities, for which there is only an either-or.

Among the psychological explanations of man we find also Windisch's explanation of 1 John; it is asserted (concerning 3:9) that the "ideal condition" of Christian sinlessness is deduced from rebirth through God's power as "a unique event with continuing results"; 3:14 is interpreted: "through conversion we have been led to life and to love"; and 4:20 is characterized as the "psychological grounding" of the commandment to love.

Baumgarten's interpretation of 1 John can serve as an illustration of the Romantic exegetical emphasis on Gestalt and personality. He interprets 1:1-4 in such a way as to reduce the historical reality of the Redeemer (by which he apparently understands only what is historically ascertainable) to the "character" of Jesus; but this is merely a negligible case among all the attempts to view Jesus as a personality. In any case, what is being asked here is unimportant for existential man in general (at least, for the New Testament personages); existential man is interested not in the personality of Jesus, but in his anxiety about his own existence or in the question of the truth of his concern. The reminder that Socrates, Caesar, Hildebrand, Dante, Goethe, and Napoleon also are figures, characters, or personalities should give us the clue that the concern here is not with what the New Testament means when speaking of Jesus. In fact, the question of Gestalt and personality is raised from the same distance, that is, the spectator's standpoint, as the questions raised by Idealist or psychological exegesis. Man is viewed here externally, as a mechanism, and his existence is not understood as something involved in the concrete moments of the here and now, as subject to time and moments of decision.

Against these examples which fail to grasp the reality of history, why do I not set up counter examples? Because exegesis which is motivated by the question of existence is to be found only in the living moment of its being practiced. It never thinks of adducing an example to show how it is done and it never thinks of asserting even that it is motivated by the question of existence. The insight into the fact that it must be so is no guarantee that it really is. And since the guarantee for the fact that the reality of history comes to expression in exegesis can always be given only through the reality of history itself, we have no criterion at our disposal to establish that this has happened. We are stuck in this situation, and the goal of our reflection can never be to do with history as we like, but only to clarify our situation completely.

If we again take up the question of where the meaning of the text lies and of its accessibility for the exegete, then it is clear that we are asking about the possibilities for our existence which arise from our encounter with history. But it is also clear that we may not expect an answer to this question, which will become a presupposition from which the text may be questioned. Then we would have control in advance over the possibilities of our existence, about which the text should inform us. We reject every exegesis which regards the possibilities of human existence as either closed or foreseeable, and we maintain that the only possible attitude is to be conscious of the problematic character of our existence. The attitude underlying the interpretation of a text may perhaps be formulated in this way: We attempt to understand the way in which the text shows its writer's interpretation of his concept of existence as the real possibility of existing. In this approach we attempt an elucidation of our own existential possibility, and thereby confront the text just as we confront other men to whom we stand in living relationship and with whom we first achieve any existence at all, that is, in the relation of I and Thou. Then it is clear that there can be no reconstruction of actual history, any more than of the relation of I to Thou, friend to friend, husband to wife, or father to child. Nevertheless, our own existence occurs precisely in these relations; in them we *are*. And just as these relations are temporal events for us, events which bear the character of decision, so then the existential encounter of history takes place in temporal moments which demand our decision.

That would mean first of all that we must give up the idea of development which seeks to comprehend actual history, for it presupposes that man's possibilities can be foreseen and controlled. We can speak of development only where we can examine the subject being developed, that is, where we know a specific man and his possibilities. "To know" in this connection naturally does not mean in the quantitative sense, but as we know a line when we know two of its points. The idea of development, then, signifies having history at one's disposal, and its symptom is the idea of reconstructability. Just as history considered from the idea of development robs our exegesis of the character of temporal event, so it is also the idea of development which eliminates temporality from history; which is to say, the really human mode of existing is eliminated. Of course, it does not eliminate measurable time, so-called objective time. But it is precisely this time which is not real time—this time serves as chronology, as a means of ordering those relations whose connection serves to clarify the idea of development, whereas real temporal events are of no consequence here. The historian of development is indifferent to how fast or how slow time passes, and for him the entire relational connection could just as well be squeezed together into one moment or stretched out to infinity. Time would not exist at all for the mind which could survey the entire relational connection; this mind could record all occurrences in a different system of order as well as in the temporal system. Reflection, for one who views history in such a way, is timeless; but the existential encounter with history is a temporal event in which the word of the text has this temporal character.

And this event—insofar as in our activity our existence unfolds as our own possibility for living—would be a free act. Naturally, this does not mean one feels induced to act on the basis of his understanding of the text; rather, the understanding itself is the act. As a free act it stands beyond my control and occurs only in decision, so that I cannot stand alongside it and control it at the same time. Therefore, it cannot become a methodological principle, but arises as a decision evoked by the question posed in the text; and to the extent that the decision is demanded by history, it is obedience to the authority of history.

The presupposition of every exegesis should be recognition of the uncertainty of our existence, the knowledge that our existence is occasioned in our free act of decision; add to that an attitude toward history which acknowledges it as authoritative and thus sees it not with the detachment of the spectator but in the light of present decision. However, before inquiring into the distinctive aspect of New Testament exegesis or theological exegesis, we must emphasize again that no new method is being put forward. The question of how far methods are really adequate for the understanding of a text, how far every concrete task of exegesis must always be methodical, is expressly set aside. The answer depends first on realizing that we do not really grasp history by a method, since the method comprehends only that which we have at our disposal. This becomes much clearer when we consider that interpretation as a rule ought to mediate the text to a third person, who, in his existential being, is also not at our disposal. As already pointed out, therefore, definitive results are not obtained by a postulated exegesis; such results, in fact, would only serve to kill history, because they lose the character of temporality and block the way to an existential encounter with history for the third person. The results of an existentially inspired exegesis therefore cannot be justified and established in the same manner as those of a methodological exegesis. The possibilities of textual comprehension can no more be limited after exegesis than before, but are as inexhaustible as the possibilities which grow out of the encounter of I and Thou.

The discussion thus far has been based on the view that it is our concern to pose the question of our existence and by so doing to encounter the reality of history. But that is an abstract situation and does not really exist, since there is no point at which we can stand outside history, and from which we could step inside it for the first time. And yet all secular exegesis, so far as it understands itself, begins precisely at that point. I cannot set myself the task of investigating how and to what extent there is concern with the question of existence and how it works in the concrete writing of history in the various areas of secular historical investigation, such as the State, literature, art, and mathematics.* In general, it can be said that interest in a

---

* However, I may well refer to Dilthey's concern for the meaning of historical interpretation and also to the continuing force of his ideas, particularly in the study of modern literature. An example is R. Unger's essay "Literaturgeschichte als Problemgeschichte" (*Schriften der Königsb. Gel. Ges. I geisteswiss. Kl.* 1, 1924). With Dilthey he views poetry as the interpretation of life, so that the history of literature becomes problematic history for him; and here "problem" is meant not as a rationalistic concept, but as an existential one. Therefore, problematic history does not become a dialectic movement of formal aesthetic concepts, but a "phenomenology of the problems of life." The riddles and questions of destiny in existence (such as nature and spirit, love and death) are the content of poetry, and thus also constitute the subject matter of the history of literature. Without a conscious position in regard to the subject matter itself, this history is not possible at all, and, in contrast to the earlier philological historical methods, it must seek to establish a connection with philosophy. In this regard it should be noted that none other than Albert Eichhorn perceived that the philosophy of history is a necessary ingredient of historical investigation, that only the person who understands the

particular area of history (if the work in it is not pure busywork) rests on a conscious or unconscious choice among the various possibilities for making human existence accessible and that, insofar as this choice results from existential vitality, this vitality will continually be effective in the historical task. This will be true precisely to the extent that knowledge in all these areas is not conceived of as a mere collection of data, but as something that leads us to understand our existence, which is stirred by the question of truth. Scholarship in these areas confronts the question of truth, and thus every advance of knowledge presupposes readiness for radical sacrifice of what was previously known—that is, it is based on radical freedom from presuppositions.

Philosophical exegesis does not finally interrogate history for specific information in some area, but is directed from the outset by the question of the possibilities of human existence, and, in fact, by the presupposition that man himself can pose the question of existence and has the possibility of free acts through which to attain to existence.

The distinctive characteristic of New Testament exegesis is that although it remains in the realm of secular exegesis it is still confronted by the New Testament contention that man does not have his own existence at his disposal in such a way that he can pose the question of existence for himself and possess the possibility of free action —all this is found only in the experience of faith. The decisive question for understanding the New Testament would then be whether or not the demand of faith is acknowledged. True, but in the face of all these considerations, the situation of the exegete would be completely impossible. For not only is the possibility of this decision of faith refused him; the New Testament even asserts that in himself man cannot know what faith is, since this knowing results only from a believing exegesis. And if he desires to pose his questions correctly, even this questioning must be a believing questioning!

Must this readiness for believing questioning be a prerequisite for the exegete? Obviously that would be as senseless as requiring him to leap over his own shadow. It shows that reflection cannot be carried out in its entirety on the basis of a principle, that is, when the exegete is viewed as standing in the unreal, abstract situation which the secular exegete seeks; when, that is, in reflection his concrete situation is disregarded. The concrete situation is precisely that New Testament

---

present is a historian (H. Gressmann, *Albert Eichhorn und die Religionsgeschichtliche Schule*, 1924, 8). He also gave a lecture on the major theological concepts (sin, faith, incarnation—*ibid.*, 13) and directed his essay on the doctrine of justification, *Apology* (1887), to an understanding of the events of the life of faith itself (p. 10).

exegesis becomes the task of the man who stands in the tradition of the church of the word. There can be such a readiness for believing questioning only if I stand in my existence under the tradition of the word, not if I view myself externally as an individual conditioned by time.

There is no more possibility of justifying theological exegesis of the New Testament "in principle," than there is a specific method for theological exegesis. A valid investigation of the text can only be a believing one; that is, an investigation grounded in obedience to the authority of Scripture. Paul demanded faith as ὑπακοή (obedience) without needing to legitimize the authority of the word; in John, the μαρτυρία (witness) is not a legitimation for the word which stands next to it, but the word itself; in the same manner, relevant exegesis of the New Testament arises only from obedience. "If any man's will is to do God's will, he shall know whether the teaching is from God or whether I am speaking on my own authority" (John 7:17). This act of obedience is the presupposition of exegesis, but it is not constantly at my disposal, since it is always an act in a specific situation rather than an expression of a fixed position on the basis of which I act, and is real only in the act itself. Moreover—and this amounts to the same thing—it is not in some abstract situation that I confront the decision whether to act, but in the concrete one in which all my existence is concentrated and brought into play.

An exegesis for which faith in the presupposition would be a theological exegesis, but it can be carried on only as a conscious risk; it cannot be established and justified, since the presupposition is not at our disposal. That settles the question, then, of whether Augustine, Luther, Schleiermacher, or even the Bhagavad-Gita must be interpreted in the same way as the New Testament. Insofar as I reflect theoretically, and put myself in an abstract, traditionless situation, there will be no difference. But whether in such an interpretation we will see the text with the eyes of faith is a question that we cannot answer theoretically.

But then exegesis is in the same situation as theology in general, which also has meaning only under the presupposition of faith although it is not in control of this presupposition, and which must be nonetheless put into practice. To give up theology would mean to give up faith, and would prove that the meaning of revelation as the justification of sinners is not understood. For theology is the conceptual presentation of man's existence as an existence determined by God. But since neither God nor existential man is at the disposal of theology, it can never speak *from* God, but only *about* God and *about* man. And it proves its validity only in the constant recollection that this speaking is that of sinful man and makes no pretense of being from God, and that it has as its justification the recognition of these limitations, since God desires to justify the sinner. To remember this, however, does not mean we have a position in relation to a presupposition we can use at will or to a hypothesis for scholarly study, but it means we are in a relationship to revelation, which is real only in the act of revealing. To renounce theology, therefore, would be to renounce faith, because it would be a failure to recognize the significance justification has for man in his concrete enterprises—in this case the theological enterprise—and a rejection of its promise for him and his work. *Pecca fortiter* is the motto here.[4]

Since textual interpretation cannot be separated from self-interpretation and self-interpretation becomes explicit in New Testament exegesis, and since, on the other hand, the self-interpretation of man as a historical individual can occur only in the interpretation of history, the result is that theology and exegesis—or systematic and historical theology—fundamentally coincide. Therefore, theology cannot set itself the task of "critical reflection on the basis of faith" and the systematic development of its assertions from a controllable datum.[5] On the other hand, in the light of the above, a biblical theology would not involve establishing a complex of historical statements or occurrences or establishing what was in the consciousness of the New Testament writers. Rather, it effects an existential encounter with the reality of history. It is necessary, to be sure, to separate the systematic from the historical task in their concrete expressions, so that their interconnection can be constantly rediscovered. The conceptual explication of man's existence, then, as it is determined by God, would be the direct theme of systematic theology, but could only indirectly be the theme of historical theology; and systematic theology would have to present directly the interpretation of man found in the texts, and in such a way that it brings this interpretation out of the concepts of the past into the concepts of the present.

Looked at in this way, theology is always a scientific enterprise, since it is the task of conceptual thinking. And its scientific nature suffers no loss by its recognition that the contents which it expresses in concepts are not rationalistic in origin. Its ambiguous situation, brought on by its particular preoccupation with man's existence, is plainer than that of other historical sciences, even though they also ultimately slip into ambiguity, since they are never undertaken by man in the abstract.

Nevertheless, theology cannot lay claim to being direct proclamation of the word. For, as scientific work, it can offer statements of only relative validity, whereas the proclamation of the word has meaning only if its statements claim to be definitive for the concrete situation (and there is no proclamation of the word other than for the concrete situation). The agitation which results because a statement of faith is not a general, timeless truth, but is real only in the act in which revelation becomes an event, is common to both theology and proclamation. But the conceptual work of theology, even in exegesis, can never be conclusively valid in the concrete moment, but must continually be improved, something which it would be meaningless to require in the same way of the proclamation of the word—if proclamation is really what it ought to be. The church must demand a constantly improved theology, not a constantly improved proclamation of the word; all it can demand of proclamation is that the word be proclaimed.

Insofar as the New Testament is the Word of God only indirectly and not directly for the conceptual thinking of exegetical theology, it is completely valid for us to draw on theological tradition to formulate its main theme as "New Testament theology." This is merely to take seriously the fact that God's Word is a hidden word spoken to man, that the revelation present in Scripture is a veiled revelation. We are confronted in Scripture, therefore, by a kind of speech which is primarily a speaking *about* God and *about* man, for it is uttered in the human sphere. Just as there is no direct encounter between I and Thou, but only the encounter concealed in the word by its being an expression of something, so there is no direct revelation, but only revelation concealed in human words. Just as this fact makes it necessary for exegetical theology to transform the statement of the text into present concepts, so objective criticism is necessary for all exegesis. We have spoken already of the formation and ambiguity of objective criticism (pp. 240-241); this ambiguity comes up again, for in transforming the textual assertion into present-day concepts, it must be shown to what extent the concern of the text receives equivalent expression in what is said. Barth is certainly right in saying that criticism must avoid the misunderstanding that it thinks the Spirit of Christ is found in competition with other spirits in the text.[6] But one must not overlook the fact that the human statements of the text cannot be regarded as direct statements of the Spirit of Christ. Furthermore, insofar as Paul speaks of the "subject," he represents a human standpoint, which not only may be compared with other standpoints, but which Paul himself may not always have accepted so firmly. If one wishes to do theological exegesis scientifically, he should not be shocked by the question: "At which particular place can one assert that the Spirit of

Christ comes to expression?" One must in fact be concerned with such a distinction; the question is reminiscent of the peculiar situation of the exegete who is moved by the question of existence and knows therefore that he has no criterion at his disposal with which to grasp decisively the reality of history (pp. 248, 249 f.). However, he cannot for this reason refuse to make definite statements, but neither can he make the nature of the text as the Word of God into a controllable presupposition of exegesis. To undertake the responsibility of objective criticism is surely no occasion for arrogance on the part of the exegete, but a constant reminder of the obligation to undertake self-criticism, self-criticism in an existential sense.

Objective criticism must not allow itself to be confused by the question of whether a passage which is critically challenged can still (since it stands in the New Testament canon) become a word of revelation. Presupposing that the critical objection is correct, the situation just referred to could indeed come about if the passage were interpreted from the perspective of other passages—through allegory, for example (which, however, can never be justified as a general method, but only in a particular context). Obviously, no one can count on this possibility. Furthermore, just as the concept of the canon is intended to guard the contingent character of revelation and avoid the misunderstanding that revelation has to do with generally discernible truths or with the faith of individuals who are especially strong in piety, so criticism must guarantee that the concept of revelation does not become a presupposition at the exegete's disposal, as though the demand for existential encounter with the reality of which the text speaks could ever be dispensed with as the presupposition (not at one's disposal) for understanding the text.

Since there is no direct encounter with God, but his revelation is hidden in the word, there can be no appeal to an inner light for exegesis, no "pneumatic" exegesis which counts on the pneuma as a possession previously bestowed on the exegete. We have at our disposal no pneuma which is not bound to the word. Exegesis can proceed only from the interpretation of the word. Since exegetical work is work with concepts, and since the word of the text is never the subject matter itself, but its expression, this subject matter becomes available to the exegete only if he understands the word. The understanding of the word is certainly loaded with all sorts of ambiguity, because words are not only the unique expression of the concrete here and now, but also have their own history; in fact, they can be the former only to the extent that they are the latter. The exegete must be thoroughly familiar with the entire history of the words of the text without imagining he has thereby grasped the meaning of a passage in the concrete here and now. Therefore all the philological historical work on the New Testament is valid, in fact, obligatory, and has its special character because the New Testament is written in Greek. This work on the New Testament is tantamount to establishing a lexicon. But since a word has no fixed meaning like a label, but is determined by its particular development from its origin through its history, and through its broader and wider context, this lexicon cannot be a reference book for students; it includes the grammatical task, as well as all research into concepts and the history of religion.

Since we can understand the words of a text only if we understand their relation to the matter of which they are speaking, we cannot approach the exegetical task as if philological historical research provides an explanation related to the era of the text as a starting place, followed then by an explanation of the content, so that, to quote Barth, "Niebergall would have the answer in Volume V."[7] It is likewise erroneous to say that historical and theological exegesis could occur in different places;[8] rather, one should emphasize that the separation of historical and theological exegesis is an untenable position for both and that no one has the right to tack a theological commentary onto a philological historical commentary. In the actual process of exegesis, the relationship of historical and theological exegesis cannot really be analyzed, since genuine historical exegesis rests on the existential encounter with history and therefore coincides with theological exegesis, provided that the validation of theological exegesis rests on precisely the same basis. And that existential encounter is not something that could be undertaken like anything else and as such find its place within or behind methodical, philological, and historical interpretation.

NOTES

1. *Lehrbuch der neutestamentliche Theologie* I, 2. Aufl. (1911), 224.
2. *Ibid.*, II, 164.
3. But Scheler, for example, is also aware of that: *Über Ressentiment und moralisches Werturteil* (1912), 25.
4. I have developed this more fully in the essay "Welchen Sinn hat es, von Gott zu reden?" *Theologische Blätter* IV (1925), Nr. 6.
5. Cf. Gogarten, *Zwischen den Zeiten* III (1925), Heft 1, 78.
6. Preface to the Third Edition of his *Epistle to the Romans* (1923).
7. *Ibid.*, p. XXI.
8. *Epistle to the Romans*, Second Edition (1922), Preface, p. 11.

THE QUESTION OF "DIALECTIC" THEOLOGY:

A Discussion with Erik Peterson*

Rudolf Bultmann

When Socrates set out to find truth in the *Discourses,* his underlying notion was that the individual man, in his empirical state, does not have truth at his disposal, but that it can come to light in dialogue, in conversation. The individual has no criterion for truth and falsehood; if in dialogue, however, one convinces or persuades the other, this constitutes a criterion. In continuous dialogue, in questioning and answering, in testing and convicting, the truth must become progressively evident. The underlying conviction in this situation is that truth was present from the beginning, but concealed, and that such dialogue partakes of this truth. But there is something else here; in subsequent speaking, truth is still present only in concealment, since the questioning and answering goes on and on. Knowledge achieves the presuppositions necessary for the validity of its assertions only step by step; furthermore, we must strive to find the presuppositions which lie deeper within the subject, in order finally to approach the presupposition which needs no other presupposition. This process is unending, and yet meaningful, for ἀλήθεια (truth) is the infinite goal, not as something which can always become a datum (even if in the infinite), but as something immanent in the entire process of dialogue (thinking). It is the "undefined middle" at any given time between two assertions. Only, one should never forget that the entire process of knowledge is dialectic, a dialogue in which no assertion taken in itself may claim absolute truth, but is truth only in relation to the middle. This relation is guaranteed by the fact that every statement must be confronted by its opposite—that it is our task to find the opposite of every statement. Truth which is known at a specific time is therefore certainly never reality, but always and only possibility. Moreover, one can demonstrate that two (or more) actual persons are not necessary to the concept of discourse, but that thinking as such is discourse which may just as well happen in monologue. The duality of dialogue has meaning only in guaranteeing the dialectic character of speaking or thinking as such.

It is also valid to say that question is answer, and answer is question in this dialogue. For if the immanent movement of *logos* occurs in the

* From *Zwischen den Zeiten,* IV (1926), issue 1, pp. 40-59.

interchange of question and answer, then every question insofar as it, as individual *logos,* shares in the *logos* of the whole releases as an answer the corresponding movement of the developing process of thought. A question contains, then, not an accidental answer, but the necessary one. The answer is determined by the question, just as the question was determined by the answer in the previous stage, and just as the new answer must open up a new question. Thus, the relation here to a presupposition (ultimately, to *the* presupposition) is basically a posing of the presupposition itself through speech, insofar as every *logos* shares in the total *logos.* We are not speaking of the accidental posing of a "working hypothesis" by some thinking individual, but of the immanent presupposition posed by all speech which claims to be true.

If truth is never reality, the possession of a datum, then it is basically only the law of knowing; that is, in the act of knowing, the one who knows comprehends nothing but the knowing itself. And if this results in the opinion that in such knowing one grasps the essence of things and of his own existence, it demonstrates that one sees the being of things and of his own self nowhere except in the various *logoi.* No one can "seriously" speak of any other being; everything encountered as an object awaits the resolution, the reduction, into *logoi.* No one can "seriously" speak of God if he fails to see that in this line of thought God can mean nothing other than the primary presupposition of all thinking, which is, at the same time, the essence of the regularity of all thinking. Even if error is avoided here, it is still true that, serious as this thinking may otherwise be, to speak of God in such a way does not actually mean to speak of *God.*

Does the speaking of God in "dialectic" theology fall in this category, as charged by Peterson as well as many others; and, since it deludes itself about its own meaning, does it lack all seriousness?

In "dialectic" theology also one is concerned with a dialogue based on the presupposition that no individual assertion is itself true or has general validity, but that it achieves its meaning only in connection with a counter-assertion on the basis of the relation of both assertions to an undefined middle. In "dialectic" theology also one speaks of the question being the answer and vice versa. But at this point it becomes clear that despite all this outward similarity something fundamentally different is involved, so that we must ask whether it is really justifiable to speak of "dialectic" theology at all. So long as the meaning of what is said is not misunderstood, however, the question is ultimately immaterial.

It is clear that we "dialecticians" use this language which says the question is the answer and vice versa only in relation to one particular question—the decisive question of man in his existence. And there is likewise one particular answer—the justification of the sinner by God. Indeed, the answer immediately becomes a question again if man comprehends it; that is, if he understands it as a statement which is disconnected from the actual event it signifies. But it does not become a *new* question; it is the *old* one, and similarly, the answer it contains is not a new one, but the old. Thus, it is not a matter of a developing process of thought, but of a continuing point or, if you prefer, of a circling about one midpoint. Every attempt "to advance" would be futile, since the person supposedly advancing sees himself immediately pushed back to the old question.

The question, in fact, is not asked from man's point of view at all, nor is the answer determined by man's questioning. As long as *man* questions, the answer is not the question (Barth, *Gesammelte Vorträge,* p. 161); the answer can be the question only if God has done the asking; that is, what is in question is the real man in his specific situation, not abstract man. Since man's existence is not at his disposal (he does not stand *alongside* it, but *in* it; he *lives* it, he *is* it as it takes place), he recognizes the question under which he stands (namely, that he is a sinner) only when God shows it to him. If *God* shows it to him, then the question is the answer; not, to be sure, because the question is eliminated or transcended, that is, understood as a step toward the answer in the continuous process of knowing, but the answer must, in fact, *be* the question (Barth, p. 167); in other words, it is the sinner who is justified.

So the essence of the answer, which is also the question, is not constituted by the movement of the *logos* or consolidated by the *logos;* it is rather the existential concreteness of man's being, which is seen not in the *logos* but in his historical reality unfolding between birth and death. Truth, which is the issue here, is not an abstract possibility, but a concrete reality. Just as the question in which we are immersed is our existential situation (whether we are aware of it or not), and is neither our subjective questioning nor a stage in the sweep of the conceptual process, so the answer is only really spoken by God—it is an *event* in which our existence is grounded anew (Barth, p. 165). At this point we fully agree with Peterson when he says: " 'The religious mystery' is there before it can be actualized by man, before faith is able to approach it, before the human will can harmonize with it" (ZZ, 1925, p. 294).

It is an *eternal* event, insofar as it never creates an actual state (neither in the empirical history of humanity nor in the history of the individual) which would be an intellectual or mental datum; it is an event continually renewed by the miracle of the Holy Spirit. But it is an eternal *event*, not something made perceptible as the eternal movement of the *logos*, but something real insofar as it comes from God and becomes an event in our temporality through the miracle of the Holy Spirit. But it is just this concept of eternal event which allows the dialectic process (let us not say method) to appear as the appropriate parlance of theology. To speak of such an eternal event as though it held still even for one moment for us to examine it and solidify it into an assertion is to falsify it; only the constant reservation that it is not meant in this way can justify my speaking about it. This reservation comes into operation in setting up the counter-assertion to the initial assertion. How this process appears is shown by Barth (p. 172), to the extent that one can "show" such a thing—basically, one cannot, since absolutely nothing can be demonstrated in the abstract. Dialogue is no fiction here; it involves the constant situation of assertion and counter-assertion about what is said by and to a specific person. On the contrary, it is the monologue form of theological development that is fiction.

This "dialectic" is no less than a dialogue which, as such, sets up its own presuppositions. But the theological dialectician is not permitted to do this (Barth, p. 174); that is, he cannot give meaning and truth (meaning and truth = reality!) to his speaking, because the presupposition is not at his disposal. His speaking is never anything but a witness to God's truth, which lies "in the middle" (p. 173). This truth is truly the event from God; it is God's act, which is neither presupposed for the speaker as the immanent law of thought which gives every statement its meaning, nor imagined as perfect knowledge at the end of the infinite path of all discourse; rather, it is something which happens (in time), something to which the speaker relates himself and to which he refers. And it is not because he must always say something new and true of God that his speaking becomes a process *ad infinitum*, but because he must continually guard the reference to what happens against being misunderstood as a reference to an objectively demonstrable fact of the history of humanity or the soul; it is after all an *eternal* event!

The "seriousness" of this "dialectic" consists in the fact that dialogue is viewed as the only appropriate form for speaking of God. It honors God in the fact that it is not deluded into thinking it can achieve the seriousness of God (Peterson, *Was ist Theologie?*, p. 7). God is not a dialectic possibility here, nor does one speak of "God in general," or of "man in general," but of revealed God and concrete

man; that is, one does not speak of empirical man (of man's experiences, and so forth), but of existential man, who does not exist in
abstraction but only in his reality.* The answer to the question "What
is theology?" at first reads[1] that theology exists only where one speaks
of God's revelation as an eternal occurrence—nevertheless, an occurrence; it says further that there can certainly be no theology which
makes general statements about God, no theology which speaks in
God's stead, no theology which claims to attain to God's seriousness.

The fundamental difference, however, between Peterson and us is
by no means expressed in this delineation. For insofar as Peterson
polemicizes against us at this point, his polemic rests on a misunderstanding (albeit, a widely held one). Indeed, what has been said up to
this point is really much more valid in reference to our other opponents than to Peterson. Our real difference with him may be explained
as follows: When the discourse of theology refers to an *occurrence*
(arising from God) as its presupposition, then the object of theology,
insofar as God is spoken of in theology, allows fundamentally no
discourse at all (we can go this far as dialecticians), and the only appropriate form for speaking of him is that of message, of proclamation.
But "dialectic" theology is aware of its direct association with proclamation (as its presupposition, not its consequence), and it is at this
point that we part company with Peterson. Because he does not derive
his theological (dogmatic) concepts from the character of their objects
as events, he therefore loses the direct connection of theology with
proclamation. Rather, he derives his concepts from the "order of being" *(Seinsordnung)*[2] by means of a so-called phenomenology. His essay
on the angels' songs of praise[3] shows very clearly how this turns out.
He first describes the mystic's "higher form of being" from the perspective of mysticism; the mystic is thus the actual object of discussion
and the discussion is basically historical. But suddenly this perspective
is changed to that of phenomenology; mysticism is seen as an object
and is lumped together with what the mystic intends and is then
regarded as the *real* mode of being.[4] Peterson constantly deals in
essences, which are in truth only concepts of an established, historical
interpretation of being at any one particular time, and which, since
they are available, have not yet demonstrated their justification and
validity. Basically, truth and being lie in the realm of *logos,* not for

---

* What does "empirical" really mean? The "empirical" man is indeed seen from
a particular perspective, in which he is perceived in the kind of looking which dis-
regards the self; that is, he is viewed as a thing of nature, not the real man with
whom we are bound from the start in being-with-another. Empirical man, therefore,
is an abstraction.

us, as he charges, but for him. For he lifts his essences from the *logos* alone. If these essences really possess authority *(auctoritas)*, according to the place they assume in revelation, it is hard to see how phenomenology can attain such authority this way, or how this authority can be any different from that which can be discerned *in* these essences by observation. Indeed, I can speak seriously of the authority of an essence only if this authority is not some property it has, but is its very *being*, and if it is so *for me*. The debate between us, therefore, would have to be carried on in an entirely different manner (and I hope it still will); it would have to be on the basis of the question of the concepts of being[5] and the question of the possibility of attaining genuine theological concepts. We agree with him entirely in the polemic against inauthentic theological concepts, against rationalism, psychologism, and historicism (thus, for example, also against Althaus). The nature of his attack on us and his specific reproaches are such that they bring out the real difference between us in this connection only indirectly or at certain points. But we must now proceed to defend ourselves.

The "seriousness" of "dialectic" theology lies precisely in the fact that it takes very seriously the dissimilarity of its talk to divine talk— that it takes seriously the ultimate lack of seriousness of its own theology and all others as well. This ultimate lack of seriousness means that all the very serious speaking about God is limited by the seriousness of God, which alone gives true seriousness, as he manifests himself in the final judgment (Peterson, *Was ist Theologie?*, p. 7). "Dialectic" theology gives expression to this reservation. Peterson's discussion would be justified only under this reservation, even if it is static discussion and does not express the reservation at all. One may naturally ask why God may not also be spoken of in a static, undialectic manner, that is, in the way Peterson says dogma is expressed. We might answer as follows: To be sure, this can and perhaps must happen, but only under the one condition that the existence of that eternal reservation, resting on God's deity and man's humanity, is so self-evident to the one who speaks in this way (even if it be the church) that it need not be given particular expression. In this case the static discussion would be dialectic in the highest sense—in its totally undialectic nature.

But this is not the case with Peterson. He thinks he has the full seriousness of God present when he talks theology, which is, in fact, no longer a "talking to," but a "talking with." He does have this seriousness, because the speaking he refers to here is not *his* speaking, but that of the church, nothing other than the extension of the awesome, eternal seriousness of God in Christ into time and the world. "Dogma consists in the extension of Christ's speaking of God, and therefore the authority of dogma is . . . the authority of Christ which expresses itself here" *(Was ist Theologie?,* pp. 21 f.). Indeed (and this is the decisive point), this "extension" is conceived as direct and unbroken, not a real extension constantly grounded anew in the Holy Spirit through God's miracle, but a simple and undialectic continuity of the history of revelation with the history of the church. Here lies our real point of disagreement.

We could perhaps accept all of Peterson's assertions and join him in stating them (as said before, we agree with him in his sharp opposition to all psychologism and historicism), but only on the condition that this continuity is broken by the reservation of the Holy Spirit, which means that the seriousness of God remains reserved to God himself and can never be delegated once-for-all to an earthly entity, even if it be the church.

Moreover even Kierkegaard may have deluded himself about the character and meaning of the dialectic process. In the very work to which Peterson occasionally alludes, *Fear and Trembling,* Kierkegaard says very clearly that the dialectician qua dialectician advances the process no further than the most ordinary and naïve man (p. 44).[6] Kierkegaard put his acceptance this way: "I cannot complete the movement of faith" (p. 44). "It is absolutely impossible for me to complete the final movement, the paradoxical movement of faith" (p. 62). "I can well *describe* the movements of faith, but I cannot *execute* them" (p. 48). In *Fear and Trembling,* faith is clearly delineated in contrast to the resignation of melancholy. Kierkegaard well knew the meaning of seriousness and intended to preserve it through dialectic. "Seriousness is just this, that Christ can make no direct communication" *(Training in Christianity,* p. 135). By making Christ speak directly we make him "into some sort of a public person as it were, almost as serious as the parson" (p. 135). "To begin by refusing direct communication—this is seriousness" (p. 140). "All Christian knowledge, regardless of the power of its expression, must be grief— that is precisely what edifies. Grief is the relation to life, *to the reality* of personality, and is for the Christian *seriousness.* The elevation of insignificant knowledge increases seriousness for the Christian to such a small degree that it is jest and vanity. Again, seriousness is what is edifying" *(Sickness Unto Death,* p. 142). "Speculation cannot . . . concern itself with sin . . . only the individual is *real,* and sin exists therefore only as the sin of the individual. That is seriousness . . . that it is my sin and your sin—and thus also the sin of the speculative thinker, who is nevertheless an individual. But if he should deny the individual in his speculation (that is, deny himself also as an individual), then he can think only without seriousness of his sin, that is, frivolously. In fact, all speculative talk of sin from an ethical viewpoint (that is, objective, correct talk) is frivolous" (p. 251). If God becomes man, "then *this fact* is the seriousness of existence. And what is serious here is that everyone should form an opinion about it" (p. 261). The person who only experiments (and that is what Peterson's dialectician would do) "knows no power above himself; and there, seriousness is missing; he can reflect only an appearance of seriousness by giving his own experiments the highest possible attention. Regardless of the fact that it seems ever so serious to him, it is only affected seriousness, and thus not seriousness at all. Real seriousness is found only in the thought that God looks at man" (p. 202). "The only seriousness is in relation to God. What is serious is precisely the fact that the task is pressed toward the highest peak, because someone is there who can apply the pressure of eternity. Seriousness lies in the fact that enthusiasm knows a power beyond itself and is accompanied by its master" *(Works of Love,* p. 154). "Seriousness is the relation of a man to God; seriousness is what a man does, thinks, and says as God is involved in it" (p. 258). Seriousness, therefore, is nothing but unconditioned reality; and the expression of the will, objectively speaking, is dialectic, just as the relation to life in general is dialectic. "The seriousness of life is to wish to be and to express the ideal in daily reality. But one must truly *wish* it, so as not—to his own ruin—to underline it quickly once and for all or to regard it as something worthless as a dream (in both cases, there is, oh, such a lack of seriousness!); he must desire it humbly in reality" *(Training in Christianity,* p. 188; cf. p. 223, concerning the dialectic of this seriousness). "That man has never known seriousness who has not learned from seriousness that one can take things too seriously" *(Works of Love,* p. 275). "One cannot speak seriously of death if he does not know enough to use the furtiveness of death, the whole melancholy cunning of death" (p. 284).

If the meaning of theological "dialectic" is clear, then our refutation of Peterson's specific charges can be readily understood. We agree with him that for the time between the first and second coming of Christ the point of *faith* has taken the place of all dialectic questioning (Peterson, *Was ist Theologie?,* p. 8). Our "dialectic" process does not have the least intention of establishing faith by the *via dialectica* or of replacing faith by it; it seeks rather to elevate itself on the *basis* of faith and attempts to speak in a compatible manner. We agree with Peterson that obedience is the true nature of faith (p. 8), that concrete obedience and concrete authority receive expression in theology, and that revelation is presupposed and operative in it (p. 9). We know as well as Peterson and Kierkegaard that the existence of the dialectician is not one of obedience, and we must keep ourselves from pretending that it is. We know as well as Peterson, therefore, that the obedience of faith is wholly undialectic.

The decisive question, however, is still the following: In what way is revelation "presupposed" in theology? In what way are concrete authority and concrete obedience expressed in it? Peterson knows as well as we do that revelation is neither a historical-empirical factum nor a hypothesis in the process of radical thinking; and his theology, as ours, desires to move beyond an abstract concept of revelation, authority, and faith. His own concept of revelation issues from his concept of man's being as an essence which assumes its definite place in the cosmos in the graduated structure of the modes of being, and has the possibility of comprehending the entire cosmic order of being by speculative thinking, and even of elevating its own mode of being to one that is higher and nearer the divine mode. This last possibility is given through the fact of creation and revelation—this is how Peterson must be interpreted. Revelation, then, is a cosmic transaction (just as man is a cosmic creature), which took place once and continues working in the form of a causal process (how else?). There can be a knowledge of revelation, then, only in the form of speculation, within which the obedience of faith accepts, on the basis of some authority, the datum of revelation, as something given.

In truth, we are not speaking here of concrete authority and concrete obedience, since we are not speaking of concrete man. For concrete man cannot be understood as an essence which has its place and thus its security in a cosmic order of being. Concrete man exists only in the specificity of his temporal being, in his historical nature—and that means in full uncertainty. Because his existence is always in time and therefore in constant flux, it is impossible for him to be incorporated into an order of being. And not only could he know nothing about a revelation that was a cosmic event, but it would not concern him in the least. Our opinion is that one speaks of the real man only if one sees that man is subject to time in a specific way. And if revelation is God's eternal event, an event which enters into our time, our history, then revelation is available to theological talk as a "presupposition" only when it pleases God to set up this presupposition, when he allows it to happen in the working of the Holy Spirit. Obedience is indeed not something that can be calculated as a datum at our disposal; whether or not it is present in our theology is decided by God. The authority to be expressed in theology is not our authority, but God's; that is, it is not a direct authority controlled by theology, but the authority of the Spirit over which we have no control. In other words, participation in the Logos, which is presupposed in theology in Peterson's view *(Was ist Theologie?,* p. 11),* is not direct, but is man's participation in the Spirit of God by the miracle of the Holy Spirit. We are not practicing a *theologia gloriae.*

But neither does all this mean that the realistic character of theological knowledge, which rests on the objective character of revelation, is forgotten or sacrificed (again, we agree with Peterson; his statement [p. 29] that in modern theology faith is an attitude of the soul is not directed toward us). It does mean, however, that the objective character of revelation does not make revelation into an establishable, objective fact, but that in revelation one is dealing with God's deed, which does not take place within any cosmic order. Therefore, with Peterson, we reject the connection of dogmatics with Idealist philosophy just as much as the demand for a "system of Christian doctrine"; and, with Peterson, we are of the opinion that to speak of the incarnation of God as a dialectic possibility means not to speak of the incarnation at all (p. 10). We also reject Peterson's attempt to turn theology into speculation about human and divine orders of being and their associations; this attempt is basically a transposed empiricism, which no more achieves the concreteness of its objects than natural-scientific empiricism does.

To be sure, Peterson is fully correct in disputing that paradox is the real meaning of revelation (pp. 11, 27). In fact, Christianity is not concerned with one or more paradoxical statements, and we might ask whether paradoxical language is not better dispensed with, since the terminology of paradox as well as that of dialectic is loaded with philosophical connotations. But there can be no serious doubt that our talk of paradox refers to the paradoxical *event,* namely, the event in which God is gracious to the sinner. As a statement it is not paradoxical in the least—it is understood quite well by the world; but as an event it is completely incomprehensible.† The paradox, therefore, is that the statement (for one can speak of an event only in a statement) about God's grace for the sinner can be uttered as a true statement. To deny the paradox would be here to assert the direct, unbroken,

---

* What does it mean after all for it to be presupposed that in theology revelation, faith, and obedience involve somehow a participation in divine Logos? How? These are the crucial questions.

† Therefore, we do not know why Peterson replies *(Was ist Theologie?,* p. 27) that the Stoic Paradox, the sage alone is king, is indeed a paradoxical statement, whereas the assertion that the cross of Christ is a stumbling block to the Jews and folly to the Greeks is not. His reason is that the cross of Christ itself is not a statement. We have just emphasized this and, because we know that both Peterson and we ourselves can express it only in the form of a statement, we speak "dialectically."

objective continuity of the event of revelation; it would be to forget
that Christ has ascended into heaven and has sent the Holy Spirit to
us (for the ascension of Christ would be an entirely superfluous miracle
if there were direct continuity of revelation). "Not paradoxical" would
not mean, say, the ruling out of faith (to speak of a theology of faith is
something which Peterson rightly guards against), but the ruling out
of miracles performed by the Holy Spirit, who alone certifies revelation as revelation (just as it is he who alone creates faith). It is, in fact,
crystal clear that there would be no theology if revelation did not
"harbor a relative discernability" (p. 11), or if revelation (that is, its
content as an assertion) is a paradox. But, surely, neither of us asserts
that. Rather we agree entirely with Peterson that if revelation is a
paradox, there is then no revelation, that is, if the content of revelation is paradoxical. In a different sense, though, it is valid to say that
if revelation as event is *not* paradoxical, then there is no revelation
and no theology, but only a science of the world or cosmological
speculation.

Thus, faith is indeed knowing—but why only to a relative degree?
Or, what does it mean to say this at this point? Faith can deal only
with knowing revelation, and, in revelation, faith is knowing in the
full sense of the word. The content of revelation is as little a paradox
as it is a mystery in which one may speak of a step-by-step or a partial
knowing. Therefore, faith is indeed knowing and theology thus is not
to be confused with literary activity (*Was ist Th.*, p. 13). This reproach
of Peterson's is only a bit of fencing on his part, for who would think
of reproaching us with confusing theology and literary activity if he
has read the Elgersburg lecture? This lecture is based on the fact that
the theologian's task cannot possibly be the same as that of a member
of a profession—and how can this be said of a writer?

This theological profession, as we see it, has the impossible task of
speaking of God. Of what else should it speak? But Peterson does not
deny us the object of theology, but only our relation to that object—
that is, our "speaking." Indeed, none of us has said or thought that
"speaking of something" is the only religious or intellectual possibility
for man (*Was ist Th.*, p. 14). But we do mean to say that man, even as
a theologian, cannot leap so far over the limits of his human possibilities that he ceases to be a ζῷον λόγον ἔχον (creature of the word);
that is, only in his speaking can he bring to consciousness in himself
and in others what he perceives and communicates; or again, "speaking
of something" is a part of what it means to be human. And since this
speaking as such can never embrace or communicate the object itself,
we assert that *real* speaking of God, whether in Christ's speaking or in

our speaking, exists only as the Word of God itself, only insofar as it is the result of the Spirit's activity. Whether or not a differentiation of terminology may be valid (and it is not our concern to dispute this) —that Christ "talks," the prophets and preachers "say," and the church and theology "speak"—anyone in the world who expresses himself in words, talks; and whether this is "talking," "saying," or "speaking," in their differentiated senses, does not depend on him. Peterson's theology, however, when it forgets this, is not a human theology but a theology of mystagogues, or, for all I care, a theology of angels and the departed.

Human words and human speech are words and speech "about something"; that is, apart from the existential situation of the speaker (and hearer), they tend to be understood basically as statements which have their meaning in themselves. An essay in *Theologische Blätter* (1925, No. 6), which Peterson criticized, tried to show that such "speaking about" has no meaning if it deals with God, and it tried to show the condition under which such a "speaking about God," which we cannot avoid, can be a "speaking from God." The answer was simply —if it pleases God. The essay said also that this answer has meaning only as the answer of faith which grasps the promise of the divine word in obedience.* To say that the possibility of speaking "from God" is only a dialectic possibility *(Was ist Th.*, p. 17) would be a statement of unbelief. But the fact that the realization of this possibility is not at our disposal is indeed security enough against the charge of confusing oneself with Christ. When this possibility is grasped in faith, no such confusion can take place, for Christ is certainly not one of the faithful. To say *that*, however, is to say that where speaking for God becomes reality, where this speaking is a gift of the Spirit, there Christ is speaking—but it is not our speaking!

But if God is the object of our human speaking, then in order to avoid philosophical dialectic and speculation, we must not forget that we are speaking of ourselves. And it is enough to say that that does not mean to speak of our experiences. It should be equally clear that we are then speaking of our *reality*, in which alone we have our being before God. For "the one who is god in isolation is not God. He could

---

* The essay neglected, though, to refer to the fact that the spoken word has its true meaning only as a word spoken *to* the hearer; in other words, that the real being of man is a being with another, or that being heard is essential for the word. Similarly, the preached word of faith is characterized in the New Testament as ἀκοὴ πίστεως (believing hearing). The character of theology, however, as distinct from preaching, is that it does not speak to concrete persons. On the one hand, the result is that theology has meaning only as church theology (since it happens in and for the congregation), and, on the other hand, the result is that as a human enterprise it can be only a "speaking about."

also be something different. The God who reveals himself is God"
(Barth, *Ges. Vortr.*, p. 169). The phrase "who reveals himself" means,
to be sure, the one who addresses our reality. As Herrmann expressed
it: "What an almighty being is in himself remains hidden to us. He
appears in that which he brings about for us. We can say of God only
what he does in relation to us."[7] Or, as we find it in Luther: "And
here we also see that to believe in Christ does not mean to believe that
Christ is a person who is both God and man—that helps no one; it is
to believe that the same person, who proceeds from God for our sakes
and has come into the world and then leaves the world and goes to the
Father, is Christ."[8] Or, finally, as Melanchthon said: *"Christum
cognoscere id est beneficia eius cognoscere"* (to know Christ is to know
his benefits). It is certainly clear that one does not thereby make himself into Christ (Peterson, *Was ist Th.*, pp. 15 f.). Does not the statement that I am a sinner and that God is gracious to the sinner speak
of God precisely to the extent that it speaks of *me*? If it does not
speak of me, it is meaningless speculation, as Kierkegaard certainly
knew (see above, p. 263). The fact that it says something real is surely
not my doing.

Nor do we remove the theologian from the human situation, for
we are not permitted to carry on a *theologia gloriae*. We do not mean
that the theologian, insofar as he speaks through the church or the
church speaks through him, has a direct authority; nor do we mean
that the Holy Spirit, the only source of life for the theologian's speaking, is at his disposal. It is not within our power to bestow on any
speakers (or singers of praise) any qualification which exceeds human
possibilities. Therefore, we are not particularly concerned with listing
a line of ancestors, in which prophets and apostles stand next to reformers and writers *(Was ist Th.*, p. 27)—especially when we reflect
on what is the most appropriate process for our theology as a human
attempt to speak of God. And it does not console us that "someone"
(who?) can say that the one speaking in theology is not the theology
professor, but primarily Christ and secondarily the church (p. 30). That
is no help at all when we want to practice theology, since we can do it
only, in fact, as professors of theology. Naturally, that does not mean
that in our opinion the language of the dogmatician is a direct speaking about that which he believes (*ZZ*, p. 296). His faith is simply not at
his disposal. In fact, we can say with Peterson that the dogmatician
presents what the church believes (*loc. cit.*); but the church is not such
an unambiguous entity for us as it is for Peterson.*

---

* Why does Peterson say moreover (ZZ, 297) that dogmatics deals with knowing the "doctrine" of a church? Why *a* church? If it does not deal with the doctrine
of *the* church, dogmatics is an abstract possibility which can realize itself at will.

Insofar as theology speaks with authority (and again we agree with Peterson here), it is not a human enterprise. It speaks with authority (and therefore "speaks") when God's Word is alive in it, when the Spirit is at work in it. And insofar as that is true, its authority is not "derived" (p. 16), that is, it is not to be pictured as a continuous emanation; it is conveyed by God's specific acts as Lord. Its significance for us who presume to speak as theologians is only that it makes theology a commission. We *must* practice theology; woe unto us if we do not! But we cannot claim direct authority for it; it has only indirect authority. We theologians do not have it so easy that we can claim authority for our statements, nor do laymen, that they can regard them as authoritative, whatever the case is for others. But precisely because only "revelation itself ultimately determines the actual essence of theology" (p. 19), there is no other theology, no speaking on the basis of revelation and obedience. But, again, even this is a theological statement, subject to the "dialectic" character of all theological thinking; for just to glance at other "theologies" can continually make our enterprise questionable in our own eyes.

Nevertheless, the commission under which theology stands is nothing but "the concrete fulfillment of the fact that the Logos of God has spoken concretely of God" (p. 14). But theology, for its part, is not yet the "extension of the revelation of *logos*" *(loc. cit.)* in the direct sense, but only in the indirect. It is a human enterprise, which takes place under a divine commission, and stands under the promise that God's Spirit wishes to make our word a living, authoritative word.

But why is *dogma* shoved in between theology and revelation (pp. 19 ff.)? We do not accept "the" dogma in any sense, and we would like to know why Peterson does not say where and what this dogma is. We recognize dogmas but we certainly do not view them as "creeds," any more than we regard theology as being part of the extension of the act of faith (p. 21). Dogmas specifically fix a theological position and participate thereby in the ambiguous character of all theology and theological authority. We certainly do not mean that historical considerations settle the issue. Theology is no more a knowing on the basis of human presuppositions than its results, dogmas, are fortuitous

---

If (as Peterson rightly says) dogmatics deals with knowing God, there can indeed be only *one* dogmatic, namely, that of the Christian church. One is served as little by the various theologians' doctrines of faith as by the various dogmatic systems of individual historical churches, each one answering the requirements of a dogmatic. The demands placed upon dogmatics are certainly not purely formal ones; they grow out of the fact that one should speak of a *particular* act of salvation (*Heilstat*) by God. Furthermore, Peterson speaks also of *the* church in general. But where is it if it is possible (and actual) that "the churches" know nothing of the fact that dogma exists (*Was ist Th.*, 24)?

academic views, or stages of a developmental process. Their meaning lies in the imperceptibility of their assertions; they have the nature of allusion, of witness to the revelation of God attested to in Scripture. But they do not thereby lose the character of human formulations, which are connected with the developmental history of human theological thinking, and from which no churchly dictum can free them. Their authority, like that of theology, is indirect; it exists only in connection with revelation. Being human words, however, dogmas stand under the judgment of the Word of God revealed in Scripture. But, again, that does not mean we play the Bible off against dogma on principle (Peterson, ZZ, p. 299), but that dogma has to legitimize itself by Scripture.*

One may formulate the difference between theology and dogma as follows: all theology tends toward dogma; theology is the process of reflection and argumentation (thus, also, criticism), always in flux, whereas dogmas are the specific results of theological work. Naturally, one may say that the church creates dogma at a specific time (ZZ, pp. 297 f.), but that is a historical judgment on our part. For to exercise *direct* authority through the creation of a dogma is no more at the disposal of a church than of the professor (one can deal here only with a church at a specific time). "The" dogma is an ideal entity; namely, perfected theology; if we had "the" dogma, we would no longer need theology. Dogma can in no way be the subject matter of theology; rather, it is its goal, its perfection. From that perspective,

---

* All this is good Lutheran thinking, according to the opening of the Formula of Concord, which reads: "We believe, confess, and teach that the only rule and norm, according to which all dogmas and all doctors ought to be esteemed and judged, is no other whatever than the prophetic and apostolic writings both of the Old and of the New Testament . . . But other writings, whether of the fathers or of the moderns, with whatever name they come, are in nowise to be equaled to the Holy Scriptures, but are all to be esteemed inferior to them, so that they be not otherwise received than in the rank of witnesses, to show what doctrine was taught after the Apostles' times also, and in what parts of the world that more sound doctrine of the Prophets and Apostles has been preserved . . . In this way a clear distinction is retained between the sacred Scriptures of the Old and New Testaments, and all other writings; and Holy Scripture alone is acknowledged as the [only] judge, norm, and rule, according to which, as by the [only] touchstone, all doctrines are to be examined and judged, as to whether they be godly or ungodly, true or false. But the other symbols and other writings, of which we made mention a little while ago, do not possess the authority of a judge—for this dignity belongs to Holy Scripture alone; but merely give testimony to our religion, and set it forth to show in what manner from time to time the Holy Scriptures have been understood and explained in the church of God by the doctors who then lived, as respects controverted articles, and by what arguments, dogmas at variance with the Holy Scriptures have been rejected and condemned" (translation quoted from Philip Shaff, *The Creeds of Christendom* [New York: Harper, 1919], 4th ed., Vol. III, pp. 93 f., 96 f.).

dogma must not even determine the inner form of dogmatics for the theologian, as Peterson rightly points out (ZZ, p. 300). The only subject matter of theology is God's revelation, through which theology is intrinsically released from the connection with the so-called intellectual sciences (Was ist Th., p. 23). To the extent, however, that critical reflection on its own labors is proper to theology, since all its results can claim only relative validity as qualified through their relation to Scripture, dogmas are, in a certain sense, the subject matter of theology.

We may reject, therefore, the alternative of having to choose between academic theological views and dogma (Was ist Th., p. 24). And if instead it is a question of choosing between academic theological views and revelation, we can decide for the latter only if we do not forget in the process that we never have revelation directly before us. The true alternative would be a choice of either academic theological views or faith in the revelation in God's Word. We know, further, that we ourselves cannot decide between these alternatives, but that it is the Spirit who gives faith.

The extent to which Peterson's entire mode of thinking results in the exclusion of the Holy Spirit becomes clear when we consider his theses about Scripture and preaching. He does not exclude the Holy Spirit from his reflections, but transforms him; everywhere and with the strictest consistency, he relates him to the institution, that is, to the church, which teaches, administers the sacraments, and preaches. But as we understand the matter, it is by precisely this process that the Holy Spirit is excluded. In this light it is understandable that Peterson shows no interest in an exact doctrine of inspiration, for example. He speaks (Was ist Th., p. 29) in a curiously undogmatic manner of theories of inspiration; whereas for us it is at this point that the question of inspiration becomes really acute.

For him, the doctrine of inspiration is replaced by his doctrine of dogma. For in spite of the above-mentioned differences between us, a common concern once more finds expression in his view here. His doctrine of dogma is really a safeguard against the concept of Scripture which takes Scripture as a compendium of doctrines—as we find in the orthodox doctrine of inspiration or in Biblicism—and against the view of Scripture as a collection of passages or speeches of prophetic personalities; in other words, it is a safeguard against the direct identification of Scripture and revelation. We agree, therefore, with Peterson, when he says that Scripture communicates the Word of God only when it is spoken (and, we must add, when it is heard). Just as he who hears Moses, Jeremiah, Matthew, and Paul hears only the *witness* to revelation (Barth, ZZ, 1925, p. 220), and the person who hears exegetes and preachers today hears only their witness; thus, exegesis as well as preaching is only the linear continuation of Old Testament prophecy, but not the continuation of that which the incarnate Logos has said of God. Actually, theology is neither the systematizing of biblical concepts and doctrines, nor the historical exposition of the faith, life, and doctrine of biblical persons. Rather, it presupposes (in the sense previously indicated) that Scripture is really the witness to revelation and speaks of revelation; in this respect, therefore, theology is really the concrete fulfillment of what the Logos of God has spoken about God, and only revelation can ultimately determine its essence (Peterson, *Was ist Th.*, p. 19). We can, then, give full assent to what Peterson said about the relation of the revelation of Christ to the prophetic word (p. 30, n. 20), assuming that what Peterson means by "event of revelation" is what we call the eternal event. We agree therefore with the following statement: "The Bible is a fully adequate medium for the prophetic utterances. But it is essential to see that Christ's message is not contained adequately in the Bible, since Christ has not only spoken God's Word, but is God's Word." But we cannot continue with the statement: "Dogma allows us to avoid the danger that, by mediating what Christ has spoken, the Bible would turn his speaking about God into prophetic utterance" *(loc. cit.).* To be sure, we see this danger also, but Peterson seems to make the mistake of eliminating the Holy Spirit and instituting a continuous sequence of revelation in dogma. The danger is not avoided in the least by having objective data at our disposal; rather, we stand in continual uncertainty, which is overcome only by hearing and believing the testimony. That is, revelation does not allow some dogma to turn it into a direct assertion; it can become an event only when the testimony is heard and believed.

Nevertheless, we agree again with Peterson's view that dogma, in a certain sense, does indeed mean deliverance—that is the case insofar as it alludes and testifies, not to Scripture, but to the revelation to which Scripture witnesses. Thus, it is the necessary expression of the life of the church, for through dogma the church guards itself against understanding Scripture directly as revelation, be it in the sense of the orthodox doctrine of inspiration, of Biblicism, or of the modern view of "God in history." And by speaking in dogmas of that to which witness is given, and thereby bearing witness, it demonstrates a seriousness about understanding Scripture as *witness*. Theology, therefore, is always exegesis inasmuch as it has access to revelation only through the witness of Scripture and seeks to grasp by exegesis what Scripture, understood as witness, says. In form, therefore, theology is always exegesis of Scripture. Its content speaks of revelation. But since revelation is the eternal event, judging or forgiving man, the object of theology is nothing other than the conceptual presentation of man's existence as determined by God—that is, as man must see it in the light of Scripture.

NOTES

1. Cf. Peterson, *Was ist Theologie?*, 5.
2. Cf. *Zwischen den Zeiten* (1925), 290.
3. *Ibid.*, 141-153.
4. Cf. H. Schlier, *ibid.*, 410, n. 1.
5. *Ibid.*, 410-414.
6. Quoted material is our translation. Page numbers refer respectively to *Fear and Trembling* and *Sickness Unto Death*, tr. by Walter Lowrie (Garden City: Doubleday & Company, 1955); *Training in Christianity*, tr. by Walter Lowrie (Princeton: Princeton University Press, 1944); *Works of Love*, tr. by David F. and Lillian Marvin Swenson (Princeton: Princeton University Press, 1946).
7. Wilhelm Herrmann, *Die Wirklichkeit Gottes*, 41 f.
8. *Erlangen Ausgabe*, XII², 163.

2

Friedrich Gogarten

BETWEEN THE TIMES

THE CRISIS OF OUR CULTURE

THE PLIGHT OF ABSOLUTENESS

THE RELIGIOUS CRISIS:
An Open Letter to Emil Fuchs
Friedrich Gogarten

THE UNCONDITIONAL SERIOUSNESS OF OUR PIETY:
A Reply to Friedrich Gogarten's Complaint Concerning
the Plight of Absoluteness
Emil Fuchs

AN APPLE FROM THE TREE OF KIERKEGAARD
Ernst Troeltsch

AGAINST ROMANTIC THEOLOGY:
A Chapter on Faith

COMMUNITY OR CORPORATE SOCIETY?

HISTORICISM

PROTESTANTISM AND REALITY:
Epilogue to Martin Luther's *Bondage of the Will*

BETWEEN THE TIMES*

Friedrich Gogarten

It is the destiny of our generation to stand between the times. We never belonged to the period presently coming to an end; it is doubtful whether we shall ever belong to the period which is to come, and, if through our own efforts we could be a part of the future, whether it would come as soon.

So we stand in the middle—in an empty space. We belong neither to the one nor to the other. Not to the one which precedes us, which would like to make us its disciples and the heirs of its thoughts and convictions. We cannot follow them. We never could. When we did, it was only to see how they worked—but never to have a model or example for our own actions. So we are berated as individualists, grumblers, and eccentrics. And we have suffered under this chiding. But we could not do otherwise. Your concepts were strange to us, always strange. When we did think of them and use them, it was as if we were tormented by an inner vacuum. Where we heard you, we heard the best and truest of intentions, but they sounded hollow, hollow, to our ears. Because we heard nothing but the best intentions. It was, though, your purpose and our longing to say more and to hear more. You spoke indeed of what was divine and not only of what was human. That was your intention.

You do not know how it tormented us that we could hear nothing more. We could not find ourselves (we sought to find ourselves in you—we did indeed) and you left us empty. The tormenting question never left us, the question of whether we, who were supposed to give everything with the word, could have anything at all to give. Indeed, we received nothing. We received much that was scholarly, much that was interesting, but nothing that would have been worthy of this word.

In our need we were often angry with you, because you left us alone—and because your words were so weak and so empty that they sank to the ground before they reached us. But mostly we cried out our question to you through all your answers to your own questions, when the agony of having nothing with which we could approach men drove us to you.

Today you also have a need, one which touches on your spiritual

* From *Die Christliche Welt*, XXXIV (1920), issue 24, columns 374-378.

existence. But it comes to you from the outside, from external circumstances. You are afraid for your learning because of the cost of printing and the price of paper. But inwardly this learning has long since come to an end.

But this is not to belittle you, certainly not. We know today that we could not expect you to answer our question, since you did not understand it and perhaps today still do not understand it. For you belong to a different period than we, who belong perhaps to none. Had we been able to make our question clear to you, we would have had the answer. Even now we have only a faint notion of the answer, but we are content that, however slowly, it does become clearer.

And because we no longer demand from you what you could not give us, we can gratefully accept from you what you do have. But we cannot carry on your work. And will those coming after us do it? I need not bother to answer that.

We never belonged to your period. In the same breath, therefore, you could express shock at both our radicalism and our reactionary attitude. We were so far from this period that we had to look outside it; Nietzsche and Kierkegaard, Meister Eckhard and Lao-Tzu, have been our teachers more than you to whom we are indebted for all our intellectual training.

Today we are witnessing the demise of your world. We can be as calm about all that concerns this decline as if we were seeing the extinction of something with which we had no connection at all. In fact, we are not connected with it. That we are nevertheless moved is only because something we have long seen is now becoming real before our very eyes. Perhaps it was in dreams that we saw it. But it was much more living, much more real than a dream could ever be. It was always an experience deep within us. It was always the presupposition of our relation to this period, but so concealed, that we were not aware of this. Therefore we recognize disintegration even in the most hidden recesses, where you do not yet see it. We saw it long before it became as evident as it is today.

We do not wish to lift a hand to stop it. What is it that we should stop? And how should we do it? All these things have long since disintegrated. They have long since been explained in terms of historical development, long since been placed in the stream of general history. That happened the moment you handled them scientifically. You could not have done it a moment sooner. Science (should I say "our" science?) directs its attention toward and can comprehend those things which are dead. And what is left of this period that has not been worked over scientifically and that science does not understand? I do not wish to reproach science. It does not kill. It is not strong enough. It can only attack what is already dead.

The stream of events in historical development simply takes all things with it. The world, even to its most distant corners, is filled with the roar of this stream.

You cannot require us to stem the tide of this decline; for you have taught us to understand it. And now we are glad for the decline, since no one enjoys living among corpses.

In all the world we see no form of life which is not being dissolved. Did you not teach us to see the work of man in each and every thing? Was it not you who sharpened our sight for the human element by subjecting everything to history and development? We are grateful that you did. You created the tools for us; now let us use them. Now we draw the conclusion: Everything that is somehow a human work not only has a beginning, but passes away again. And it passes away when the human work overruns everything else. I have said already that it happens when science grasps it. It can do just that in the moment that man has won out. Now is the hour of decline.

We see the disintegration in everything. That means we are acutely sensitive to the human element. We feel how it has asserted itself in everything today—including the most refined concept of God. And we raise the question, in all seriousness, whether today there are any men who can really conceive of God. We know that he has never concealed himself from the simple (do you understand this word?). We are so deeply immersed in humanity that we have lost God. Lost him. Yes, really lost him; there is no longer any thought of ours which reaches him. None of our thoughts reach beyond the human sphere. Not a single one.

We know that now. And in the face of this recognition it is as if we had never known anything before.

Is it any surprise that we have become distrustful right to our fingertips of everything which is in any way the work of man? Yes, it is a surprise even to us. For if the distrust of what is human still mainly determines our feeling, then this distrust, which questions everything, is only possible because there must be in us a germ of the knowledge of the opposite, of that which is not human.

We cannot, however, conceive of God. But we can know more and more distinctly what he is not, what he cannot be. We can no longer be deceived and no longer deceive ourselves into taking the human for the divine. We lose a great deal thereby, but nothing which we could regret. The wavering confusion of the divine and the human in all our concepts, words, and deeds was too long a tormenting anxiety. And if this purely human world were all that remained to us, even that would be an answer, following that miserable game of hide-and-seek in which we did not know at any given moment whether we were dealing with the human or with the divine.

Therefore, we were jubilant over Spengler's book. It proves, whether or not it is true in detail, that the hour has come in which this refined, intelligent culture, through its own intelligence, discovers the worm in itself, the hour in which trust in progress and culture receives the death blow. And Spengler's book is not the only sign. Whoever reads can find it in nearly every book and essay, even if they only raise the question of the "why" that is the driving force behind them. Should we not then begin a massive program of reflection? Or are there theologians (what has become of this word?) who chatter about this culture and show that it really is not so bad and that everything will soon be all right again?

There were periods when we thought we could work toward a coming, new culture, and we believed that it would bring wholeness. Its image loomed large and rich before our souls. But this dream is over.

Not only have we become distrustful of the human element in what others did, but much more so of the human in our own actions and plans. And this distrust cuts us off from those who set the tone of our age.

It is not that we reject what they do. But we see that they are the same as those whom they replace. It is only that they go at their task in the opposite way.

The fact that they operate in a human sphere, remote from everything divine, is hidden from the older generation, and even now they continue to deceive themselves about it; whereas their successors recognize the fact and operate in this way consciously. We can understand why they do it. (Indeed, it was from them that we learned to understand almost anything.) They saw through their long-standing pious error—but not entirely. Otherwise they could not have thought that their work would succeed if they knew nothing more than how to do consciously what their predecessors had done unconsciously, to their own destruction—that is, to build a world by human will and human wisdom.

And, to be sure, there is much good will here, and this fact makes us feel ashamed when we cannot join in with a full commitment of our power and convictions. But we cannot. Although we feel the allure of the courage, the impartiality, the indifference toward things meriting no consideration, and the youthful vigor exhibited by this period, and although our human sense of justice really draws us toward those ranks, because as men we must have some place to stand in time, yet our thoughts and aspirations seek a different goal.

There was finally an opportunity to raise questions about God. The times fell asunder and now time stands still. For one moment? For an eternity? Must we not be able to hear God's Word now? Must we not be able to see his hand in his work now?

Therefore we cannot yet run from one period to another, however much we would like to. The decision must first be made here. Until now we could do nothing wholeheartedly. We have been standing between the times for so long. This is a terrible human plight. For there everything human crumbles in disgrace, including everything which was and is to be. But now if we fully comprehend this plight we can ask about God. Then the question does not get entangled in the human and find false answers in it—false because the answers are human and not divine, regardless of our good intentions. When it comes to divine things, good intentions do not count, not even the best. We know now how far the question must reach; our distrust of the human outlines the area it touches (one must add today that the entire occult-scientific other-worldliness of the human element belongs to this area)—and it will direct us there again and again.

But will it take us further?

No, it will take us not one step further in historical development or toward deliverance from human confusion. We are in a different realm and are looking for something other than progress—interest in cultural opportunism no longer moves us.

We have, therefore, no suggestions about how to make improvements. Those who are practical, of course, will all ask about that. The only practical suggestion we can make is the following (and it is not really practical, since it cannot be carried out by good intentions alone): to recognize with dismay—if even only a few people realize it today—that clever suggestions can no longer help in the situation in which we all find ourselves.

Do we still not understand that our hour (it does not pass as usual ones) is probably the hour of repentance? Or can we repent and in the same breath develop our program for what is to come?

We should guard ourselves in this hour from nothing so much as from considering what we should do now. We stand not before our own wisdom, but before God. This hour is not our hour.

We have no time now. *We* stand between the times.

THE CRISIS OF OUR CULTURE*

Lecture Held on October 1, 1920, at Wartburg

Friedrich Gogarten

OUR CONCERN

There are events which are of such crucial importance that any attempt to deal with them prematurely is disastrous. At the beginning of the war, someone made the ironical remark that the man who uttered with such feeling that maxim about a transformation of all attitudes because of the war considered this maxim valid, but valid only as it was applied to others. This, of course, would exemplify the disaster in its most extreme form. Today our world is experiencing a convulsion—of which the war was but a mild omen—and the tragedy of such a self-deception, which has in fact already had a large number of traceable consequences, would be merely laughable compared to the tragedy this self-deception will result in if it is re-enacted today.

Let us take a closer look at this self-deception. Perhaps we will thereby provide ourselves at the outset with some clarity as to our basic relationship to every happening in the world; for it is this very clarity with which we will concern ourselves in the course of our reflections together.

At the root of this self-deception lies the notion that one has perceived an event before it occurs, so that the event once realized confirms him in the conviction that his perception was valid. And one can find adequate support for this notion at all points. However, whatever the event in question happens to be, the notion is correct only as regards changes upon the surface—mere shiftings-about of the existing matter. Basically, everything remains *what* it was, if not *as* it was. How much, in fact, everything does remain the same is proved by the very man who seeks to demonstrate to another how profoundly the convulsion proceeding from the event in question has worked. So profoundly (he claims) that all men should revise their outlooks and change themselves. He alone is in the right and is able, come what may, to remain the same person he has long since been, by reason of his prescient perception.

Amusing though such a person may seem, once we have recognized him; garrulous and superficial though his cogitations may then appear

* From *Die Christliche Welt*, XXXIV (1920), issue 49, columns 770-777; issue 50, columns 786-791.

—our smiles fade when we comprehend that his attitude is the very one which we ourselves customarily adopt in the face of events, and that this same attitude will certainly render every event—whatever blessings it may promise—completely barren. And this barrenness, considered in terms of that point of view to which we wish to attain, is not just an omission, not just a lack, but is a corrupting and annihilating doom. For we seek that point of view from which the course of events is something more than just a colorful, varying series of changes. So regarded, the various forms which things assume finally become less important than the enjoyment of the changing scene and its continuously transformed variety; and all guilt and tragedy finally become nothing more than the deepest, most darkly glowing colors in the whole picture. But from the point of view which we now hope to attain, the present moment, that is, the moment which demands to be lived precisely now, is that moment which demands *nothing more,* in fact, than to be lived precisely now.

THE PSYCHOLOGICAL, PHILOSOPHICAL, AND RELIGIOUS POINTS OF VIEW

But to be *really* lived—from a psychological viewpoint, this means that the moment refers all energy, awareness, and a complete sense of responsibility to itself, so that there remains no possibility of its being regarded as one moment among many. Nor is it possible, from this point of view, to raise oneself above the present moment, or to leave it (for the purpose of meditative or evaluative observation) amid the inscrutable row of moments which precede and succeed it.

Philosophically formulated, really living the moment means referring the contents of the moment—whatever they may be—to the Absolute. This, too, requires that the moment and its contents be torn from the relativity and flux of the stream of time. Whatever precedes, whatever succeeds, the present moment must be referred to it in rigid order and must derive from it its meaning and purpose. Past and future therefore cannot remain as they were. From within the perspective of this one moment and from within the referring to it of both time past and time to come, past and future take on—if I may dare this expression—the dynamic form of the one moment. Within this dynamic form, they become the "body" of the one moment, as in its lightning-fast progress it dries up the uniform river of time, in which one wave is identical with another.

Religiously formulated, really living the moment means that, from the point of view which we are now in fact seeking, the immediate moment requires nothing but to be immediately lived; it means—religiously expressed—an encounter with God in the moment. Accordingly, this moment, regardless of its immediate form, acquires a content which tolerates absolutely nothing besides itself. Nothing remains, either of that which preceded the moment or of that which will succeed it, including that rigid order of which we have just spoken. For there is now nothing which could be ordered. There now exists only the one moment and its content. Nor does there any longer exist that lightning-fast movement—here there exists nothing but the pure present, the moment, brought to its final perfection.

What the Concept of the "Human" Means According to the Psychological, Philosophical, and Religious Points of View

But will we not deprive ourselves of an understanding of this perfection if we consider it in any sense a human product?

The psychological viewpoint of which we have spoken sees only the human product. From this point of view, man as he actually is, with his contingencies, weaknesses, and virtues, his insights and his errors, remains an essential factor, or even *the* essential factor. According to this view, if the psychic tension and concentration be but slightly relaxed, the powers of reflection will then have unrestricted scope and an incontestable right to make the moment a part of an infinite and uniform series where it is only one among many.

The philosophical viewpoint removes at least contingency from the human product. Philosophically considered, accidental psychic concentration is not decisive, but is a matter of indifference. The philosophical point of view is true when it proceeds strictly according to some principle by which the philosopher connects the moment with the Absolute. And even though the rigidity of this ordering, of this regularity, is identical with the love of the Absolute, which like all love desires a union with the beloved, it remains bound to the discursiveness of reason and can never be anything but a rigidly ordered motion *toward* the Absolute. Man will always be *here* with his reason, and the Absolute *there*. And the moment is between them like an electric spark between two poles, except that it is timeless and therefore an eternal motion, an eternal striving; because it is unceasingly in motion, this very moment has a unity of its own.

From the religious viewpoint, however, this motion is no longer seen as a motion from one thing to another, that is, from man to God. Nor does the eternal striving come into consideration; it is meaningless here, for a thousand eternities would not suffice to walk the path which leads from man to God. And should this motion, this ceaseless striving, remain, it will be the most miserable of torments; for with every step one takes along this path, the distance increases, while the prospects of ever reaching the end diminish.

The religious point of view has meaning only insofar as it retains nothing but God, only insofar as everything human disappears from it, only when it crosses the border into a realm different in its very roots, and only when man's busyness ceases and God's activity begins. Therefore, what occurs in this moment no longer belongs to the general relativity of events, nor can it spring from that context of events and man's event-determining energy or passivity; nor can it have any influence—as cause or effect—upon the general development of world history. However, in order that we do not make a false start and slip at the very outset from a religious into a moral viewpoint, it is necessary to observe that we are speaking not of that which will occur on the strength of this perception which we have won, but rather of that which was occurring in the moment, i.e., of what the content of this moment was, precisely when we turned our attention to it. What happens in this moment, then, is exclusively God's act, and will remain so.

Because it is recognized as God's own act, it is recognized as something new—something absolutely new—and it would be so, even if it were (regarded from the outside) something old and long since familiar. And even if it had been predicted long ago by a brilliant and profound seer, it would still be—and is—something different. For when the seer sees the new which he prophesied, he sees only a change within the old, but he does not see the new which is in contrast to the old and its mutations, and which is something really and completely new, something absolutely different. On the contrary! And the effect, when a man claims to have come face to face with this newness by virtue of his predictions—even if his predictions be centuries ahead of his time— is like that of an unintentional joke. For it is quite amusing to hear someone speak with great familiarity of things from which he is universes distant, separated from them by precisely this alleged familiarity.

For surely the total transformation, the μετάβασις εἰς ἄλλο γένος is possible only when the human element disappears, leaving no trace. And this is, in fact, the first condition for any sort of religious contemplation—that man as an active factor be eliminated, or, to express it positively, that God be recognized as the sole agent.

We cannot remind ourselves too often of how greatly the religious point of view, in so doing, contradicts every other way of thinking— especially every usual and accustomed attitude. Here, everything— and in every respect—goes against appearances; this contradiction cannot be smoothed over with psychological or religious-psychological approaches, nor by means of an equation of God's activity with the creative directness of man, nor by translating God's activity into man's subconscious or unconscious. God does not require man to be in a comatose state in order that he may work and reveal himself here on earth. Whenever he works and reveals himself, he does it before the clearest, most self-aware of man's conscious states. The flight into that comatose state of the human consciousness, i.e., into the subconscious and into so-called "creativeness," is not at all what it gladly convinces itself to be, a flight from humanity and a manifestation of the desire to escape from everything human. On the contrary, it is a flight from God and a manifestation of the desire to escape from the clarity which surrounds him. It is the last attempt to give to man what belongs to God. But this desire, too, must be overcome. This last circle must be broken out of if we are to enter that other realm, in which things can be seen from the religious point of view.

THE RELIGIOUS POINT OF VIEW: AN INTERTWINING OF A TOTAL VALUING WITH A TOTAL DEVALUATION OF THE WORLD

We should by now have arrived at that point of view we have been seeking, and from which we wish to consider our theme.

But before we proceed, let me say something more about the nature of this point of view. We will then be able to proceed with greater confidence, as it is of the greatest importance that we acquire this point of view in its purest form, unsullied by other intellectual attitudes and stances, and that we retain it in all its purity. And it is equally important that we constantly renew our awareness of how very —if I may so speak—vulnerable this position is. Therefore, we may confidently apply a great part of our thought toward attaining to and maintaining this point of view in a pure form. For if we succeed in this, then we will stand in the very center of our theme, not only in the sense that we will be speaking about it, but also in the sense that we will realize it in our own actions.

Let us say it at once, with all possible precision and concreteness: this means that we ourselves will fulfill the crisis of our culture, the only crisis which for us, as religious men, is worthy of consideration; and which for us—again, as religious men—is absolutely necessary, which amounts, in fact, to the test which decides whether we will be able to see the world and all that happens therein in the light of God.

Winning this point of view in all its purity depends completely upon whether we are successful in seeing the event in such a way that it no longer belongs to the general human stream of events but becomes and remains God's most personal act. Here, then, is the greatest difficulty presented to us by every religious manner of thinking which is religious in its substance, and not just in its posturings and rhetoric. Here is the point from which, to cite Luther: " . . . Adam fell. But ye are few, who are come so far as to completely believe that he is God, who makes and creates all things. For such a man must have died to all things, to the good and the bad, to life and death, to heaven and hell, and must confess from his very heart, that he can do nothing by his own powers" (W.A. XXIV, 18).

This Lutheran "But ye are few, who are come so far . . . " should serve as a warning, if we think that it is really not all that hard to arrive at the belief that everything which happens is an act of God. In the sort of directness which asserts this, you will not find one trace of God.

We must have "died to all things, to the good and the bad, to life and death, to heaven and hell." That is what such a belief amounts to. It means that we have been taken outside of our ordinary existence and—most important of all—that we will remain outside of it. By saying this, I wish to indicate that we are not concerned with ecstatic states, which come and go, last but a little while, and which release us from the usual run of things only by means of optical illusions. On the contrary, we are concerned with the act of seeing beyond everything which might otherwise determine our life and our reality, but a "seeing beyond" not in the barren sense of seeing nothing at all, or of ignoring things. The world in which God acts is not a barren world, nor is it a miraculous world of paradisaical curiosities; it is this very world which we daily see with our own eyes, in which we carry out our daily tasks, but it is at the same time a completely different world which we can see and yet not see, if our eyes have not been opened to it. This act of seeing beyond, this state of having died to all things, is an ambivalent thing: it is a total valuing of everything of which our usual life consists and which constitutes our usual reality. Usual life and usual reality, according to Luther, include good and bad, life and death, heaven and hell. And this seeing beyond, this state of having died to all things, is at the same time an unconditional valuing of everything which exists for us, that is, of the same things which we totally devalued.

That which compels us to both an unconditional valuing and a total devaluing is one and the same thing: the knowledge of God's reality. In the light of this, everything—good and bad, life and death, heaven and hell—becomes worthless, an insubstantial wraith. For in this light is revealed the fact that all reality has become a mirror in which man observes his own essence and tries to make his smallness and wretchedness a bit less shabby than it really is. This is why reality cannot endure before the light of God. However, once God's light has shone upon reality and everything has disappeared before it—pride, unworthiness, egocentricity, sloth, arrogance, and anxiety, and all the things which claimed the reality of this world as their property and their salvation—when these things have disappeared, then the world becomes anew the pure creation of God, and all things and events become the mirror of divinity.

But, let it be noted, man cannot have merely the one or the other, the valuing without the devaluing, nor the great Yes without the great No.

Surely, for us too, this total devaluating cannot exist without that highest valuing. Herein we can see the distinction between our viewpoint and that usual method of criticism which derives from the immanent context of things and takes only their current form to task and which believes in progressive and gradually improving change. Our critique, our great No, comes from a position utterly beyond the things of this world and brings them and their worth completely into question. For us there is no continuous improvement and change, or even if there is, we are indifferent to it. For us, there can be nothing but a drawing back into the original creation, into the origin; there can be nothing but a rebirth through the Spirit of God and a complete renewal. This is not a renewal from this one point in the general evolution of things, restricted and determined in a thousand ways, but rather a renewal from the eternal origin of the creation, from that eternal Word of God, "which has been said from all eternity, and which will always be said."

This is what I meant when I said that the purity of the point of view from which we wish to consider our theme depended upon our success in regarding the event which we desire to contemplate not as belonging to the context of general human events, but as something which is and will remain God's most personal act.

Once More, This Intertwining

There is another point which we must deal with in the interests of clarity.

The religious way of thinking, which we are practicing here, can be had only in this tension and dialectic peculiar to it. More exactly: one cannot *have* it, one can only practice it with all possible concreteness. Otherwise it will remain an empty husk, without content. We have already seen that we cannot have that total devaluing without that highest valuing. Vice versa, we cannot have that highest valuing, which is the faith that every event is God's personal act, without that total devaluing. Before we can arrive at this faith, we have to pass through the deepest skepticism, the darkest pessimism. Once again, I will let Luther speak for me: "In all his works, God does thusly—if he wants to make us alive, he slays us; if he wants to make us holy, he torments our conscience and makes sinners of us first; if he wants to draw us up to heaven, he thrusts us first into Hell."[1]

Therefore—and this is what we wanted to clarify here—any objective certainty is out of the question for the religious way of thinking. We have already said it—in such directness, there is not one trace of God to be found. There is nothing there to find except human— and only human—traces. Every objective ascertainment, that is, every ascertainment which has not already died to all things, and which proceeds purely from man, will find nothing but man and this world, man-determined down to the least particle and permeated with human intelligence, human myopia, and human egocentricity. Whenever we claim to have found God in *this* world, we have found nothing but an idol; this happens more often than we think, since it is rarely noticed, when everyday terminology is used in naming it. God has no place in a world until man first utterly annihilates himself. We speak now not from some ideal situation, but from the actual situation in which we human beings here on earth find ourselves. And this actual situation is one of apostasy from God, of godlessness. No debate should be required to prove the truth of this assertion—if anyone should demand it, then I refer him to the great religious men of all times, for whom without exception this assumption about the actual situation was valid. It is the "gain"—a gain which makes one very suspicious of their religious genuineness—of the more recent founders (or, more precisely, improvers of religion) to have asserted that this assumption is no longer valid and to have replaced it with that other assumption: Man is good.

But perhaps they had a faint inkling of something correct. For beside the sentence "God has no place in a world until man first utterly annihilates himself," we now place another: "Once God's reality has been recognized, there is no place left in the world for man, and man's personal existence is abolished." Then man stands again, as God's creation, at the origin of things, where things are still with God, and where the Word of God sounds above them: And God saw everything that he had made, and it was good. Then there exists no longer that two-ness, that dualism, according to which God stands here, man there. Then there exists nothing but God and God's reality, God's creation, and man within it like the breath in a living body, completely interwoven with God, one with his will and his life.

But we cannot maintain the foregoing and then assert our own existence; or, differently put—we must not mistake this knowledge of the origin for the knowledge of what developed itself out of that origin. But this world, in its deep, despairing godlessness, is as little a development out of God as the prodigal son was the messenger and image of his father when he went out into the world.

But, yes, he *was* the messenger and image of his father. As he wasted himself in the brothels of the great city, only then did he become his father's messenger; his message in everything he did concerned the incredible kindness of his father, who had given him freedom even in this filth and perdition. And he was the image of his father, when in his final despair he remembered his father and was confident that he might dare return to him, in spite of everything.

He was, then, messenger and image, but he was neither of these, considered in himself. Between him and the father stood the terrible Fall. And then the kindness of the father and the memory of him became a sentence of death: "Father, I am no longer worthy to be called your son."

Surely, this sentence of death is the entrance to life. And the entrance is here alone. Only after one has passed through it can one apply to this world and to our own actions the knowledge of the origin, the knowledge that all that happens is God's act. But this does not amount to placing ourselves back into the world. It is not an assertion that the world as it is is of God's making and therefore good and deserving of affirmation without reservation. The world as it is is a falling-away from God and the horror and the aimless, self-consuming longing of godlessness, and it deserves therefore to be negated to its very core.

This is, to anticipate, the crisis of culture, presented in the only way which can have meaning for us, and presented not as being imposed upon us by our own time and its events, but as being fulfilled, brought to completion by us. And a religion which has to reconcile itself to this world as it is (i.e., as it is determined by past and future, caught in the endless chain of so-called evolution), a religion which cannot announce with good conscience for its first and last message: "The Kingdom of God is at hand," such a religion is itself drawn along into the contingencies from which it should be freeing us, and it will dance the insane dance of world history and so-called evolution. Such a religion has fallen from its origin, and its distance from God is indicated by the fact that it regards a sense of longing as its finest feeling, and as the feeling most expressive of its nature.

And when the hour strikes, and the immanent strength dies out of that greater context of contingencies which we call culture, then this religion—which is perhaps the closest, most direct, and most subtle expression of the immanent strength of a culture—will die too. And precisely because it is the most direct and most subtle expression of this strength, this religion will give the first signs of the approaching end and will anticipate the end in its own fate. But the more robust and cruder cultural formations will endure a good while longer, as if nothing at all had happened to them.

THE DECISIVE QUESTION

Thus we have asked the question which for us, face to face with our theme, is decisive.

For I am certain that you will not have expected me to paint you a detailed picture of our time and culture in its present condition and then say, "Here and there things are in bad shape," and then suggest, "Here and there we ought to do this and that, and with a little bit (or a lot, according to your temperament) of faith in God, everything will get better again." If this is what you want, you can read it to satiety in any newspaper or periodical, even though—surely with some justification—you will not find overmuch weight laid on the "faith in God" there. You might sooner expect me to take for granted this general picture of our culture and then to make an attempt at estimating how deeply the crisis we are experiencing today has penetrated, to consider whether the crisis might not have some prime cause which we could then assault with assembled forces. And if our fellowship here were not a religious one, then you would have every right to expect me to treat my theme in this manner.

However, our gathering here is a religious one, and in everything we do here we are concerned with religious self-contemplation. Therefore, I take it for granted that we should inquire into the religious significance of our theme. Our present situation in regard to this theme is clearly one of being confronted in all earnestness by this question: Do we today have a religion which is being drawn into the crisis of culture and which must therefore defend itself against the crisis? Or do we have a religion which itself precipitates a crisis of culture, a crisis which is only being mildly hinted at, parabolically announced by the other crises, and which reveals itself within and through the immanent evolution of culture itself?

The answer which we will give to this question is the same as the position we took in regard to the crisis of our culture. I ask your indulgence while I make the antithesis explicit. Let me say that I do not wish to offend by my sharpness, but I consider it necessary for the sake of clarity. We must be absolutely clear about this antithesis, this either-or, because we are concerned about a clear understanding as to where our place in the world should be and what sort of task we should fulfill therein. We have, then, either a religion which seeks to be the soul of culture, which, therefore—to resume the expression we employed before—is itself that strength immanent in the larger sphere of contingencies known to us as culture, and at the same time the most subtle and direct expression of that strength. Or else we have a religion which is a constant crisis of this and every culture.

RELIGION: THE SOUL OR THE CRISIS OF CULTURE?

I say expressly "of this and every culture" in order to eliminate at the outset a misunderstanding. For someone will immediately object that this antithesis is no antithesis at all, or at least, it need not be one. But if that religion which seeks to be the soul of culture be profoundly enough conceived, then it is at once the critical crisis of culture as well. For it is then that which never allows culture to pause at the level which it has just attained; it is the germinating and always progressing image of the perfection of culture; it is the vitality of culture, which never rests, and which constantly assumes new forms. Religion, to borrow a phrase from Spengler, is then the potentiality which desires to become reality in culture and is that constant state of becoming which is continuously breaking out of the rigidity of that which has already come to pass. It is that which opens up the depths of the unconscious and the sources of creativity which inject fresh impulses and psychic health into a culture. I hope that this is a fairly accurate and not unjust elaboration of the sort of religion which we are now speaking of. There is no doubt whatever that it has tremendous importance for culture and tremendous influence upon the psychic health of a culture. It is in fact the very life of culture and therefore the cause of those crises which every culture must struggle through, as well. But this sort of religion is what it is only insofar as it is within the culture. It is itself a part of those conditions and contingencies which, taken all together, go into the making of a culture. It is in fact immanent in culture, and, if the culture dies, then the religion inevitably dies too. Its mythology may be immortal, and its sacred documents may be critically compiled by philologists with the greatest care and read by literary amateurs with the greatest enthusiasm, but they will no longer have a formative effect upon our lives. As religion, they will be dead and will live on only as curiosities, preserved—if at all—as exotic curiosities.

I would like to make this one further remark: Even if religious documents fall victim to this fate, this does not prove that these documents come from such a culture-determined religion. Whatever is visible in this world is visible only within the form of the currently ruling culture, and as long as it possesses this worldly visibility and worldly form, it will always be possible for it to succumb to the fate of every culture, i.e., to death. And it will always so succumb as long as there are men who see and yet do not see, who hear and yet do not hear, and in whom the original creation does not live.

The antithesis remains, then, between the one religion, which seeks to be the soul of culture, and the other, which is an absolute crisis for this and every culture. For even though this culture-religion signifies a crisis for culture, it is a crisis only in an immanent sense (i.e., it is a crisis from within this culture), the transitory, current crisis which every culture passes through at the turning points in its development. It is not, however, that crisis which jeopardizes this whole culture in all its potential and actual dimensions, nor that crisis which destroys this culture's naïve confidence in itself and its naïve faith in its unlimited endurance and more or less continuous development. And when the downfall of this culture finally occurs—and it can happen at any time, be it from Russia, or from the infamous ice-ages, which always ultimately freeze Troeltsch in his reflections upon culture—when, I say, the downfall finally comes, then the religion of this culture will fall, too. And this can only be considered good, for what would there be for such a religion to do, once its culture had disappeared? It would have to build itself over again from the bottom up; it would have to become timely again. But it is likely that religion will die away completely in that cultureless time which comes between two cultures. Until then, this religion can do nothing but work against the downfall with all its powers and present itself as the best medicine for a culture which has become exceedingly weary and pessimistic. This will have to be done with great zeal, for the declining culture will hardly be willing to heed such "agitatory" voices—primarily because it will in the meantime have reached the stage in which it perceives that its condition is the consequence of its religion's death. May it not be true that, in this case, it is the culture which is in possession of the more profound perception?

RELIGION: A MYSTICAL RETREAT FROM THE WORLD, OR COMPLETE WORLDLINESS?

One more thing, namely, the argument that this crisis which we are currently experiencing is not the one which will lead to the final downfall of our culture. This argument can hardly be proven, but there is a very good possibility that this crisis is not the final hour of our culture. If this is true, then we have gained time—in this case, a very little time. For once one has ventured into religion, he becomes involved in at least the tendency to escape from time. (Whether this tendency becomes reality is another question.) Simultaneously, he gains the ability—dependent upon the absoluteness of his escape from time—to return to the present time with everything which he is and has, including religious thoughts which are utterly distant from and superior to this world and time.

Culture-religion is capable of neither the escape nor the return; naturally, it also has the tendency to remove its whole being from the stream of time. But does it in fact do this? It does not do it to the extent that it utterly negates time and its content, which is culture, with all the accretions and values of culture. On the contrary, the culture-religion defends itself violently—for its own peculiar nature is at stake —against that way of thinking which does intend an utter negation, namely, against the attitude which regards the world in its present state as the world of apostasy, of the Fall, and of original sin. The culture-religion knows no apostasy and no original sin; it knows only evolution, development, progress. And if it wishes to get outside the flow of time, to come into contact with eternity, then it submerges itself into the fecund source from which all evolution derives. But this submersion is in truth nothing but an abstracting from time and reality; it is—if I may return to what I said at the outset—an act of ignoring, rather than an insight; it is an evasion, not an elevation. In practicing this submersion, the culture-religion leaves time and reality where and as they are; it does not take all time and reality along with itself, in order that it may place both them and itself before God's annihilating holiness.

For God's holiness annihilates, not just for the sake of annihilation, but to save us so that we may live. "When God wants to make us alive, he slays us," says Luther. This is the reason for the annihilation. Luther does not say "he plunges us into creative directness," nor would he ever say that, for he knows all too well what precedes this creative directness, not soon forgotten by the man who has undergone it. Then, too, this creative directness is not the final, profound ground and source from which all life flows, but at the most a consequence, a psychological datum. The last and deepest source reveals itself only at that point at which all our foundations have been destroyed, have become worthless and meaningless, have become one with sin, separation, and the falling-away from God. Here and only here, in this annihilation, can creation become creative; in this state of utter debasement—and only here—can the divine values arise; and only in this state of meaninglessness can the eternal meaning of all things shine through. In this state of sin, God makes us holy.

There exists one and only one possibility of freeing oneself from the world and time, and it exists at this aforesaid point, where God's holiness annihilates both world and time. But this is not that silent, sweet, mystical departure from the world and time, nor is it a skeptical secession from the affairs of the world. To be sure, this latter action—the skeptical secession from worldly concerns—is a conscientious fulfillment of what the present time demands of us; but it is otherwise a retreat into a refined, intellectual realm, which endures forever, and which the tumult of this world never penetrates, or—even if it does—penetrates it from such a great distance that the confusion and tumult become but a gentle, playful tinkling.

This sole possibility of escape from the world and from time demands that we do not free ourselves from either world or time, not even to the extent of a single fiber of our being; that we, on the contrary, take world and time upon ourselves, shirk not one difficulty and assume the burden of all responsibility for everything which exists or happens.

The Unavoidable but Untenable Situation: Man in the Middle Between Self and God

Here there can be no question of an evolution or unfolding development rising out of a profound, generating source in accordance with a hidden but immanent law to which religion, by its nature, is supposed to adjust itself. Here there is only the independent act which takes place at this very moment, simply because I exist and live face to face with this world, which I recognize as my world and for which I bear all the responsibility.

Everything I have ever done before points to this one act, this one moment; in this act all my actions meet, and each brings with it, time and time again, this whole world and time as its burden and guilt. For there is nothing discrete in this world; all things are intertwined and interacting. Therefore, nothing good can be isolated or distilled from evil. One or the other: the world is either entirely good or entirely evil.

And seen from within the human perspective, the whole world is evil. Well, no, not from within the human perspective—from a purely human standpoint the world is as we usually take it to be: a mixture of good and evil. But then good and evil become relative concepts, which is to say, the good is whatever is not evil, and vice versa. But then both good and evil are deprived of their absoluteness, their demonic and unconquerable power. And then we have nothing but bourgeois virtues and bourgeois vices, made out of that which has the power to build and destroy worlds and to make a travesty of the divine creation.

So, from a purely human point of view, the world is not entirely evil. But it is entirely evil when man looks at it with the eyes of God. To see as a man, but with the eyes of God! Then the demonic, godlike power of evil becomes visible, that power which passes nothing by, which grazes everything with its poisonous breath, including the finest and noblest thoughts and deeds of which man is capable.

But the situation in which man sees with God's eyes is in itself untenable. It becomes impossible as soon as we recognize it as that futile situation in which we wish to maintain ourselves as human beings beside God, in which we want to see with God's eyes and yet remain human beings.

THE DECISION

And then the light of God shines forth upon the world and upon us in all its purity, no longer refracted by our human nature; and the power of God can go forth freely, no longer repressed by our own will. And now "the whole world is evil" can become "the whole world is good." "A Christian is holy in body and soul, be he layman or priest, man or woman."[2] "One should allow the blessing to remain upon the whole man, soul and body, for whoever is a Christian is blessed through and through, along with everything he sees, hears, and feels, in order that the Word may be widely and effectively propagated" (W. A. XXIV, 251).

Here there is nothing but grace and miraculousness. One should not intrude here with psychological explanations or with possible psychological interpretations. Everything depends upon our recklessly breaking out of this last circle, exploding it so thoroughly that it will never again be able to restrict our thoughts. In the words of Ludwig Rubiner: "The soul is the last barricade against life in the spirit, against unconditional access to God, against our progress toward the Absolute."[3] Or if you prefer Luther's voice: "God wants us to be built not upon uncertain remorse, but upon his certain promise, so that we may endure all distress."[4]

It is crucial that we do not become confused at this point and commence with our human questions, and that, where God's light shines, we do not try to produce clarity for man by using human light. Everything which separated us from God is now cleared away, and we stand naked before him, retaining nothing for ourselves. And it is equally crucial that we do not again place ourselves between self and God.

Here there is only one explanation and only one revelation: Jesus Christ. But what do explanation and revelation mean here? They mean that the explanation and revelation cannot be separated from that which is to be explained and revealed. Jesus Christ is identical with the act of God and with the annihilation of this world; he himself is the original creation. There is nothing simpler than the fact that

God helped mankind by means of a man. And this fact is true only in its final, most profound simplicity. But this final, most profound simplicity is this: Man cannot have God without God.

THE JUDGMENT

We have now to consider the direct application of the insight which we have attained in our deliberations to our contemporary situation, that is, to the crisis of our culture, in which we manifestly find ourselves today. But I can really say nothing more than I have already said; I can only concern myself with a greater elucidation of it.

The sense of what I have been saying up to this point is—to sum up—as follows: religiously viewed, every crisis of culture is but a mild omen, a parable of that total crisis which religion means for every culture. On the other hand, if the crisis has fateful consequences for religion, if the crisis attacks religion itself, then this is an unmistakable indication (even if the fateful threat is very distant) that the religion was long since lost, had lost itself, in fact, because it became infected with culture.

But the significance of this crisis, which threatens gradually to make inroads upon religion, is not that the prestige of religion within culture will diminish or that the numbers of those who profess this religion will decrease. These are otherwise important matters, but in our present concern they are utterly insignificant. The significance, which is a symptom of the disease, lies in the fact that the adherents of religion will become greatly preoccupied with effecting a union of religion with culture and with setting culture on the right path again by means of religion. When this situation exists, culture inevitably becomes the goal, and religion becomes merely a means to that goal—the most subtle, most serious, and most intellectual means, to be sure.

But a cultural crisis can never embody the fate of that religion which has not gone astray; rather it only sets religion the task of fulfilling what it (the crisis) can only begin and only then begin (and then only parabolically) if religion fulfills it: that is, the act of judgment. But not that judgment which is pronounced from a detached position, which consists in evaluation and condemnation. This is the judgment of the moralist, who produces his legalistic yardstick, lays it upon cultural reality, and proceeds to diagnose our shortcomings. Nor do we mean that most popular judgment, so gladly pronounced by those people who (as they innocently but significantly say) are "in a movement," who have discovered some random shortcoming in our culture, ferreted it out of every corner with idiosyncratic zeal, and now, because they find it everywhere, mouth their clichés. Wherever such people do some good, may they be blessed a thousand times. But their activity is only a drop in the ocean.

Nor, do we mean that judgment which culture passes within, for, and upon itself. When this occurs, culture makes approximately the following pronouncement: "Everything had to happen as it did, in accordance with the great laws of evolution and history. Bring on the last act! And then we'll get ready for the next drama."

The judgment which religion passes on culture is in its essence of another sort. It does not attack random shortcomings, one here, one there, as do all moralists who want to censure this or that failing. It not only attacks an entire cultural epoch, passes sentence of death upon it, and issues the death warrant; it attacks culture *as* culture. And we must go even further; this judgment is not directed to one particular time, or lifted from the whole of time, but directed to all time itself. This judgment does not attack a particular part of the world, lifted from its surrounding parts—it attacks the whole world.

But do not think that this means only that this one particular culture, which is the only one we are dealing with, will therefore disappear within the world which is now summoned before the court, and that this judgment is therefore only a game, that at the last moment I will issue one of those popular and easily employed abstractions which are usually brought up when religion speaks about the last things, and which it uses to shirk reality.

Turn about and see whom the judgment goes against! Against this whole world, surely. But the world is silent and dead, and it is pointless to demand a reckoning from it. There remains, then, only the man who established the court of judgment and summoned the whole world before it, that is, the religious man himself. For this is the man who sees and hears in this world, who even now sees and hears the judgment. Whether or not he is the only man in the world who sees and hears is of no importance; he, at any rate, sees and hears the judgment which falls upon the whole world and all of time. And he cannot separate himself from this world, cannot place himself beside it and say: "Here is the evil, imperfect world, and here am I, the good and pure man of God." The whole world points to him and says: "Here is the man in whom I recognize myself as that world upon which judgment must fall." And all time advances toward this one moment and points toward it, as if it would say: "Here is that in which I will finally become manifest, and in which I can proclaim my guilt."

This, then, is the judgment which religion passes upon culture, the judgment which is identical with that cultural crisis which is itself identical with religion.

WHAT, THEN, SHOULD WE DO?

A word, in conclusion, as to the question "What, then, should we do?"

This question will certainly be asked, and I am aware of its presence in my own thoughts. But there is nothing to be done: we must recognize that the question is a last-ditch attempt to shirk the one thing which really should be done. And that one thing is precisely what we have been doing, provided that my words were not empty and that my thoughts were not merely a theoretical, speculative game, but a realization—and that thing consists of withstanding the judgment, which, however, means letting the judgment be carried out of its own accord. (Surely, I can so speak without the risk of giving up the last, highest activity of which man is capable.)

Here is the unalloyed, creative activity of God. Does it not suffice, that we let him act? All that is necessary, all that remains, is to open all eyes to that which we now perceive, in order that all men may endure the judgment. But will this come to pass if we flee the judgment and say to God: "Wait a bit, until we have fetched the others also"? This is what we used to do, and we fled the judgment long enough that we should certainly know by now that by so doing we will not bring one single soul to God. Rather, we will deprive him of the one which we already intended to give him—our own. As it turns out, we will remain exactly where we finally found ourselves—in the annihilating, creating act of God. That is, exactly at that point from which Jesus Christ speaks today, just as he spoke two thousand years ago: Repent, for the Kingdom of heaven is at hand.

NOTES

1. Walch, XVIII, 2119.
2. *Bonner Ausgabe* II, 318.
3. *Der Mensch in der Mitte,* 184. Aktionsverlag.
4. *Bonner Ausgabe* II, 98.

THE RELIGIOUS CRISIS:

An Open Letter to Emil Fuchs*

Friedrich Gogarten

It will probably not contradict your own view for me to say that the situation in which we theologians and churchmen find ourselves drives us to decision more forcefully every day. And I will also be in agreement with you if I sketch our situation in this way: On the one side is Christianity, on the other side our nation and other nations; and we, the theologians, stand between them, responsible to others for nothing more and nothing less than Christianity itself.

You yourself have so described it in your response[1] to Wilhelm Schäfer's essay about the Wartburg conference.[2] To be sure, you put it in these words: Our task today is to create a Christianity which sees its universal task and at the same time can give strength to the laborer and to the socialist.

Permit me a few words in reaction. I direct them to you not only because you have mentioned me in your response as one engaged in this task—meaning an engagement in it as you conceive such a task, although contrary to all my own insights and intentions—but above all, because for a long time now the thought has plagued me that even with the best of intentions we theologians are on the wrong path, and because I know of few pastors of any time whose intentions and activities would seem to me so pure and intelligent as your own. Pardon me, if I, being younger, say that to you, but I must, in order to make perfectly clear what I wish to write.

Let me sketch our situation again, as we both see it: On the one side is Christianity; on the other side is man; and we are in the middle between them. But in the middle as what? That appears to me to be the decisive question. Two things are possible here—we are either arbiters or mediators. To be an arbiter means to stand between the two parties as a third party and negotiate. To be a mediator means to stand in that place where the two parties stand sharply opposed to each other, where they confront each other in harsh antagonism. In this case we cannot be a third party, for we are the battleground on which both parties wage their fierce attacks and their sharp conflicts.

Now I cannot help but have the impression that we today are definitely arbiters, and our best and purest intention is directed to-

---

* From *Die Christliche Welt*, XXXV (1921), issue 8, columns 142-145. This text from *Die religiöse Entscheidung* (Jena, 1921), pp. 5-11.

ward nothing more than arbitration. That means arbiters with respect to both sides, toward Christianity and toward man. I can offer no direct proof for the way things stand. In any case, in your response I find evidence of this arbitration toward both sides. The fact that I find it in you both convinces and frightens me more than if I found it in many other pastors. For an understanding of our situation and a determination to understand it, whatever the consequences, appear to me to be not at all widespread. Therefore, those who see clearly and wish to see clearly under all circumstances should communicate all the more frequently and openly and help each other to attain clarity at all costs.

In your response I find arbitration in favor of man in the fact that you speak of the cultivation of piety. I believe I know well what that is, and I admit to having practiced such a cultivation long enough, or at least having wished to do so. But I also believe that this cultivation does not attain what it ultimately intends, not by far; namely, the seeing and hearing which man can never get by himself. For they can only be given him by the one who is seen and heard. It is impossible to foster them by cultivating any sort of good and joyous soul-stirrings and emotional urges. I do not want to say even one more word to stimulate such processes. And even if I would like to (in that case I would be aware that their cultivation would be the most complete means of blinding and deafening possible; if, indeed, men have any kind of power in that situation), I could scarcely account for doing it in our blatantly dilettante, theological manner—all religious-psychological practice to the contrary—rather than with the extreme virtuosity and finesse of the anthroposophists, who practice technique precisely as technique and therefore have success upon success, and this by no means with only the worst of men.

But permit me to say more clearly why I consider the cultivation of piety to be an arbitration in favor of man. It appears to me that we are a long way from seeing or even suspecting our real plight, if we still think we can help men in some way. In that case we still know nothing of that hopeless plight of absoluteness. I intentionally use this uncommon word, because we have dragged the usual words all too much into the realm in which we can do anything with a more or less good will, and where we think we can deal with our sinful plight by the cultivation of piety. But in fact, we would first of all have to cultivate sin or at least the sense of sin. Then we would be among those who understood something of piety and would know where its cultivation must begin. Indeed, it is no accident that the summons to pietism was expressed recently in the *Neues Werk*. But those people know nothing of the plight of absoluteness and will find no knowledge of it

on the path of pietism. They, too, are arbitrating, even without knowing or desiring it; they see only a piece, only one side, of the plight,
the side which allows this or that part of it to be altered, as is the way
of arbitration. Only with the seeing and hearing that sees and hears the
Absolute, and that thus can only be given by the Absolute, does anyone see and hear the whole plight; we mean the plight which remains
the same in relation to each and every concern of man and which, once
one has seen it, gnaws at everything and brings everything good into
question. For this reason arbitration in favor of man is inadequate; it
is still merely the reverse side of arbitration in favor of the other party.
I find it also in your brief essay; for example, in the place where you
set up for us the task of creating a Christianity which recognizes its
universal duty but which at the same time specifically gives support
to the socialists and the laborers.

I believe I understand you correctly when I say that you pose this
task because you consider Christianity to be the revelation of God,
which alone can help us out of our embroilments. Naturally, you do
not see in Christianity merely a product of human cultural history
which may have proven itself very helpful in many exigencies of history and which must be applied again today with a few contemporary
alterations. If I understand you correctly, you see in Christianity a
revelation of God which must be re-worked each time in the form of
the currently dominant climate and views in order to bring to that
generation the help which a revelation of God can give.

I well know with what great seriousness this concept has been
worked through in the urgent desire to save Christianity for our time,
when it ran the danger of being thrown aside as a remnant of a world
view which was no longer valid. And if it were concerned with that
which was only a product of human cultural history, then I would
not know what position one should take in relation to this ingenious
operation other than admiration. For out of this product of a totally
different culture, long since dead and buried in all its other aspects, or
at least preserved only in museums, this undertaking has produced
something which we might accept as one of us, decorous, and reason-
ably able to move about. However, what has been so solicitously and
dexterously transformed into something contemporary strives to be
something totally other than a product of human cultural history. And
its relation to its specific cultural manifestations cannot, therefore, be
a relation of its being to its more or less perfect facade, although the
facade will be brought to fulfillment with the passage of time. Rather,
it is a relation of the most intolerable opposition, of the unconditional
either-or, of a conflict which will never be ended. It is the relation of a

conflict, of an either-or, which we shall not abolish or end by regarding it *sub specie aeterni*. For we are never simply observers, but we exist in time; and this fact is ultimately the most important thing about us—indeed, it is only for its sake that we are making these reflections. With just this existence *sub specie aeterni* we come into the most extreme plight, into the sharpest contrast to the "eternal," into the most decisive either-or—either us or eternity. Whoever thinks that there could be here a "not only . . . but also," even if only to bring about objective cultural and historical reflection; that there could be a neutral, calm mixture of what we are and what eternity is, or an investing the form of our time with eternity on the basis of comprehensive, fundamental knowledge and the free, creative act; he does not know what we are *sub specie aeterni*, and eternity has not even entered his thoughts.

It is indeed possible that in this consideration what we customarily call Christianity may be lost—and we mean not only its history but also what we consider its essence. But that does not concern us, not at all—what does concern us is the eternal, original act of God which first set this entire history in motion (must we perhaps say, which turned history loose?). No one need call our attention to the fact that the categories of cause and effect are not operative here. I know also that I have still said very little when I say that the category of "being born anew" is valid here, that is, the categories of birth and death. Thus, the only relationship at this point would be that of absolute opposition. However, if we also know nothing of the original act of God, then precisely through this unknowing we know of the real impossibility of our existence and of the necessity of getting out of this situation. If reality, which if it exists at all can be only a divine reality, proceeds out of this necessity, which is a divine necessity, just as does the impossibility of our existence, which corresponds to this necessity, then we shall probably have to achieve that history of Christianity anew. For if it really is the history of Christianity, if it is itself that of which it reports, that which was set in motion and (now I no longer need ask) turned loose by God's original act, then it must contain an abundance of new life in itself. And we will not allow ourselves to miss one pulse-beat of that life in this world of death. To be sure, we are men and our lives belong to God and thus may only be perceived by reflection which is subject every moment to that restless opposition which is our only connection with everything divine and which indeed will rule our whole inner being. For what we are in being born anew we are in God; but we ourselves remain men. And even if we place our whole being with all its impossibility and sin into God's being in believing defiance or in bold fullness—and God's overpowering, original being forces us to do so—still this deed and this belief in which it takes place are ours; and perhaps the opposition between God and us is the greatest, and our knowledge of it clearest, here where it is completely surrounded by the peace of God.

Therefore, it must indeed be the case that one hears the No more than the Yes, conflict more than peace, in the words we speak here. And it should not surprise anyone very much if the Yes remains as good as unheard when it refers to what was most clear and most established. In fact, it is the real Yes for us men in this life only when it is encircled by the No. Luther, who was by no means untutored in these affairs, had this to say about it: "We know that Christ himself could not have taught the gospel without chastizing. And wisdom complains that its discipline has been scorned. It is the salt of the earth— it stings in order to purify, it punishes in order to heal, it chides in order to bless, it kills in order to bring to life. Whoever says otherwise does not preach the gospel, but prattles mere flattery."[3]

If it is as I have said, that the relation of the original act of God— to which we refer when we speak of Christianity—to its specific cultural manifestation is not the relation of its essence to the form of its manifestation, which can always be improved, but the relation seen in terms of the manifestation of irreconcilable opposites, then it is clear that no one can ever achieve Christianity for himself and his contemporaries by transforming or re-creating its form according to the dictates of the times. Whoever begins there may intend to mediate between time and eternity; but even with the purest of hands and with the best of intentions he still can lay hold only of time. And if we desire Christianity, we try to lay hold on eternity, the divine act itself; a human impossibility, but a divine necessity. In Christianity there is only the act of putting oneself in the middle between self and God; it means, however, not being a third party any longer, not putting oneself alongside self and God; it means standing where "wisdom stings in order to purify, punishes in order to heal, chides in order to bless, and kills in order to bring to life."

NOTES

1. *Frankfurter Zeitung* (1920), Nr. 799.
2. *Ibid.*, Nr. 786; reissued as: "Drei Briefe mit einem Nachwort an die Quäker" (München: Verlag Georg Müller).
3. Walch, XVIII, 1316.

THE UNCONDITIONAL SERIOUSNESS OF OUR PIETY:
A Reply to Friedrich Gogarten's Complaint Concerning
the Plight of Absoluteness*

Emil Fuchs

Dear Friend,

May I address you in this way and eliminate the formalities between us? I feel the need to do so, since we are wrestling together with
the most profound aspect of the human soul. Reading your open letter
was a time of meditation for me, a time of self-examination, encourage-
ment, and pleasure.

I also felt deeply how wonderful it is for you who are younger to
begin influencing life at a time when we are so oppressed by the full
seriousness of all the questions of life and death. How laboriously we
had to make our way through experience and decision to our present
resoluteness. But perhaps we do, in fact, bear in ourselves an experience of the divine from those stable times which ought not to remain
unheeded.

I was touched in a particularly profound way by your statement:
"We will not allow ourselves to miss one pulsebeat of that life in this
world of death."

Indeed. That above all else! In her tale "The Vision of the Emperor," Selma Lagerløf has the Emperor Augustus experiencing the
great miracle—and later building a temple to it. When I read such
stories as a child, it always seemed impossible to me that those involved
did not do more. Should they not have withdrawn and given themselves entirely to the miracle? No! That is the frightening aspect of
man's destiny and being. He builds a temple to the miracle, perhaps
even in his heart—but surrenders its power and meaning again and
again to everyday reality, which is nothing, truly nothing, to the person who bears in himself an intimation of the eternal.

To take the eternal seriously as reality is, to my way of thinking,
piety, "faith," as Luther calls it. Men who are only a little sicklied o'er
by piety, that is, who bear it as a bruise of sentimental feeling on an
otherwise healthy skin of worldly wisdom and adjustment—previously
I thought I had to shake them and rattle them, now it is sufficient to
divorce myself from them. They are most frightening when they have
the audacity to preach God, and at the same time, set up and ad-
minister their life and their church according to the considerations of

---

* From *Die Christliche Welt*, XXXV (1921), issue 9, columns 153-157.

worldly wisdom. Here, it seems to me, lies the mortal peril of our evangelical church. Even the most authoritative among the authoritative cannot completely range themselves on the side of the reality of the eternal, but direct the church according to the insignificant considerations of earthly accommodation.

Do I wish to recast or help to recast Christianity's revelation of God for our time? Indeed, am I a Christian?

I openly admit that I can give no quick or certain answer. To grasp the reality of the eternal is always the affair of the individual man, always a personal and decisive issue. There is nothing to "renew" here. Each person can only be what he is, grasped by that primeval force whose certainty appears to us again and again as the wonder of all wonders.

Thus, what I am is seen by the way I am, and since the voice of that primeval force rings out to me from Jesus, Amos, Paul, Luther, it is completely natural for me to enter into an intimate relation with them and to enrich others by leading them to these figures. Nor am I conscious of a wall between me and a Rabindranath Tagore. There I see that in other forms and feelings reality is being taken seriously, a reality sacred in contrast to everything transient and earthly.

If that is piety, can it be cultivated? No, it cannot. You are entirely correct in remonstrating with me for this unfortunate expression and clarifying for me how very dangerous it is to use it. We ourselves often do not notice how much we become accustomed to traditional errors, especially in our terminology. The reality of the eternal either enters into a man's being or it does not. We can cultivate only feelings or emotions, and if "pious" feelings and emotions become rampant because others cultivate them, we have just that sickly hue of piety. Piety of this sort is fraud, and the strong and true scorn it.

We can just as little mediate or adapt piety. This would always mean causing people to take into their lives something which in others had been great, true, and powerful, but which in them would remain alien; it could assume power, truth, and life only if it were the same reality in them as it had been in the others.

What did I intend by that unfortunate term? First, the formation of a community of the truly devout, so that we might truthfully and resolutely approach each other and seek satisfaction for that burning desire which basks in the reflected beams of the primeval force of the greatest experiences of other human souls. I have this desire and consider it one of the strongest elements in all piety.

What we can do further, as individuals and as a community, is to confront the others in all seriousness, and attempt to shake them out of the torpidity into which the miasma of counterfeit religion or events of earthly significance have brought them.

And we can struggle against all the crassness, triviality, and bitter burdensomeness of life, which choke and kill the living power, truth itself, of many men's souls before they have a chance to defend it.

At the same time, we can strive to draw as many as possible into the community of our life of the soul, so that they may learn once more to accept this life as truth and to give themselves to it. Only then will their souls find the capacity really to accept the being of the eternal as it relates to them. Such a band of truly devout men could not help but become a contagious power in the guidance of the life and conscience of our people. That is what I termed "creating a new Christianity." No one can create piety, but we can well create a community of devout men with the power to lead various groups.

It is possible to smile at the helpless attempts of insignificant men to improve that which destiny has laid upon humanity. For me, however, the great moment at which I became certain of the unconditional reality of the eternal was when I saw that you must regard each of these human souls as unconditionally important; you must seek communion with them untiringly and bring them to themselves; you must fight against all the banality and crassness that choke the human soul. If I forsook that, I would no longer be taking the eternal seriously, as it has entered my life. I am unable to find joy in anything which I do not at the same time turn into a means of making other men's souls more alive and more true. Even my family life is something I wholeheartedly enjoy only when it is at the same time an open community for anyone who is susceptible to the gentle influences which originate here and are able to awaken and strengthen souls.

The overwhelmingly great experience of my piety is the fact that we insignificant, earthly men are instruments of the inexpressibly powerful One. Through us he does that great deed, greater than we imagine, the greatness of which is reflected in its true reality, there, where a real community of souls is formed, where the true life of the soul exists, and where he surrounds us.

But for me, all that is the work of culture. It transforms humanity into a community of souls and—let us use here the old, sacred expression—into the Kingdom of God, even though more is expressed in that term than we can grasp. Therefore, true art must set forth for us the life and being of the soul. Law must limit baseness and conflict; every day we must all fight, struggle, create, and mold, in order to more intimately understand the people who make up our circles. Everything material is merely a means of preparation. But the material also effects an alleviation of life, so that more souls can mold themselves freely, and fewer and fewer be crushed by the pressure of the purely earthly. The great bane of those who are insignificant, weak, and earthly is that the economic aspect is always becoming dominant and they remain stuck in what should be only a detour on the road to truth.

And now you smile perhaps, as so many others do. To many, it is already a breakdown to take the earthly and external element at all seriously.

But I am fully committed to taking my stand in the place where millions upon millions are deprived of their humanity by the pressure of miserable circumstances. It is totally impossible for me to have all this freedom of soul—and to consent to their being deprived of it. And when one of them perishes or suffers injury, I must go over and strive to rescue him from his narrowness and gloom, so that his life becomes broad enough and free enough that his soul can be a soul, and live, and embrace the reality of the eternal with its whole strength. Thank God that such work in no way diminishes the life of the soul, but intensifies it in resolution and strength, in which the reality of God is revealed anew. Thus, I can belong only to a religious community which desires to sustain everyone. That is why I am a pastor. And that is why I belong, in spite of everything, to the national church. That is why I am searching for ways by which we, the pious, can awaken and strengthen the lives of the people, even at the risk of error and human weakness.

Oh, I know well enough that one can take his place among the struggling masses of men and become as weak and insignificant as they are, serve the material world as they do, recognize the power of the status quo and submit to it as they do, tolerate art as a pleasing intensification of life as they do, eat and drink with them, court and be courted, and allow prosperity and social status to become one's goal in life; there is a tremendous danger in working with men in their "culture." But it is dangerous only for the person who has not dealt seriously with the eternal. And can he be brought to account? The serious man stumbles, and adapts himself more than he ought. He is dragged farther and farther. This oppressive struggle is his destiny. To assume a fully uncompromising stance by withdrawing from the communities of those who are only half alive—into individualism, sects, social settlement—is impossible for me, pleased though I am with those who walk this path genuinely and unreservedly.

Do you know E. T. A. Hoffmann's *Märchen vom Goldenen Topf*? (Tale of the Pot of Gold). To some the pot of gold is the whimsical, comical Mr. Archivarius Lindhorst, in all his quaintness, someone not to be taken seriously—but to the perceptive eye it is the sublime power of destiny-laden creativity. That is true for our culture as well—and for us all.

For me, not religion, but God himself, is the supporting strength of culture, which is "culture" only so long as it is related to God, whether it is aware of it or not.

What you call "cultural religion" strikes me as only a surrogate. Indeed, it lacks the seriousness which is all important.

It is well for us if we are supported by a faith which will not allow us to be deceived by the immensity and wonder of our being and its relationships.

And the "No"?—is it not the entire, resolute, powerful act of living, which only the soul takes seriously, and which serves only it, whatever the circumstances? It is the act of living which passes with a smile over the external advantages and positions which others purchase for themselves at the cost of their deepest truth. It is the great, great joy which fills life among the disappointments of earthly things—a joy found in the rising feeling of the infinite reality to which one belongs. It is the patent capacity to see and accept in the other person his own truth and soul rather than his exterior, even when he considers himself important.

Yes—my "No" is always a "Yes"! Just as I am about to say "No," that other, before whom I must reverently bow, appears to me out of some concealed little corner of man's stunted nature, through the figure of Mr. Archivarius Lindhorst, and I must say: Yes, Eternal One, here also I must serve and love you, and cannot be distant from that which in its time you wish to make into new heights and new brilliancy.

Is it only that we are speaking different languages? To a certain extent, yes, because I sense again and again how close we are in our feelings. But there is more. Only a ray of reality ever shines through us insignificant men, a ray which grasps us and does with us what it will; and it is often different from our view of it. Thus are all our formulations so varied and inadequate.

This is why I am not trying to instruct or convince you. I am wholly satisfied if my words stir in you what your words stirred in me —the great feeling that here a human soul in its own way has truly looked into the divine reality and taken it to heart. Wherever people feel that, they belong together and their differences will enrich each other's lives. Let us together continue to seek the way of unconditional seriousness for ourselves and for our office.

AN APPLE FROM THE TREE OF KIERKEGAARD*
Ernst Troeltsch

It is the fate of our circle, which is already small enough and without influence in the church, that apples of Eris are always being tossed into it. They stir up everyone, excite many, and in the end both attract new members and disgruntle the old. It makes our circle exciting, but it also makes it a mirror of the whole exceedingly difficult situation of German Protestantism, which is partly a wing of the conservative form of the State and its ruling class, partly the early Lutheran religion of the peasants and the middle class, partly a semi-scientific culture-religion, and partly an experimental field of religious subjectivities. There is something of all these, especially the last, in our small group. It is held together by its size, and, in spite of everything, by the personal trust of its members in an honest exchange of ideas; thereby forming a microcosm of honest and amiable Protestantism, with the consequence that from time to time apples of discord are tossed into our midst from all sides and friendly controversy, albeit with inward anxiety, is constantly stirred up. Pastor Gogarten has thrown in the most recent such apple, an apple from the tree of Kierkegaard. The effort has been increased by the fact that a writer, supposedly from his aesthetic pleasure in sharply honed paradoxes and a sense of the tragic either-or which inflames the imagination, has declared himself for Gogarten in a large daily paper and dealt contemptuously with everything else. This aesthetic pleasure in paradox has for a long time been the effect produced by Kierkegaard, himself half-artist, half-aesthete, who has always stirred non-Christians more deeply than Christians.

I could not attend the recent Eisenach colloquium. Otherwise, I would have participated in the discussion; the more so because I had the feeling Gogarten was essentially attacking me. Whether he correctly grasps my views or—especially in the concept of development, which is one of the most complex problems for me—ascribes a more trivial view to me than I actually have, is something I would like to leave out of consideration here, since it is basically a personal matter. I have continually regarded the relation of Christianity and culture as a very difficult open question, and have therefore repeatedly emphasized asceticism in both its Catholic and Protestant forms. To be sure, asceticism is only one side of the issue, and the pressures of life have

* From *Die Christliche Welt*, XXXV (1921), issue 11, columns 186-189.

always added to or twisted it in some way. Essentially, this is a theoretical and historical judgment. Gogarten's letter to Pastor Fuchs shows that the concern is with more general matters, primarily those involving pastors; I wish to limit myself essentially to his letter in what follows, inasmuch as he shows by practical applications how to understand the issue more clearly.

Like Kierkegaard, Gogarten speaks of the "Christianity" which corresponds to no church or confession or historical form, but is wholly personal and private, deriving from a very sharp radicalism against the world, the nation, the State, culture, and church, but which, understood intuitively in terms of general radicalism, is seen, profoundly and accurately, to be the Christianity of Christ. Just as God is supposedly in radical opposition to the world, can intervene in it with a freedom that transcends reason and logic, and wishes to throw it back, in its fallen state, to the excruciating sense of its nothingness; so in this view, Christianity is to be thoroughly judged and condemned by the Absolute in the supra-temporal moment of the personal confrontation of God and man. Indeed, this is to happen so thoroughly that man becomes unable to transcend himself, and thus renounces any attempt to communicate and transmit this condition of soul to others. The encounter with the Absolute, its radical contrast to the world, the self-indictment of man in the absolute situation, and the disregard of all mediation between God and the world, which according to Kierkegaard is the essential interest and work of all churches—that is the Christianity of absoluteness or of the either-or, of genuineness and of depth of soul, of historical reality and of the idea. Nothing further is permitted in connection with this emphasis. While Kierkegaard mainly attacks the churches, Gogarten attacks culture, its social demands and scientific concepts, all of which are historical or intellectualistic. The natural sciences are more remote from Gogarten; otherwise he would similarly stigmatize any settlement with them. His position, like that of Kierkegaard's, appears to be religiously based, but like it, is connected with very subtle and currently very modern theorems concerning the relative and the Absolute, intuition and rational knowledge, time and the moment; it is also expressed in very philosophical language.

This position is camouflaged with appeals to Jesus and Luther. But one must remember here that, for Jesus, the either-or was the decision for the coming, imminent Kingdom of God, which would then provide the positive content of religion and its relation to the world. As for Luther, we should not forget that the radical slaying of "the old man" corresponded to the birth of "the new man," and that

this new man, even in Luther's thought, had to work out his relationships to the "world." Anyone who appreciates his experiences in
the first realm ought not overlook the no less basic and painful experiences in the second. We must not forget that beginning in Paul's
day, as the utopian hopes of the imminent coming of the Kingdom of
God faded, the early church accommodated itself to the world on
every hand and retained its old radicalism in its core only, in the form
of asceticism and monasticism. Only in this way did the church become an entity of historical reality at all, and its historical descendants,
the Protestant churches, had to follow the same path of mediation, in
a somewhat different way. Apart from the necessities of life and the
concessions expressed already in Scripture (especially in Paul), this was
occasioned by something in the Christian concept itself—we think of
the continued belief in creation, the world-encompassing unity of God
embracing all exigencies, and the indefinable element of sympathy for
everything human and natural in Jesus' concept of love. Only the
small, consistently chiliastic sects were able to renew the either-or of
Jesus, and then in a more acute form; only mystical immersion could
replace it by an equally radical, psychological dualism. The accommodations to the world, which are never absent, even under these
conditions, and the secularization, which always sets in after such
harsh beginnings, become all the more interesting. Kierkegaard himself, in his ancestry and training as well as in mentality and ultimate
direction of life, belonged in this realm of sectarian religion and correspondingly fought for a purely individual and abstract, a purely
personal and absolutely radical, Christianity. He was disposed to a
particularly profound exposition of this contrast, especially in the
aesthetic-artistic period of his life in which he often discovered the
boundary of what was morally permissible and developed to the nth
degree the penchant in modern psychology for all that is cunning and
concealed. This rejection of the contrast which lay deep within his
own being led Kierkegaard to those ingenious controversies with the
Romantic and pantheistic philosophy of development, which actually
brought out very grave problems and drove Kierkegaard himself to a
harshly pietistic and fully psychologized dualism. His total loneliness
and eccentricity, which appear to be related to a psychopathic condition, and his early death exempted him from the necessity of working
out that side of his religion which is positive, affirmative, and comes to
terms in some way with the world. It was indeed the sensing of difficulties at this point which allowed Kierkegaard to become more and
more reckless and bitter in his polemic against worldly, accommo-
dating, and ecclesiastical Christians, whereas he had once passionately

opposed only the accommodation of the world and God in German speculative philosophy. In the end all he had was more polemic, nothing positive—it led only to self-judgment, arising from the "absolute situation" in relation to God.

That is easy to understand. For it cannot be denied that in the modern world Christianity—churchly and non-churchly—has been caught up infinitely more into secular culture, modern science, social problems, politics and economics, than were the Catholic and early Protestant churches. The modern world relies completely on man's power and autonomy and believes that in science man finds the director and organizer of his autonomy. We have only to think of Giordano Bruno and Bacon, who have marked out the same path from opposite sides. This attitude makes the position of every form of religiosity, and especially Christianity, extremely difficult. Modern life is full of these difficulties, and it is entirely true that modern accommodations to the world have reached correspondingly much farther than those of the Catholic and early Protestant churches.

Gogarten senses in these accommodations the loss of the radical either-or, of radical Christian dualism. For that is what he understands as "absoluteness." I can indeed sympathize with that, and I assume that Gogarten's psychological conditions are somewhat similar to Kierkegaard's. Social Christianity that accommodates itself to the economy and the wooing of the masses appear to have especially revolted Gogarten. Much like Kierkegaard, Gogarten severs the knot which centuries, with good reason, have tied; a knot which, to be sure, has become quite complicated in the modern world, and which all too many people go on tying with honest, though facile, hands, without a notion of its danger and difficulty.

If such a position as Gogarten's is rooted in inner, personal necessity, it is difficult to deal with. Logical and historical reasons, moreover, are of no use to the "youth" of today. Anti-historicism, irrationalism, intuitionism—things with which we older people have concerned ourselves passionately and scrupulously—have already become comfortable and pleasant dogmas for many of the young. One can contrast only the instinctive, ultimately inward, religious position which he has grown into. Indeed, in the end that is really what is decisive and essential; but it does not develop in anyone simply without historical or cultural reflection or serious thinking, as our most recent experiential Romantics would have it.

Therefore, my personal position, from which I now must speak, is, in contrast to Gogarten's, a wholly instinctive and naïve concept of religious dualism. God's being and continuous creative activity may be completely groundless and supra-logical. They may produce a constantly new reality as a constantly new creation out of the depths of life. But they are not opposed to the world as Gogarten has it; they carry the world in themselves; they are themselves the life of the world, constantly dividing themselves to become finite life in its fullness and to raise the finite out of self-love and self-glorification to union with God and service to him; they are themselves constant self-repudiation and constant self-incorporation. The result, for a finite being, is the necessity of a revolutionary conversion, a fundamental change of direction of his life and being. This necessity, however, grows out of the inner depth of his being and is already latent in his love of self and of the world; this conversion bursts out of the unavoidable catastrophe in those beings who are organically connected with the ultimate ground of things. The fact that this connection is such a diversified one for the conscious life seems to be rooted in predestination; and that such a diversified connection works wherever the possibility exists seems due to both the extent of faithfulness and the surrounding influences. Then this inner revolution is surely the most profound revelation of God; but alongside it there are a thousand others—for the whole world is God's. And then the primary task is to unify and mold the ever-available raw material through selection and affirmation, so that its formation can be an expression of the vital powers thus achieved. Each period and each living man must create the principle and ideal of this formation for himself.

I do not wish to ask which influences might take part in the expression of religious feeling. Nor do I wish to ask whether anyone "still" wishes to call it Christian; I myself attribute this attitude of life essentially to "Christianity," without asserting that that is its essence. I say only that it stems from Christianity. Neither do I ask whether this is a possible position for pastors, who must unfortunately always legitimize their positions on the basis of the Bible. And I do not ask whether this attitude is effective for the masses or relevant to our youth today. I ask only about the source of my life and what my position is if I must characterize Gogarten's as intellectually impossible for me.

In saying all that, of course, I am speaking more against Gogarten's Eisenach lecture, or, more specifically, against the critique of my position which I see there, than against the practical applications which are evident in his letter to Pastor Fuchs. I took from it only a few characteristic traits which seem to me to be more understandable there than in the lecture. I am only setting up the counter-position, just as, in fact, Gogarten is only pointing out his own position. In both cases the basis is so deep and involved that it cannot be spoken of here at all; anyway, foundations as such are not to the taste of modern Romantics—a certain sign, incidentally, that their taste cannot last very long.

For my part I do not wish to pursue any further the pastoral question touched on in the letter to Pastor Fuchs. It is certainly a difficult one. But Gogarten would then have to draw the same conclusions as did Kierkegaard in his complete rejection of the church and cultural accommodation, which go together so closely—or, in case he rejects these conclusions, he would have to modify his presuppositions. In Gogarten's theology of the absolute moment, there would be no pastors, no church administration, no mission, and no sermons on education and counseling. If anyone desires these results, he must necessarily attack "accommodation," and the only question is how he can effect this within the narrow Protestant adherence to the Bible and the Creed. The Catholics, with their strong, sacramental-liturgical inclinations and their neutralization of every discussion of derived dogma, have it easier here. But these are ancient questions, constantly re-examined, to which I can say nothing new and which I must leave to those concerned. They do not have an easy task, and—more than lofty critiques, which are far too easily given—they deserve sympathetic support.

AGAINST ROMANTIC THEOLOGY:

A Chapter on Faith*

Friedrich Gogarten

The decisive question is whether it is appropriate to think of
the relation between God and man in terms of categories drawn from
organic life. If it is appropriate and they are used in this way, statements such as the following necessarily lead to positions essentially
different from mine. Troeltsch says, "God's being and continuous
creative activity . . . carry the world in themselves; they are themselves
the life of the world, constantly dividing themselves to become life in
its fullness, and to raise the finite out of self-love and self-glorification
to union with God and service to him; they are themselves constant
self-repudiation and constant self-incorporation."[1] And it is the "completely earnest acceptance of the eternal as the power behind all being
and duty, as the reality embracing all greatness in man" of Heumann
and Fuchs.[2] However, those who have objected to my theses have
limited themselves to making their opposition known and have only
hinted at their own positions. At any rate, this has been done clearly
enough to reveal their basic outlook. And this outlook, as we see from
their use of categories of organic life to describe the relation of God
and man, is for all of them the Romantic.†

I suppose this assertion will to some extent astonish Troeltsch.
Since he is eager to go on the warpath against contemporary Romantics, we might think his position would be anything but Romantic. In
fact, in his last essay against the Romantics,[3] in which he gives a brilliant and extraordinarily instructive survey of the new Romantic
scholarship, which in its most cultivated and tasteful form developed
from the circle of Stefan George, Troeltsch fails to relate the sense of
superiority with which he deals with this new school to his own position; rather, in speaking of these brilliant Romantics, he refers first

* From *Die Christliche Welt*, XXXVI (1922), issue 27, columns 498-502; issue 28,
columns 514-519.

† Since I will bring Erich Foerster into the discussion which follows, I would
like to state at the outset that he is an exception to this verdict. His own position,
at least to the extent that it is evident in his lecture on "Marcionistic Christianity"
(*Die Christliche Welt* [1921], Cols. 809 ff.), is so edifyingly ethical that it never
comes to grips with the actual theological problem, in spite of all attempts. Richard
Wilhelm could even refer to it, with good reason, as a fine presentation of Con-
fucianism. It should be noticed as a somewhat surprising fact that Johannes Witte
explicitly cites Hermann Keyserling as an authority against Wilhelm.

to the technology (Spengler!) of philological research—whose dominance, by the way, he attributes to the leader of the George school,
Friedrich Gundolf—and then even more to industrial technology, and
ultimately to the harsh economic needs of large modern populations.
But where Troeltsch does refer to his own position, as in the essay
already cited, it is quite clear that his basic attitude is in fact no different from that of the modern Romantics, in spite of all his attacks on
them.

I would like to give the basis for this assertion, even though, according to Troeltsch, bases are not to the taste of Romantics. I do not
do this without emphasizing my obligation to Troeltsch precisely at
the point at which I oppose his views. For at this point I have learned
much from him; and his works have helped me more than a little in
"historical and cultural reflection," through which, unlike the most
recent experiential Romantics, if Troeltsch is correct,[4] I have come to
a clear understanding of my own position. I believe I can perceive
the theological consequences of Troeltsch's pivotal and frequently
reiterated judgment that, for him, in the "immense transformation in
the modern intellectual climate, history has been incorporated into the
framework of universal occurrence."[5] Any theology that tries to steal
past this insight, by whatever means, is condemned. And we can only
be grateful to Troeltsch for having pronounced this verdict on traditional theology. With the application to theology of the recognition
of the universal validity of historical thought, he is in a position to
free theology from the indecision with which it vacillates between
God and man, not risking a decisive step toward one or the other, and
coming to a knowledge of neither. Troeltsch's insight threatens theology with the total loss of its subject matter. For its object, the divine
event, is its object no longer if this event has become just one among
many in the generality of history; that is, if it has ceased to be divine.

But that this insight threatens to deprive all theology of any object
whatever is no objection against it; in fact, it is just the opposite—this
can free theology from its indecision. It can confront theology with the
problem which is rightly its only problem—that of revelation. But we
can then no longer accept revelation as an object; and indeed, it is
not. Not if it really is to be God's revelation and not the revelation
and expression of a human spiritual condition, as the Romantic view
would have it. There is every reason to make a very sharp distinction
here, if one is willing to acknowledge what is involved. If theology
nevertheless makes revelation the object of its knowledge (and if theology is to exist at all, it will not be able to refrain from doing so), it
will have to remain conscious of what it has done. Only then can it

refrain from confusing its own object with revelation, and from coming to terms with this confusion as a factor given in its own existence, and therefore not to be neglected. It is a confusion, by the way, which infiltrates not only theology, but influences everyone who not only relates himself to revelation in belief (that is, allows it to be the subject), but also thinks about it, makes it an object. And who then does not repeatedly fall from the posture of belief to the posture of thought and knowledge? From this perspective, we could say the task of theology is none other than to expose this confusion; that is, to continually demonstrate the fact that thought about God and about his revelation can never have an object. No one ought to say that the task is too small and too negative. For it consists in nothing more nor less than the clarification of that faith which is really faith; that is to say, faith, as long as it is faith, does not make revelation its object, but lets it be its subject. (The limitation is necessary, for what faith does not constantly fall prey to the danger of becoming "knowledge" and thus ceasing to be faith!)

I said that this insight of Troeltsch's could have brought theology again to a decisive confrontation with its problem, the problem of revelation, and thereby freed theology from its indecision. However, in Troeltsch's own theology, this has not been done—for the probable reason that for Troeltsch this insight has always been and still is that of a historian. He thinks that since in the modern intellectual climate history has without exception been incorporated into the framework of universal event, "direct, religious feeling can be directed only toward the supra-historical, toward God himself."[6] But has "direct religious feeling" at any time been directed toward anything but the supra-historical, toward God himself? It has never been directed toward anything which could have been incorporated into the framework of universal event. If it really was what it was presumed to be—faith—then that toward which it was directed was so transformed that it was identical with its perceptible historical object only in an amazingly indirect manner. On the one hand, this incorporation into the framework of universal event can be quite irrelevant as long as the event is considered purely for itself, as it might be according to the laws of historical causality. On the other hand, however, as soon as universal event is brought into relationship with the ground of this transformation, the incorporation assumes great significance, a significance which real faith can never overlook (or it would not be faith). In any case, "direct religious feeling"—that is, faith—has never been directed toward anything other than the "supra-historical," God himself. But the decisive criterion here is whether faith really is that which it is said to be, whether it is aware of that transformation; I could even say, whether it is aware of that amazingly indirect identity of that which it sees or imagines as its perceptible object with that which can never be its object, and is absolutely impenetrable, inscrutable, and unknowable. What this says is that the "direct religious feeling" directs itself toward the historical as well as the supra-historical. For only then can we speak of that amazingly indirect identity of the historical with the "supra-historical," which faith accepts.

It will quickly be observed that what I call "transformation" here is something very different from what Troeltsch intends. Troeltsch is aware that faith, "where it has applied itself to historical facts," transforms "them into non-historical realities."[7] But since Troeltsch conceives of faith Romantically, as completely mythopoeic "religious imagination,"[8] he can also conclude that this "transformation can continue only so long as the alleged historical bases have not become the object of real historical investigation."[9] If Troeltsch knew that faith is never what he allows it "only" to be, namely, "faith in a concrete concept,"[10] but that it is faith in something which is absolutely non-perceptible and non-concrete for us, for whom everything necessarily becomes a content, an object, a thing,* he would know also that all "actual historical investigation," including its results and the entire "collective instinct of the modern spirit, which assumes a view of history different from the medieval and ancient one,"[11] cannot in the least hinder faith from carrying out this transformation. The only thing historical investigation can do is force faith to perform its transformation and prevent its becoming a sentimental, speculative, or ethical substitute for religion, as is so often the case, according to Troeltsch, in modern thinking.[12]

Since Troeltsch's decisive insight that faith is fixed "solely on the supra-historical, on God himself" is always conceived of solely as a historical judgment, it is not surprising that he has never gone beyond Romantic concepts in his theology. His concept of faith, for example, is Romantic in all its aspects. This is true equally when Troeltsch defines faith as "a mythical-symbolic-practical, peculiarly religious way of thinking and knowing, proceeding from historical-personal impressions";[13] when he holds that "origins of such faith are found only in naïve men and naïve social classes";[14] and when he says that "the insight of faith is related to the totality of a spiritual, collective power,

---

* Let me ask here an admittedly superficial, but perhaps still necessary question: Can God and whatever might be divine become concrete, perceptible, and, in Troeltsch's sense, believable for us as long as we are who we are?

grasped essentially through act and will; a power which . . . radiates from intensely religious individuals."[15] All this is pure Romantic subjectivism, which insists on its Romantic polarity and is only intensified in the statement that "the individual remains bound to pre-history and accumulated collective experience," and that "this collective experience receives at historical focal points new, creative impulses, which are a powerful intensification of the otherwise irrational new formation found in even the most minute process."[16]

The same proof could be offered for all the other theological concepts with which Troeltsch has dealt. My concern, however, is not merely to show that his theology is Romantic, but primarily that Romantic theology cannot do justice even remotely to theological problems such as the concept of God. It cannot grasp the real problematic and dialectic nature of these problems, since the extent of its tensions and dialectic antitheses is too limited.

I could easily demonstrate this shortcoming by considering the concept of God, where Troeltsch's view is the direct opposite of mine.[17] But the conciseness and irregularity of this formulation might lead too easily to misunderstandings. Therefore, I prefer to retain as my example the problem occupying the center of Troeltsch's thinking as well as of contemporary theological thought. Troeltsch has formulated it with great precision in his book *Die Absolutheit des Christentums und die Religionsgeschichte*. It is the problem which today is designated "faith and history."

Troeltsch says the problem of history is "not the either-or of relativism or absolutism, but a combination of both."[18] He characterizes this combination more precisely as the "constantly new, creative synthesis, which gives the Absolute a form possible for a given moment, yet carries in itself the feeling of a pure approximation of true, universal, and ultimate values."[19] In order to indicate at once where I wish to differ with Troeltsch, I have tried to formulate the problem as it must in my opinion be formulated—it does not deal with an either-or of relativism and absolutism, nor with a combination of them; it can deal only with a both-and.* And this both-and is by no means a "constantly new, creative synthesis," but nothing other than *faith,* which in no way "gives the Absolute a form possible for a given moment," but believes in the pure, full presence of the Absolute in

---

* Someone may wish to remind me of the directly contrasting formulation which I used, for example, in my letter to Fuchs (*Christliche Welt*, 1921, cols. 142 ff.). That would be a gross misunderstanding; we are dealing not with formulations, but with an issue, which one cannot be painstaking enough in keeping free from easy formulations.

the present. Nor does this both-and "carry in itself the feeling of a pure approximation of true and ultimate values"; it believes in the absolute distance of this moment and itself from "true and ultimate values," that is, from God.

It is a mistake for Troeltsch to think that what he calls "the constantly new, creative synthesis" is a combination of relativism and absolutism, for the antitheses here touch neither the relative nor the Absolute. Strictly speaking, Troeltsch ought not to speak of the Absolute here at all, for the Absolute really means that which is an absolute contrast to all that is conditioned or relative; it is free of all connections. It is then totally inconceivable that the Absolute could have a form possible for a given moment, one that is conditioned by the moment and its situation. It is likewise inconceivable that there could be an approximation of the Absolute, that is, a situation conditioned by something other than the Absolute. The instant one places the Absolute under a condition, that is, the instant one speaks, for example, of a form possible for a given moment, he is no longer dealing with the Absolute, but with what is conditioned and relative. But it is worthwhile to look closely at the nature of this conditioned result which is produced as soon as the Absolute is subjected to a condition. Once it is brought into relation to the Absolute, it is in that relation conditioned absolutely. If I may so put it, what is thus conditioned has an inverse relationship with the Absolute. It is the not-Absolute; that is to say, as it is related to the Absolute it is not this thing or that thing, which are after all conditioned and determined by this or that—thus, these things, instead of being the not-Absolute, would only be "not this" or "not that." Its only characteristic, however, is that it is not the Absolute which it was, or, more exactly, which it should be. Thus, the "form possible for a given moment" would not be a mere form of the Absolute, that is, a conditioned absolute, but the Absolute itself. And yet, it is not the Absolute and cannot be in any way. For a conditioned absolute has inevitably ceased to be the Absolute. If we conceive the Absolute strictly, as indeed it must be conceived if we are to include it in our thought structure at all—if, that is, Troeltsch's synthesis would really become a synthesis of the Absolute and the relative—then Troeltsch's position is in truth disclosed as the negation of the Absolute. What he calls "the form of the Absolute possible for a given moment" and with which he, in fact, understands culture and its finest, most intimate structure, religion, is then acknowledged by the claim of its approximation of "true and ultimate values" in complete distinction from the Absolute. And I was therefore right, when, in my Wartburg lecture, I said that culture, together with culturally conditioned religion, must be sternly rejected. But what religion is not culturally conditioned, Troeltsch will ask? He has already asked it, and rightly so. But since he asks as a historian and a Romantic, he will not answer, "Revelation" (which, to be sure, is not a religion), although this answer would enable him then to ask the decisive question.

All that has nothing to do with an "inner, personal necessity" and is not "the instinctive, ultimately inward, religious position which [one] has grown into," as Troeltsch defines it in the traditional Romantic fashion.[20] But that is a position which is taken up by anyone who devotes himself in a "passionate and scrupulous concern" for the concept of the Absolute, without which there can be no clarity on "anti-historicism, irrationalism, intuitionism," things which can easily become, somewhat frivolously expressed, "comfortable and pleasant dogmas." Troeltsch thinks this is what happens for many of the younger generation,[21] because they have realized that these things are without decisive significance for the problems resulting from the concept of the Absolute. For in this concept we are dealing with contrasts quite different from historicism and anti-historicism, rationalism and irrationalism, and the like.

It is, however, valid to say that the Romantic position is an instinctive, ultimately inward, religious position which one has grown into. If it is not true generally that this position has always been and still is a Romantic one, it is true at least in our times. Which one of us is not a Romantic in his "instinctive and naïve" spiritual attitude (we ought to notice the contradiction here!—but this contradiction, or confusion, is the essence of Romanticism)? And this attack on Romantic theology does not mean that my Wartburg lecture is completely free from Romanticism. However, I do not find its remnants —which are not insignificant or without danger, and which are still in my lecture, and which I have tried to overcome in my subsequent works—in the same place where Troeltsch looks for them. I should not neglect to say here that my standing controversy with Troeltsch, from which I have learned so much ever since my student days when I heard him lecture and studied under him, has in the end not helped me to see how much of the "instinctive, ultimately inward, religious position which [I have] grown into" remains in this work, my first attempt to get free from Romanticism, that is, free from this position into which I have grown.

Troeltsch thinks that in my "theology of the absolute moment" there would be "no pastors, no church administration, no mission, and no sermons on education and counseling."[22] There is, though, certainly no theology without the "absolute moment," not even Romantic theology, whether in the form outlined by Troeltsch or in the form of orthodoxy. Troeltsch has shown that orthodoxy is impossible, and even if I am right in my objection to his own theology, this rendering of orthodoxy is still valid. He himself asserts the necessity for overcoming theology, which he understands as the expression of a position which has been grown into in his statement that "even the religious element of life belongs to merely given drives" and therefore "needs to be elevated into the sphere . . . of what ought to be and what is objectively necessary."[23] He does not, however, get on with his theology without "the absolute moment"; on the contrary, the Absolute is as good as the center of his theology and is the decisive problem there as in every other theology. In any case, I maintain that Troeltsch's attempt to achieve the Absolute through a "combination" with the relative leads him irredeemably away from the Absolute. And there is a second byway: the isolation of the Absolute and the relative, instead of their "combination" and "mediation." When Troeltsch characterizes my theology as that of the absolute moment, he probably means a theology of the *isolated*, absolute moment. In that case, I admit that he is right; such a theology must lead to a "complete rejection of the church and of the transmission of culture."

In spite of Kierkegaard's last book, *The Moment*, it is questionable to me whether he ever set forth such a theology (see the note about "My Productivity Considered as 'the Correlative Factor' to the Existent" in the selection from Kierkegaard's journals, *Buch des Richters*, edited by Gottsched). Kierkegaard was a dialectician and wielded the method of "indirect knowledge" with inexorable consistency; thus, we can now make statements only with extreme caution, a caution which Kierkegaard perhaps did not possess, because he believed in revelation.

Long ago, Marcion may have had such a theology. This presupposes that Foerster's presentation of it in his lecture "Marcionite Christianity"[24] is correct. However, it would be a considerable "blunder" if Foerster considered my theology a "renewal of Marcionism," as he does in the lecture. He could make this blunder, as I see it, only because he has overlooked, as have Heumann and Troeltsch, the fact that my theology is dialectically determined throughout; that is, that no statement in my theology ought to be taken without its counterstatement, its opposite. If I may suppose that the formulations in Foerster's "Preface" to his lecture are not entirely unrelated to my Wartburg lecture, held one year before his in the same circle and characterized then, jokingly, as "speaking in tongues," such a dialectic appears so unusual to him that he invokes against it the "ethics of logic." But that cannot move me to forego this dialectic. I am convinced that without it every one of the opposites given with the concept "God," and without which God absolutely cannot be thought of, remain hopelessly concealed from us. On no count, though, should it be said that this dialectic cannot be expressed differently from the way I express it. For example (the question is whether this is not so much a possible example as an unavoidable necessity), it can take the form of the graphic, extremely concrete, Pauline and Lutheran expression "in Christ." Characteristically enough, Foerster "prefers" to say "in God,"[25] rather than "in Christ," and Troeltsch also agrees on sociological grounds.*

I believe I am not very far from this "in Christ" when I formulate the present problem as the both-and of the Absolute and the relative. And when Troeltsch submits that I should not overlook the "basic and painful experiences" of Luther in the area of "accommodation to the 'world,' " I believe I can confidently follow his admonition without being forced to a fundamental revision of my theses. For in dealing with Luther, we must remember not only, as Troeltsch admonishes, "that the radical slaying of 'the old man' corresponded to the birth of 'the new man,' " but even more that this "new" man is by no means the "new" man of Romanticism; he is not "creative" man, nor is he Foerster's "unconditioned, genuine soul, which has carried out the *metanoia,* the reflection, to its final conclusion."

May we ask when this "final conclusion" is reached in reflection? As a basis for this question, allow me to cite a passage from Luther: "I wish to confess the following: I do not desire, even if it were possible, a free will, a will which would allow me to strive for blessedness . . . for then all of my work would be as fruitless as beating the air, and my conscience would never be sure about how much it should do in order to satisfy God, even if I lived and worked until doomsday. For whatever I might do in the way of earthly works there would still be kinks in my conscience about whether the works pleased God or whether he required still more."[26]

But we will have to be acutely aware of the fact that this "new" man is "new" solely in Christ, *sola fide,* "through faith alone." In this situation, the factual—if you please, the historical, psychological—

---

* Cf. "Die Bedeutung der Geschichtlichkeit Jesu für den Glauben," 30: "The connection of the Christian idea with the centrality of Christ in cult and doctrine is not a conceptual necessity, following from the concept of salvation . . . it is socio-psychologically indispensable for worship, administration, and outreach, and that should suffice to justify and maintain the connection."

presence and continuance of the "old" man is at the same time both shatteringly asserted and denied in our being, and this is done again and again.

That is the posture of man in the both-and, and I can also say, that is the posture of the man of faith. The image of the man walking on the precipice, which Karl Barth uses here, well expresses the matter. And if Foerster says, in contrast, that "such a sight would seem terribly strange to the millions inhabiting the plain," then I would like to know how these inhabitants are disposed toward the first of Luther's 95 theses, which surely does not imply a settling down in the plain.

As concerns the "relation to the world" of this man and his position, whatever is intended for the "old" man is likewise true for the "new." For he is never one or the other, nor is he, as all the Romantics think, first one and then the other; if we must isolate them, man in this posture is neither—he is both the "old" and "new" man. But it always seems to me that it is proper for us to see the relation first from the standpoint of the "old" man. (This psychological succession does not change the essential temporal unity. And the Romantics, historians, psychologists, and sociologists would do well, before claiming victory, to undertake some fundamental reflection on the difference between "believing" and "knowing." In order to undertake such reflection, they would have to cease being Romantics, historians, psychologists, and sociologists.) For it seems to me that "sin" and "guilt" are real facts which give us solidarity with the "world," with civilization, culture, church, and "religion," which urge us to cooperate with them, and which hinder the emergence of an either-or or even a "nevertheless" from the both-and. (I wish also to admonish against misunderstanding this "guilt" in any historical, psychological, or sociological, i.e., Romantic, sense.)

If "guilt" is the bond which ties us to the world, then no one will any longer undergird and standardize his work in the world and on the world with Idealistic and Romantic demands and requirements; and all thoughts of culture as the "approximation of true and ultimate values" will be over. In any case, no one will allow the norms for his activity in the world to be derived from any Idealism, no matter how well formulated. And since Idealism finds its culmination in its ideal of the State, it will be necessary to be especially careful with respect to any Idealist ideology of the State, be it Marxist or neo-German.* The summons to order and to the issue at hand will be recognized as valid for all those who are in search of suggestions for establishing a

---

* Friedrich II was certainly no Idealist; he was rather a cynic (an intellectual attitude not so distant from the one suggested here).

"new" world with the stormy question "What should we do?" (But does anyone ever, regardless of his attitude, not belong to this group?) The summons is: Repent, for the Kingdom of God is at hand. Repentance, however, is not, as Foerster explains, a reflection which is carried out to its final conclusion; rather, the peculiar aspect of repentance is that it begins precisely when it has been carried out to this so-called final conclusion. If anyone says then, as Foerster does, that while denying culture and the world we forget that we affirm them with our actual behavior; or if anyone says, as does Troeltsch, that we must accept as the consequences of our view "complete rejection of the church and of transmission of culture," then we can only conclude with some astonishment that the decisive word has not been heard or understood here. It is the word of sin and guilt, which man cannot annul or avoid.

NOTES

1. See above, pp. 314 f.
2. *Die Christliche Welt*, 1922, Nr. 6, Sp. 93.
3. In Schmoller's *Jahrbuch*, 45. Jg., 4. H.: "Die Revolution der Wissenschaft."
4. Above, p. 314.
5. *Gesammelte Schriften*, 2, 826.
6. *Ibid.*, 826 f.
7. *Religion in Geschichte und Gegenwart*, 2, 1450.
8. *Gesammelte Schriften*, 2, 826 f.
9. *Religion in Geschichte und Gegenwart*, 2, 1450 f.
10. *Ibid.*, 1448.
11. *Gesammelte Schriften*, 2, 826.
12. *Religion in Geschichte und Gegenwart*, 2, 445.
13. *Ibid.*, 1440.
14. *Ibid.*
15. *Ibid.*, 1442.
16. *Ibid.*, 1454.
17. Above, p. 315.
18. *Die Absolutheit des Christentums*, 2, Aufl., 58.
19. *Ibid.*
20. Above, p. 314.
21. *Ibid.*
22. Above, p. 316.
23. *Gesammelte Schriften*, 2, 620.
24. *Die Christliche Welt*, 1921, Nr. 45, Sp. 809 ff.
25. *Ibid.*, Sp. 826.
26. Walch Edition, Vol. 18, p. 2474.

COMMUNITY OR CORPORATE SOCIETY?*

Friedrich Gogarten

It is entirely justified to ask whether this question can still be seriously posed today. If we call community the form of common life constituted by individuality, will, and the convictions and consent of the individual, and if, in contrast, we call corporate society the form of common life in which an authority not resting on the will of the individual and not resulting from it unites individuals without reference to their wills, then our present situation is the result of a long development, beginning four hundred years ago with the rise of the modern world, which has undeniably brought the first form of common life, community, to prominence. This is not to say that the form already prevails, but that it is the uncontested goal. Indeed, it appears today to be perhaps the only possibility for regaining a common life.

There is no question that all forms of the common life of man, from the State to the church and from the school to the family, which formerly enjoyed totally unquestioned validity, are today shaken right to their roots. The objective forms, valid independent of the consent of the individual, have burst asunder and released the individual. We may complain about this and think it is merely the rebellion of the individual, and that force must be used to re-establish the authority of the forms. But this force is simply no longer available, and no complaining about the wicked, modern world nor praising of the good old days will re-establish it. Nor would it help if somehow external, material force were available again. We are concerned here with intellectual decisions. To bring these objective forms forcefully to bear would, according to the contemporary outlook, be ethically unacceptable and such a project would be condemned to defeat from the outset. If those objective forms of common life once had authority over the will and consent of the individual, it was only because the individual and his will were considered to be not only not good, but evil, requiring thorough constraint. And no form of common life, not even in its ultimate and highest intentions, was concerned with forming an ideal of the individual or community. There was no such thing as an ultimate goal, only the desire to bring the given opposites into relation to each other, if possible without friction, but, in the event of even the roughest friction, without timidity. There was no desire to use

* From *Von Glauben und Offerbarung* (Jena, 1923), pp. 63-83.

these objective forms of common life to educate the individual and thereby release him from compulsion. The corporate society was not at all concerned, even after infinite development, in becoming a community in which there was no longer the opposition of compulsion and freedom, authority and individuality, and which might furthermore be characterized by the freest harmony of the individuals bound together in it.

In a word, this concept of corporate society, of the forms of common life, and thus of individuals and individuality, is by no means idealistic. It has no infinite, eternal goals. It is limited in every respect, not just in comparison with an idealistic concept of community in the broadest sense of the term. Its goal—if it may be called that, and perhaps we ought rather say, soberly and unidealistically, its purpose —is not creative life, but purely and simply obedience and order. It has no faith in the infinite capacity for development or the consummation of individuality. For modern thinking and feeling, however, that means it has no faith at all. And because this is how it appears to modern man (who now prevails even in the most conservative and orthodox circles), this concept of corporate society is condemned from the outset.

To modern thinking and feeling, where faith is accorded infinite possibilities of development, this concept appears not merely reactionary, but, much worse, a symptom of fatigue which must be sharply combated. We may even ask (and individualistic liberalism, naïvely believing in the concept of development, not only asks the question, but answers it) whether anyone who has such a concept of corporate society does not set himself in opposition to what God says very clearly to men in history and the development of history. We could think that history, which with the rise of the modern world produced individualism, after the establishment of individualism by the powerful activity of German Idealism, pronounced its verdict against the objective, authoritative corporate society in favor of the community which is individualistic in the deepest and truest sense. We could speak of evident disobedience to the will of God where this decision does not ensue, and when it happens—as it does—that someone prefers not to seek in the general disillusionment of these days or in neurotic frustration the reason for the failure to recognize this decision.

It can be recognized already, from these considerations, that the decision between community and corporate society does not involve merely an isolated question about which people may differ and still remain basically in general agreement. This difference pervades everything. Here there are two views which diverge in every aspect, the least as well as the greatest, the most external as well as the most inward, and which are mutually exclusive. Thus, we are not dealing with a polarity in which one view can free the other from onesidedness and supplement it, but with a distinct either-or. Nor are we dealing with a contrast in the way in which information and views are shared, in the sense, say, that the form of communication would be aesthetic and artistic one moment, and scientific the next. The question then remains whether we are dealing with a contrast of two cultures. And that appears to me to be a question which must be painstakingly considered and repeatedly asked. In fact, it must be based on the following consideration: Whoever decides for the objective corporate society, rooted in authority, and against the individualistic community, based on freedom, stands today in a fatal proximity to reactionaries, to Romantics, to those who expect deliverance from the Middle East, Russia, China, or India, and to all sorts of other subjects of prejudice. If from this company any sort of harmony results among those who want to justify and improve culture, it would, in any case, have to do only with the question of the contrast or combination of two cultures, and to this almost any answer can be given. There would not be, as we usually think in such cases, two cultures in opposition to each other, but at best only the remnants of cultures. For where a culture begins to justify itself and reflect on itself, there we find only a few unstable and lonely intellectuals dreaming their dreams. The question of whether this contrast is dealing with two cultures ought to be asked repeatedly in order to alert us to the danger of the question of truth unintentionally becoming a question of this or that culture. For this either-or is the either-or of truth or falsehood.

It is clear that no historical development can alter the truth, even if this development has brought about a highly developed and even brilliant culture. This presupposes that there is culture in the sense understood by the intellectual cultural dreamers. Any development, even the most brilliant culture, must justify itself before the truth. And it is impossible to see why a centuries-long development, or the most brilliant culture, could not be shown to be a frightening mistake when measured by the truth, even if this error so pervaded the entire spiritual life of a period that it would seem hopeless and impossible to ever get free from it, since it would still permeate every idea. This could be the case, since there would be no word whose meaning would be free from this error. For through centuries of earnest and painstaking work, words would have taken on the content of this erroneous concept. (But it is inconceivable for individualistic thought that error and serious scholarly work need not be mutually exclusive.) Anyone who knows how much a word with its given, traditional content directs the paths of thought knows how difficult it is to give new meaning to words, to uproot them from their course and guide them in the way which thought wishes them to go.

There is something else which is even more important to recognize. If our question deals with the contrast of truth and error and not merely with the contrast of two periods, generations, or cultures; that is, if we are concerned not with an accidental but, as it is sometimes said, with an absolute contrast, then it is easy to see that it is essentially not merely an error of a period, generation, or culture, but an error which constitutes an abyss before which everyone constantly stands who is concerned about the truth. This is so if truth is one, and therefore, pictorially speaking, not a broad field on which everyone can move according to his own individual pleasure as his creative fancies are inspired, but a narrow, overgrown, and hard-to-recognize path through a bottomless swamp where every false step brings the peril of sinking from sight. If error is frighteningly near, and if we guard this knowledge as something which must be continually regained, then we are indeed saved from unintentionally confusing the decision between truth and error with the decision between two cultures. And we will also be prevented from developing a program for a new, authoritative, objective culture and falling thereby into the company of progressives, reactionaries, or any other cut of Romantics who carry on a most superfluous operation—the establishment of culture, the deepening of culture, or whatever else. And certainly no one would think of inviting his readers to undertake the establishment of an authoritative corporate society. For, since corporate societies cannot be directly established, that would actually mean establishing a community, a community with the purpose of propagating an objective corporate society and combating communities that have purposes. Anyone doing this would show that he does not know what he is saying or what he wants. No one can hold any longer to aims which are far reaching and move in some way toward world betterment if he presumes to deal with truth. For then he must deal with that which is closest to him—himself; and in such a way that he is constantly alert so as to make the right decision between truth and error. To avoid falling into the swamp of error, or I could also say, of individualism, let it be expressly said that this decision is not dredged up from the creative depths of the individual, but is nothing more than objective, rational knowledge of truth and obedience to the truth. That is no sort of individualism. What is at stake here is not the creative development of one's own self, but self-knowledge.

The intention and task of such a consideration can be only this and nothing else. In the end, it is this not at all personal but rather extremely objective task and work which binds the reader and writer together. And no one would for a moment retain this obviously limited connection—should I say, community?—if he felt instead any direct expression of the soul, if, that is, he wished to experience a direct contact between souls. If anyone wishes to retain this connection and to fulfill the task given by it, he must have previously perceived the fateful error of individualism—not merely the error of a superficial, but of a very profound individualism, whose error and guilt become greater the more deeply they are grasped. Besides the aesthetic concept of individualism, which is customarily used in the so-called religious movement today, there is a still more profound individualism, namely, the ethical and speculative.

In a report of the Wartburg Conference of the Alliance for Contemporary Christianity, Emil Fuchs[1] has singled out the will to truthfulness as the real substance of the community between such otherwise divergent men, which in his opinion this Alliance tries to bring about. In contrast to this community he places another, rooted in the same concepts, confessions, worship, and ceremonies. And he feels that the overcoming of all these things is a prerequisite for unity in the new covenant. This appears quite broadminded, tolerant, and undogmatic, but actually it is not. For if it is not a proclamation of the purest subjectivism and the most uninhibited caprice, if, on the contrary, it is a well-considered and well-established view, then unavoidably its presupposition is that true desire in its authenticity and individual man in his individuality, his individual particularity, are the actual reality, divine life, and thus truth itself. No one can make truthfulness into a standard if truthfulness is not in itself the truth. Or else, he does not know what he is saying. The result is a surprising picture in which the modesty with which individualists of all kinds set up truthfulness alone as the ultimate standard, by which they measure others, and by which they themselves wish to be measured, has as its presupposition faith in the one truth. The result, then, is that the individualist himself, in his truthfulness, in his individuality, is the truth.

Since, according to individualism, the individual in his individual being is the truth; and since in his own knowing, if it is only his own personal knowledge, he knows the truth itself; and since in his own seeing, if it is only his original, creative seeing, he sees the truth itself, then truth can never be an object, something outside the individual, something known, something seen. It is always in the individual, in his being and doing that are most personal and most active, i.e., his original, creative being and doing. Indeed, the being and doing of the individual is then the living essence of truth. And every objective being, everything known, seen, or effected is only the expression or symbol of a truth which is itself never seen or effected, but which only sees and effects. It could also be said that truth is only in individuality: to characterize its core and basis in one word, truth is in the I. To be more precise, it is not in the I seen as an "it," as an object, as something conceivable, as a thing; but it is the pure "I-am." The only thing it can say of itself is—I am. And even that is not stated precisely. But the unspeakable cannot be spoken. That which is not and can never be known is not knowable; indeed, truth itself does not know itself, for this self would already be something known, only an expression, a symbol. It can only know, be, or operate, and can do this only as pure I, as individuality.

The extent to which individuality in its pure individual being, or truth in its pure truthfulness, is presupposed here as the one, universal truth becomes even clearer if we ask how this individuality becomes community. I scarcely need say here that we are not asking about a simple, empirical juxtaposition of men in time and space, but about the innermost connection of man's being—community. But this is the question of how the I can come to itself. It is the essence of individualistic community that its members should be in contact with each other in their pure and most profound individuality. As Fuchs puts it in his report, "all persons will find joy in the truth and truthfulness of others, and out of this joy in one another, will desire to become the source of power for one another." That means that one self desires to come into contact with another self; it desires to become one with the individual life of the other in order to draw power from the other to nourish its own particularity. Were it not that truthfulness and individuality, in their innermost being, were regarded as the one truth, living in everything and self-attesting, a community between these individualities, each having its own particular truth, would be absolutely impossible. Men would be infinitely, hopelessly, and incurably lonely in their innermost being. And because they would be individualities enclosed within themselves, they would be shut off from every other individuality. There would be no way from one to another. Each one would live in a separate world—a world which could be only his own. Even where the longing for community became unbearable, each person would have to leave all others alone, however close they were to him. Wherever a person was isolated, he would be totally isolated, in touch with no one else. There to his torment he would know only himself; there the most yearning cry for companionship would be heard only by his own ears, and he would hear no reply except his own interminably repeated, unanswered cry.

That can be different only if every individuality is in its own innermost being the one truth. Then it is one with all others in itself, in its own being. And since its own works, its own views, are only symbols of its own being, of the one truth, so also the works and words, the life lived by every other individuality, are signs and references to the deeper life and being, to the unspeakable and unknowable truth itself. Through all that, it is in direct contact with other individualities.

But, as much as one individuality is in contact with another, as much as they would like to become one, there is never here an individuality of one which is not already included in the other. It does not give its life a new tone, but only awakens what was already latent in it. "I have the other only if and when I recognize his particular beauty and help him achieve his beauty, as he helps me," as a representative of this view says in characteristically aesthetic categories.[2] This community is truly an individualistic one. It is a community in which the I exists solely and completely alone. And its song is "I am I." That is all, yes, the one and only thing, that its members call out to each other. But they need no other song. For it comes from the deepest individuality and it can sound forth only from there; moreover, if individuality in its innermost, individual being is its actual, real being —the being which establishes everything else and carries it in itself, then it is God's own being, and only then is "I am I" a song of jubilation and the joyful cry of the released I. If this "I am I" comes from the deepest, purest level of individuality, where it exists only in itself, and if individuality is divine in its foundation, then it is not only a man, or, if I may so put it, a human, who sings this song, but in him who is divine in the depths from which the song comes, the eternal deity itself sings, and it sings its own majesty, the eternal "I am that I am," and truly no man could say happier, more blessed, or stronger words than these to another.

If these presuppositions were proven false, then this cry of jubilation would in truth be a terrible lament of the man caught in the shameful and terrifying prison of his selfhood, the man who yearns for the other who is to shatter this horrible prison for him. And this lament would be that much more terrible if man did not understand it in its true sense.

Let us therefore test both presuppositions. The first is that man can realize his individuality at its deepest, purest level. And the second is that individuality at this level is divine.

GOGARTEN: Community or Corporate Society?   335

If by the term "individuality" we mean the innermost being of
man, something not determined by circumstances, not conditioned by
this or that, not in any sense an object, but the being of being, the
life of life, the pure, eternal I-am, then by all means it is divine. For
God alone is the life of life, the being of being—only the divine is not
an object, a this or a that; only the divine is unconditioned. But
whether man is this individuality and whether he can ever become it
is another question. Do the divine "I am that I am" and the human "I
am I" really mean the same thing? In other words, is the I in the
eternal, pure I-am, which is eternal and divine, the same I as in the
second case? Is it a statement of identity to say "I am I"? Or is there
not a gaping contrast between the first I, the I from eternity, from
God, through which I exist, and the second I, which I am now in this
temporal moment? Is it not a contrast as large as that between time
and eternity? And can anyone seriously ask whether this contrast can
be abolished in human life? One could think that possible only if he
had not clarified for himself the meaning of the first I in the statement
"I am I." It means being one with God, being a child of God; it means
an image of God; it means pure, joyous, guiltless being in God. The "I
am I" of man has come from this. Have we no ears to hear the word
that contemporary man experiences a frightening absence of thought
as soon as he speaks of the eternal, of his own being in relation to
eternity, if he thinks this "I am I" is the same in any way as the divine
"I am that I am"? And yet, contemporary thinking as a whole rests
on this error, on this blasphemy. That we wish to be like God is the
continually repeated error through which we all, from the beginning,
have become, and become anew every moment, who we are. It is always
the same sin—that we wish to put man in God's place. We repeatedly
echo God's words: "I am I." And we would all like them to mean—
and the Idealists and individualists and mystics are even convinced
that they do mean—I am the Alpha and Omega, the beginning and
the end, who is and who was and who is to come. And regardless of
who speaks these words, they always mean merely "I am I"; that is,
they indicate only a narrow, painfully narrow, suffering, and lonely
I, separated from every Thou, from God and man, and full of desire
for God and all creatures. Furthermore, it means that no destiny or
fate has maliciously made me so; no, I am I and there is no third entity
on which to shove the responsibility. The guilt is mine. It means that
it was not fate or God who made me into the I that I am. It is I, ever
since I have existed. This guilt is my being throughout the time that
I was and am and am to be.

And if these words "I am I" are understood in their deepest sense
as man's cry of despair, if all pride and conceit and finally too all

callousness has disappeared from these words, then they mean (and right from the outset nothing but this) God, be merciful to me, a poor sinner!

We have seen that the form of mutual human relationship which we called community is totally individualistic in essence. That means it stands upon the I, upon its will, its impulses, its truthfulness. Community—assuming that it is realized—would indeed be nothing more nor less than revelation, the unfolding of the I in its deepest essence, of individuality in its original form, in its immediacy. In other words, the problem of community here is not how the I comes to the Thou, but how the I comes to the I. And this is meant in both senses implied in the statement, which in the end may prove to be one and the same, to be identical. According to this view, the I comes into community with the Thou only if the Thou, which is sharply contrasted to the I, impenetrably foreign, incomprehensibly other, is transformed into an I which desires nothing more than to be and live out its pure I-ness. But because the Thou, which, as the Thou, remains more remote from me than heaven is from earth, discloses itself to me in its I-ness, its individuality, its particularity, I would need to become a pure I; I would need to wish nothing other than to disclose myself and live in my deepest, most personal selfhood. In this self-disclosure, the I of my own self would open itself to me, the I of the other would open itself to me, and the pure, eternal I of the deity would open itself to me in the harmony of my I and the I of the other.

This would be the perfect individualistic community, a community where only the I, oneness, individuality, freedom, spontaneity, and immediacy would exist; a community in which there would be no force, nothing in common, no one confronting me; there is no Thou, neither the Thou of man nor of God. For God would have become the pure, eternal I. More precisely, God would have become the pure, eternal I for me. But that means and can mean nothing else but that I would have become the pure, eternal I of God.

Individualistic community and everything associated with it stands or falls with this statement, this assertion. An example is the whole culture of individualistic personality of recent centuries and of those to come, insofar as it is still claimed they will bring the fulfillment and deepening of individualism, as its exponents maintain in an attempt not to lose from the start the battle against the deplorable condition of contemporary individualism. It does not much matter whether the individualist accepts verbatim this fundamental statement of individualism. Individualism pretends mostly to be aesthetic, and religious individualism especially is almost always aesthetic individualism, with religious emphases. That is basic, since individualism is of aesthetic origin, and has its justification as well as its limitation within the aesthetic sphere. A basic obscurity of thought is concealed in carrying over aesthetic categories and principles into a fundamentally different area, that of religion. Here, the religious-aesthetic individualists can do quite a piece of competent work on themselves. But it can only be done under the condition that they cease to be individualists, at least in this work, and that they recognize the authority of truth, which is not an individualistic truthfulness, but one before which even the most sincere individualistic truthfulness is shown to be a fateful error.

We acknowledged that, in sharp contrast to individualism, the ultimate meaning of "I am I" is not the divine "I am that I am," but the very human "God, be merciful to me, a sinner." Here, the I has yielded its dominant position. It is no longer the sole reality, and definitely not the ultimate genuine reality. God cannot become the I for me if his I and mine are of the same essence, and impossible to distinguish. Rather, God is the Thou, only the Thou. And thus the same severe, harsh, unceasing contrast between God and man is established as between I and Thou. Individualism knows that a boundary is drawn between the I and the Thou which renders any essential, substantial community between them impossible. Because it desires this community it transforms the whole world of God and men into the I, and cannot avoid doing so. Therefore, all Thou is of necessity dissolved into the I. And therefore, the I must be its sole and only reality.

But for the same reason, individualism collapses in its entirety and individualistic community proves itself a phantom at that moment when a Thou rises up which eludes that transformation into an I, a Thou which will not allow itself the inner, immediate community in the I-ness and mystical I-feeling. This Thou arises the moment the I recognizes that it is not the sole and only reality—when it recognizes that the world is broken up into I and Thou.

With this recognition, the problem of the relationship of man to man arises anew. The problem cannot be solved any longer by the individualistic community, whose problem was how the I comes to the I. The real problem is how the I comes to the Thou. And that means the Thou who can never become the I, but who continues to confront me in the stern, harsh contrast of the Thou. The individualistic solution of realizing community by turning the Thou into an I no longer exists. This solution is now recognized as a monstrous self-deception, in which the real problem of the Thou and its contrast which was to be overcome is simply set aside; and it is a truism to say that when each person has become a pure I, the contrast will no longer exist and community will be realized.

Between the I and the Thou there is a relation which transcends the dimension of the momentary and accidental only by virtue of a third entity. And this third entity can only be something extracted from subjectivity and individuality in the same way that authority is. Or (and this is the second possibility) the relation consists in the unconditional subordination of one to the other, of the I to the Thou. But the I and the Thou can never be connected in essential unity, as individualistic community intends. In other words, there is no direct community between the I and the Thou, but only an indirect one. But a community in which the enduring and separating contrast is mediated, I would term a corporate society.

At this point we encounter a difficult, perhaps the most difficult, question about authority. Who is the authority? Where is authority possible at all?

We saw that authority is not possible in the acceptance of individualism, regardless of how it may be constituted. Authority and individualism are mutually exclusive. Thus, no one can assert individualism, even if only to work at bringing it about, and then, finding that it will not work otherwise, admit some authority. Every form of individualism, the tamest or the most unreasoned, makes any sort of authority simply impossible. This is the situation of our culture; if you please, of our time. It is so in law and the State, work and art, marriage and family, and school and church. The desire for authority makes sense only if it is recognized that individualism, in any form it assumes, is an error. For there can be authority only where the Thou confronts me indissolubly, ineffaceably, and inflexibly. But there is and there can be no such thing in individualism, since individualism is the fundamental dissolution of the Thou into the I.

Since authority is a spiritual reality and its force (if one may use that term) is not the force and necessity of an event, it can be authority only as the Thou, as the authority of the Thou. However, we should not confuse authority with the power of persuasion, which a leader, even a brilliant leader, in the camp of the individualists, may have in contemporary movements. For one recognizes himself, his own innermost I, in a leader, especially one of genius. And the harmony with the leader is nothing but the harmony with one's own I and not with the Thou. For we follow the leader because of his genius and individuality, because of his comprehensive and intensive I-ness, in which we find our own I and strengthen it in the power and intensity of the leader. To be a leader is not something anyone gets from himself; one is a leader only in relation to his supporters and their acceptance of him. The supporters choose the leader, but the leader does not choose his supporters. When the leader loses his genius, he loses his following. But if he wishes to have authority, he must give up any attempt to influence his following with his genius, individuality, and I-ness. That means that man as man never can and never will have authority. For in the moment that he as a man wishes to exert authority, he places his I, his genius, in the place of this authority.

Therefore, only the Thou of God can have authority. God alone is the pure, absolute Thou, with whom we can in no way equate ourselves, and whose authority is not established through our acceptance of it, nor abrogated by our rejection of it. It is the Thou of God which makes us the I that we are and which allows us to recognize our "I am I" as "God, be merciful to me, a sinner." It is God's absolute Thou which really allows us to discover in our lostness our profound, impenetrable loneliness.

We have understood nothing of what we have considered up to this point if we seek to rediscover authority, this Thou of God, in inner experience; if we assert any sort of direct certainty of this authority, a certainty originating in the creative depths of our I; or if we wish to equate this authority of God in some way with individual regularity, that is, with our genius or the ultimate deepest being of our nature. God's Thou never becomes our I, in spite of Angelus Silesius, indeed, in spite of Eckhart, which means even more. It remains God's Thou; it is as remote, as alien, and as unapproachable as every Thou. Only it is even more remote, more alien, and more unapproachable, since it is the eternal Thou of God.

We may ask how we can have knowledge of God if the relation between the I and the Thou, the human I and the divine Thou, is as we have stated. The answer can only be that God imparts himself to us on his own initiative. And if we do not fall back into individualism, it will be clear that this communication is genuine and not a Platonic, Idealistic self-remembrance. For God remains the Thou and in no way becomes the I. Thus, there is no *unio mystica* between God and man, God and soul, no sort of direct contact or experience. There is nothing of the sort. There can be only a hearing of his Word. For the Word is the only form of communication between the I and the Thou.[3] But I remind the reader that this Word is not the mystical word of inner experience, for then we would only hear our I, and not God's Thou. God's Word can be a word only from the outside. And this divine Word is God's authority.

We have already seen that relationships among men can exist

only under authority. We have seen also that there is no authority apart from God. Let us put it more precisely so that the error of individualism does not creep in again and so that this authority, rooted in God, is not confused with the originality of man: there is no authority apart from the authority of God's Word. Thus, there can be no relationship among men apart from God's authority, that is, apart from the authority of God's Word. Furthermore, the relationship among men, which from the start and more than any other exists under God's name and which we call the church, cannot be constituted by human, individual, religious emotion or by human, religious experience, not by the will to truthfulness or "by the joy of the one in the particularly of the other," but solely and exclusively through the fact that God's Word is preached and heard in the church. The organization of the church is not established by the intimate community of its members, edifying and strengthening each other with their individuality, but by nothing more or less than the preaching of the Word of God in the church. Thus, it is not an individualistic, personalistic community, but an authoritative, objective corporate society.

What that means is understood only by the person who has recognized the boundaries and essence of the I and that in its deepest sense it means not, as individualism would have it, creative, original life, but guilt and sin. Thus, the point is established at which the most complete equality, and thus an absolute bond and solidarity, is reached in a corporate society in which the existing contrasts are not somehow abolished, but are robbed of their power. Only those contrasts are absolutely abolished which owe their significance to their religious nature, that is, the contrasts between the priest and the laity, the leader and the follower, the genius and the masses.

Indeed, Romantic individualism will also claim this profound equality and the community given with it. But it will and can establish this equality and community only out of the individual, creative experience of sin (the reader will pardon this expression; it is intended only as a clever phrase), which must then be required of every individual. And since we are not dealing with this or that specific sin, which would indeed establish a difference rather than an equality between persons, but with total sinfulness, the impossible demand for the realization of individuality at its deepest, simplest level will be raised again; but only in the light of the objections to it. Despite this, the degree to which the same thing is still meant here, namely, the impossible demand for realization of individuality at its simplest, deepest level, results from the fact that this total sinfulness of individuality appears only as the dialectic reverse of its perfect divinity. And the same answer we gave to the question of whether a realization of individuality at its simplest level is possible is valid also for the total sinfulness of individuality. And since individuality is rooted in the same unrealizable presupposition, this community, which is supposed to be constituted by the individualistic experience of total sinfulness, is merely a phantom.

It could be argued that this judgment must refer also to the corporate society, which we previously said includes a complete equality, and thus an absolute bond of solidarity among its members. But the constitutive aspect of this society is definitely not an individualistic experience; its presupposition is not the realization of individuality at its simplest, deepest level. The presupposition is instead the I's renunciation of the claim to be the true and only reality. And it is not a renunciation which stems from the I's immanent fatigue or despair; if that were the case, we would be back with Romantic aesthetic individualism and its phantom community. The renunciation intended here is possible only through knowledge of the divine Thou and obedience to its authority, which can come, however, only from an active hearing of God's Word.

Just as the total sinfulness of individuality shows itself to be the dialectic reverse of its perfect divinity in the view of Romantic aesthetic individualism, so forgiveness is seen here to be the divine answer to the sin of men, and thus also divine sanctification of all human life. But this answer does not happen through a dialectic conversion, but solely (and one cannot stress this point strongly enough) from an active hearing of God's Word.

The result is that the corporate society constituted by the authoritative Word of God is not only the society of total sinfulness, but also the society of the saved. The knowledge or experience of this total sinfulness, however, is not the result of a realization of individuality in its simple form, but the hearing of divine judgment; similarly, this sanctification is not the result of such a realization of individuality. This sanctification exists only where God's Word is heard and believed. "For wherever I believe the Word . . . I must forthwith confess that I, with all I can do, am done for."[4] This sanctification will not forget that its reverse side is total sinfulness. And it will make no difference whether we make the one side or the other into the substance and constitutive element of all human life and thus all common life. No one will find a different substance or constitutive principle. In any case, no one will be able to use this sanctification to somehow establish an ideal community among men, in which the contrast of force and opinion, authority and freedom, I and Thou, would become an unmediated, direct unity; nor will it bring about some sort of ideal condition on this earth in God's name. If anyone wishes to know how the common life of man is shaped according to this view in law and politics, in marriage and family, in work and art, in school and church, he would probably do better to begin with total sinfulness—then as far as possible he will avoid the danger of forgetting what it means to say "we have become a new creature, after being completely corrupted and slain."[5] In any case, it would no longer be individualistic or idealistic. No one would then understand the nature of another individual's being nor would he be understood. But how much depends on this! If anyone believes in God's Word on God's authority, then he is understood by God in his deepest and highest, most external and most inward, existential being; to "help [the other] achieve his beauty, as he helps me" is not possible here, for the eyes which see deeply do not find "beauty," but guilt and sin. However (and this is the most important), he can forgive all the sins of the other in God's name and by God's Word.

NOTES

1. "Kunstwart" (December 1920).
2. Mensing, *Freie Volkskirche, Blatt für Gegenwartschristentum*, 1922.
3. I cannot omit referring to the important and beautiful book by Ferdinand Ebner, *Das Wort und die geistigen Realitäten* (Innsbruck: Brenner-Verlag, 1921).
4. *Erlangen Ausgabe*, 20, 142.
5. *Ibid.*, 127

HISTORICISM*

Friedrich Gogarten

The historicizing of all our thinking has been carried out today
to the extent that it has become impossible for any of our ideas to escape it. This historicizing threatens to abolish absolutely every idea
which requires a norm or might tend to be a norm itself. For it is its
nature to place all forms of human life, even those of highest normative validity, in the flow of history, of development, and within this
development to allow every individual form to be its own standard, its
own norm. In the process, all norms are abolished. A norm can exist
only if it is subject to another law than that governing the development of the manifestation for which it is to be the norm. The only way
out would be for the final goal of history itself to be this norm to which
the separate manifestations, the succession of which constitutes history,
would be subjected. But this way too is no longer open. Even this final
goal and this concept of being which has become reality, both of which
the Enlightenment and Hegel wished to exclude from the historicizing of all other occurrences, have meanwhile become "historical." Historicizing has been carried out today so thoroughly that even these concepts, freed from development and relativity, which were supposed to
be the norm for all the individual stages of development, are recognized in their historical conditionality—they are totally contingent
historical manifestations made into absolutes. And they are thus finished as norms. Even the final way out, that which leads to total relativism, is shifted here to a desire to creep silently out of history by
means of a delicate, aesthetic attitude. The apparent superiority of
such a relativistic gesture is recognized here as the fatigue of a culturally decadent period.

Practically speaking, that all means a tremendous convulsion of all
authorities and norms and the forms of human life which they support. The indisputable validity which nearly all of them possessed in
the past is brought into question. And this is not done only by men
who are revolutionaries in principle, as the middle class, which has an
interest in this indisputable validity from more than one point of
view, would have us believe. The grounding of all these institutions
exclusively in the historical-empirical and the stripping away of all
their absolute validity is taken care of by contemporary science, which

* From *Zwischen den Zeiten*, II (1924), issue 8, pp. 7-25.

is thoroughly historicized in its methods; by so doing it has emphatically shattered, more fundamentally than any revolutionary could, all authorities and norms, "all eternal truths, whether the ecclesiastical-supernatural which claim the highest authority, or the eternal truths of reason and the rational constructions of politics, law, society, religion, and morality, or political pressures toward education, which relate to worldly authority and its dominant form."[1]

Briefly stated, this is the intellectual situation of the present, as Troeltsch has repeatedly clarified it afresh in his writings, and which has become the starting point of his work and the stimulus for his task. As he formulated it himself in his most recently published posthumous work,[2] this task consists of "an examination of the basic concepts of all theology," a task in which he was engaged in *Die Absolutheit des Christentums und die Religionsgeschichte*,[3] which summarizes his previous works. It is the examination of basic theological concepts from the perspective of the universal historicizing of thought. His conclusion is that theological positions are stripped of their claim to be absolute norms, and, like other conceptual positions, are placed in the stream of history, and are revealed as purely historical structures.

It is quite easy for Troeltsch to enter into controversy with one of the two schools into which he divides theology, the orthodox-supernaturalist school. He shows how this school uses miracle as the base of its claim that Christianity is the one and only truth, the inner miracle of conversion. But since an inner miracle can be proven as such only by an external miracle that penetrates the external course of history and its causality; and since, for this purpose, the validity of the direct and exclusive effectiveness of God must be claimed for all of redemptive history, to Troeltsch, who proceeds from the presupposition of the complete historicizing of all thought and events, the theory of this school is an impossibility. For the uninterrupted continuity of historical events can concede any exception to its validity only by denying itself. And it makes no difference if we submit extra-Christian and extra-biblical events to historical method for research and interpretation. For the characteristic of the modern historical method is that it subjects everything to itself without exception. If anyone acknowledges its validity at even one point, he can never withdraw from its consequences. It is Troeltsch's great contribution even to orthodox-supernaturalist theology that he made this clear and demonstrated it repeatedly. In this respect, the task of supernaturalist theology, instead of retreating to the "abstract impossibility of a strict denial of miracles,"[4] would be to subject the historicizing pointed out by Troeltsch in all contemporary thinking to a thorough critical examination, in relation to all history, not only to redemptive history, and to investigate the truth and reality of this historicized thinking. That would certainly mean that the presupposition of this supernaturalist theology, the separation of redemptive event from profane, and the apologetic nature of the thinking closely connected with this separation, would be totally overthrown. But there will be more to say about that.

Troeltsch enters into a much more penetrating discussion with the second of the two schools into which he divides theology—the idealistic-evolutionist. Indeed, it can be said that Troeltsch's thinking, to the extent that it is theological in the stricter sense, consists largely in the critical discussion with this idealistic-evolutionist theology. As a theologian, Troeltsch himself stems from this school. According to him, its theory is "the attempt, rejecting all reliance on the miraculous, to demonstrate the validity and significance of Christianity in a purely historical manner and without falling short of the self-assurance of the doctrines of the early church."[5] This theory received its classical formulation from no less a figure than Hegel. Its basic concept, which underlies all of its different expressions, is the equating of Christianity with the concept of the absolute, perfect religion: In Christianity, the perfect religion has appeared in history. All other religions still express the truth of God, but in an incomplete form. They prepare the way for and find their fulfillment in Christianity. According to Troeltsch, however, the "rainbow [of these constructions] can only brighten the fog of a still highly unformulated historical knowledge."[6] The idea of an absolute religion is obtained not from history, but from the concept of the absolute itself. And progressive historical research has shown that Christianity can never be understood as a simple idea, but only as a historically contingent manifestation of a highly limited, individual and historical kind, arising out of a thousand contingencies and influences. The concept of a historical realization of a universal concept, in this case the concept of the absolute religion which would be the driving and shaping force in all religions, contradicts the essence of historical reality. Historical reality recognizes only limited, contingent, individual manifestations. As Troeltsch has shown, however, the most recent and significant theological school, that of Albrecht Ritschl, has made a virtue out of necessity. Since the concept of an absolute religion is an impossibility, the Ritschlian school emphasizes the historical character of Christianity and, out of the particular historical appearance of Christianity and its "individual-historical" claim to absolute revelation and redemption, advances it as the norm for all other religions. Troeltsch shows, however, that they operate here with an ambiguous concept of the historical: in reference, on the one hand, to all non-Christian manifestations, they draw these relativistic conclusions and, on the other hand, in reference to Christianity, they use this concept without these consequences, for in Christianity it is the "individual-historical" claim to the absolute quality of revelation that should establish this use. As concerns this theory, *mutatis mutandis,* what was said about the orthodox-supernaturalist theory is valid—that it is basically nothing other than a watered-down supernaturalism.[7] In view of this, it is necessary to clarify anew our thinking concerning the concept of the historical and its consequences, and thus also concerning the thorough historicizing of contemporary thinking.

Troeltsch's own solution to the problem of how Christianity comprehended entirely as a purely historical manifestation can still be made the basis for a system of norms is as follows.

Just as surely as there is no universal concept of religion present in all empirical religions and evolving in them out of distortion and imperfection, and just as surely as Christianity in particular is not this universal concept, it can still be asserted with all justification that there is a common element in all religions. In fact, this element is a common goal, valid for all religions. And this goal is "the productive power in the idea of goal-setting, in the forward-driving unrest and yearning, and in the confrontation with the purely natural world itself."[8] And Troeltsch says of this goal and this power of personalism that among all the great religions Christianity is its "strongest and most concentrated revelation." It has assumed "a unique position because it alone has achieved the separation of the higher and lower worlds, the effect of which is felt everywhere; and by means of a higher world has covered over, changed, and finally abolished the reality that is material, factually given, and traditional, and all this through uniting redemptively the souls bound in the world and in guilt to the love of God which takes the initiative and lays hold on them."[9] The acknowledgment of the validity of Christianity as the culmination of revelation rests "on the needle point of personal persuasion"[10] just as personalism is to be accepted as a valid goal solely through personal persuasion. But Troeltsch is of the opinion that the history of religion permits the certainty that Christianity can be considered as this culmination and, at the same time, "as the point of convergence of all recognizable directions of religious development."[11] That does not mean the realization of a universal concept of religion through Christianity. For Christianity is this culmination precisely in its historical particularity and in its wholly individual character. Nor can it mean that it is the final culmination of religion. However much Christianity in its historical particularity may be the actual culmination for us in our particular historical situation, this historical conditionality does not exclude the possibility of a still higher revelation, even if we can say absolutely nothing about it. According to Troeltsch, it is sufficient for us that Christianity assumes the highest validity in the world in which we live.

This was the solution as Troeltsch presented it in *Die Absolutheit des Christentums und die Religionsgeschichte*. As early as 1912, in the preface to the second edition (the first appeared in 1902), Troeltsch observed that the statement of the problem was no longer the same as when he wrote the book; in the intervening decade it had been greatly sharpened. That decade produced (not to mention other works) Troeltsch's research compiled in 1912 in his great work *Die Soziallehren der christlichen Kirchen und Gruppen*.[12] And in the next decade came the research published as *Der Historismus und seine Probleme. Erstes Buch: Das logische Problem der Geschichtsphilosophie*, which clarified the situation even further. Both these works lead beyond the understanding of the problem as stated in *Die Absolutheit des Christentums*, since in *Die Soziallehren* a much deeper insight into the limitation of Christianity for the individual was achieved. According to this study, Christianity is completely dependent upon the cultures in which it develops. Thus, its concept of personalism is not universally human, but specifically Western, European, and thus transmitted only with difficulty to a different cultural context, for example, to Indian culture. As a result, the concept of supreme validity and especially the concept of the convergence point of all acknowledged directions of religious development, both of which were claimed to the fullest for Christianity, would be significantly abridged; indeed, the second would be entirely abolished. Christianity remains for us Europeans the supreme revelation, "the face of God turned to us." Its "validity consists primarily in the fact that we have become what we are through Christianity alone, and only in Christianity do we possess the religious powers we need." However, we thereby admit that "other groups of mankind in relation to completely different cultural conditions feel the relation to the divine life as individuals in a completely different manner; and similarly their religion arises under these conditions, a religion from which they cannot free themselves as long as they are what they are."[13] In the second of the major works just quoted, the problem, since valid norms are to be achieved exclusively on the basis of historical thinking, is carried beyond the narrow framework of theological interrogation to the universal realm of history; and it is applied to cultural, political, ethical, social, artistic, and scientific norms. That is a completely consistent development. For only in this extension of the inquiry is the total meaning of the problem demonstrated. In looking for the supreme validity of a religion, it makes no sense to compare it with other religions if the validity of each is conditioned by the culture of which it is a part. If someone wishes to compare at all, he must compare entire cultures and weigh them against each other; religions are simply a part of these cultures, albeit perhaps the most important part.

It is obvious, however, that, under the given presuppositions, a comparison of values is impossible here. Troeltsch feels obligated to call attention even more sharply than in his book of 1902 to the fact that a possible union of different religions and the impulses at work in them "cannot lie in one of the historical religions themselves, but that they all point in a common direction and all strive from an inner impulse toward an unknown ultimate culmination, at which and only at which the ultimate unity and the objective-absolute can exist."[14] Troeltsch asserts a very close connection between religion and the entire realm of cultural, historical formations; and it appears as if at the very least Christianity is totally subjugated to Western culture. If Troeltsch says that he always finds in this connection the real religious element to be the more and more self-sufficient and particular autonomous power of life, and if this should mean there are no norms at all without there being first a religious norm, then it becomes clear how urgent it is that these questions be solved, and how it is, in fact, that a "new hour in world history" has arrived for Christianity. For Christianity has the task of helping an anarchical world to achieve principles and norms. But it is also clear that the statement of the problem has become exceedingly acute and difficult—it is no longer meaningful to try to help Christianity attain normative validity by keeping it away from the tendencies of modern historicized thinking which dissolve norms and destroy authority or to limit the event of Christianity to being a special event or one based upon a special causality and set apart from all other events, from "worldly" events. There are only two possibilities here. On the one hand, we can acknowledge Troeltsch's position as correct, primarily his decisive thesis of the complete historicizing of our thinking. Then, regardless of our theology, be it orthodox-supernaturalist or idealist-evolutionist or Ritschlian, we must take the step with Troeltsch to the recognition of the philosophy of history as the science which truly establishes norms.[15] We may question whether Troeltsch still accorded the establishment of norms to theology in his book on the absoluteness of Christianity. In it, he makes a confession of Christianity "insofar as it is understood in its total historical manifestation."[16] This is basically the same idea which he sought and finally set up as providing the actual norm, or indeed containing the norm in itself—the idea of Europeanism. However, in *Absolutheit* he viewed this idea essentially from the perspective of Christianity, that is, theologically. Later he viewed it essentially from the perspective of Europeanism, that is, of cultural philosophy. Such a statement as "the great religions appear indeed to be substantiators of the great racial spirits, just as the races themselves are substantiators of the biological-anthropological forms"[17] shows how far he was willing to go.

It is unnecessary to say that Troeltsch's transition from theology to philosophy of history, from Christianity to Europeanism, is not accidental and does not rest on the personal peculiarities and interests of a single man. Rather, with this transition, which is accompanied by penetrating historical and philosophical work, he brilliantly represents and justifies the actual and long-since-ensued abandonment of theology for historical philosophy, and of Christianity for the idea of Europeanism, and therefore his work is an even greater shock for those concerned, namely, theology and Christianity.

The only possibility with which Troeltsch confronts contemporary theology, regardless of which direction it takes, is that of withdrawing as a discipline which establishes the real and final norm, surrendering this role to the philosophy of history, and becoming itself a pure, historical science whose task is to investigate Christianity. But this could only mean acknowledging as justifiable a condition which has long existed, and the resulting, bitter task would be to become fully conscious of all the consequences. The other possibility would be that of questioning Troeltsch's decisive thesis—the complete historicizing of our entire thinking. Naturally, that does not mean questioning whether this historicizing has actually occurred. It is beyond question that it has occurred, and occurred to the extent that Troeltsch claims. But we must question whether it was justifiable. This is not the old apologetic problem of keeping Christianity and biblical history from incorporation into a general historical context; the question is rather whether the event in its entirety must remain concealed and divorced from historical thinking, because historicized thinking moves in an unreal sphere, one which the event has a priori made unreal. Thus, theology would be confronted by an immense task, but a task which is ultimately its own—that of being the discipline which establishes the real and ultimate norm. If what Troeltsch says is true, that "there is no formation of standards without the concept of God" (and theology cannot well assert the opposite), then this first and crucial formation of standards would become the task of theology.

It is surely no accident (I allow myself to suppose that in this regard accidents do not easily occur in the language, or rather, jargon, used here) that, where Troeltsch says there is no formation of standards without the concept of God, he adds—without any qualms—"or some analogue to it."[18] Thus, the plainly idolatrous and delusive aspect of this, and not only this, philosophy of history reveals itself with shocking clarity. It becomes clear in the fact that the assertion that the concept of God somehow stands behind all thinking as the presupposed conception of things implies some vague notion, which cannot be further defined, the name of which is finally immaterial. For this final unity of thought, beyond which one cannot go, is the place of absolute stillness and not of fundamental decision; hereby, in spite of Troeltsch's energetic denial, the thoroughly contemplative nature of this thinking is irrevocably established. And it is not as difficult as Troeltsch thinks (p. 113) to anticipate the connection between this stillness in the religious idea and the infinite work of history, over which are written the irreligious words "life process of the absolute" and not the word "decision." Therefore, we cannot say that every basic assertion presupposes a real and thus incomprehensible, unthinkable, and thoroughly non-contemplative encounter with God which determines everything else as it works itself out. And we can certainly not put "some analogue" in the place of this encounter. If, however, the foundation already is a movement based on pure non-reality, we cannot hope to subsequently encounter some reality or other. So the task of theology remains; and with the miscarrying of this philosophical-historical attempt, it is more urgent and probably more difficult than ever before.

Having indicated provisionally the error of Troeltsch's theory, I would like to say with all the more emphasis that his achievement appears to me to be of the greatest significance, and that no theology may hope to achieve anything significant without fundamentally coming to terms with Troeltsch. After his work, every theology which does not attack the problem of historicism to the full extent to which he has raised it will be unfruitful from the outset. And in coming to terms with Troeltsch, there must be the constant awareness that it is not a question primarily of his theory, with which he tried to achieve norms by means of and in spite of the historicizing of thought; rather, it concerns first and foremost this general historicizing of thought. It cannot be said often enough that this historicizing is not Troeltsch's theory, but a fact, which he has demonstrated to its full extent, with all its consequences. This discussion is all the more difficult since our own thinking shares in this historicizing. Our entire education is historical. And no educational reforms, however radical, can escape this fact. At this point, only the most thoroughgoing deliberations can help us. The clear penetration of historicism and its presuppositions, given to us in Troeltsch's last works, contributes more than a little.

In an essay which first appeared in 1898,[19] Troeltsch said that historical method emerged from a supposition which was entirely metaphysically determined; in fact, as he said then, it emerged from the presupposition of the interrelatedness of the universe including the activities of the human spirit. In his great work on historicism, he discussed in detail these basic metaphysical presuppositions of historicism and of the historical method. The essence of historicism can be most thoroughly understood from Troeltsch's perspective. The basic metaphysical supposition deals with a concept which, as he expresses it, lies at the boundary of science and can no longer be justified by strictly scientific methods (p. 173). But its significance is so great that "the great fundamental and basic questions about the nature and content of scientific investigation" (p. 687) can be answered only on its terms. Without "history's retreat in such a manner to its periphery in a mystical background of the All, not even the self-sufficiency of its logic and method can be upheld. It would become a totally incomprehensible paradox in the strictest sense of the word" (p. 87). Only in historicism would there be the guarantee "that the historical movement rests ultimately in a final unity, which eludes expression only by its own being in motion and which is thus very inadequately characterized by the words 'unity' and 'all'" (p. 173).

Thus, the decisive concept of Troeltsch's philosophy of history, the concept of individuality, must be seen entirely against this background and is deeply colored by it. At the same time, however, it is closely connected with the clear, observable, logical, and empirical areas of this philosophy of history. For it is exceedingly important to Troeltsch to remain in close contact with empirical investigation and its rational, practical methods. One can say that his great work *Der Historismus* is a philosophy of individuality in terms of its concepts which constitute historical reality. Accordingly, the significance of the concept of individuality for empirical, historical investigation is established in the first of the book's four chapters. What this means is immediately clarified when we notice that Troeltsch states (p. 201) that this chapter, which bears the title "Das Wiedererwachen der Geschichtsphilosophie" ("The Reawakening of the Philosophy of History"), should really be called "Naturalism and Historicism" (which now is the title of only the concluding section of the chapter). The concept of individuality, which constitutes the historical subject matter in contrast to the natural-scientific, is not the general concept of "law in relation to individual cases, but the concept of the unity of life [Troeltsch also speaks of individual totality—see p. 32] with its elements; this is no abstract view of events which are always the same, but the always perceptible representation of innumerable individual acts in a totality which embraces them all" (p. 120). Historical reality and, with it, historical investigation are distinguished from natural-scientific reality and investigation. The metaphysical content of the concept of individuality is established in the next two chapters.

In the second chapter, which, as Troeltsch said in the passage mentioned above, should really read "History and the Doctrine of Values" (the actual title is "Concerning Standards for Judging Historical Things and Their Relation to a Contemporary Cultural Ideal"), the decisive concept is "relativity of values." It means "the interaction between the actual and what ought to be, an interaction which is always plastic and creative and therefore never timeless or universal" (p. 211). Thus, the concept of individuality contains "not simply the pure, actual particularity of a specific historical-spiritual complex, but a specific individualization of the ideal or what ought to be" (p. 201). Troeltsch achieves this interaction of what is and what ought to be, the historically relative and the normatively valid, in the concept of individuality; he does it by considering the deepest core of individuality, the so-called I, not "as something isolated and empty, something equipped only with the formal capacities of imagining, feeling, and willing, but as something virtually and specifically enclosing cosmic consciousness to an extremely diversified extent in itself or, the other way around, involving cosmic consciousness as the I" (p. 209). Individuality then ceases to be merely factual. It shares in the "value" of the absolute, but only because it is relative in its historical nature. Thus, it is a "value relativity" in whose "relativity an absolute becomes active and creative" (p. 212).

In the third chapter, which deals with the historical concept of development and universal history, the idea of the participation of the finite spirit in the infinite spirit is further developed and, at the same time, the concept of historical development established. Basically, this concept is nothing but the concept of historical individuality fully developed and fully active. "The essential and individual identity of finite spirits with the infinite spirit" (p. 677) allows individuality to participate in the "dynamic unity of life" of the infinite spirit, through which the unity of life itself comes into movement, into a process in which it can develop. Thus, in the last analysis, the movement, the process, of history is the movement of the divine life itself. Besides

that, however, this identity of finite spirits with the infinite spirit
allows individuality to share in the concrete content of the infinite
spirit. We have already seen how individuality becomes an individualization of what ought to be. But the significance of this participation is
not yet thereby exhausted. Rather, it helps Troeltsch solve the problem of the knowledge of the "other being," an exceedingly important
problem for history: "by virtue of our identity with cosmic consciousness we bear the alien spirit in us and can understand it and feel it as
part of our own life, and simultaneously as something strange which
belongs to its own monad" (p. 684). On the basis of the knowledge of the
other being thus achieved, it is possible to recognize and understand
even alien individualities historically, that is, in their active movement.
And they need not be merely individual personalities; they can also be
supra-personal entities, such as perhaps the Renaissance or the War
of 1870-1871 or Capitalism or Christianity or Western culture. For
even if at first the concept of development "is restricted to the understanding of single, self-contained entities which can be surveyed adequately and authoritatively" (p. 658) then "the separate entities naturally go on to form themselves into connections and sequences which
are real and causal and which can be perceived. . . . In this way there
arises universal history, the natural completion and crown of history,
the comprehensive achievement of the concept of development" (pp.
688 f.). For Troeltsch, however, the concept of universal history does
not mean a history of all humanity, for the individuality of humanity
as a whole cannot be observed. If anyone desired to invent such a history (and it can only be invented), he would lose all contact with reality
and its empirical investigation. But if he wished to keep in view everything he knew about humanity, he would have to halt in pure contemplation of what is at hand, since, as a result of its incompleteness, he
can achieve only a kaleidoscopic view of humanity. However, in a
world which exists in dire spiritual exigencies and "wishes to be sure
of its own essence and meaning" (p. 692), what is described above is
not the significance of the whole historical enterprise. The world is
helped only by a universal history which comprehends and presents
a very broad and yet definitive individuality, which is what this world
itself is in its present, concrete, and real causal unity. Such a history
would be "the developmental history of Mediterranean–European–
American culture" (p. 690). The only meaning which Troeltsch can
ascribe to the philosophy of history is to be found in "one's own position and positive cultural contributions, a meaning fundamentally opposed to all inclinations and attempts at an exclusively contemplative
and, in this sense, universal view of history" (p. 708).

The final chapter of the book describes this expanded concept of individuality as the concept of the structure of Europeanism. Europeanism is the individual unity of life of the West. This concept of structure should "extract from universal-historical development the great, elemental forces which are immediately significant, effective, and concrete." Furthermore, it has "to make these basic forces understandable in their original sense and in their development from the historical movement in order to determine the decisive emphases for our historical remembrance, to arrange them with reference to the present, and finally, to comprehend the evolving relationship, in the modern world, of these basic forces with one another and modern life" (p. 765). The "contemporary cultural synthesis," which we so passionately seek today, would result from this concept of structure. Thus— and with this Troeltsch concludes his book—"the concept of structure means to overcome history with history and to prepare the stage for new creative activity" (p. 772).

Troeltsch was not able to write the second volume of his great work, which was to offer a philosophy of history, or the universal history of the West, and then a contemporary synthesis of culture, for which the first volume paved the way. The first volume, however, appears to me fully sufficient as the basis for a critical discussion. In it he provided the key to the problem of historicism. Only with these fundamentals may a critique begin which is concerned not with details but with the total picture. And the critique which we intend to make of Troeltsch's theses concerns the total picture. So the question is not whether the historicizing of thinking has actually taken place to the extent asserted by Troeltsch. We acknowledge his assertion that all thinking is historicized and that this complete historicizing is a necessary consequence of accepting the authority of the modern historical method at any point whatsoever; consequently, once such a partial recognition is accorded, all attempts to exempt particular aspects from this historicizing are untenable and rest actually on a misunderstanding about what the modern historical method is. It is Troeltsch's great achievement, the decisive significance of his life's work for the whole of theology, that he has provided clarification here; and it will not detract in the slightest from this significance if our critique of him proves correct. Our question, then, is not whether the historicizing of all thinking has actually occurred or whether Troeltsch's conclusions are correct, but whether the historicizing which actually did take place is valid. Nor do we ask this question in the old theological sense of restricting it to so-called *Heilsgeschichte*; that is, whether this histor-

icizing is valid with respect to *Heilsgeschichte,* in which case its justification with respect to so-called secular history is readily admitted.

According to Troeltsch, the key to the problem of historicism is
given in the concept of the "essential and individual identity of finite
spirits with the infinite spirit" and in the consequent "intuitive participation of finite spirits in the concrete content and the dynamic
unity of the life of the infinite spirit." For "by virtue of our identity
with the cosmic consciousness we bear the alien spirit in us and can
understand it and feel it as part of our own life, and simultaneously as
something strange which belongs to its own monad."

These two statements contain all the elements which constitute this
concept of history; and I add, the concept of history as Troeltsch
established it, a concept which is not concerned with a pure contemplative approach to history, but wishes to achieve from history a "contemporary system of culture which will determine the next direction
for the future" and thereby wishes to accomplish a "historical act" (p.
120); thus, it desires not to write history but to determine history.
Erudition is not Troeltsch's goal; rather, "the powers we need above
all, responsibility and the will to creativity," which should emerge
from this erudition (p. 82). But that which constitutes history in this
not merely contemplative but responsible sense is, on the one hand, its
encounter with another man, the Thou—the other being, as Troeltsch
characteristically puts it—and, on the other, an encounter with God,
or something analogous to God, says Troeltsch (again characteristically)
as we saw above. The first notion, the encounter with another man,
gives history its real content. History does not exist for man in isolation
from community. For him there is at best only a self-unfolding, just
as every organic entity must unfold itself according to inner necessity.

When Troeltsch says the concept of historical development rests
"on the intuition of the alien spirit" he refers to the same situation
as above. Of course, this situation does not exist when man is not released in this way from his isolation and consequently not placed in
the historical realm, in the sphere of history, by an "intuition of the
alien spirit." The second instance which constitutes history, the encounter with God, makes history into real history, since only the
encounter with an unconditioned entity allows an event to be more
than an alteration and gives it the double edge necessary to call man
to decision.

When Troeltsch says the problem of value "is the primary great
problem of all philosophy of history, putting all else into a secondary
position," he refers to the same situation. But this situation is negated
and the event in which history occurs not called into the realm of de-

cisive encounter, if Troeltsch seeks to solve the problem of value with the concept of individuality. That is especially true if he makes individuality into a creative entity, allowing it to be that which ought to be, something imposed; and does so by allowing the finite spirit to share in the infinite spirit and its absolute value. In saying that real history is not an unequivocal encounter, that is, an encounter between two men, we are saying nothing different from what Troeltsch himself says. If it were only that, there would be no way to guard it from dissolution into relativism and naturalism, that is, into an exclusively natural process. Real history, however, is an encounter with a twofold meaning—the encounter with another man and the encounter with God. And the one encounter is like the other inasmuch as neither is possible without the other. For an encounter with a man, which is not at the same time an encounter with God, would be merely a natural process following the laws and necessities of physics and thus not really an encounter with man. History must always involve three realities—God, Thou, and I.

All this says nothing different from what Troeltsch also says. He, however, wishes to understand this double encounter and thereby history by reducing these three realities ultimately to one (thus paving the way to the "historical act") and by making their mutual involvement into an inner movement of the life of this one, a "life-process of the absolute." This reduction refers to his theory of the fundamental and individual identity of finite spirits with the infinite. In this way, history, for Troeltsch, becomes a "life-process of the absolute" or a "possibility of divine spirit" (p. 212). And man knows about history as a result of the intuitive participation of the finite spirit in the infinite. However, the threefold dimension of real history has changed here into a presentation which is flat and two-dimensional. This is a withdrawal from the *actio* back into the *contemplatio*. And regardless of what happens on this contemplative plane, no amount of contemplation, scientific statements, or interpretive investigations will bring about the smallest act, unless one considers a new interpretive investigation of history to be a "historical act."

But even the spirited "contemporary synthesis of culture" will activate itself only in the timelessness of scholarly contemplation. The real present—and thus real history—exists only in time, in the three-dimensional world of real occurrences. But there is no transition from the two-dimensional interpretation or representation to this. And the intuitive participation of finite spirits in the infinite is unable to do more than help man draw himself, his own "present," into contemplation and transform it into the two-dimensional picture. It appears that

Troeltsch himself feels that he remains in the contemplative, figurative realm with this theory of the fundamental and individual identity of finite spirits with the infinite spirit and therefore does not advance beyond it to action. He is content to let this theory be a myth, as he thinks Platonic and Christian doctrines have been. He seeks the way out of this problem, then, not with the absolute, but with the finite spirit and its historical act. Here he develops his doctrine of the "leap . . . by which we come out of the past and into the future through our own decision and responsibility" (p. 178). The real venture of this "leap," says Troeltsch, consists in the fact "that we dare to consider, comprehend, and pursue a flashing concept of reason as the emanation of divine life" (p. 185; cf. pp. 167, 172, 175). We notice, however, that this act does not lead out of the realm of contemplation; it is itself nothing but contemplation, introspection.

But can anything else remain as a "historical act" when the three elements necessary for a historical event are reduced to one? And what is this remnant when its core is nothing but belief in a myth?

At the decisive points of his book, Troeltsch has indicated in detail that historicism has its point of departure in the philosophy of consciousness, which was founded by Descartes and has influenced the thinking of recent centuries (cf. "Naturalism and Historicism," pp. 102-110; "History and the Doctrine of Values," pp. 200-220; and "History and Epistemology," pp. 656-693). Troeltsch himself goes back to this point of departure. But he sees the error in the way this point of departure had previously been viewed. According to Troeltsch, we may not view consciousness "as enclosed, substantial, individual consciousness," nor as "transcendental consciousness in general." In both cases we arrive at only general concepts and never at the comprehension of history as individual reality. Troeltsch says that instead of this we "must regard the I as a monad which participates in the total content of reality by means of the unconscious or of its identity with total consciousness, and which as a result contains in itself the 'external world' —the material world as well as that of other souls. As a result we will, in specific circumstances, bring the portions of the all, which are experienced by the individual consciousness, into relation to our own I as the reality of our own experience, and supplement the inner connections of this experience with logical means far beyond our conscious experience" (p. 675).

We have examined the consequences and the content of reality of the "history" to which this theory leads. We will not be astonished at these consequences if we keep in mind that what is later to be discovered in this concept has been put into it a priori. Thus, the problems are set up in such a way that they are disposed of from the outset. If the problem of history is the question of the actual, real encounter with God and with man, it is answered here with the statement that the three realities are contained in the one consciousness, and this consciousness—and here is the answer—need be conscious only of itself. But this fails to take into account the fact that a question which the consciousness asks itself cannot be a real question, but that it, together with the answer already implicit in it, is only the unfolding of a presupposition made earlier. Troeltsch thus disposes of the problem of history from the outset by making the "other being" and God the content of consciousness by means of the theory of the identity of finite spirits with the infinite spirit.

NOTES

1. Ernst Troeltsch, "Die Krisis des Historismus," *Neue Rundschau*, XXXIII, 573.
2. *Der Historismus und seine Überwindung. Fünf Vorträge*, 1924.
3. 2. Aufl., 1912.
4. *Die Absolutheit*, XIX.
5. *Ibid.*, 23.
6. *Ibid.*, 41.
7. *Ibid.*, 48; cf. Troeltsch's *Gesammelte Schriften*, II, "Historische und dogmatische Methode in der Theologie," 729-753.
8. *Ibid.*, 74.
9. *Ibid.*, 86.
10. *Der Historismus und seine Überwindung*, 71.
11. *Die Absolutheit*, 89.
12. English translation: *Social Teaching of the Christian Churches*, 2 volumes (New York: Harper & Row, 1960).
13. *Der Historismus und seine Überwindung*, 77 f.
14. *Ibid.*, 82.
15. Cf. *ibid.*, 110: "If one no longer acknowledges the norms of life in ecclesiastical dogma, or in its offspring, rationalistic dogma, then history is the only source and philosophy of history the only solution for these norms."
16. *Die Absolutheit*, 82. In this connection compare also the following statement: "As such, it combines Israelite prophecy, the preaching of Jesus, the mysticism of Paul, the idealism of Platonism and Stoicism, the medieval fusion of European cultural unity with the religious idea, the Germanic individualism of Luther, and the conscientiousness and activity of Protestantism."
17. *Der Historismus und seine Überwindung*, 80.
18. *Ibid.*, 184.
19. *Über historische und dogmatische Methode in der Theologie;* republished in *Gesammelte Schriften*, II, 729.

PROTESTANISM AND REALITY:
Epilogue to Martin Luther's *Bondage of the Will**

Friedrich Gogarten

Protestantism has long since made its peace with the spirit of
the modern world. Sometimes it has done so with a bad conscience—
as quietly as possible. That, however, can be called peace with the spirit
of the modern world only because it is peace with the spirit of the
world in general. In that case it retains its own form, but atrophies and
becomes unreal since it cuts itself off and leads an isolated existence
in its churches and communities. It scarcely dares look at its adversary
and shies away from forming any definite conceptions of him. It prefers to deny his existence and behave as though nothing had changed.

And sometimes Protestantism has made its peace with the modern
world deliberately and with a good conscience, and as a result has been
almost fully absorbed. To justify this, it sets up the dogma of the identity of Protestantism and the modern spirit. And in order to have historical proof for this identity directly at hand, it considers—today one
must say, it considered—the so-called modern period as beginning with
the Reformation. As a result it was natural to regard the modern
period as largely the creation or effect of the Reformation and as permeated by the Protestant spirit.

However, the more the modern spirit understood itself and its
origin, the less the dogma could retain this form. The cleavage between
the modern spirit and the Reformers was relentlessly widened by the
exponents of this spirit. And there is no need to turn to particularly
radical persons, who from some kind of animosity saw the cleavage as
deeper and broader than it really is. Even Dilthey can say that "this
entire concept of life which constitutes the presupposition of the
Protestant doctrine of justification as the central conviction of the Reformers" (namely, "the assertion of the all-penetrating feeling of inability to do good works, the total other-worldliness of the Creator and
Judge of the world, his absolute justice, and the demands which his
holiness makes on his creatures, in spite of their innate inability") "is
a thing of the past and thus the doctrine of justification by faith no
longer has meaning for us." It now has only historical interest.[1]

The contrast between the modern spirit and Protestantism is thus
put forward with all the clarity needed or desired. This contrast is not
in the least modified by Dilthey's statement that the enduring result

* Text from *Glaube und Wirklichkeit* (Jena, 1928), pp. 13-43.

of the Reformation is, first, release from the dominance of the hierarchy, and, second, the basing of religious conviction on inner experience. This first result, after all, is a purely negative definition of freedom, and such a freedom has no relevance for the modern spirit. It would be a permanent result of the Reformation only if freedom had the same roots now as then. The fact that the modern world can adduce it as such proves that the roots are not the same. For to the person whose culture "is characterized by the tremendous expansion and intensity of the concepts of freedom and personality,"[2] freedom, as freedom, is a positive value. It was not that for the Reformers. For them, the positive aspect, the sole source of the meaning of freedom, was bondage. To demonstrate this is the intention of this essay. The issue with freedom is the same as that of the second aspect, the basing of religious conviction on inner experience. It is true here also that in the modern view inner experience as such already has its own content. This too was not so for the Reformers. This is proven by their sharp opposition to the sectarian and mystic teaching of the inner light toward which, on the contrary, modern men are strongly drawn.

Nevertheless, some have wished to hold to the continuity of Protestantism with the modern spirit and have therefore distinguished within Protestantism between an old and a new Protestantism. Old Protestantism belongs to the so-called Middle Ages and new Protestantism to the modern world. And the transition point from the Middle Ages to the modern period is no longer the Reformation, but the century of the Enlightenment, in which a new Protestantism developed. In the new Protestantism "the end of medieval culture is effected; and authoritarian State-church culture gives way to the beginning of modern, church-free, individual culture."[3]

To be sure, this matter of continuity is a strange thing. Careful investigation shows that it applies at practically every point not to Protestantism proper, but to the Anabaptists, the sects, the mystics, and the humanists of the Reformation period. And where Protestantism proper comes into consideration, it can be said, as Troeltsch himself does, that the "grandiose political and economic consequences of Calvinism" are "contrary to what was intended."[4] And this is true not only for cultural consequences, but for those in the area of faith. Here too it is the Anabaptists, spiritualists, mystics, and not least the humanists, whose effects still endure, not the Reformers. And if, as Troeltsch reports, Semler, "the father and pioneer of a Protestantism which thinks and reacts historically and critically, could express as self-evident that everything achieved by the new theology was already present in the great and remarkable Erasmus,"[5] we must add that a single glance at Luther's book against Erasmus (De Servo Arbitrio) suffices to show that such a theology can have nothing to do with the Protestantism of the Reformers. If the strongest historical significance of Protestantism may then be its effect on the religion of the modern world,[6] and if the casual relation between Protestantism and the modern world may be seen most clearly there, then (presupposing that one is not disposed toward every little change in Protestantism and does not see its essence to be a chameleon-like possibility of transformation), it is quite clear that the historical significance of Protestantism for the modern world is ultimately negative. Basically, Protestantism only eliminated the obstructions which the Roman Catholic system, in spite of all its splendor, had, in conformity to its nature, placed in the path of the new world. Those are Troeltsch's own words, which he, in fact, uses in speaking of the significance of Protestantism for modern culture.[7] In the light of all that he says, however, they can also be applied to the significance of Protestantism for modern religion.

The attempt which, though resulting from the recognition of the contrast between the modern spirit and the Protestantism of the Reformers, still sought to demonstrate a continuity between them demonstrated instead that there is no such continuity. The new Protestantism, which was supposed to go back beyond the old (whose radical opposition to the modern spirit is admitted) and establish continuity with the decisive doctrines of the Reformers, has really nothing in common with them. Troeltsch says that "where the way of personal conviction became more important than the goal of supernatural salvation"[8] Protestantism made the enthusiasm of Anabaptists and mystics and humanistic, philological-philosophical theology its own and "opened for them the door to *commercium* and *connubium*." But he overlooks the fact that it is a very deceptive *commercium*. Protestantism no longer enters this door, for the simple reason that it has been eliminated here. Into its place steps a religion of "seeking God in one's own feeling, experience, thinking, and intention."

Troeltsch's attempt to demonstrate continuity between Protestantism and the modern spirit is an attempt, in spite of its denunciation by the modern world, to maintain the peace which Protestantism has made with that world. He carries on this attempt completely at the expense of Protestantism. What Troeltsch says in general about the significance of Protestantism for modern culture—that "it has achieved neither an inner strength for itself nor a creative strength for culture"[9]—is valid as well for this enterprise of seeking continuity.

The controversy between Protestantism and the modern spirit, inevitable in view of the clear contemporary recognition of their opposition, is still to be entered into. And now may be the time to get on with it. For today, for the first time since its inception, the modern spirit is shaken to its very depths. Even such a free spirit as Troeltsch was so taken in by the unquestionable validity of the modern spirit that it never occurred to him to seek to justify it in the eyes of Protestantism. It did not occur to him even when he came face to face with the danger, which he considered never very far away, that the concept of freedom and personality by which, in his view, modern culture is characterized, is threatened by this same culture.[10] This indicates the great extent to which the modern spirit dominated his thought and his entire outlook on life. And what Guardini says of the inner distortion caused by Protestant individualism (although this is how Guardini puts it, he actually means modern individualism, which is essentially different from Protestant individualism; we will say more about this) is valid not just for Catholics. This individualism was "not only convinced that it represented the religion and the spiritual attitude of the truly worthy man, but it also brought Catholics to share in this feeling. For a long time it was able to impose a second feeling, a kind of pariah feeling, on many Catholics, superimposed on their consciousness of their worth."[11] What Guardini says here is equally valid for Protestants.

It should not be imagined that the triumphs to be won in this controversy between Protestantism and the modern spirit will be cheap and that we will celebrate an easy and joyful re-entry into the old, long-empty house of Protestantism. There will be nothing at all to celebrate. On the contrary we will have to force ourselves to realize some very bitter facts—unless, of course, self-knowledge, especially at a time like this, is not bitter.

It will not be possible to avoid the first, very bitter realization that Protestantism shares most extensively in the rise of the modern world. This appears to contradict the previous assertion that there is no continuity between Protestantism and the modern spirit. But previously the issue involved the question of whether the modern spirit was the legitimate continuation and development of Protestantism. The answer was No. It is a different matter to ask whether Protestantism participated in the rise of this modern spirit which is definitely not homogeneous with it. The answer here is Yes. And these words already indicate what sort of participation it is.

Regardless of the fact that the unity and limitations of the society given to the West throughout many centuries by the Catholic Church were already broken in many places even before the Reformation, there is no doubt that the Reformation dealt this society the decisive blow. With full knowledge of what they were doing, the Reformers tore down the limits and boundaries, the norms and principles, by which the world, which always presses toward the unlimited and the boundless, was protected from chaos by the church and by which it was held together as cosmos. The Reformers based and justified their action on the grounds that these limits, principles, and norms were actually—in their judgment—human discovery and human caprice. The fact that the church claimed sacred and conscience-binding validity for them made the attack against them an obligation, an obligation which no reservation or danger could cancel—not even the danger of the dissolution of the bourgeois world and its set patterns. But the Reformers did not seek this freedom just for its own sake. They did not want merely to exchange bonds for freedom, but to tear down these false, illegitimate ones. Those bonds consisted of the church's claim to dominate the life of secular society and its institutions of family, State, and so forth, and indeed to do so with the same conscience-binding authority it demanded for itself in the religious realm. This claim was rejected. Of course, it was not rejected in order to leave civil life—family, State, and society—completely autonomous. This life was subjected to itself and its own laws, but it derived its by no means loose bonds from the recognition of the sinfulness of all human life. Thus, civil life became totally secular and was subjected to an order based on this present world. For its part, however, this world, if the word is to have any meaning at all, was subject to real limitation by another world, and it could not easily have been freed from that relationship, as it is in the modern age. And if it often enough makes no difference whether the life modern culture attempts to live (as Troeltsch says it does) appears as a purely human life or as a life filled in its entirety by God's Spirit,[12] then it may be assumed that this life is neither human nor divine but is only a phantom. In respect to this "inner-worldliness," which can be considered characteristic of modern culture, we can say that the Reformers' view of secular life was rooted in the reality of that life. The liberation of the life of society from the restrictions of the Catholic Church, brought about by the Reformation, was conceived of as being in accord with the restrictions of the laws to which all reality knows itself subject, not as its theoretical but as its real limitations—and only as it is limited is it reality.

It takes little reflection to realize that man shrinks back from reality more than from anything else. The recollection of how long and how deeply the world was bound to the church suffices for understanding that this bondage to reality was very promptly exchanged for a bondage of secular life to the church, a bondage which was much easier to endure and, which is more important, easier to maintain. It was all the easier to carry out this exchange, because the authority of the church was maintained in the religious realm. Of course, the damage which the Reformation inflicted on ecclesiastical culture could not very well be undone simply by reintroducing this culture in Protestant territories with the prescribed modifications. On the contrary, the multiplicity of types of ecclesiastical culture, which by its nature and its claims must be a unified whole, completely disrupted it and permitted modern culture with its ideal of secularity and freedom to win a total victory. And since Protestantism could no longer maintain an ecclesiastical culture in the territories it controlled, it either limited itself to the nurture of an unfruitful inwardness, or, as we already noticed, as "neo-Protestantism" it was totally absorbed by modern cultural forms.

So Protestantism was in fact involved in the rise of the modern world—it made a breach in the bronze wall within which the medieval Catholic Church had enclosed the world. This act is significant enough to merit great admiration. And this has been abundantly accorded it. There is no question that immense forces were unleashed by this act of liberation. And this unleashing is a Protestant act and is itself good, genuine Protestantism, for it is a direct result of the thorough secularization of culture. It is good genuine Protestantism in spite of the fact that it happened completely against the will of and with the greatest misgivings on the part of the churches of post-Reformation Protestantism. But the fact that these forces remain unfettered and as a consequence are today, before our very eyes, engaged in the task of destroying the world is also a direct result of Protestantism, because Protestantism has not fulfilled its obligation to the world. Protestantism in its essence is not freedom for freedom's sake. It is properly understood only as the strongest kind of bondage. But it is not a bondage, as the modern concept of freedom and personality would have it, to a God who speaks to man in this freedom and reveals himself to man. That "bondage" would be merely another word for the boundless freedom which is based only on itself, on its limitlessness. For us, who are finite creatures in every connection, that means it can never be a real bondage. As Luther said, refuting Erasmus, one of the fathers of "neo-Protestantism," it is only a dream that "the situation of man is as if he had never been corrupted by sin and only the external appearance of his body and limbs can be seen."[13] Protestantism is a bondage through the revealed God, who has entered the finite world. *This* is the only real bondage, for it is a bondage through finite reality. This is the bondage which Protestantism still owes it to the world to provide; and Protestantism, since it can no longer keep the world in confinement through its old ecclesiastical structure, has had to let the world be unrestrained as it moves unmistakably toward chaos.

Protestantism's controversy with the modern spirit, which may be imminent today, is therefore not merely a theoretical concern. Protestantism can carry on this controversy only if it does its work in the world, if it provides as sole bondage for the world not a bondage of man to himself—and thus not slavery to arbitrariness and all human passions—but a bondage to reality. This controversy is not concerned with the means and establishment, in retrospect, of how the forces of history or of development have brought it about, but with the determining of guilt. And regardless of the fact that past generations may be guilty a thousand times over, the contemporary generation shares this guilt. For what was left undone then is still undone, and what was required then is still required.

So it is not a matter of trying to re-enact the lives of the Reformers. Our task today (as our world has become lawless, it cries out for laws; and as it has become unreal, it hungers for reality!) can have nothing to do with reviving historical recollections. The Reformers were not humanists and were anything but initiators of a historical approach to biblical writings. And it would make no sense for us to try to become humanists today with their help. If we did, we would break down the connection we seek to establish with them. The only significance of our concern with the Reformers is that they can open our eyes to reality. No one can relieve us of the responsibility of seeing reality for ourselves. But we have not yet seen it and are not on its track; we do not yet have a feeling for it if we are content with seeing the Reformers, regardless of how precise and correct our historical vision is. "We are all required to die and no one can die for another; each person himself must be armored and equipped to do battle with the devil and death. We can certainly cry out to the other, console him, and exhort him to patience and conflict and battle, but we cannot do battle and carry on the conflict for him; each man must stand alone in his trench and confront his foes, the devil and death themselves, and press alone into battle with them. At this point I will not be with you, nor you with me."[14] This, since it is true for every encounter with death, also holds true for every encounter with reality.

It is probably correct that every period sees and comprehends about every other period only those things which affect it in its own present relationships and pressures. But it is also true that a period which has not yet encountered reality and been instructed by it, but which seeks to govern life by its own teachings and ideologies, will find in another period to which it might turn for instruction or whatever else, only teachings and ideologies. It will never be able to see where that period really is or where it encounters reality.[15]

Wherever men and times encounter reality and are engaged in coming to terms with it, they are necessarily referred beyond themselves to the reality with which and from which they live and in which they become real. And they are pointed beyond the doctrine which they themselves develop about this controversy and this encounter. This is not as if they had a low estimate of the significance of this doctrine. On the contrary it is pursued with the same seriousness and responsibility as everything else which concerns reality and the attempt to come to terms with it. The doctrine itself participates in reality; but only as a doctrine. And precisely because it is taken with full seriousness as a doctrine of reality, it cannot pretend to be reality, even in the form of myth or symbol. Nor can it pretend, as a doctrine of reality, to bear a mysterious power in itself, which it mediates to the person who accepts it. Nor can it transform itself into fiction. It remains what it is, nothing but a doctrine, because it is merely a doctrine of reality, pointing to reality; but it participates in reality only in this manner.

The doctrine of the Reformers is of the same character. We all know with what care and seriousness they developed their doctrine. Nevertheless, the same thing happens to it as happens to those doctrines which do not nearly so forcefully and firmly point to reality— it becomes fixed and is taken for reality itself. In accepting the doctrine, we think we have reality. Soon after the Reformers, indeed right under their gaze, Protestant doctrine began to turn rigid and dogmatic. The change had already been completed by the time of the Formula of Concord.[16]

When under the influence of the modern spirit, scholars did away with the rigidity of doctrine, put aside dogmatism, and, as they said, went back to the meaning of doctrine, viewing it as merely a dated expression of a truth which is timeless, they seemed to have arrived at a deeper understanding of the Reformers. Troeltsch characterized this momentous transformation of Protestantism achieved by German Idealism, as translating "Protestant Christianity into general truths of reason."[17] It was momentous because reason—unlike that of the Enlightenment which dealt with a highly sterile and, because of its emptiness, easily exposed "intellect"—dealt in this instance, as Troeltsch formulated it, with the "value-determined substance of life in its emergence from unconsciousness into the clear, conscious comprehension of its full theoretical, aesthetic, ethical, and religious content." However, it is true of this doctrine in a way in which it cannot be true of Reformation doctrine as seen by the Reformers, that it is myth and symbol, and thus, "perfect knowledge" is itself "union with God."[18] This then characterizes the core of the religious doctrine of the modern spirit, that is, the immanence of God in spiritual life.

Indeed, an exceedingly important element of Protestantism is grasped here—that truth and reality exist only in the most personal participation, the most subjective truthfulness, the freest decision. That is probably what Troeltsch means by his statement that Luther, in contrast to the Catholic, objective, sacramental view, draws religion into the conceptual sphere. Reformation doctrine describes this element as its unavoidable presupposition by saying that it is only the doctrine of reality and in no way reality itself. Thus, man is referred to reality itself. In Reformation doctrine man is left alone with himself and reality, and made to depend entirely on himself. That is the sole, unprecedented, serious aspect of the Reformation's "concept of personality" and Protestantism's "individualism." In fact, this extremely important and basic element of Protestantism appears to have been salvaged from the rigid dogmatism of old Protestant orthodoxy by its modern re-casting. It is at this decisive point, then, that the continuity between so-called neo-Protestantism and the Reformers would be preserved. But it only seems so. In truth, it is the impassable gulf between what is called neo-Protestantism and the modern spirit on the one side, and the Reformers and their Protestantism on the other, which is demonstrated here.

I said that modern doctrine is myth and symbol, but Reformation doctrine is not. It can be said that modern doctrine considers the perfect expression of its knowledge to be "union with God." From this perspective, the meaning of modern doctrine becomes clear, as does the structure of reality of which it speaks. In contrast to Reformation doctrine, it refers not to the object, but to the subject; more than this, since it is knowledge and thought, it not only refers to the subject, but it is the actual expression, the actual substance, the actual reality of the subject. Thus, it is, or (since such perfection is unattainable) would be—in its perfect expression of the absolute subject—God himself.

It is then clear that salvaging the subjective element of Protestantism, of which the modern spirit boasts and which is the basis of its claim to be related to Reformation Protestantism, takes place at the expense of the complete subjectivizing of reality. The subject alone is real here. There can be no other reality. In one of the most recent and characteristic publications of "Idealist-Christian" neo-Protestantism,[19] it is said that all objectivity can be only conceptual objectivity and, since it is "nothing but a completely subjective mental fiction," has no value. How could it be otherwise if one has turned the subject, the idea, the I, into the sole principle of reality? And how could it be otherwise in such an absolutizing of the subject, of the I, than that all reality is lost; since reality is an irrevocable contrast, an irresolvable conflict of subject and object, of I and Thou?

The modern concept of personality is thus no more than an absolutizing of the subject, the I. If this concept were intended to be nothing more than a model of the I, if it observed the boundary of pure ideality of thought and did not forget that with this absolutizing the sphere of reality is forsaken—in that case there would be no objection to it. Such modesty, however, is not practiced. Releasing or detaching the I from the sphere of conditionality, of relationship, of contradiction, and elevating it into the sphere of idea, of freedom, of pure I-ness, which means here personality, is considered the achievement of reality, or appears to be reality itself. And the concept of God's immanence is the most comprehensive and ultimate expression of the actual meaning of this view.

The force of the subjectivity of the modern spirit and its blindness to everything real (which is no longer a riddle for the person who recognizes its essence) prevent us from seeing that there is no trace of this concept of personality in the Reformers. In the strict sense, we cannot speak at all of a *concept* of personality in the Reformers, while the I of the modern spirit is completely an *idea* of personality. The I spoken of and asserted by the Reformers is in no way an idea; it is far from the pure subjectivity, the pure I-ness, which determines the thinking and view of life of the modern spirit in its entire sweep. The subject with which Reformation doctrine is concerned and seeks to relate to reality, and of which it is absolutely not a subjective expression, becomes real or comprehends its reality only if it acknowledges the bonds and the limitations imposed by the object. In contrast to the modern idea of personality, it can also be said that the subject, this I, which is the concern of Reformation doctrine, becomes aware of its reality when it dispenses with its absolutizing, with its pure, free, unlimited and unconditioned I-ness, and its complacency in its selfhood. Only then does it grasp its reality. For the I does not have its reality in its pure I-ness, but only in its relation to the object, in its being conditioned by the Thou. And only if it dispenses with its own absolutizing, its free, creative, absolutely unlimited and unconditioned I-ness, can it acknowledge these conditionalities and relations and connections and give itself to them with all its yearning, will, and desire.

Can it dispense with all that? That is the problem here. This is quite contrary to the modern spirit's concept of personality, the realization of which depends specifically on its no longer being bound to or determined by the object, on its striving for unconditioned freedom and pure I-ness with no modifications. It is not too difficult to recognize that we are dealing with total, mutually exclusive contrasts. The modern concept of personality seems to signify the absolutizing of the subject, of the I; all objects are imposed upon the I, and are to be transformed and absorbed in I-ness and its freedom; thus, the I is imposed upon itself, an entity constantly created anew out of the boundlessness of its own freedom; the I in the modern concept of personality is therefore the absolutely creative I. If so, it is in complete opposition to the concept of man intended by Reformation doctrine, in which every object is something given and the I knows itself to have been created by the same power that created the object. Here all depends on allowing the given to have validity as such. What is given is the subject and the object, I *and* Thou, creature *and* creator. The distinction of one from the other is given. It is to be acknowledged and respected. Therefore, their unity is not something to be attained. If this is dualism, it is the harshest dualism.

The subject cannot claim to be the real principle of reality. Reality is subject *and* object, I *and* Thou, in their givenness and in their given distinction and opposition. And the monstrous claim of the I to be the real principle of reality is recognized here as the idolatrous arrogance of the creature wishing to make himself the creator.

It is quite clear that this view is far from the concept of God's immanence and that absolutely no transition or continuity can exist here. And to say that the trans-subjectivity or the objectivity of God is only conceptual[20] is nothing less than an explicit renunciation of the Thou, which always confronts us as a real Thou. Whoever says this closes his eyes to the most elementary fact of our life, admittedly difficult to endure and to respect, the contrast of Thou and I; to give up this contrast is to give up reality.

According to Protestant doctrine, God and man are related as Thou and I, in their essence unmixable, as given in the original differentiation and original relation. The relation with God is restricted to the area constituted by the I and the Thou. But this area is none other than the whole world. For only here is there a world, a cosmos; the world consists of that realm which is ordered solely and strictly through the world-creating power of the tension-filled relation of Thou and I, and is determined by it in the remotest corners and the smallest of the things which fill it. If this realm is no longer determined in this way, we have in it only senseless chaos, only the illusion of an ordered world.

This is the same as to say that the relation to God can be only an ethical one and that only that world and that life are real which are

ethically determined. But we still have not demonstrated the ultimate
or deepest ground from which all reality emerges. It is indeed true
that genuine, real relation to God must necessarily prove itself in
moral action, and that life which is not morally determined is not life
in reality, is not real life. All this, however, is still not the ultimate
word. The real relation between Thou and I, in which the Thou
remains Thou and the I, I; in which the Thou is the first word and
the I the second word; in which, therefore, in and through the Thou,
I becomes the real I, the concrete, fulfilled I, for the first time—this
relation, this reality of I and Thou is not yet designated by the moral
act.

The moral act, which claims to be ultimate and to be the foundation of reality, and which does not accept itself as the result or effect
of another reality, contains its law within itself. It is here if anywhere
that the I is the first word. That I give myself my own law and that
I do not accept it from another, from a Thou, is the nature of the
moral act, understood in this way. The essence of the moral act is
unlimited freedom, which rests in itself, in its own freedom, and that
means here, in its own boundlessness. The moral act which is based
on its pure moral essence is essentially isolated—it is not the relation
of Thou and I. In fact, it does not even know the Thou. It acknowledges the Thou only as acting in unison with the I. Only in this way
can it avoid the danger that threatens every relation between men—
that one man misuses the other as a means. But the price paid for
avoiding this danger is nothing less than loss of the Thou and of the
encounter with the Thou. From the perspective of the moral act the
only relation possible between men is the consciousness that they are
in unison with one another and are driven by the same impetus of
freedom. The only possibility of speaking with God or man is to speak
with oneself in one's innermost being. And the only possibility of unity
between God and man is in man's unity with himself in his ultimate
ground. The ultimate and most profound thing which can be said
here about the relation with God is Ovid's *est deus in nobis*. God
must "become the thought, word, and deed in man himself." To be
consistent, we must say that the "God beyond us," in contrast to the
"God in us," "cannot come to us."[21] Of course not, for here the I is
enclosed in itself, and no ray of light can penetrate it unless that
light comes from within. Here, the I is not merely the first word; it is
the only word which characterizes reality.

The moral act has so little chance of establishing reality, of becoming the living, concrete reality of Thou and I, that where it is
made the final ground of reality, not only does the Thou disappear,

but the I with it. For the I that is the subject of the moral act based entirely on freedom is not the real I, but the idea of the I which is free from all limitations, all conditions, all external influence. It means only that the subject of this act, ultimately and solely based on freedom, is the I which is freed from its conditionality and limitation to the Thou; that is, it is I without Thou. And that means it is a completely unreal I. Wishing to create reality for the I by proclaiming "God in us" is nothing but an act of despair. After all, this "God in us" is as unreal as the I for which it is supposed to create reality.

The I does not become real by penetrating man's innermost ground and calling this depth "God in us." The I becomes real only in the encounter with the Thou. But the Thou can never be in us; it can never be a part of our I. To be sure, we greatly yearn for the coalescence of the Thou and I. Nothing is more difficult for us than to respect these boundaries and to endure this separation. But not to do so means not to endure and respect reality. Reality means neither I nor Thou. That is, reality is not a unity, but a duality. For it means I *and* Thou. But I and Thou are connected only in a firm, irresolvable opposition of their entire being. They are related only in their pure opposition, which absolutely nothing can divert or obstruct. An impassable boundary is fixed between them. This boundary, however, is the reality of the I and Thou. The I is the real I and the Thou is the real Thou only where this boundary is respected, where the boundary and the claim of the I and Thou are preserved. And there is no more hopeless separation and forsakenness than that which man experiences when he tries to cross this boundary. For then he gives up himself and the other, and does not accept reality where it encounters him, at the boundary between I and Thou, a boundary to be preserved and maintained. Since this boundary is the reality of I and Thou, it is the key to all reality. If man does not accept reality here in the only place it can be found, in the contrast of I and Thou, if he wishes to find it in the coalescence of I and Thou, he exchanges reality for all his innumerable passions, noble and ignoble, and for illusion and unreality.

If one holds firm to the I and Thou as never under any circumstances to be given up, that is, as bound together in the strict, irrevocable contrast of their being, then he can venture to give a name to this basic and original relation, to *his own* reality, which is the reality of all realities, that is, love. I repeat, one can venture to name it only if he understands as a truth, never to be sacrificed, that the boundary between Thou and I, you and me, should never be crossed;

and that should anyone nevertheless cross it, he exchanges reality for illusion, love for passion.

No word in our speech is so full of passion as the word "love." And when reality is exchanged for passion, it makes no difference whether that passion is the vilest or the noblest. When we speak of love today, we speak of the most consuming, burning passion for reality. But that is precisely what love is not, what it cannot be, if it is true that it is reality itself.

What we said of the moral act, based on the I and its freedom, holds true to an even greater extent for the love which is passion and eros. There is no Thou for this love. The moral act is different from love primarily in the fact that the moral act knows the Thou only as being in unison with the I. Therefore, it does not recognize the insurmountable boundary between them. To a very great extent, then, it is always alien to reality. Eros, however, is aware of this boundary; it is aware of its pain. But eros desires unity and therefore does not tolerate the claim of the boundary nor respect the division. Eros wants no part of the Thou. And even if it did it would be only as its own creation—and consequently not as Thou. For the Thou can never be the creature of the I. In eros the I desires itself and never anything but itself. And thus, in its insatiable hunger, its indefatigable creative urge, eros attests the unreality of the I that is obsessed with its passion.

What we previously said holds true—no one makes the I real by going back to his innermost being, even if that being is eros itself. And to say that the I becomes real only in encounter with the Thou is still not to say that the I becomes real only when it loves the Thou. That cannot be the meaning of the assertion that love is reality. Even in loving the Thou, we have not yet transcended the limits of the moral act or of eros. To be sure, the I will show its reality by loving the Thou. But man as the I becomes real only by being loved—by being loved with a love which is not passion, a love in which the loving person does not seek himself or the reality of his I. Testimony to this love, which again is not a passion, can be given only by an act (any other witness is invalid here) of a person who has experienced it as a reality, a person who knows himself loved with such love, a person who has found the reality of his own being, his own I in this love, because the power of all passions is broken before the reality of love, and the folly of the sham reality of eros is recognized.

Man can never be the one who loves in the sense of controlling that love. Only God can be that, for he alone is real in and of himself.

I intentionally said that man can testify that he has experienced this love. Of course, the only true and real testimony is that of an act.

Nevertheless, human love, regardless of how pure or strong it is, always remains only a reflection of divine love. And only as long as it is such, only as long as man does not think he loves in his own strength, can his love be witness and fruit of divine love. Only then can it be love and not passion.

I am merely drawing the conclusion from all we have discussed thus far when I assert that absolutely nothing remains of Protestant Christianity in that "transformation of Protestant Christianity into general truths of reason"[22] which Troeltsch puts forth as "neo-Protestantism." Troeltsch thinks that the main question for those who hold to the "general truths of reason" is no longer what it was for the Reformers—how one finds a gracious God—but whether God exists at all. It is not simply, as Troeltsch thinks, that the problems which fired Reformation Protestantism "grew cold";[23] but that the God who is the Thou to man, in whom man comes to his I, and before whom it seems "that he and God are alone in heaven and earth and that God has to deal only with him"—this God becomes an empty scheme, a universal concept of a "god in general." And the God who is gracious to man and loves him becomes a generalized rational truth of the love of God. The total loss of content which occurs in this "transformation of Protestant Christianity into general truths of reason" is very clear here. For if there is one thing which can never become a generality, it is love. Even the most vigorous conviction that God is love is still not love itself. As Wilhelm Herrmann has shown in discussing Bousset,[24] we may remain in the error of orthodoxy, which thinks it sufficient to accept a doctrine of the love of God, and take the doctrine of love instead of love itself. Here, however, we do not arrive at reality, which is contained solely in the contrast of Thou and I. Or we may fall back into the subjectivism of knowledge, about which, Troeltsch explains, it is a miracle that "man can grasp such a concept in his weakness and sin."[25] Instead of the faith of the one who is certain that God speaks to him as his Thou, as one man speaks to another, we have, before we realize it, a "religion of seeking for God in our own feelings, experiences, thoughts, and desires."[26] No doctrine can take the place of real life, whether it be a doctrine objectivized into dogma or a subjectivized one of the love of God carried to a perfect knowledge in which one experiences "union with God." At this point the whole issue rests on real love; that is, on whether I encounter the Thou of God, whether God himself, which means nothing less than *my* God, encounters me as the Thou in whose reality I become real, find my reality, and am delivered from all passion.

There can be no serious doubt that there is only one Thou which can encounter me—the Thou of man, the human Thou. It must be a Thou which is as conditioned, bound, relative, limited, and non-absolute as my I. And that can be only the human Thou. Thus, there is only one possibility of being loved. That is to be loved by another human being.

To be sure, we have made it clear that no man has the power in himself to love wholly without passion. And the divine Thou encounters us in a man who loves us with this wholly passionless love; who encounters us really as Thou; whose Thou is directed toward us in such a way that he does not seek himself in us, but seeks only us; who gives himself to us—but not as others do, who with this giving wish to take us and win us for themselves all the more thoroughly and completely, and in this most passionate giving still seek only themselves, and give themselves to us only to establish their own I, their own self, in us. The divine Thou encounters us in a man who gives himself to us and in that offering gives us only his Thou; that is, in the man who specifically preserves our I as I and does not overstep the boundary or fall under the domination of passion. For no man has in himself the reality which makes him completely free from all lust for reality and from which he can achieve the love which is patient and kind, is not jealous or boastful, not arrogant or rude, does not insist on its own way, is not irritable or resentful, does not rejoice at wrong, but rejoices in the right, bears all things, believes all things, hopes all things, and endures all things.

However, this love, this man, does something more to us. By encountering us as the Thou without violating our I, by respecting the boundary—and now it is clear what it means to say, by loving us—he forces us, in his love, in the pure gaze of his Thou, to see him as Thou; that is, he forces us to respect the boundary drawn between him and us. The one so loved by this dispassionate love can no longer wish to absolutize himself, can no longer wish to be self-sufficient and rooted in his unconditioned freedom. The one so loved by this love and placed by it before the boundary, before this boundary of his which is drawn by the Thou who loves him, must recognize his claim to identity with God, his wanting to be like God, as the sin from which no fiber of his being was ever free nor will ever be free as long as he intends to live in himself, in his own power. The sacrifice of his faith is this, that he surrenders this claim at the feet of the man who wishes to be nothing more than just a man, nothing more than a man created by God and living wholly from the Thou of God; thus, one who can love the person who encounters him as Thou, the Thou who is real and therefore bestows reality upon him.

This is one result of this encounter—that man recognizes his sin, his wanting to be like God. The other is that the man on whom reality has been bestowed in the encounter with the Thou of God (in the New Testament, it reads instead, "on whom life has been bestowed") will necessarily be reminded through every Thou he henceforth encounters of the life imparted to him through the Thou who encountered him in the dispassionate love which belongs to reality. And this reality which he has received as a gift is revealed to him in his ability to love every Thou who encounters him, whether friend or foe, and in such a way that he does not seek in the Thou his own reality, his self, his I, with eros-ridden passion, but instead gives of his own life, of his own reality. Thus, as Luther puts it, man begins "to well up in divine love."[27] But that should not be interpreted to mean that man in this encounter now "overflows with love." It is merely to say that he *can*. The source has been tapped; the well dug. Man has been placed with his I at the boundary; he has felt his reality in the encounter with the Thou who loves him without passion and whom he can love without passion. He knows that his salvation rests "in God's promise" and not in his own freedom and its works—and that it is therefore secure. He has tasted of that life which alone is life. And he knows he can have that life and that he himself is real only by not breaking out of this bondage to the Thou of God and the further bondage to the Thou of his brothers, which is the result of the first bondage. "If you know that you have a good and gracious God, through Christ, who desires to forgive your sins and never think of them again, and if you are now a child of eternal blessedness, a lord over heaven and earth with Christ, then your only task is to set out to serve your neighbor."[28]

It is indeed no accident that the first thoroughgoing controversy between Reformation Protestantism and the modern spirit, the controversy between Luther and Erasmus, dealt with the question of freedom of the will. For the contrast between Reformation Protestantism—in which reality means the encounter of Thou and I—and the modern spirit—in which reality is ultimate truth, a general truth establishing all reality, namely, the truth of freedom—is nowhere as obvious as in this controversy. The doctrine of free will is the decisive point which shows continually whether one lives in reality or merely in the illusion of reality; that is, whether it is in the encounter with the Thou that one finds his real life and knows it to be rooted, or whether it is in the constantly renewed and repeated attempt to absolutize his own I. (In that case it is all the same in the final analysis whether we seek this objectivizing in achieving a generalized rational truth or in the formation of an individual, rational "truth" of our own individual beings. The first goes back to humanism by way of the Enlightenment, and the second to the extremists of the Reformation period by way of Romantic Idealism. In both cases, however, reality is limited to the I.) The reality that is found solely in the encounter with the Thou is reality just as it is, an absolutely determined reality. It is precisely what it is, as it is, as it is here and now, at this one, specific time— reality resting entirely upon decision. Here we encounter decisions which really earn the name, because they are irrevocable.

Where reality is not the unfolding of the I but the encounter of I and Thou, decisions are not merely the subject's own internal develop-ment, but are encounters with the Thou. They are not conditioned primarily by the infinite, creative possibilities of the I, but by the Thou; and they would not be decisions, that is, they would not be encounters with the Thou, if they were not conditioned and deter-mined by it. But this is by no means to say that the responsibility of the I is called into question. On the contrary, only here can there be true responsibility to the claim, the question, with which the Thou confronts the I. They are posed by the Thou. And even the ultimate claim and the final question are not posed by man for life, but they are posed to man. The doctrine of freedom of the will is protected here from any confusion with determinism. Between the Thou and the I there is no determinism, only responsibility.

Where the I itself, however, initiates reality, and where reality is nothing but the creative unfolding of the I, there are no irrevocable decisions, since the possibilities of the I are by definition unlimited. Instead there is development. And this development embraces all "de-cisions," even erroneous ones. Decisions are annulled and cease to be decisive when they are placed in the context of development. They drift to a middle ground; they become neutralized. But in the process the decision ceases to be a decision. And so for the modern spirit, the decision to commit sin is not "world-shattering but is simply incorpo-rated into the development of the good."[29] The case is the same as in Luther's reproach of Erasmus: "You think both God and the devil are far from us and merely watch to see which side we will choose with our free will. And you do not believe that God and the devil, as two kingdoms in eternal conflict, have a powerful influence and drive in the human will; since the human will must be like a slave, indeed, like a horse obeying its rider."[30] But if one applies the doctrine of bondage of the will to the remote God, then it is inevitable that this doctrine becomes determinism and deprives man of nothing less than his humanity, and makes God into an idol of rigid, objectified mech-anism. Under such conditions the doctrine of the bondage of the will, which means nothing other than a bondage of the real, "existential" man to the real God, that is, to his God, cannot be understood. When it is taken from the realm of the here and now, the unique, the actual, and put into the realm of the general, the conceptual, the ideal, it no longer signifies foreknowledge and predestination by the living God, but becomes determinism and fatalism. Belief in this doctrine is worlds removed from "arguing about whether I am elected or not."[31] The strictness with which belief in the bondage of the will is excluded from general application and from all rational certainty and reflection is characterized by the following passage from Luther: "I believe that we should trust God's grace, but remain uncertain concerning our own and others' future perseverance and election, as it is written, whoever stands ought to be careful that he does not fall."[32]

There is a sharp distinction here between that certainty of salvation which rests on revealed grace, and the certainty of election in terms of a hidden predestination known only to God. The meaning of the doctrine of the bondage of the will is seen in this distinction and in the fact that certainty of salvation is asserted, and certainty of election excluded. This eliminates any possibility that assurance of salvation could somehow be based on knowledge or on experience or works. In the most thorough manner imaginable, certainty of salvation is detached from any basis in the subject, man, and the I is turned toward the Thou through which it lives; man is turned toward God, who justifies him. The only way to attain to a full certainty of grace is through unconditional commitment to God, which signifies the last uncertainty, and which would constitute, "if God so willed," a readiness for "death and hell forever."[33] The distinction between the revealed and the concealed will of God, far from introducing a division in God's will, shows that it is rather the *Deus absconditus,* the hidden God, who foreknows and foreordains and desires the death of the sinner, who more than anything else points us to the *Deus revelatus,* the revealed God of grace.[34] And it is the doctrine of the bondage of the will which is the strongest expression of the bondage of the created I to the creating Thou, of responsible man to God, who lays claim to him.

We said at the outset that the essence of Protestantism is bondage —in fact, a bondage to finite reality. Thus, we are opposed to the usual view, which claims to find the essence of Protestantism in freedom. If one desired to understand this freedom only as man's being freed from the claim of his I, autonomous, grounded solely in his conscience and in his autonomy and self-discipline, and as being in his freedom, directly connected with the divine essence, indeed, carrying this essence in himself—if one, that is, desired to understand this freedom as man's release from all these claims, then we could, if need be, declare ourselves in agreement. However, the freedom in which one claims to find the essence of Protestantism is to be understood precisely and completely in the sense of this claim of the I; and not only in regard to man himself, but also to the shaping of the political and social forms of human life. In both connections, therefore, freedom cannot be accepted as the peculiar characteristic of Protestantism.

By all this we are not in the least denying the release brought about by Protestantism from the Catholic Church and the Middle Ages. It should be stated, however, that this release was not brought about for the sake of absolute freedom, as though freedom were the most profound and final word to be said to the world; but for the sake of a different bondage. Very briefly we could characterize the difference as follows: the bondage to contrived, arbitrary laws, consecrated and validated by the church, was to be replaced by the bondage to and through that reality which, precisely because it is reality, is divine, and whose laws require no human consecration or declaration of validity.

I asserted at the beginning that Protestantism is responsible to the world for establishing this bondage but has allowed the world to slip into the chaos of license. The world remains a victim of this chaos even today. Protestantism has its work cut out for it here. But it cannot do it if its last word is freedom, for freedom means license, unconditioned, unlimited license. But neither can it carry out its task if the bondage which we think ought to be its final word is not a bondage to reality, that is, if it is anything less than a bondage to God.

What is true of Reformation doctrine in general is also true here: almost before the very eyes of the Reformers there was a regression from what they intended and initiated. Although their task was to release human life in all its functions from the fetters of medieval-ecclesiastical culture, a new ecclesiastical culture began nevertheless to arise from their work. The only difference was that now the churches did their work in the interest of the State, or even more in the interest of the ruling class; and thus, ecclesiastical culture lost its grand proportions and its universality. According to the degree to which every court-chaplain became a pope, everything became smaller and more inadequate than it had been in the culture dominated and inspired by the medieval Catholic Church.

The modern spirit's giving to the world and the institutions of human life their own rights and independence seems to reflect a deeper understanding and a re-acceptance of original Reformation intentions.

But again it only *appears* so. For the autonomy of things, to which the modern spirit believes we ought to surrender everything, is in truth not the law of *things* at all. After all, it is completely impossible that a system of thought should be able to comprehend the world and its laws at any specific time if that system has no place for the Thou and if that system must transform the Thou into the I in order to under- stand it. It can only be that this autonomy of things is in truth merely the autonomy of the I, which wishes to portray itself as alone domi- nating things—dominating them unilaterally from its own perspective. Thus, this system of thought conceives of all institutions and functions of human life, such as marriage, school, church, State, economy, art, and science from the point of view of the subject, the I. The laws and norms which this system of thought sets up for real institutions, and not merely imaginary ones, cannot really be their norms and laws. And if these norms, laws, and ideals are applied to them, as has been done since the beginning of the modern period in the eighteenth century, the result can be only the destruction of those institutions and their dissolution into the same unreality in which this subject-dominated thinking leads its spectral existence.

The only help against this existence is to recognize the error of this kind of thinking, the sin of the false claim of the I, and to open our eyes to the Thou.

NOTES

1. W. Dilthey, *Das Erlebnis und die Dichtung*, 4. Aufl., 1913, 151.
2. Ernst Troeltsch, *Die Bedeutung des Protestantismus für die Entstehung der modernen Welt*, 2. Aufl., 102.
3. *Ibid.*, 63.
4. *Ibid.*, 86.
5. *Ibid.*, 100.
6. *Ibid.*, 92.
7. *Ibid.*, 86.
8. *Ibid.*, 100.
9. *Religion in Geschichte und Gegenwart*, 1. Aufl., IV, Sp. 1916.
10. Troeltsch, *Die Bedeutung des Protestantismus*, 102.
11. *Kirche und Wirklichkeit. Ein katholisches Zeitbuch*, ed. Ernst Michel, Jena, 1923, 177.
12. Troeltsch, *Die Bedeutung des Protestantismus*, 15.
13. Cf. 124 of my edition of Luther's work, *Vom unfreien Willen*, Munich, 1924.
14. Luther, *Sämtliche Werke*, Erlangen Ausgabe (henceforth cited as E. A.), 28, 205 f.
15. Cf. Eberhard Grisebach, *Probleme der wirklichen Bildung*, Munich, 1923.
16. Cf. W. Herrmann, *Verkehr des Christen mit Gott*, 7. Aufl., 1921, 179; Eng. trans.: *Communion of the Christian with God*, p. 224.
17. Troeltsch, "Protestantisches Christentum und Kirche in der Neuzeit," 698, in *Kultur der Gegenwart: Geschichte der christlichen Religion*, 2. Aufl.

18. *Ibid.*, 457.
19. Karl Bornhausen, "Est Deus in nobis," *Die Christliche Welt*, 1923, Nr. 49/50.
20. *Loc. cit.*
21. *Loc. cit.*
22. Troeltsch, *Protestantisches Christentum und Kirche*, 698.
23. *Ibid.*, 605; cf. also *Die Bedeutung des Protestantismus*, 98.
24. Wilhelm Herrmann, *Gesammelte Aufsätze*, Tübingen, 1923, 165.
25. Troeltsch, *Protestantisches Christentum und Kirche*, 457.
26. Troeltsch, *Die Bedeutung des Protestantismus*, 98.
27. Luther, E. A., 11, 2. Aufl., 339.
28. Luther, E. A., 15, 2. Aufl., 42 f.
29. Troeltsch, *Protestantisches Christentum und Kirche*, 701.
30. Luther, *Vom unfreien Willen*, 271.
31. Luther, E. A., 1, 2. Aufl., 261.

32. Luther, *Briefwechsel*, ed. Enders, IV, 51. Compare here also Karl Holl, *Gesammelte Aufsätze zur Kirchengeschichte*, I, Luther, 2. Aufl., Tübingen, 1923, 112 and 152.

33. Luther, *Römerbriefvorlesung*, ed. Ficker, II, 215.

34. Otto Scheel, in II of the supplemental volume of the Braunschweiger Lutherausgabe, 540; see also Ferdinand Kattenbusch, "Deus absconditus bei Luther," in the memorial volume for J. Kaftan, Tübingen, 1920, 187 and 203.